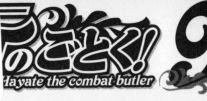

Hayate the combat butler 9

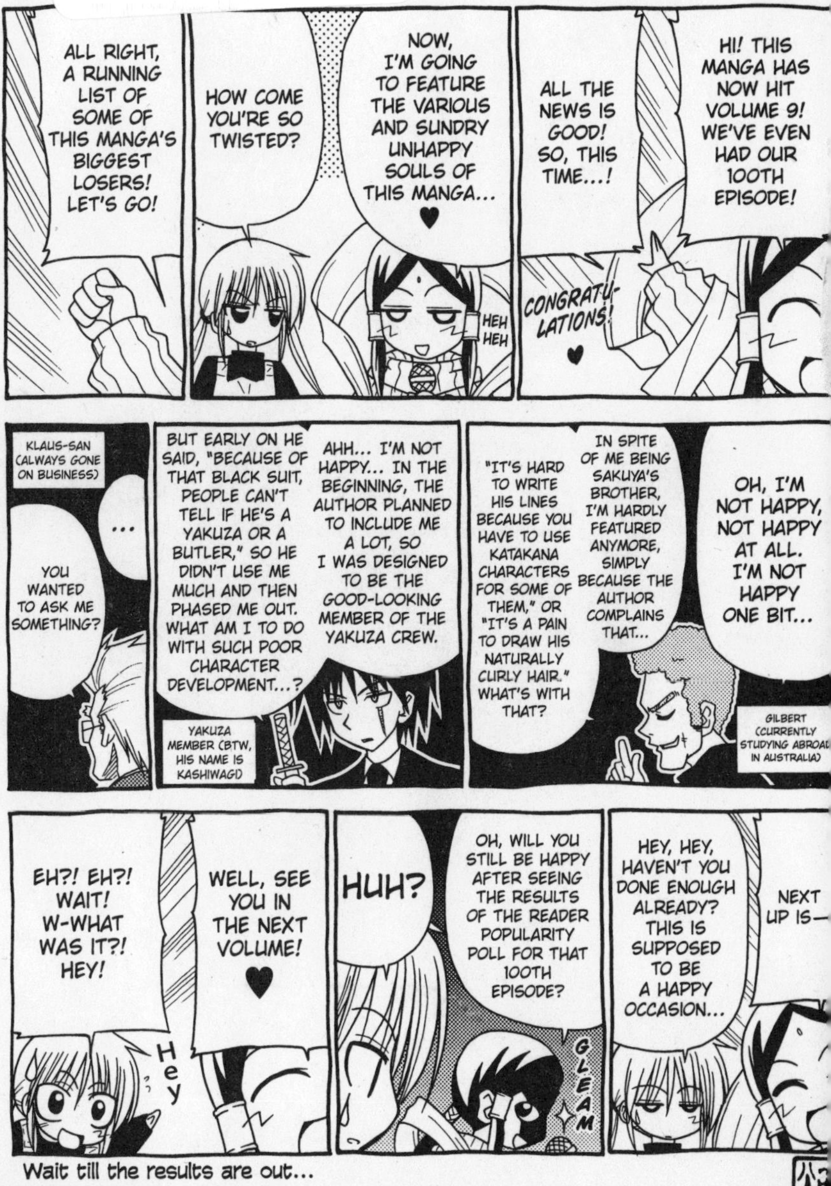
HI! THIS MANGA HAS NOW HIT VOLUME 9! WE'VE EVEN HAD OUR 100TH EPISODE!
ALL THE NEWS IS GOOD! SO, THIS TIME...!
CONGRATULATIONS! ♥
NOW, I'M GOING TO FEATURE THE VARIOUS AND SUNDRY UNHAPPY SOULS OF THIS MANGA... ♥
HEH HEH
HOW COME YOU'RE SO TWISTED?
ALL RIGHT, A RUNNING LIST OF SOME OF THIS MANGA'S BIGGEST LOSERS! LET'S GO!
OH, I'M NOT HAPPY, NOT HAPPY AT ALL. I'M NOT HAPPY ONE BIT...
IN SPITE OF ME BEING SAKUYA'S BROTHER, I'M HARDLY FEATURED ANYMORE, SIMPLY BECAUSE THE AUTHOR COMPLAINS THAT...
"IT'S HARD TO WRITE HIS LINES BECAUSE YOU HAVE TO USE KATAKANA CHARACTERS FOR SOME OF THEM," OR "IT'S A PAIN TO DRAW HIS NATURALLY CURLY HAIR." WHAT'S WITH THAT?
GILBERT (CURRENTLY STUDYING ABROAD IN AUSTRALIA)
AHH... I'M NOT HAPPY... IN THE BEGINNING, THE AUTHOR PLANNED TO INCLUDE ME A LOT, SO I WAS DESIGNED TO BE THE GOOD-LOOKING MEMBER OF THE YAKUZA CREW.
BUT EARLY ON HE SAID, "BECAUSE OF THAT BLACK SUIT, PEOPLE CAN'T TELL IF HE'S A YAKUZA OR A BUTLER," SO HE DIDN'T USE ME MUCH AND THEN PHASED ME OUT. WHAT AM I TO DO WITH SUCH POOR CHARACTER DEVELOPMENT...?
YAKUZA MEMBER (BTW, HIS NAME IS KASHIWAGI)
KLAUS-SAN (ALWAYS GONE ON BUSINESS)
...
YOU WANTED TO ASK ME SOMETHING?
NEXT UP IS—
HEY, HEY, HAVEN'T YOU DONE ENOUGH ALREADY? THIS IS SUPPOSED TO BE A HAPPY OCCASION...
OH, WILL YOU STILL BE HAPPY AFTER SEEING THE RESULTS OF THE READER POPULARITY POLL FOR THAT 100TH EPISODE?
GLEAM
HUH?
WELL, SEE YOU IN THE NEXT VOLUME! ♥
Hey
EH?! EH?! WAIT! W-WHAT WAS IT?! HEY!

Wait till the results are out...

HAYATE THE COMBAT BUTLER
VOL. 9

STORY AND ART BY
KENJIRO HATA

English Adaptation/Mark Giambruno
Translation/Yuki Yoshioka & Cindy H. Yamauchi
Touch-up Art & Lettering/Hudson Yards
Design/Yukiko Whitley
Editor/Kit Fox & Shaenon K. Garrity

Editor in Chief, Books/Alvin Lu
Editor in Chief, Magazines/Marc Weidenbaum
VP, Publishing Licensing/Rika Inouye
VP, Sales and Product Marketing/Gonzalo Ferreyra
VP, Creative/Linda Espinosa
Publisher/Hyoe Narita

Printed in Canada

Published by VIZ Media, LLC
P.O. Box 77010
San Francisco, CA 94107

10 9 8 7 6 5 4 3 2 1
First printing, November 2008

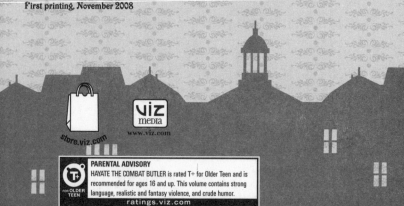

Hayate the Combat Butler

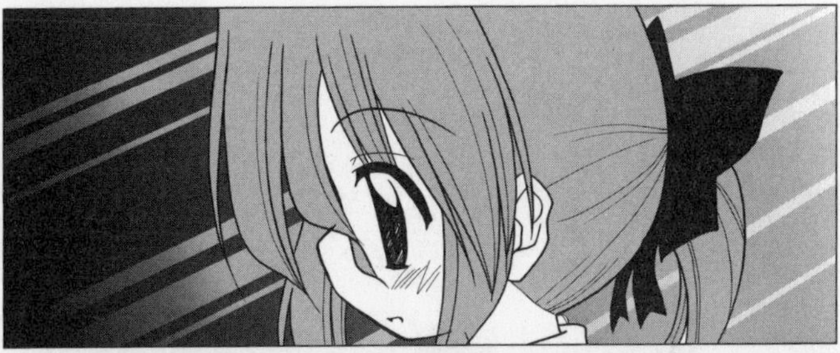

9

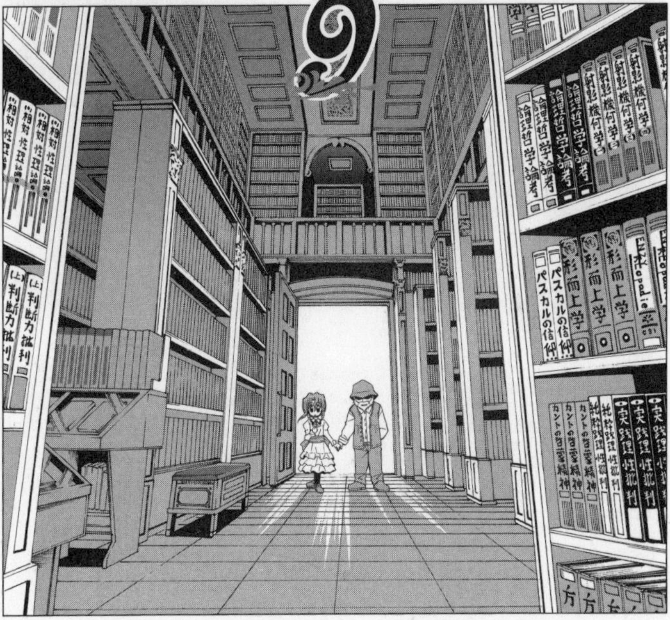
射影幾何学
論理哲学論考
相対性理論
形而上学
パスカルの信仰
判断力批判
実践理性批判
カントの啓蒙精神

KENJIRO HATA

Math I

Grad... ...Wataru Tachibana

...olve the following simultaneous equation.

2-5 { (1) $3x^2 - 6x - 2 > 0$
      If $x^2 1/1 - 8 < 0$

is.

CONTENTS

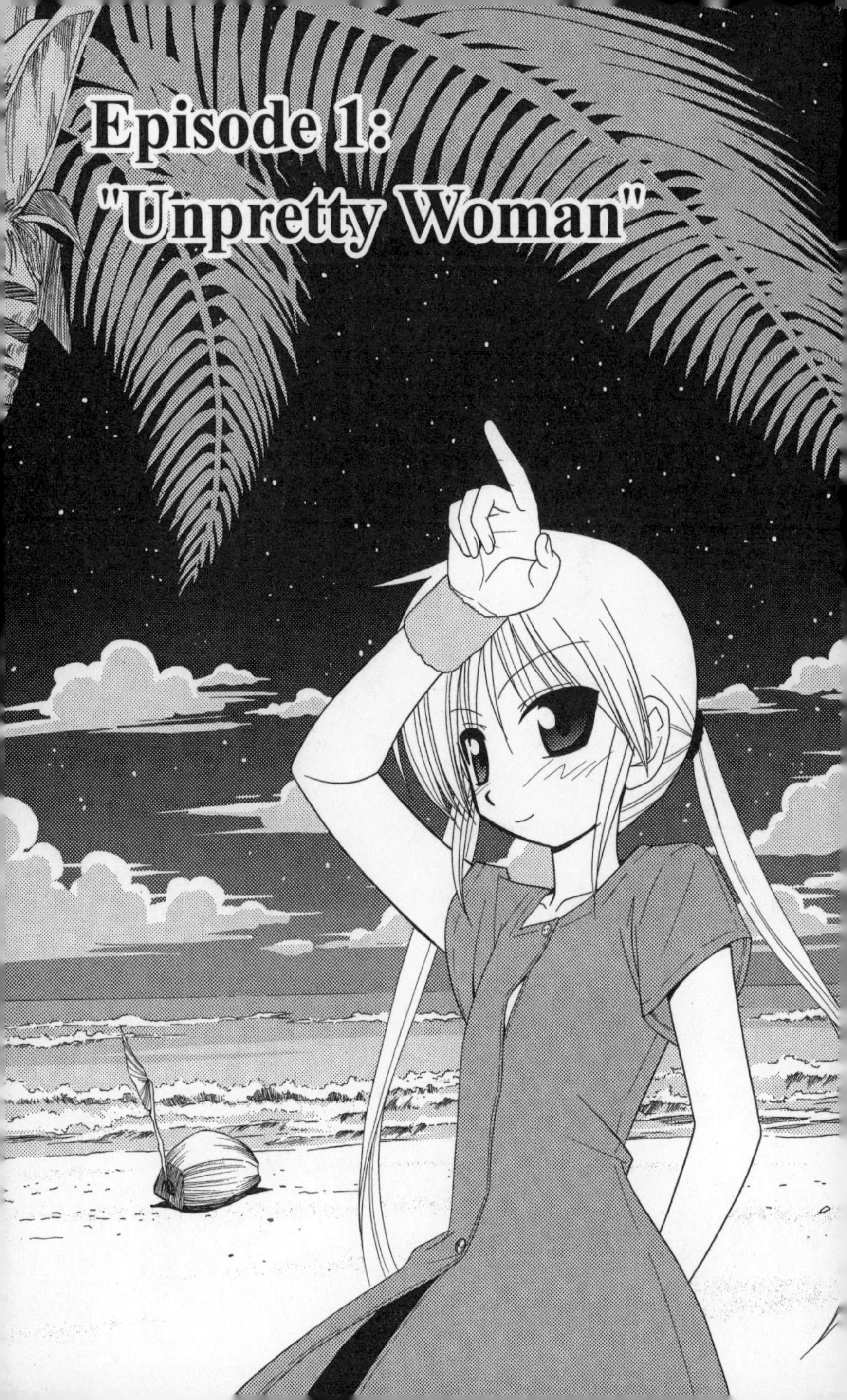
Episode 1:
"Unpretty Woman"

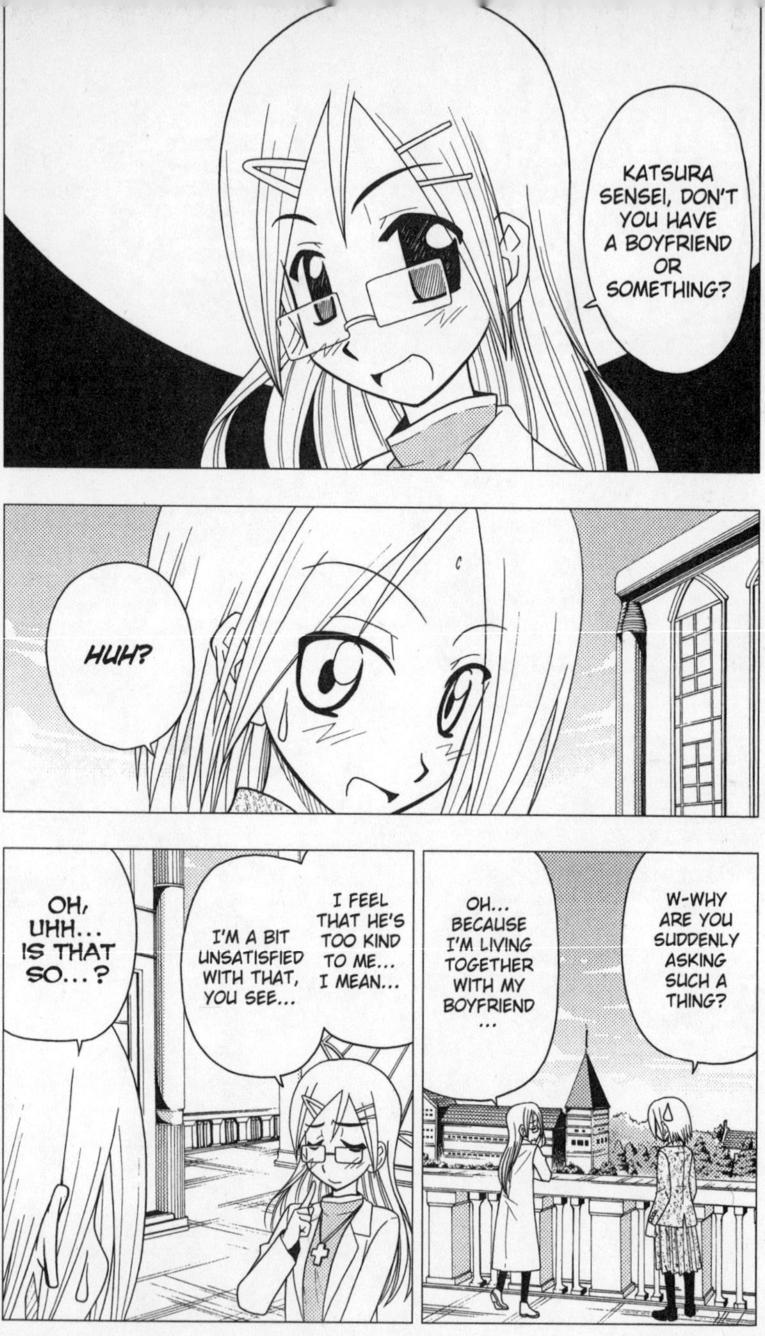
KATSURA SENSEI, DON'T YOU HAVE A BOYFRIEND OR SOMETHING?
HUH?
W-WHY ARE YOU SUDDENLY ASKING SUCH A THING?
OH... BECAUSE I'M LIVING TOGETHER WITH MY BOYFRIEND ...
I FEEL THAT HE'S TOO KIND TO ME... I MEAN...
I'M A BIT UNSATISFIED WITH THAT, YOU SEE...
OH, UHH... IS THAT SO...?

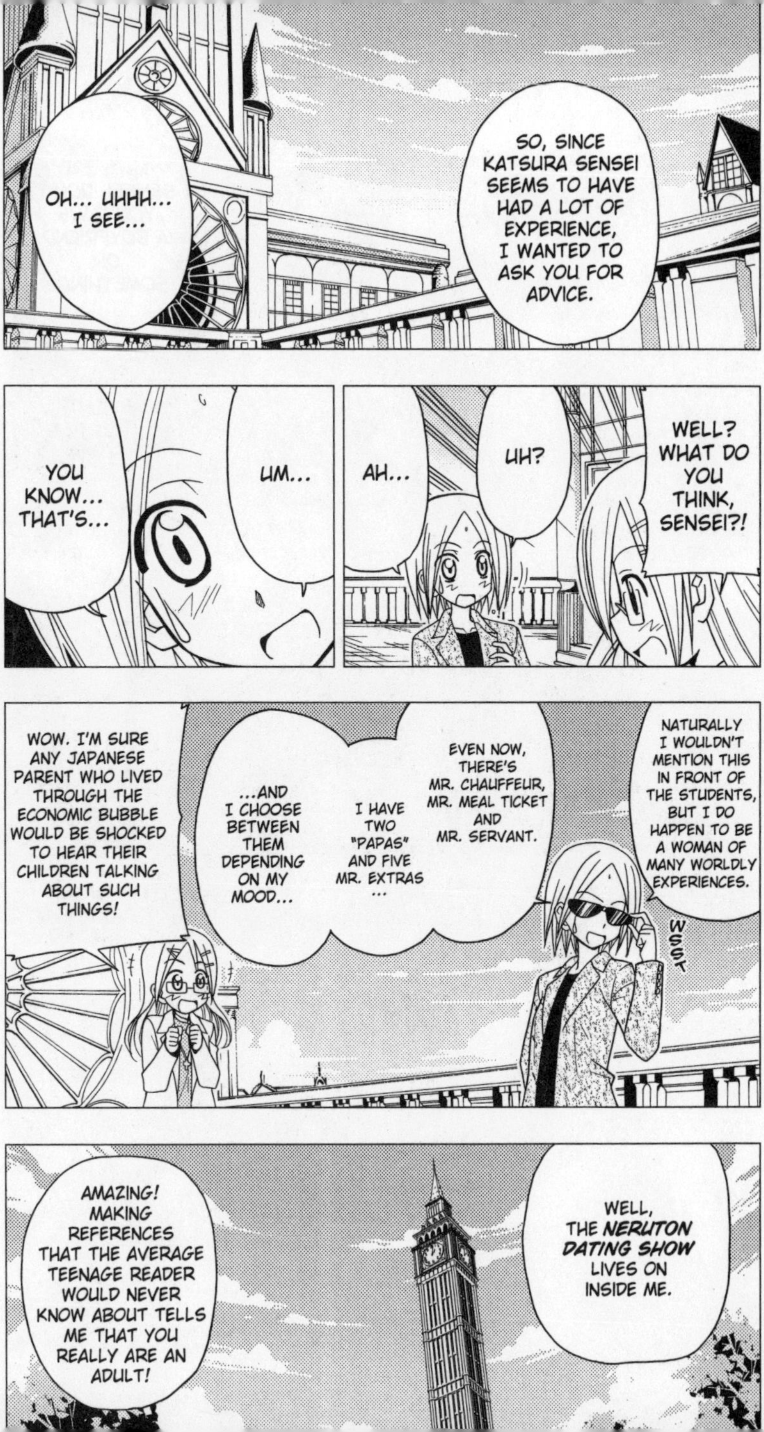
SO, SINCE KATSURA SENSEI SEEMS TO HAVE HAD A LOT OF EXPERIENCE, I WANTED TO ASK YOU FOR ADVICE.
OH... UHHH... I SEE...
WELL? WHAT DO YOU THINK, SENSEI?!
UH?
AH...
UM...
YOU KNOW... THAT'S...
NATURALLY I WOULDN'T MENTION THIS IN FRONT OF THE STUDENTS, BUT I DO HAPPEN TO BE A WOMAN OF MANY WORLDLY EXPERIENCES.
WSST
EVEN NOW, THERE'S MR. CHAUFFEUR, MR. MEAL TICKET AND MR. SERVANT.
I HAVE TWO "PAPAS" AND FIVE MR. EXTRAS ...
...AND I CHOOSE BETWEEN THEM DEPENDING ON MY MOOD...
WOW. I'M SURE ANY JAPANESE PARENT WHO LIVED THROUGH THE ECONOMIC BUBBLE WOULD BE SHOCKED TO HEAR THEIR CHILDREN TALKING ABOUT SUCH THINGS!
WELL, THE *NERUTON DATING SHOW* LIVES ON INSIDE ME.
AMAZING! MAKING REFERENCES THAT THE AVERAGE TEENAGE READER WOULD NEVER KNOW ABOUT TELLS ME THAT YOU REALLY ARE AN ADULT!

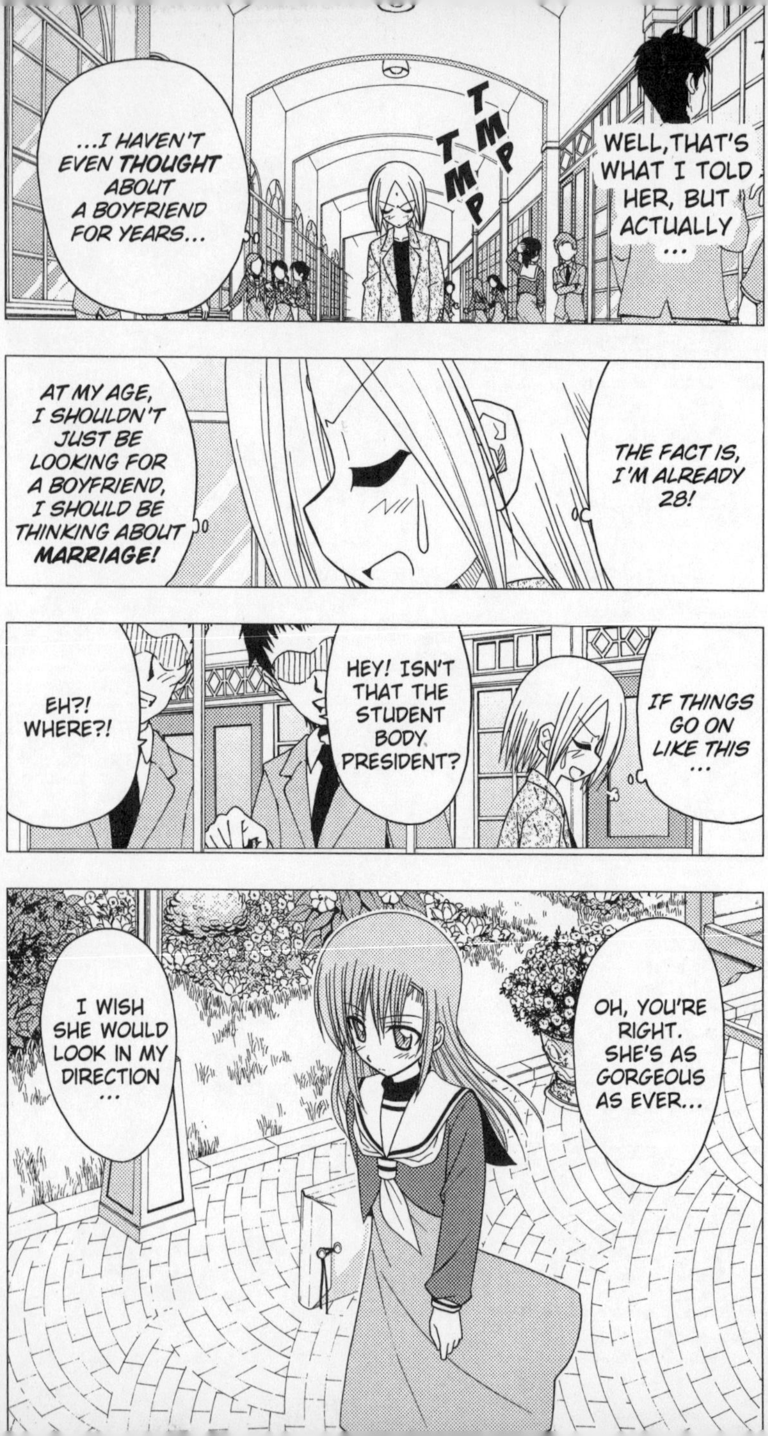
WELL, THAT'S WHAT I TOLD HER, BUT ACTUALLY ...
TMP TMP
TMP TMP
...I HAVEN'T EVEN THOUGHT ABOUT A BOYFRIEND FOR YEARS...
THE FACT IS, I'M ALREADY 28!
AT MY AGE, I SHOULDN'T JUST BE LOOKING FOR A BOYFRIEND, I SHOULD BE THINKING ABOUT MARRIAGE!
IF THINGS GO ON LIKE THIS ...
HEY! ISN'T THAT THE STUDENT BODY PRESIDENT?
EH?! WHERE?!
OH, YOU'RE RIGHT. SHE'S AS GORGEOUS AS EVER...
I WISH SHE WOULD LOOK IN MY DIRECTION ...

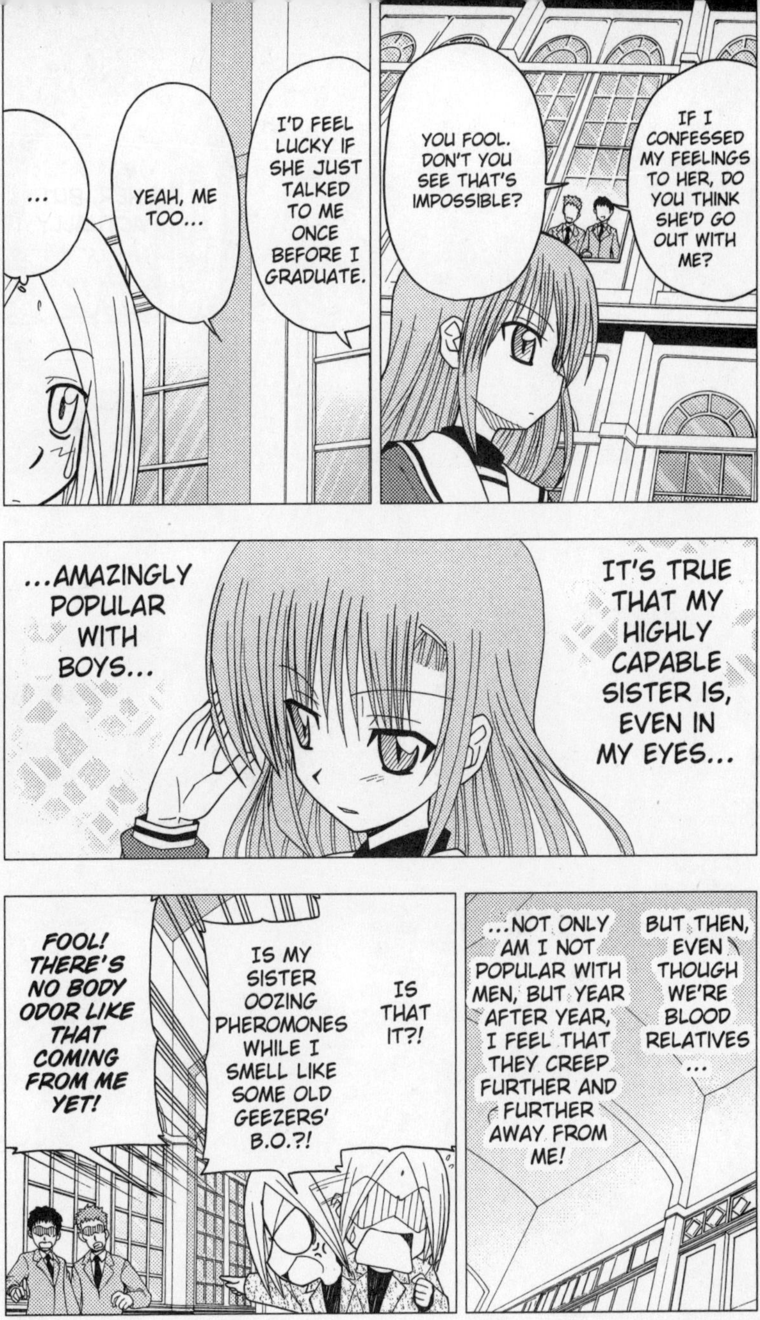
IF I CONFESSED MY FEELINGS TO HER, DO YOU THINK SHE'D GO OUT WITH ME?
YOU FOOL. DON'T YOU SEE THAT'S IMPOSSIBLE?
I'D FEEL LUCKY IF SHE JUST TALKED TO ME ONCE BEFORE I GRADUATE.
YEAH, ME TOO...
...
IT'S TRUE THAT MY HIGHLY CAPABLE SISTER IS, EVEN IN MY EYES...
...AMAZINGLY POPULAR WITH BOYS...
BUT THEN, EVEN THOUGH WE'RE BLOOD RELATIVES...
...NOT ONLY AM I NOT POPULAR WITH MEN, BUT YEAR AFTER YEAR, I FEEL THAT THEY CREEP FURTHER AND FURTHER AWAY FROM ME!
IS THAT IT?!
IS MY SISTER OOZING PHEROMONES WHILE I SMELL LIKE SOME OLD GEEZERS' B.O.?!
FOOL! THERE'S NO BODY ODOR LIKE THAT COMING FROM ME YET!

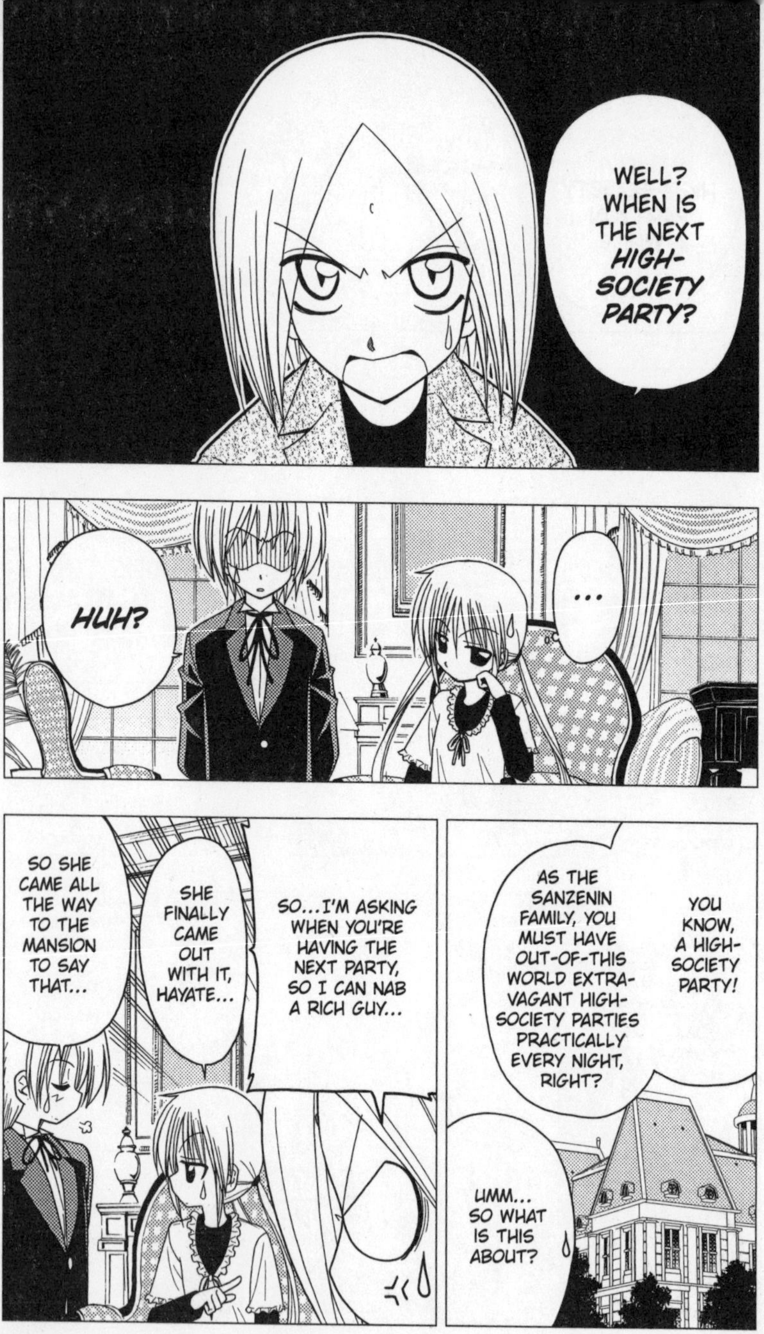
WELL? WHEN IS THE NEXT HIGH-SOCIETY PARTY?
...
HUH?
YOU KNOW, A HIGH-SOCIETY PARTY!
AS THE SANZENIN FAMILY, YOU MUST HAVE OUT-OF-THIS WORLD EXTRA-VAGANT HIGH-SOCIETY PARTIES PRACTICALLY EVERY NIGHT, RIGHT?
UMM... SO WHAT IS THIS ABOUT?
SO...I'M ASKING WHEN YOU'RE HAVING THE NEXT PARTY, SO I CAN NAB A RICH GUY...
SHE FINALLY CAME OUT WITH IT, HAYATE...
SO SHE CAME ALL THE WAY TO THE MANSION TO SAY THAT...

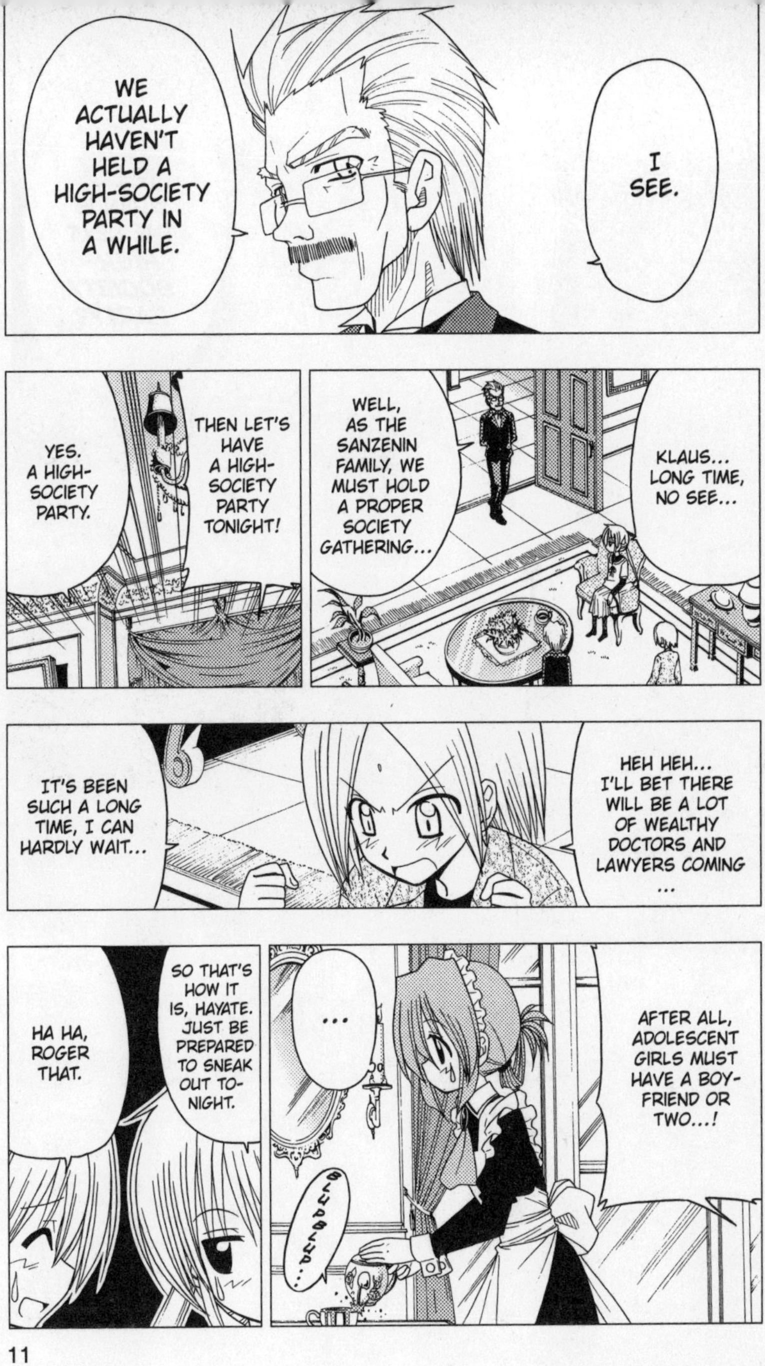
I SEE.
WE ACTUALLY HAVEN'T HELD A HIGH-SOCIETY PARTY IN A WHILE.
KLAUS... LONG TIME, NO SEE...
WELL, AS THE SANZENIN FAMILY, WE MUST HOLD A PROPER SOCIETY GATHERING...
THEN LET'S HAVE A HIGH-SOCIETY PARTY TONIGHT!
YES. A HIGH-SOCIETY PARTY.
HEH HEH... I'LL BET THERE WILL BE A LOT OF WEALTHY DOCTORS AND LAWYERS COMING ...
IT'S BEEN SUCH A LONG TIME, I CAN HARDLY WAIT...
AFTER ALL, ADOLESCENT GIRLS MUST HAVE A BOY-FRIEND OR TWO...!
...
BLUBBLUB...
SO THAT'S HOW IT IS, HAYATE. JUST BE PREPARED TO SNEAK OUT TO-NIGHT.
HA HA, ROGER THAT.

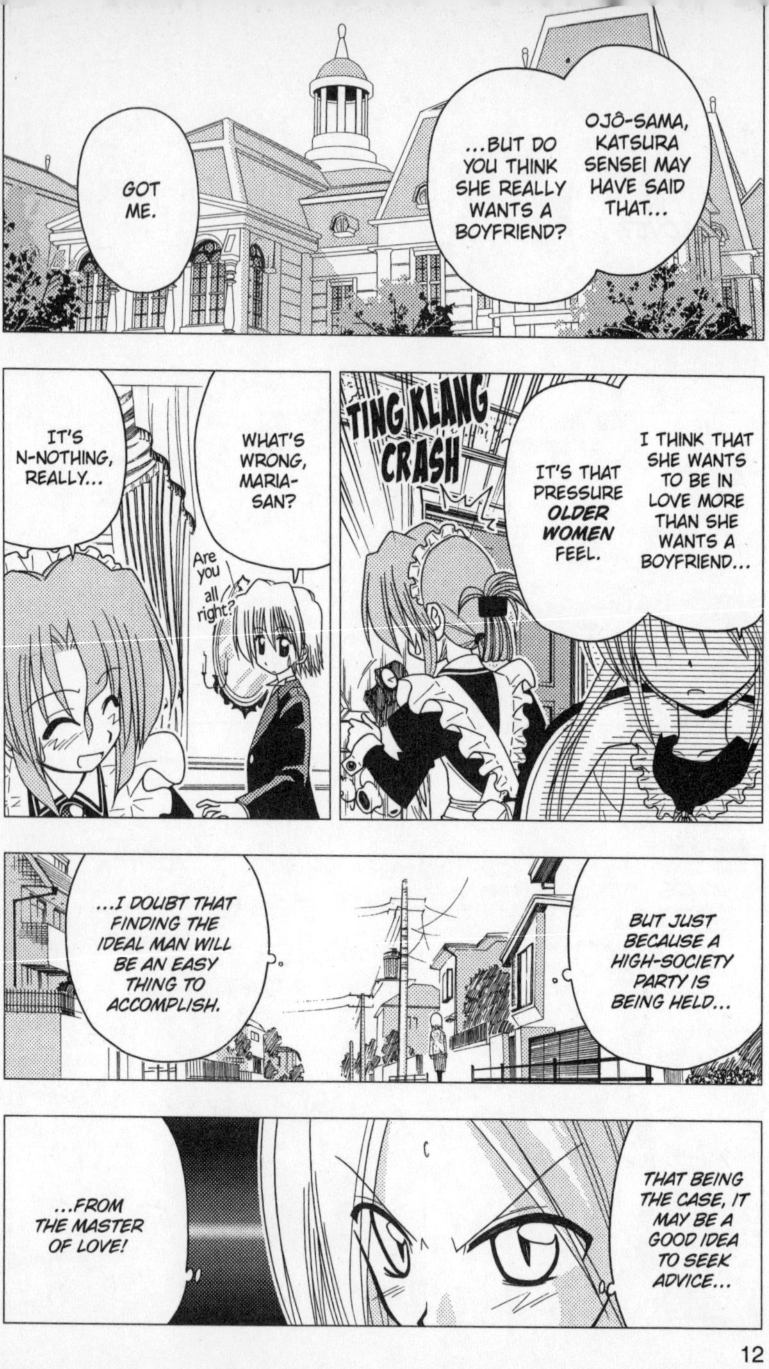

OJÔ-SAMA, KATSURA SENSEI MAY HAVE SAID THAT...
...BUT DO YOU THINK SHE REALLY WANTS A BOYFRIEND?
GOT ME.
I THINK THAT SHE WANTS TO BE IN LOVE MORE THAN SHE WANTS A BOYFRIEND...
IT'S THAT PRESSURE OLDER WOMEN FEEL.
TING KLANG CRASH
WHAT'S WRONG, MARIA-SAN?
IT'S N-NOTHING, REALLY...
Are you all right?
BUT JUST BECAUSE A HIGH-SOCIETY PARTY IS BEING HELD...
...I DOUBT THAT FINDING THE IDEAL MAN WILL BE AN EASY THING TO ACCOMPLISH.
THAT BEING THE CASE, IT MAY BE A GOOD IDEA TO SEEK ADVICE...
...FROM THE MASTER OF LOVE!

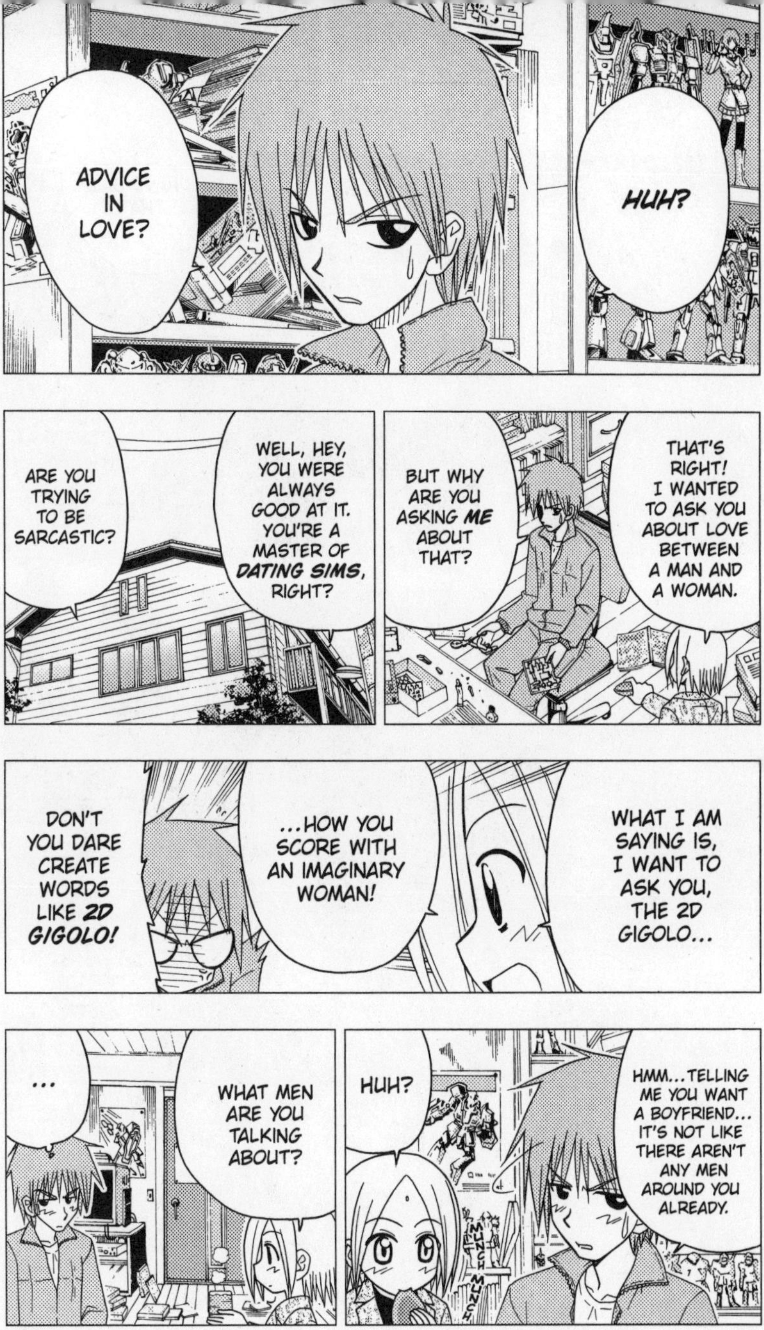
HUH?
ADVICE IN LOVE?
THAT'S RIGHT! I WANTED TO ASK YOU ABOUT LOVE BETWEEN A MAN AND A WOMAN.
BUT WHY ARE YOU ASKING *ME* ABOUT THAT?
WELL, HEY, YOU WERE ALWAYS GOOD AT IT. YOU'RE A MASTER OF *DATING SIMS*, RIGHT?
ARE YOU TRYING TO BE SARCASTIC?
WHAT I AM SAYING IS, I WANT TO ASK YOU, THE 2D GIGOLO...
...HOW YOU SCORE WITH AN IMAGINARY WOMAN!
DON'T YOU DARE CREATE WORDS LIKE *2D GIGOLO!*
HMM...TELLING ME YOU WANT A BOYFRIEND... IT'S NOT LIKE THERE AREN'T ANY MEN AROUND YOU ALREADY.
HUH?
MUNCH MUNCH
WHAT MEN ARE YOU TALKING ABOUT?
...

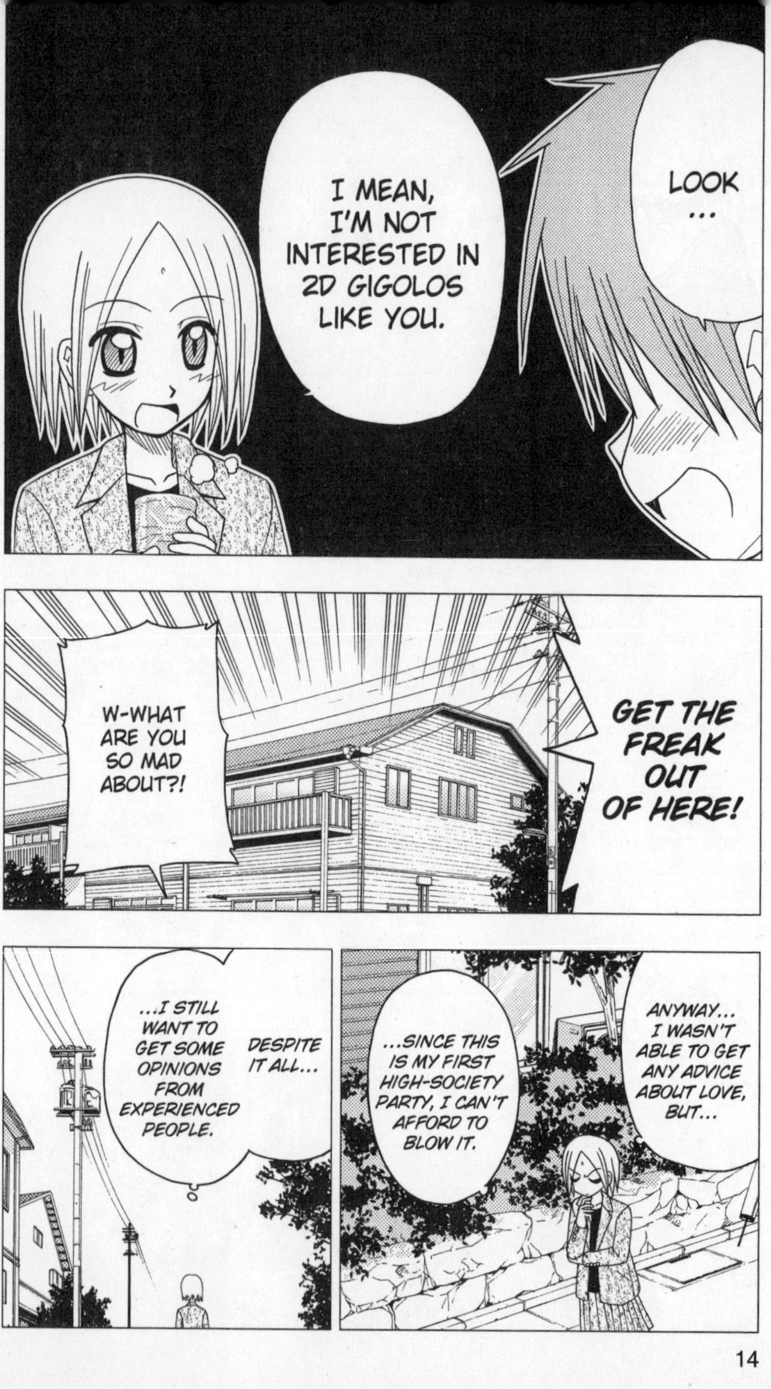
LOOK ...
I MEAN, I'M NOT INTERESTED IN 2D GIGOLOS LIKE YOU.
GET THE FREAK OUT OF HERE!
W-WHAT ARE YOU SO MAD ABOUT?!
ANYWAY... I WASN'T ABLE TO GET ANY ADVICE ABOUT LOVE, BUT...
...SINCE THIS IS MY FIRST HIGH-SOCIETY PARTY, I CAN'T AFFORD TO BLOW IT.
DESPITE IT ALL...
...I STILL WANT TO GET SOME OPINIONS FROM EXPERIENCED PEOPLE.

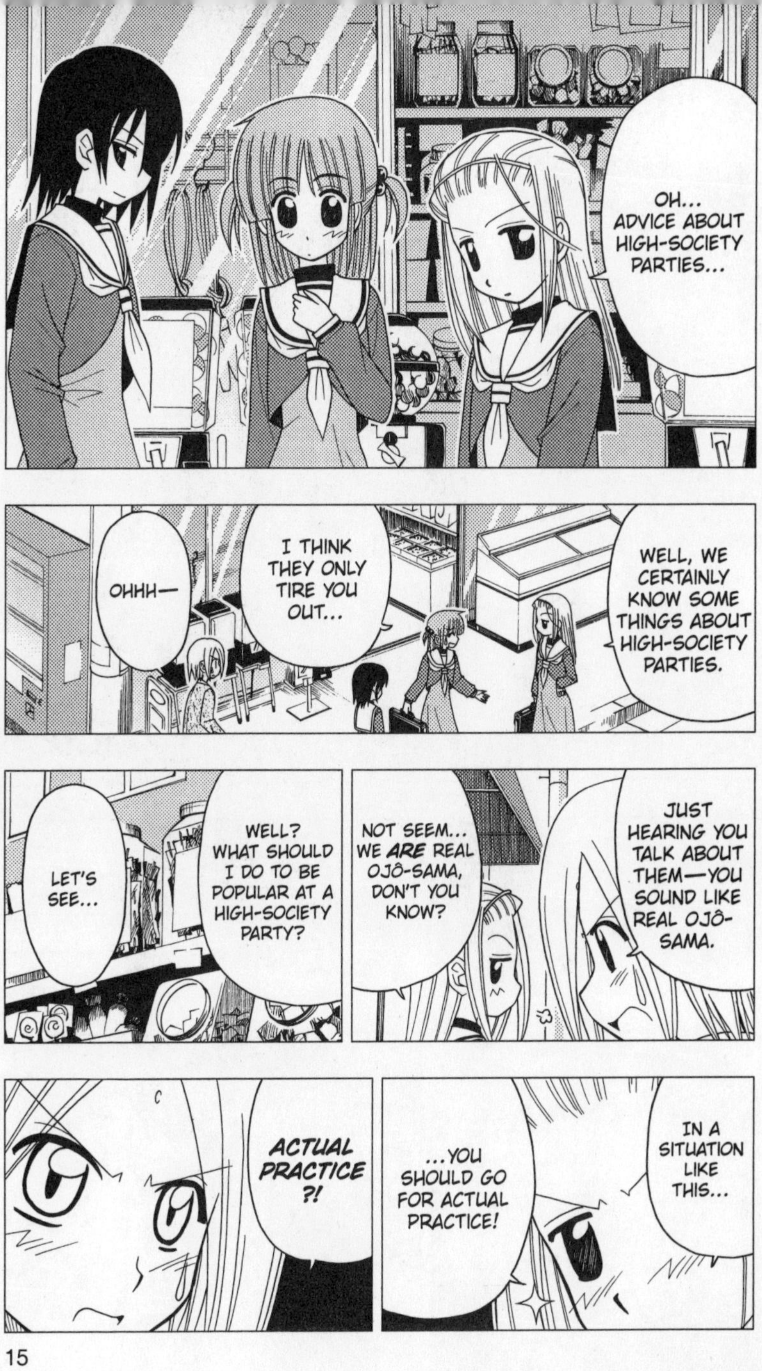
OH... ADVICE ABOUT HIGH-SOCIETY PARTIES...
WELL, WE CERTAINLY KNOW SOME THINGS ABOUT HIGH-SOCIETY PARTIES.
I THINK THEY ONLY TIRE YOU OUT...
OHHH—
JUST HEARING YOU TALK ABOUT THEM—YOU SOUND LIKE REAL OJÔ-SAMA.
NOT SEEM... WE *ARE* REAL OJÔ-SAMA, DON'T YOU KNOW?
WELL? WHAT SHOULD I DO TO BE POPULAR AT A HIGH-SOCIETY PARTY?
LET'S SEE...
IN A SITUATION LIKE THIS...
...YOU SHOULD GO FOR ACTUAL PRACTICE!
ACTUAL PRACTICE?!

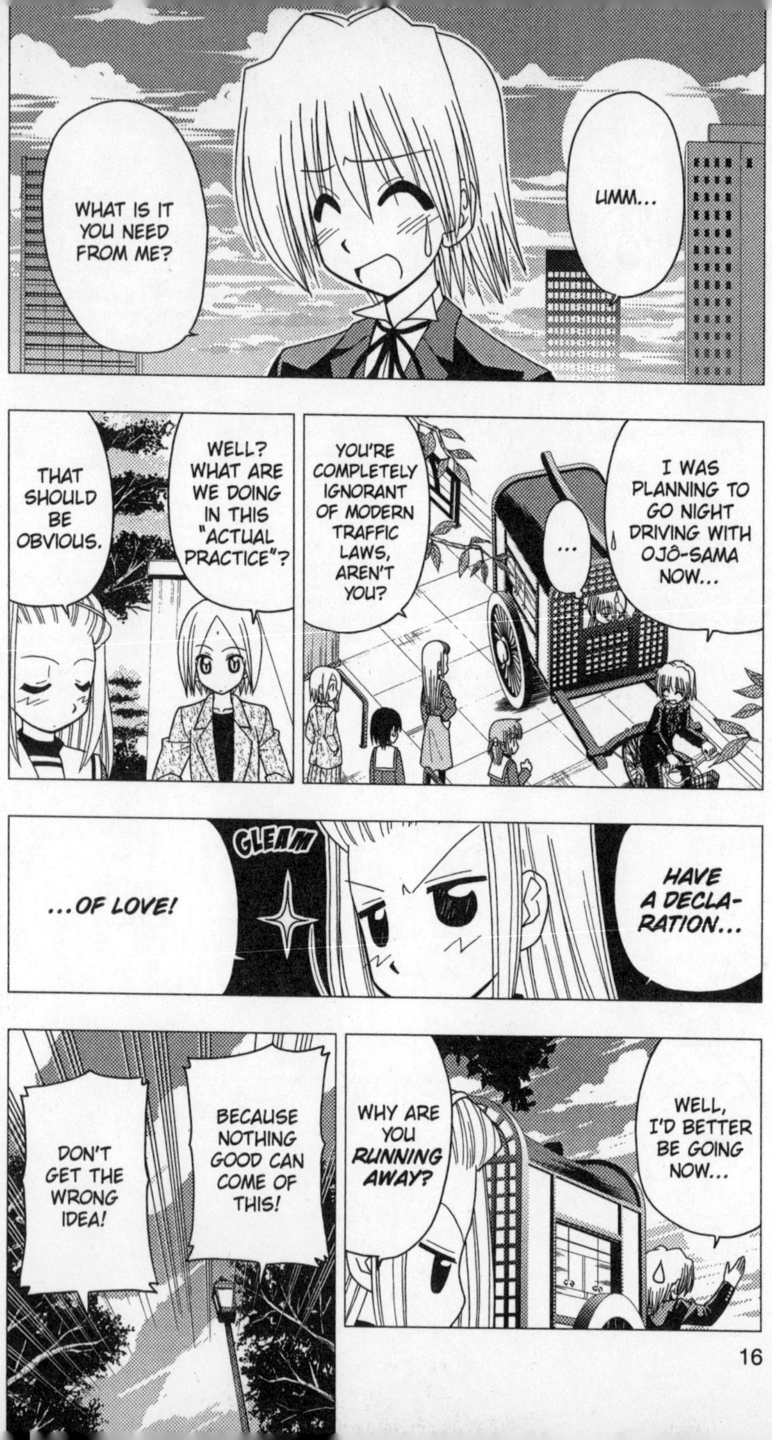

UMM...
WHAT IS IT YOU NEED FROM ME?
I WAS PLANNING TO GO NIGHT DRIVING WITH OJÔ-SAMA NOW...
...
YOU'RE COMPLETELY IGNORANT OF MODERN TRAFFIC LAWS, AREN'T YOU?
WELL? WHAT ARE WE DOING IN THIS "ACTUAL PRACTICE"?
THAT SHOULD BE OBVIOUS.
HAVE A DECLARATION...
GLEAM
...OF LOVE!
WELL, I'D BETTER BE GOING NOW...
WHY ARE YOU RUNNING AWAY?
BECAUSE NOTHING GOOD CAN COME OF THIS!
DON'T GET THE WRONG IDEA!

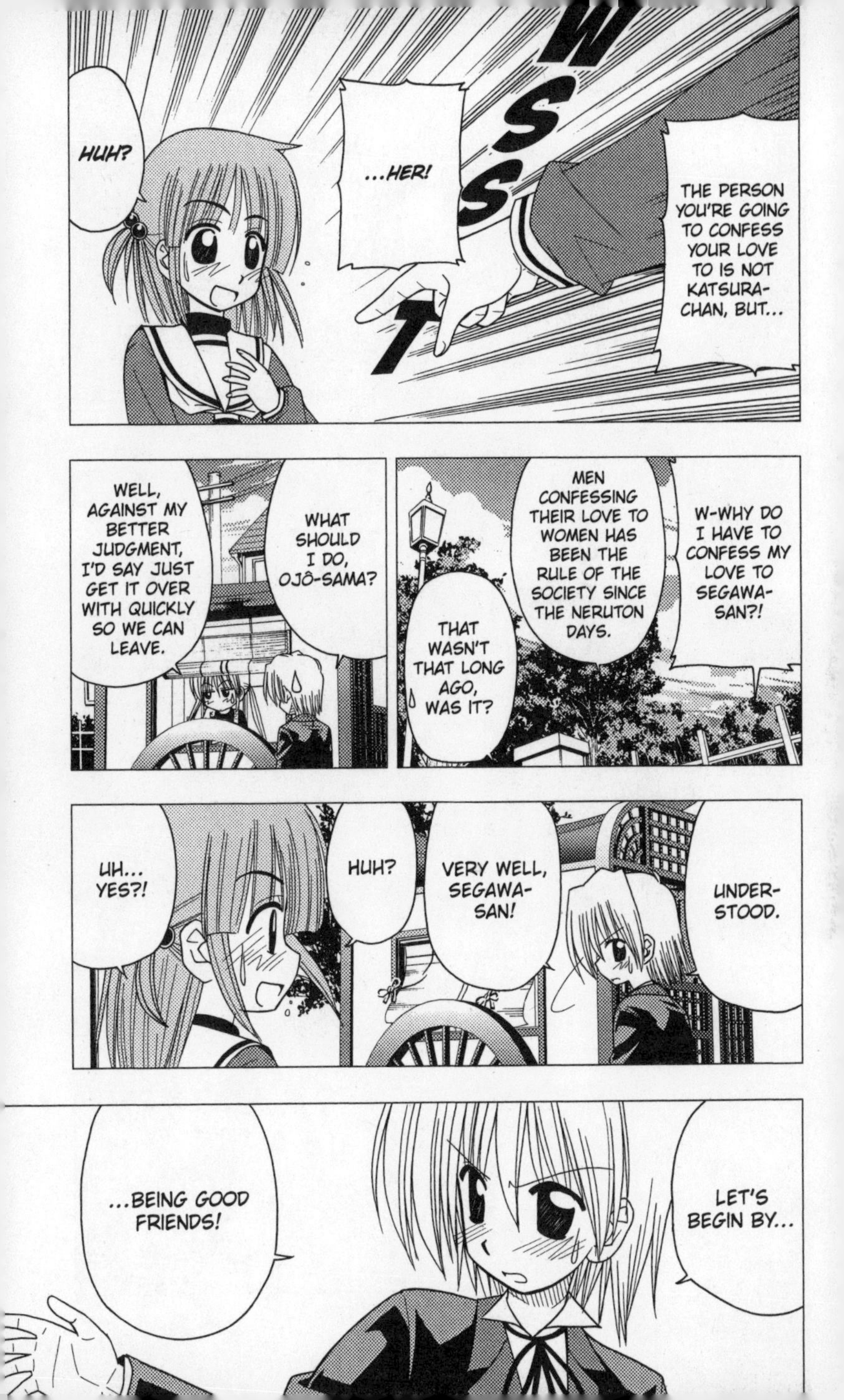
THE PERSON YOU'RE GOING TO CONFESS YOUR LOVE TO IS NOT KATSURA-CHAN, BUT...
WSS
...HER!
HUH?
W-WHY DO I HAVE TO CONFESS MY LOVE TO SEGAWA-SAN?!
MEN CONFESSING THEIR LOVE TO WOMEN HAS BEEN THE RULE OF THE SOCIETY SINCE THE NERUTON DAYS.
THAT WASN'T THAT LONG AGO, WAS IT?
WHAT SHOULD I DO, OJÔ-SAMA?
WELL, AGAINST MY BETTER JUDGMENT, I'D SAY JUST GET IT OVER WITH QUICKLY SO WE CAN LEAVE.
UNDER-STOOD.
VERY WELL, SEGAWA-SAN!
HUH?
UH... YES?!
LET'S BEGIN BY...
...BEING GOOD FRIENDS!

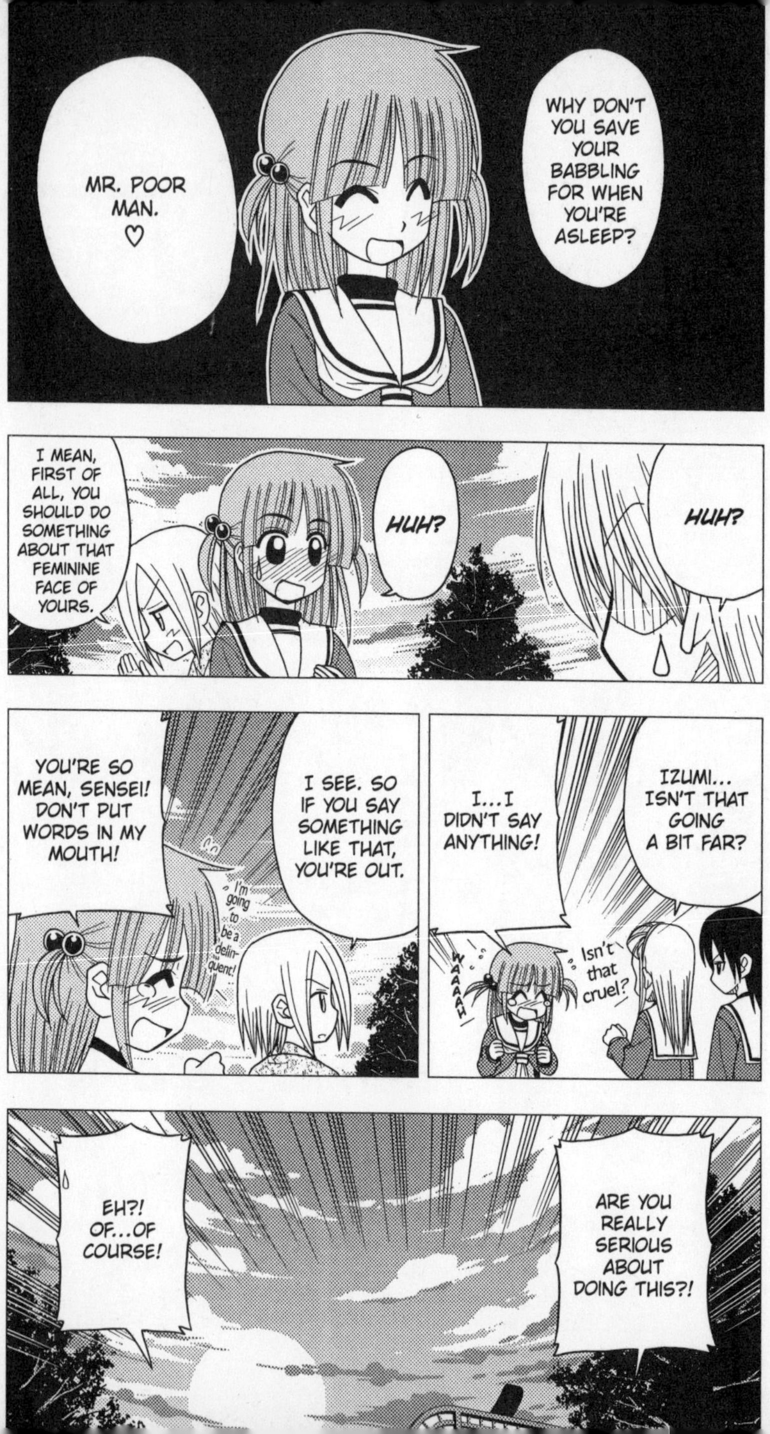
WHY DON'T YOU SAVE YOUR BABBLING FOR WHEN YOU'RE ASLEEP?
MR. POOR MAN. ♡
HUH?
HUH?
I MEAN, FIRST OF ALL, YOU SHOULD DO SOMETHING ABOUT THAT FEMININE FACE OF YOURS.
IZUMI... ISN'T THAT GOING A BIT FAR?
I...I DIDN'T SAY ANYTHING!
WAAAAH
Isn't that cruel?
I SEE. SO IF YOU SAY SOMETHING LIKE THAT, YOU'RE OUT.
YOU'RE SO MEAN, SENSEI! DON'T PUT WORDS IN MY MOUTH!
I'm going to be a delinquent!
ARE YOU REALLY SERIOUS ABOUT DOING THIS?!
EH?! OF...OF COURSE!

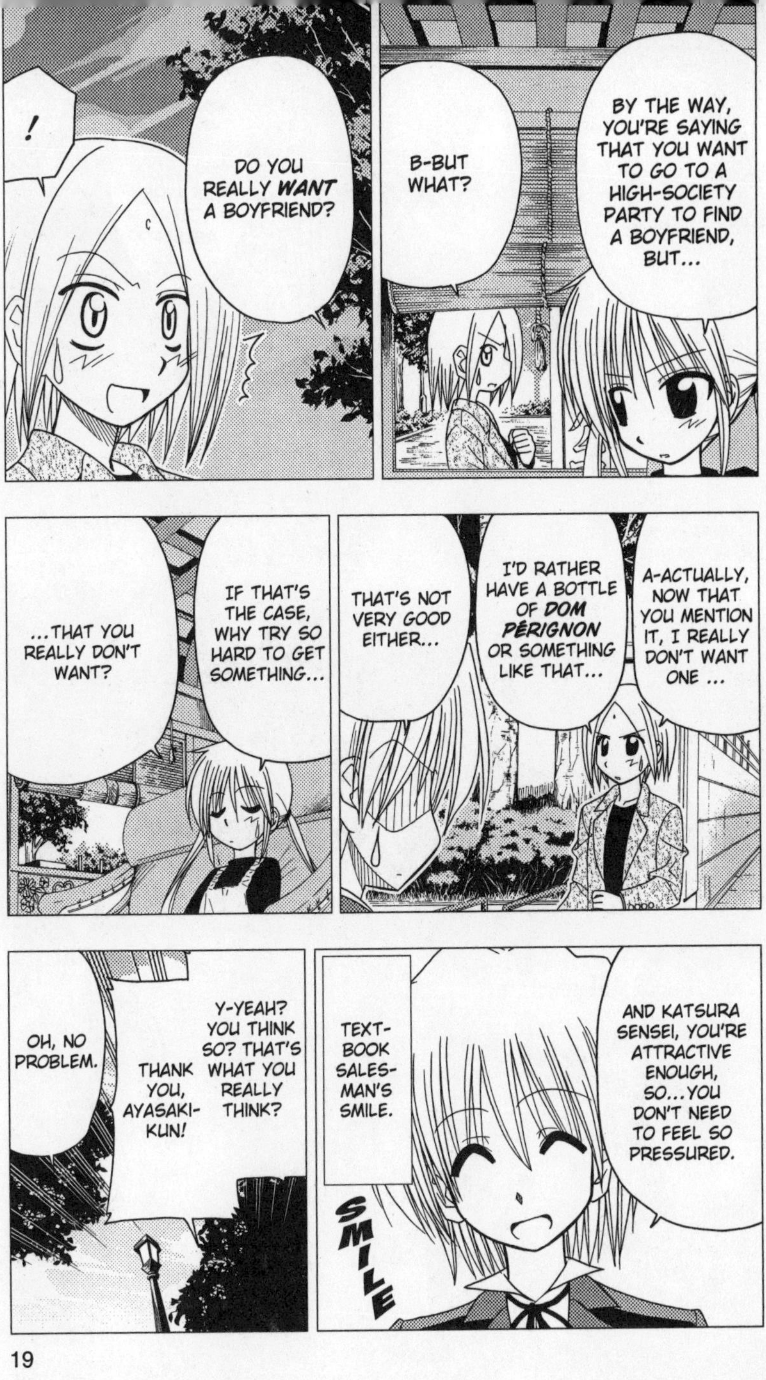
BY THE WAY, YOU'RE SAYING THAT YOU WANT TO GO TO A HIGH-SOCIETY PARTY TO FIND A BOYFRIEND, BUT...
B-BUT WHAT?
DO YOU REALLY WANT A BOYFRIEND?
!
A-ACTUALLY, NOW THAT YOU MENTION IT, I REALLY DON'T WANT ONE ...
I'D RATHER HAVE A BOTTLE OF DOM PÉRIGNON OR SOMETHING LIKE THAT...
THAT'S NOT VERY GOOD EITHER...
IF THAT'S THE CASE, WHY TRY SO HARD TO GET SOMETHING...
...THAT YOU REALLY DON'T WANT?
AND KATSURA SENSEI, YOU'RE ATTRACTIVE ENOUGH, SO...YOU DON'T NEED TO FEEL SO PRESSURED.
TEXT-BOOK SALES-MAN'S SMILE.
SMILE
Y-YEAH? YOU THINK SO? THAT'S WHAT YOU REALLY THINK?
THANK YOU, AYASAKI-KUN!
OH, NO PROBLEM.

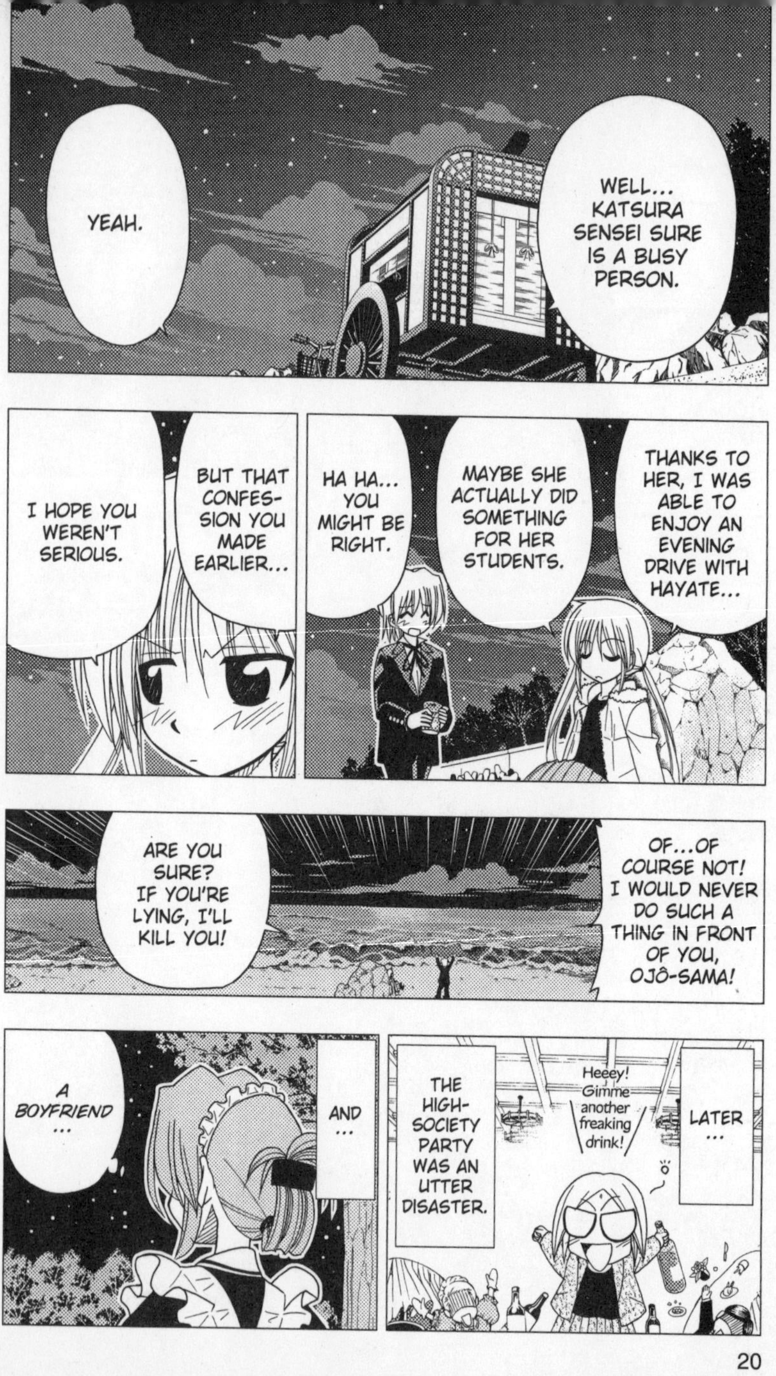
WELL... KATSURA SENSEI SURE IS A BUSY PERSON.
YEAH.
THANKS TO HER, I WAS ABLE TO ENJOY AN EVENING DRIVE WITH HAYATE...
MAYBE SHE ACTUALLY DID SOMETHING FOR HER STUDENTS.
HA HA... YOU MIGHT BE RIGHT.
BUT THAT CONFESSION YOU MADE EARLIER...
I HOPE YOU WEREN'T SERIOUS.
OF...OF COURSE NOT! I WOULD NEVER DO SUCH A THING IN FRONT OF YOU, OJÔ-SAMA!
ARE YOU SURE? IF YOU'RE LYING, I'LL KILL YOU!
LATER...
Heeey! Gimme another freaking drink!
THE HIGH-SOCIETY PARTY WAS AN UTTER DISASTER.
AND...
A BOYFRIEND...

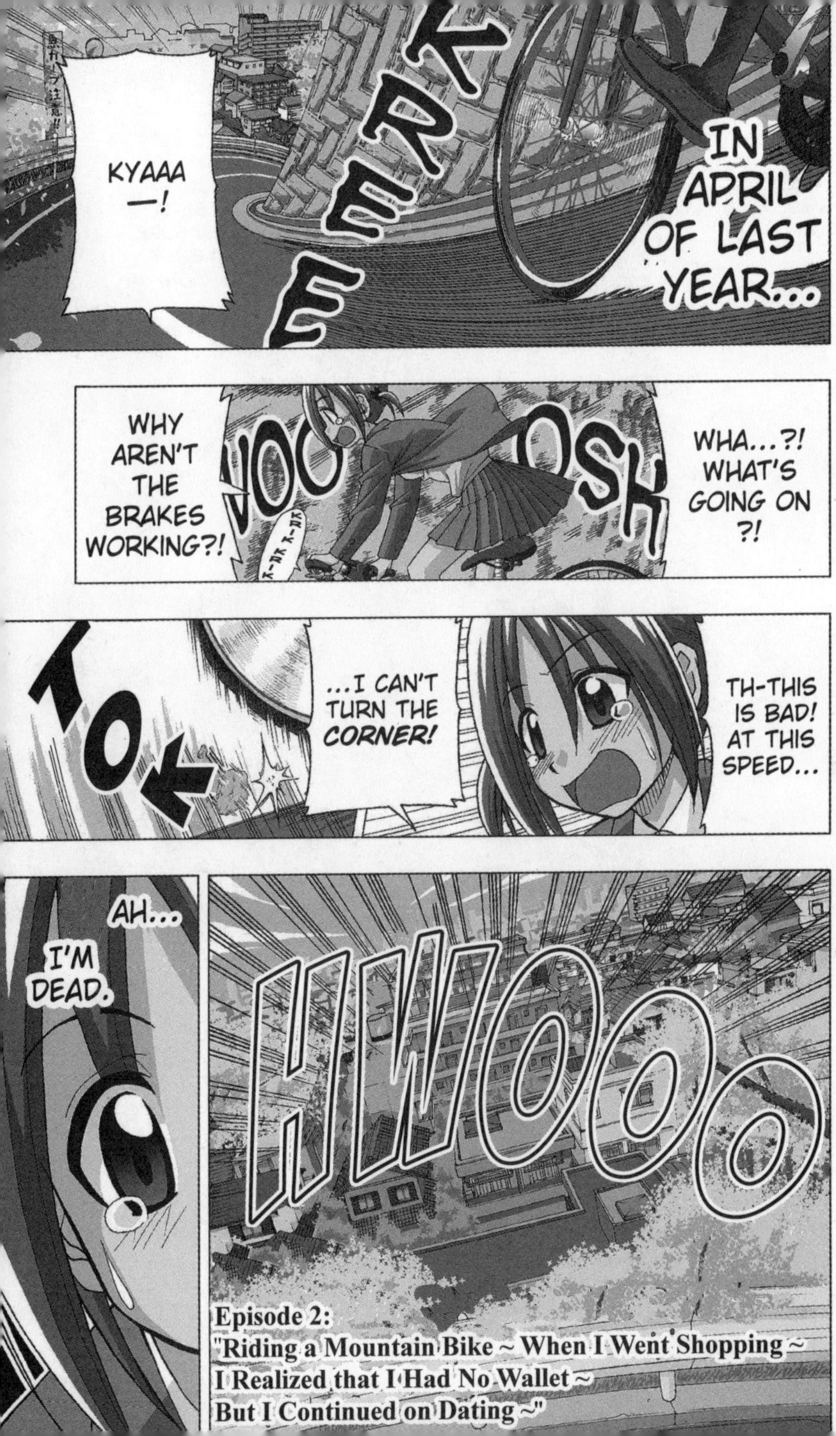
IN APRIL OF LAST YEAR...
KREEE
急カーブ注意!!
KYAAA—!
WHA...?! WHAT'S GOING ON ?!
WOOOSH
KRIK KRIK
WHY AREN'T THE BRAKES WORKING?!
TH-THIS IS BAD! AT THIS SPEED...
...I CAN'T TURN THE CORNER!
TOK
HWOOOO
AH...
I'M DEAD.

Episode 2:
"Riding a Mountain Bike ~ When I Went Shopping ~
I Realized that I Had No Wallet ~
But I Continued on Dating ~"

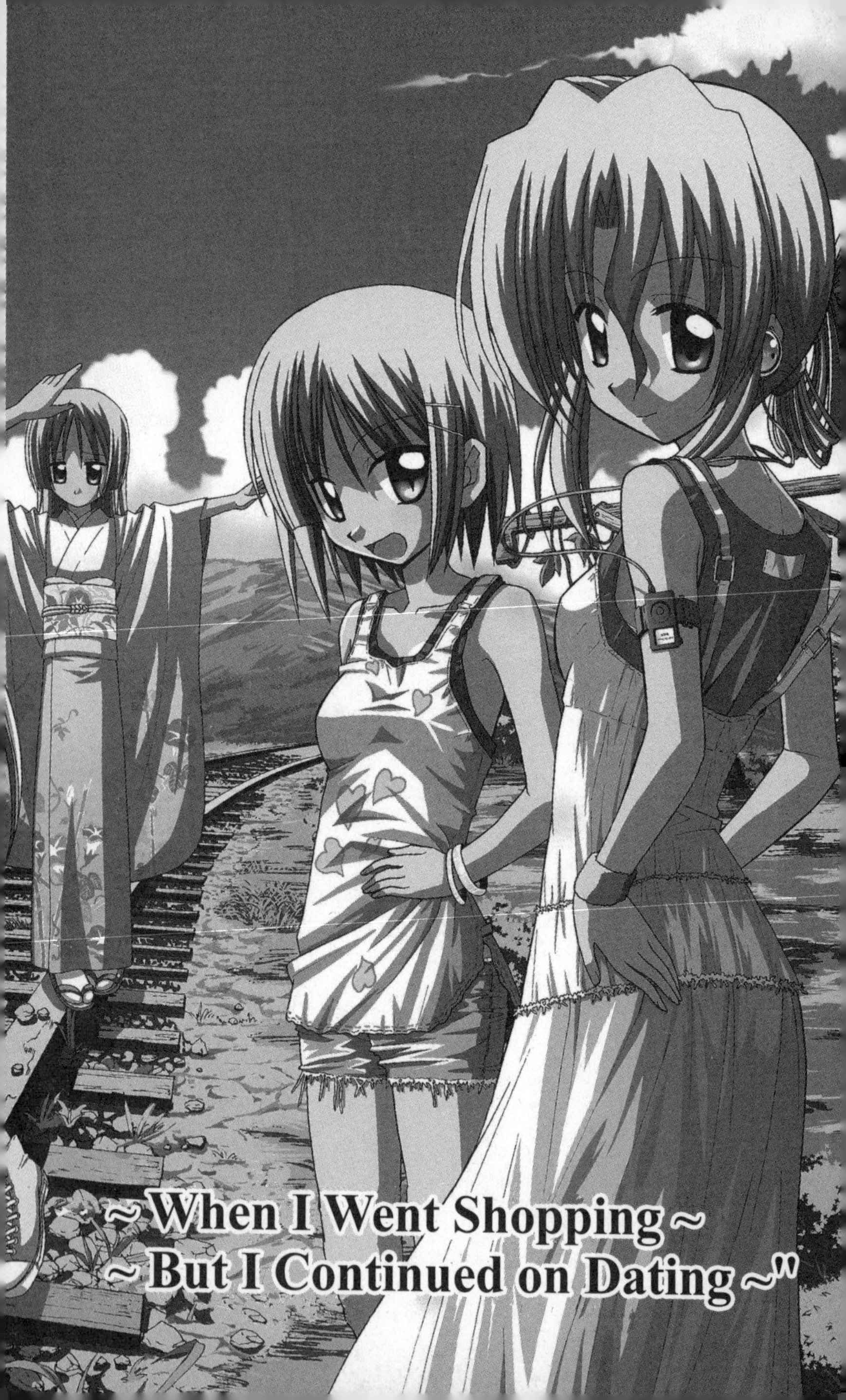
~ When I Went Shopping ~
~ But I Continued on Dating ~"

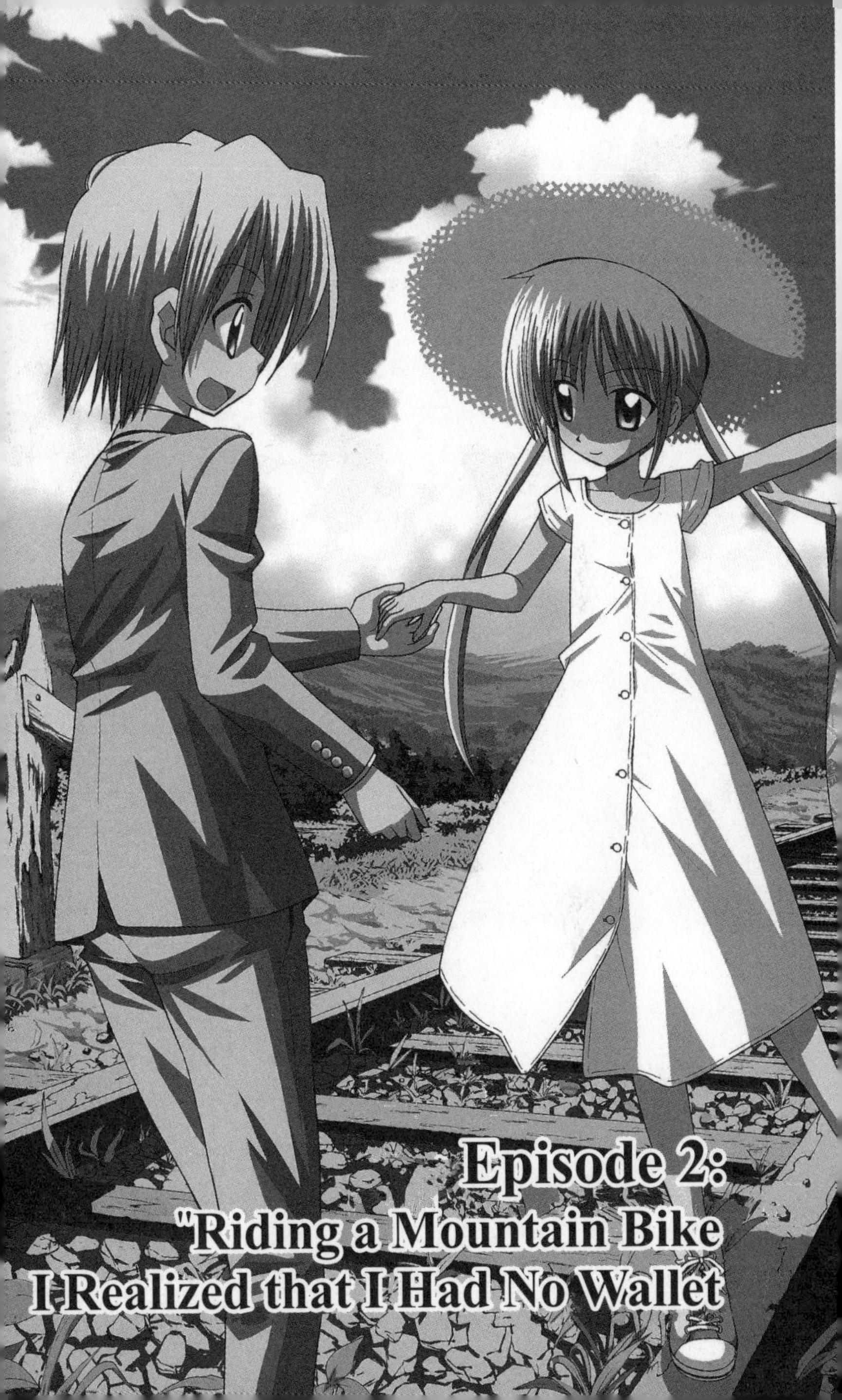
Episode 2:
"Riding a Mountain Bike
I Realized that I Had No Wallet

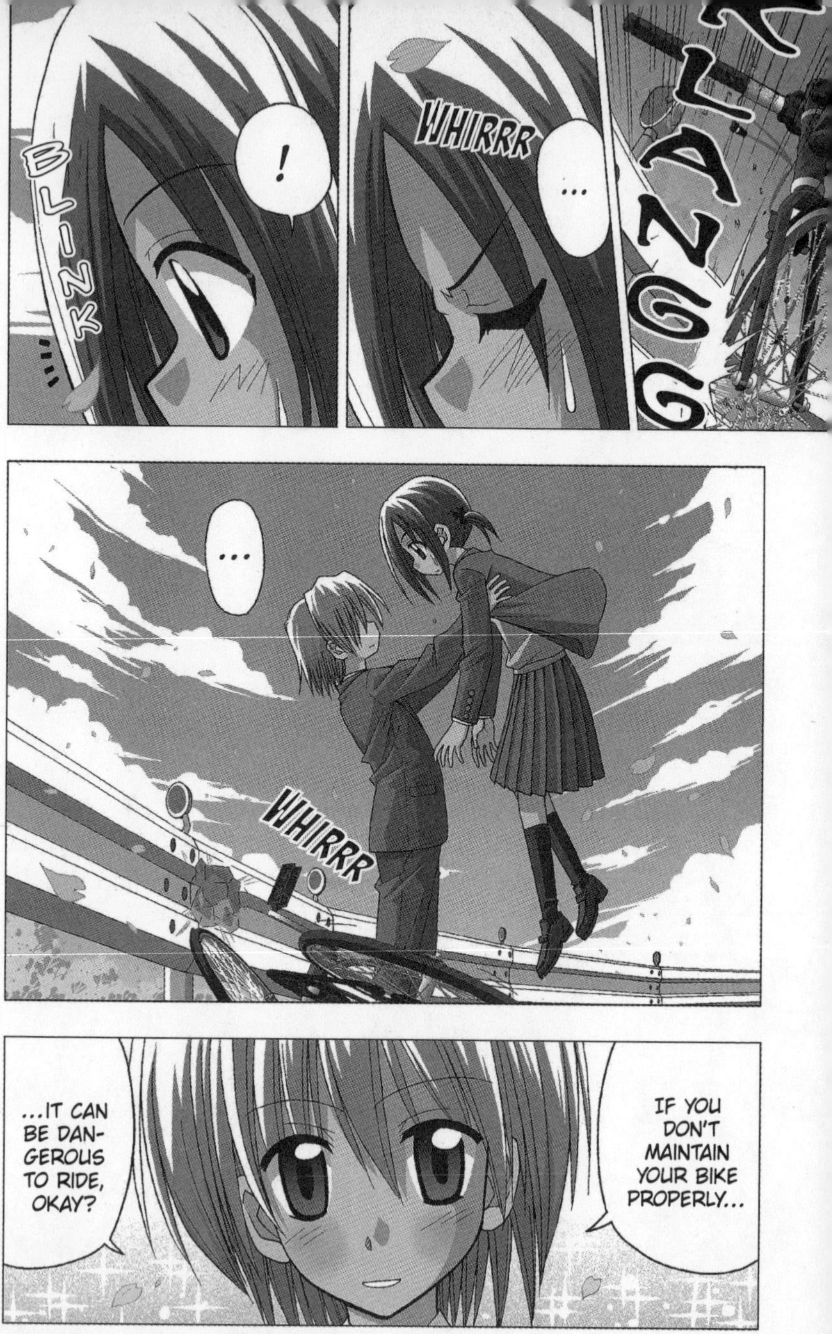
KLANGG
WHIRRR
...
!
BLINK
...
WHIRRR
IF YOU DON'T MAINTAIN YOUR BIKE PROPERLY...
...IT CAN BE DAN-GEROUS TO RIDE, OKAY?

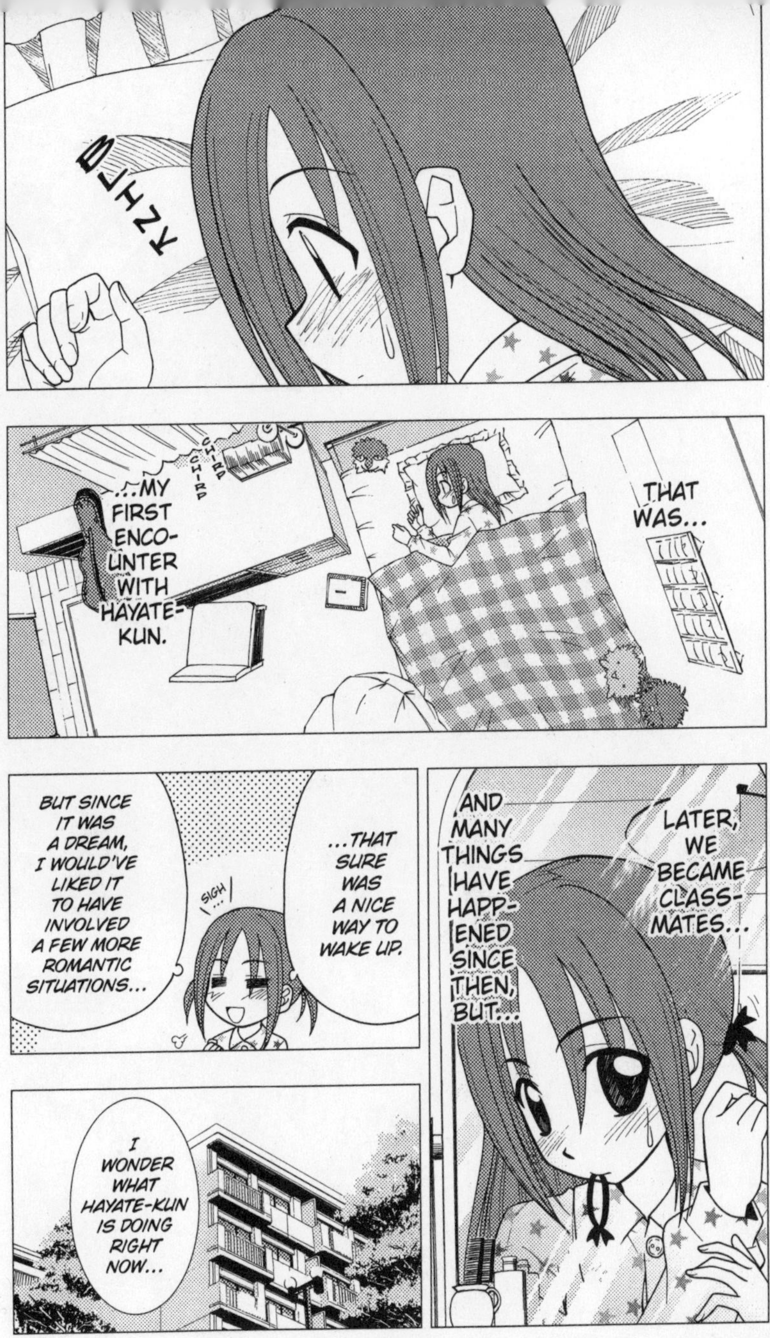
THAT WAS...
CHIRP CHIRP
...MY FIRST ENCO-UNTER WITH HAYATE-KUN.
LATER, WE BECAME CLASS-MATES...
AND MANY THINGS HAVE HAPP-ENED SINCE THEN, BUT...
...THAT SURE WAS A NICE WAY TO WAKE UP.
SIGH...!
BUT SINCE IT WAS A DREAM, I WOULD'VE LIKED IT TO HAVE INVOLVED A FEW MORE ROMANTIC SITUATIONS...
I WONDER WHAT HAYATE-KUN IS DOING RIGHT NOW...

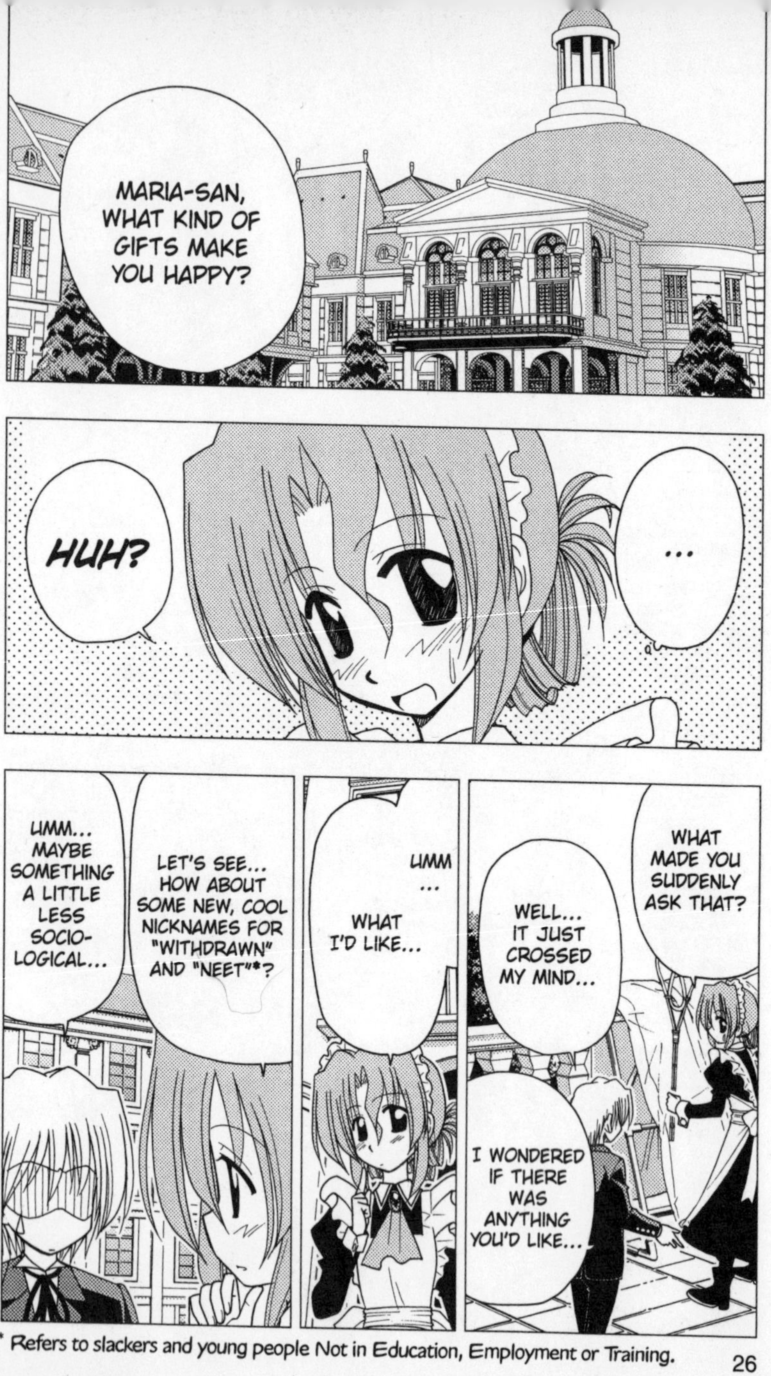
MARIA-SAN, WHAT KIND OF GIFTS MAKE YOU HAPPY?
...
HUH?
WHAT MADE YOU SUDDENLY ASK THAT?
WELL... IT JUST CROSSED MY MIND...
I WONDERED IF THERE WAS ANYTHING YOU'D LIKE...
UMM ...
WHAT I'D LIKE...
LET'S SEE... HOW ABOUT SOME NEW, COOL NICKNAMES FOR "WITHDRAWN" AND "NEET"*?
UMM... MAYBE SOMETHING A LITTLE LESS SOCIO-LOGICAL...

* Refers to slackers and young people Not in Education, Employment or Training.

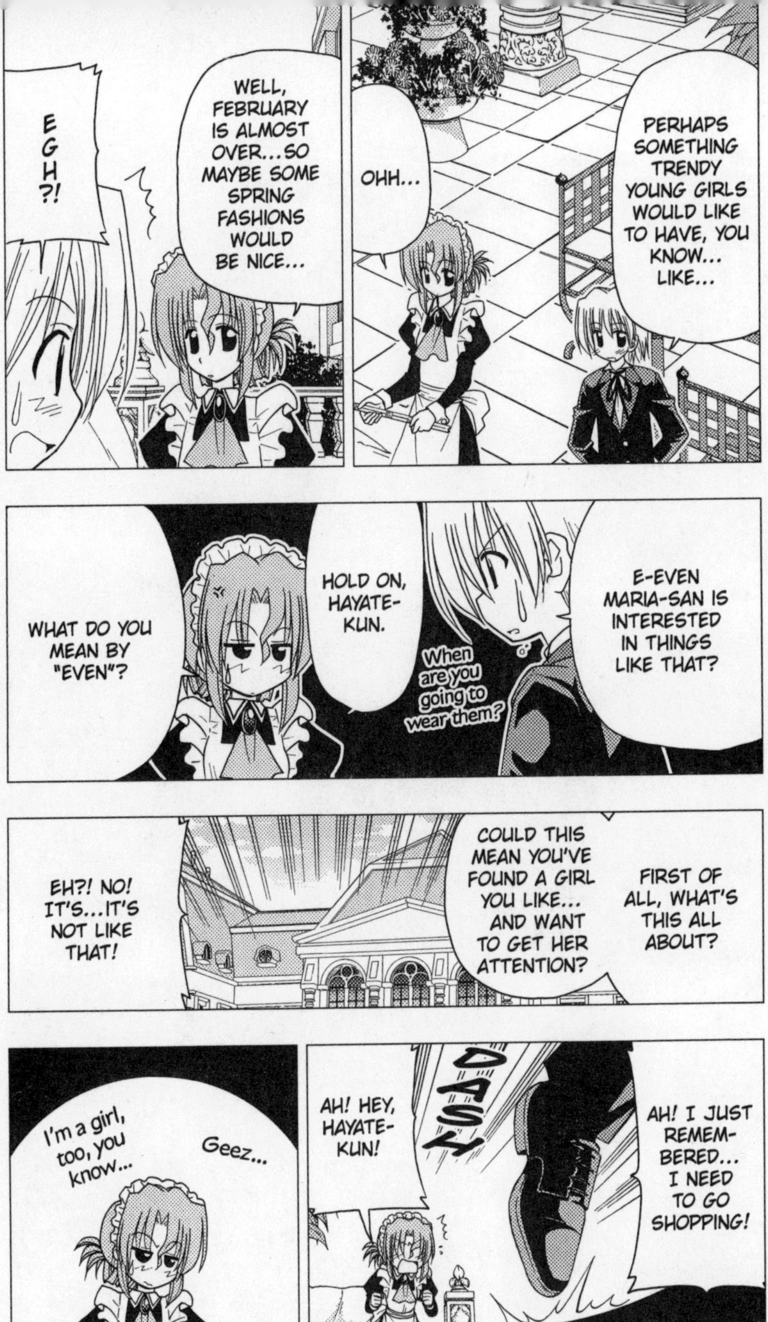
PERHAPS SOMETHING TRENDY YOUNG GIRLS WOULD LIKE TO HAVE, YOU KNOW... LIKE...
OHH...
WELL, FEBRUARY IS ALMOST OVER...SO MAYBE SOME SPRING FASHIONS WOULD BE NICE...
EGH?!
E-EVEN MARIA-SAN IS INTERESTED IN THINGS LIKE THAT?
When are you going to wear them?
HOLD ON, HAYATE-KUN.
WHAT DO YOU MEAN BY "EVEN"?
FIRST OF ALL, WHAT'S THIS ALL ABOUT?
COULD THIS MEAN YOU'VE FOUND A GIRL YOU LIKE... AND WANT TO GET HER ATTENTION?
EH?! NO! IT'S...IT'S NOT LIKE THAT!
AH! I JUST REMEMBERED... I NEED TO GO SHOPPING!
DASH
AH! HEY, HAYATE-KUN!
Geez...
I'm a girl, too, you know...

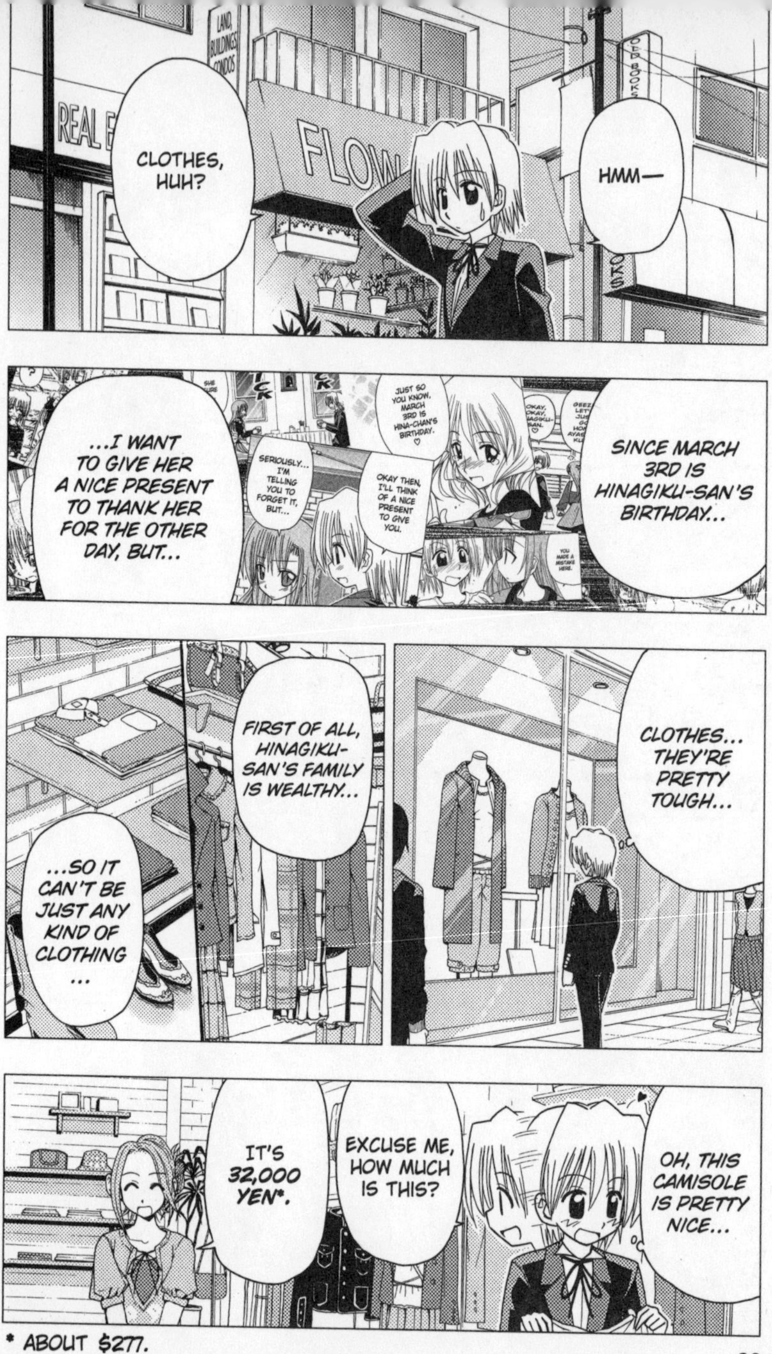
LAND, BUILDINGS, CONDOS
OLD BOOKS
HMM—
CLOTHES, HUH?
SINCE MARCH 3RD IS HINAGIKU-SAN'S BIRTHDAY...
OKAY, OKAY, HINAGIKU-SAN. ♡
JUST SO YOU KNOW, MARCH 3RD IS HINA-CHAN'S BIRTHDAY. ♡
OKAY THEN, I'LL THINK OF A NICE PRESENT TO GIVE YOU.
SERIOUSLY... I'M TELLING YOU TO FORGET IT, BUT...
YOU MADE A MISTAKE HERE.
...I WANT TO GIVE HER A NICE PRESENT TO THANK HER FOR THE OTHER DAY, BUT...
CLOTHES... THEY'RE PRETTY TOUGH...
FIRST OF ALL, HINAGIKU-SAN'S FAMILY IS WEALTHY...
...SO IT CAN'T BE JUST ANY KIND OF CLOTHING ...
OH, THIS CAMISOLE IS PRETTY NICE...
EXCUSE ME, HOW MUCH IS THIS?
IT'S 32,000 YEN*.

* ABOUT $277.

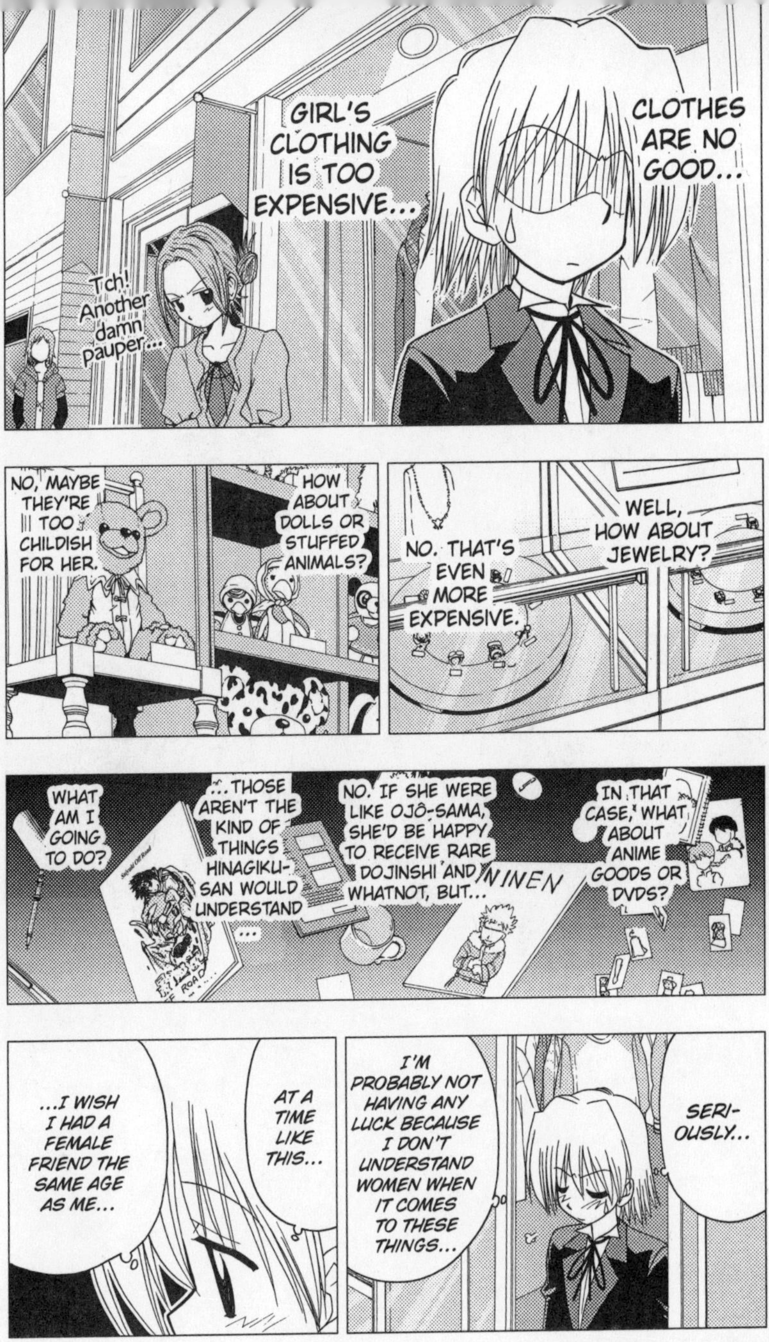
CLOTHES ARE NO GOOD...
GIRL'S CLOTHING IS TOO EXPENSIVE...
Tch! Another damn pauper...
WELL, HOW ABOUT JEWELRY?
NO. THAT'S EVEN MORE EXPENSIVE.
HOW ABOUT DOLLS OR STUFFED ANIMALS?
NO, MAYBE THEY'RE TOO CHILDISH FOR HER.
IN THAT CASE, WHAT ABOUT ANIME GOODS OR DVDS?
NO. IF SHE WERE LIKE OJÔ-SAMA, SHE'D BE HAPPY TO RECEIVE RARE DOJINSHI AND WHATNOT, BUT...
NINEN
...THOSE AREN'T THE KIND OF THINGS HINAGIKU-SAN WOULD UNDERSTAND...
WHAT AM I GOING TO DO?
SERIOUSLY...
I'M PROBABLY NOT HAVING ANY LUCK BECAUSE I DON'T UNDERSTAND WOMEN WHEN IT COMES TO THESE THINGS...
AT A TIME LIKE THIS...
...I WISH I HAD A FEMALE FRIEND THE SAME AGE AS ME...

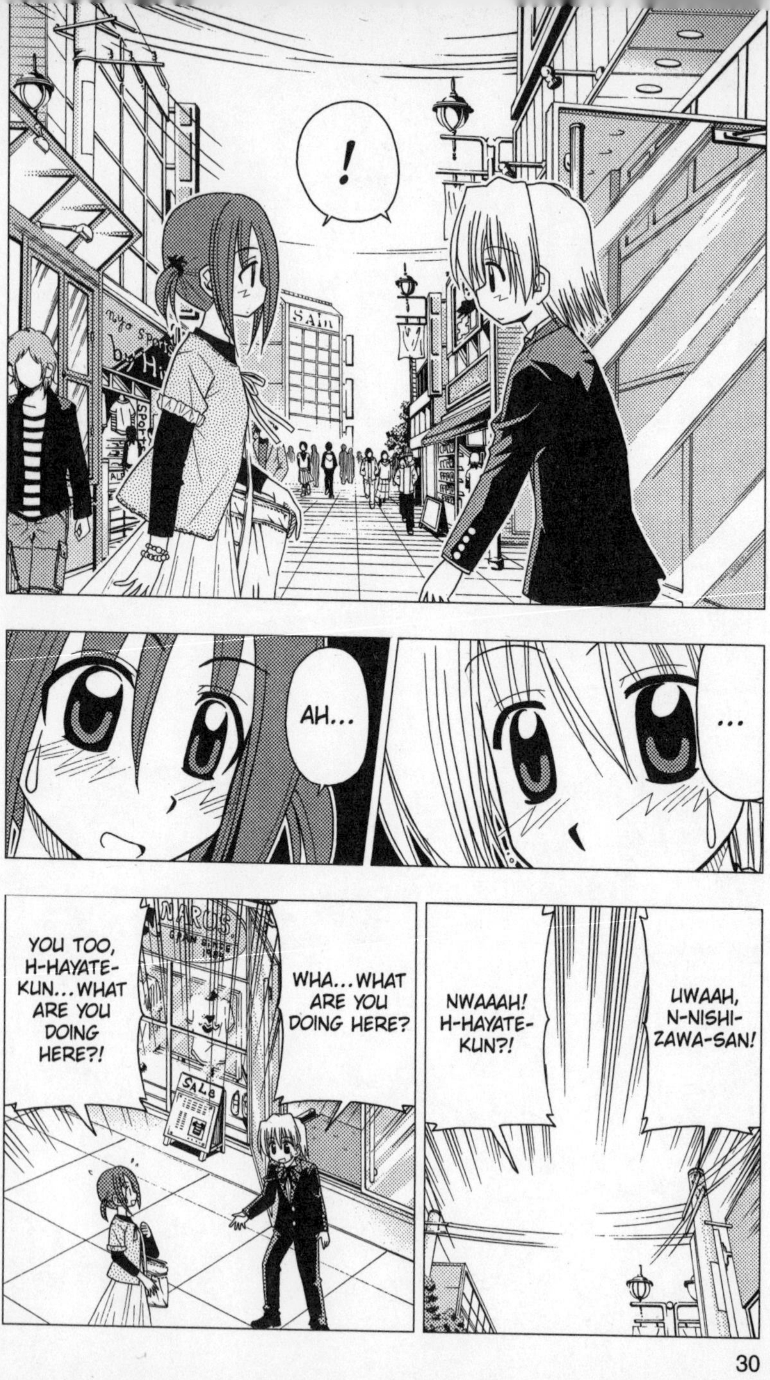
!
...
AH...
UWAAH, N-NISHI-ZAWA-SAN!
NWAAAH! H-HAYATE-KUN?!
WHA...WHAT ARE YOU DOING HERE?
YOU TOO, H-HAYATE-KUN...WHAT ARE YOU DOING HERE?!

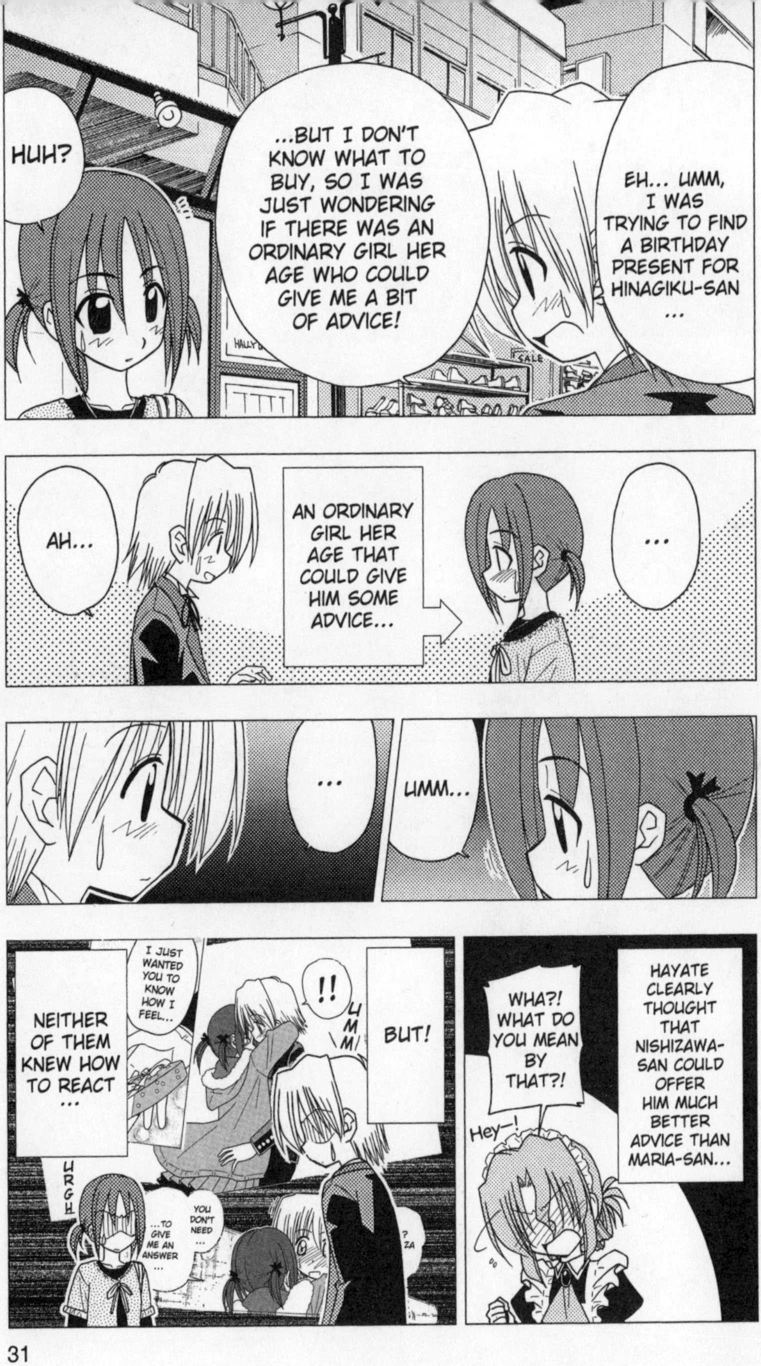
EH... UMM, I WAS TRYING TO FIND A BIRTHDAY PRESENT FOR HINAGIKU-SAN ...
...BUT I DON'T KNOW WHAT TO BUY, SO I WAS JUST WONDERING IF THERE WAS AN ORDINARY GIRL HER AGE WHO COULD GIVE ME A BIT OF ADVICE!
HUH?
...
AN ORDINARY GIRL HER AGE THAT COULD GIVE HIM SOME ADVICE...
AH...
UMM...
...
HAYATE CLEARLY THOUGHT THAT NISHIZAWA-SAN COULD OFFER HIM MUCH BETTER ADVICE THAN MARIA-SAN...
WHA?! WHAT DO YOU MEAN BY THAT?!
Hey—!
BUT!
!!
UMM
I JUST WANTED YOU TO KNOW HOW I FEEL...
NEITHER OF THEM KNEW HOW TO REACT ...
YOU DON'T NEED ...
...TO GIVE ME AN ANSWER ...
URGH

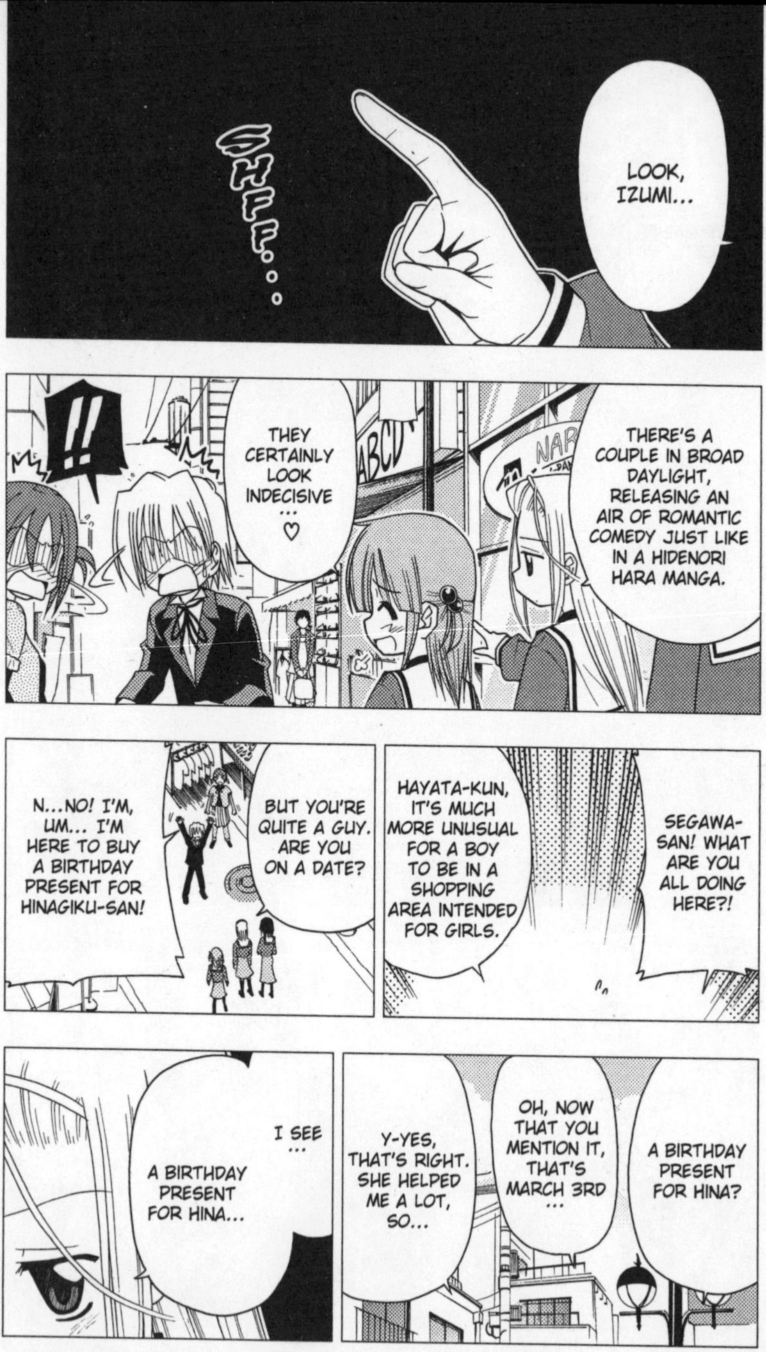
LOOK, IZUMI...
SHFF...
THERE'S A COUPLE IN BROAD DAYLIGHT, RELEASING AN AIR OF ROMANTIC COMEDY JUST LIKE IN A HIDENORI HARA MANGA.
THEY CERTAINLY LOOK INDECISIVE ... ♡
!!
SEGAWA-SAN! WHAT ARE YOU ALL DOING HERE?!
HAYATA-KUN, IT'S MUCH MORE UNUSUAL FOR A BOY TO BE IN A SHOPPING AREA INTENDED FOR GIRLS.
BUT YOU'RE QUITE A GUY. ARE YOU ON A DATE?
N...NO! I'M, UM... I'M HERE TO BUY A BIRTHDAY PRESENT FOR HINAGIKU-SAN!
A BIRTHDAY PRESENT FOR HINA?
OH, NOW THAT YOU MENTION IT, THAT'S MARCH 3RD ...
Y-YES, THAT'S RIGHT. SHE HELPED ME A LOT, SO...
I SEE ...
A BIRTHDAY PRESENT FOR HINA...

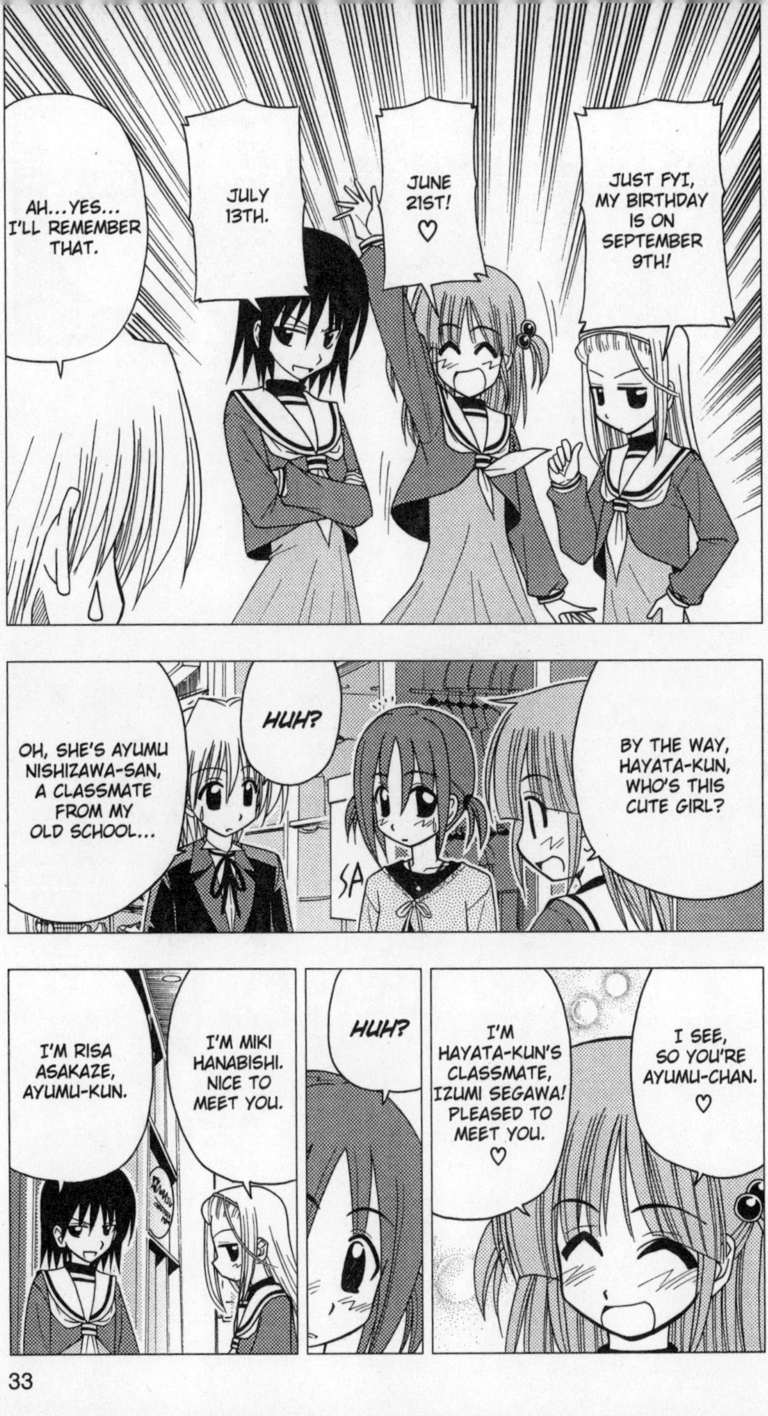
JUST FYI, MY BIRTHDAY IS ON SEPTEMBER 9TH!
JUNE 21ST! ♡
JULY 13TH.
AH...YES... I'LL REMEMBER THAT.
BY THE WAY, HAYATA-KUN, WHO'S THIS CUTE GIRL?
HUH?
OH, SHE'S AYUMU NISHIZAWA-SAN, A CLASSMATE FROM MY OLD SCHOOL...
I SEE, SO YOU'RE AYUMU-CHAN. ♡
I'M HAYATA-KUN'S CLASSMATE, IZUMI SEGAWA! PLEASED TO MEET YOU. ♡
HUH?
I'M MIKI HANABISHI. NICE TO MEET YOU.
I'M RISA ASAKAZE, AYUMU-KUN.

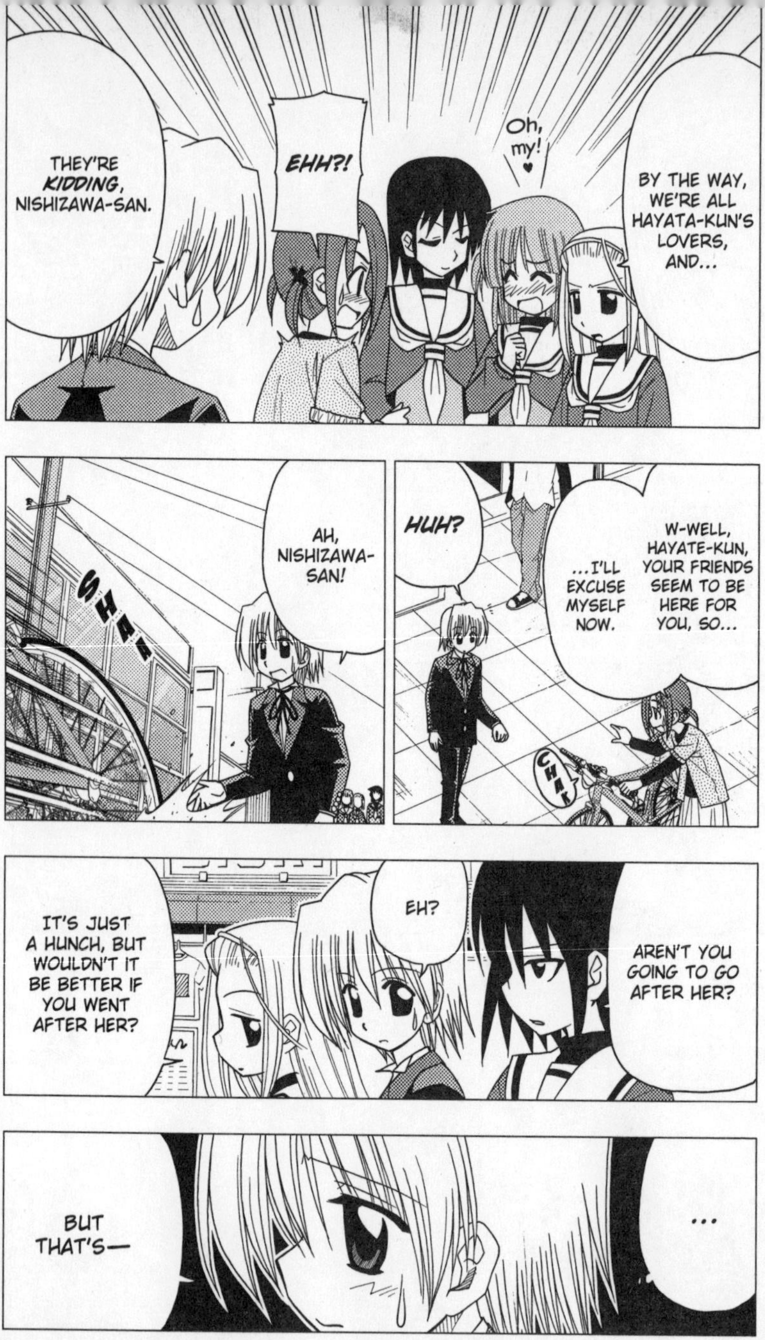
BY THE WAY, WE'RE ALL HAYATA-KUN'S LOVERS, AND...
Oh, my! ♥
EHH?!
THEY'RE *KIDDING*, NISHIZAWA-SAN.
W-WELL, HAYATE-KUN, YOUR FRIENDS SEEM TO BE HERE FOR YOU, SO...
...I'LL EXCUSE MYSELF NOW.
HUH?
CHAK
AH, NISHIZAWA-SAN!
SHAA
AREN'T YOU GOING TO GO AFTER HER?
EH?
IT'S JUST A HUNCH, BUT WOULDN'T IT BE BETTER IF YOU WENT AFTER HER?
...
BUT THAT'S—

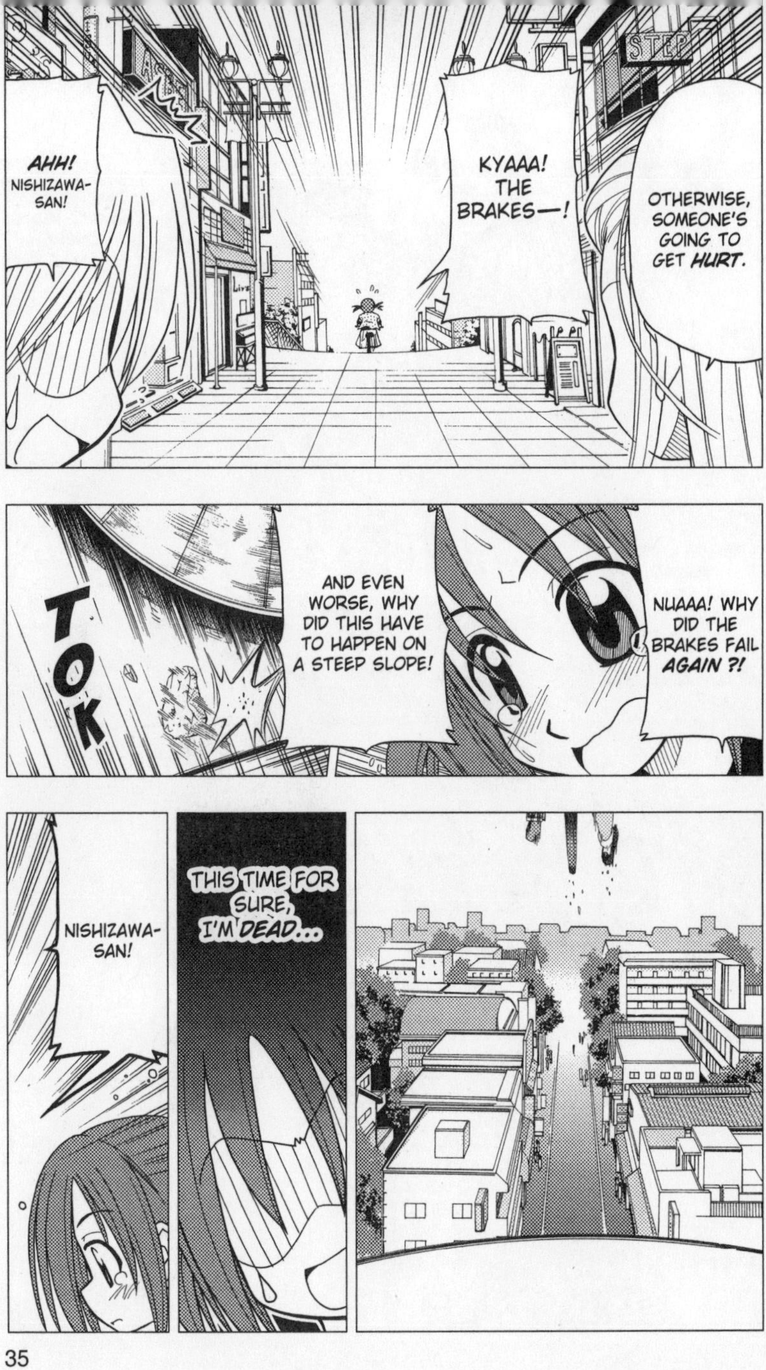
STEP
OTHERWISE, SOMEONE'S GOING TO GET *HURT*.
KYAAA! THE BRAKES—!
AHH! NISHIZAWA-SAN!
NUAAA! WHY DID THE BRAKES FAIL *AGAIN* ?!
AND EVEN WORSE, WHY DID THIS HAVE TO HAPPEN ON A STEEP SLOPE!
TOK
THIS TIME FOR SURE, I'M *DEAD*...
NISHIZAWA-SAN!

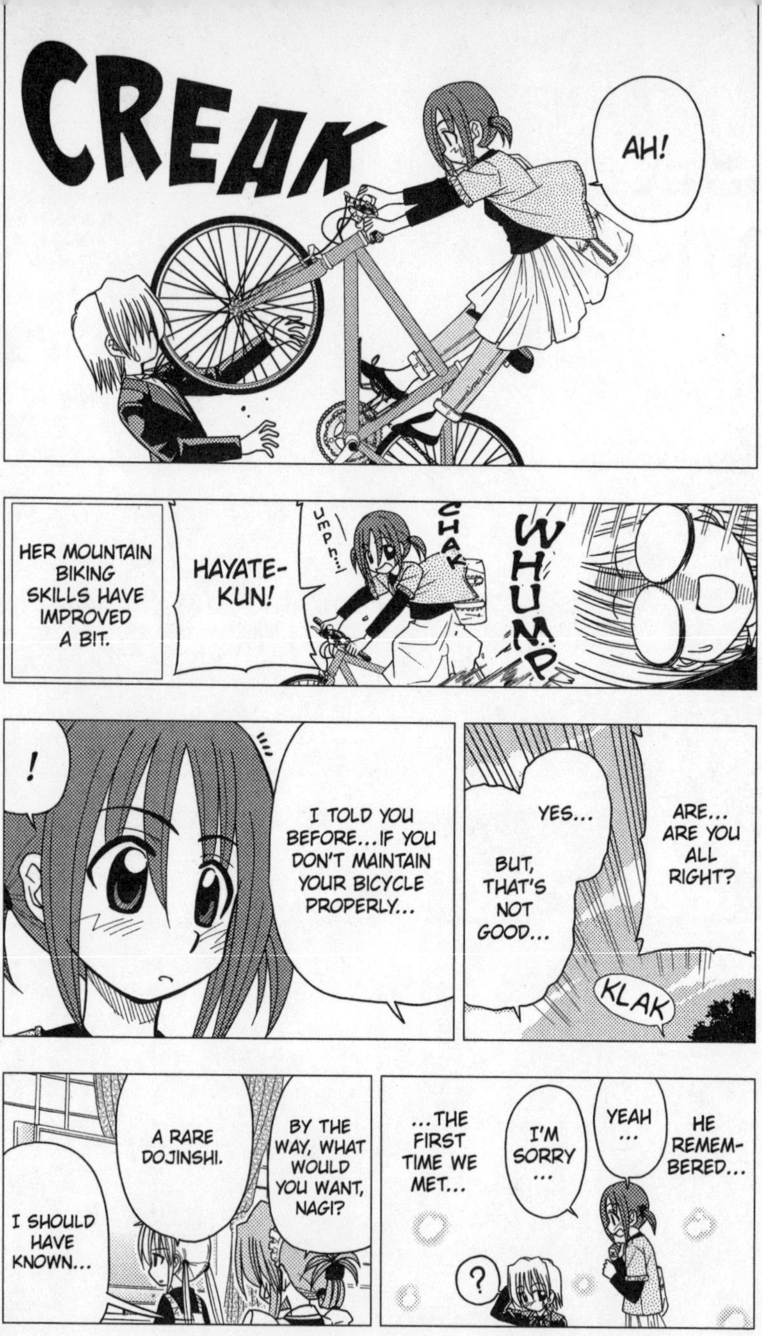
CREAK
AH!
WHUMP
CHAK
Umph...!
HAYATE-KUN!
HER MOUNTAIN BIKING SKILLS HAVE IMPROVED A BIT.
ARE... ARE YOU ALL RIGHT?
YES...
BUT, THAT'S NOT GOOD...
KLAK
I TOLD YOU BEFORE...IF YOU DON'T MAINTAIN YOUR BICYCLE PROPERLY...
!
HE REMEMBERED...
YEAH...
I'M SORRY...
...THE FIRST TIME WE MET...
?
BY THE WAY, WHAT WOULD YOU WANT, NAGI?
A RARE DOJINSHI.
I SHOULD HAVE KNOWN...

Episode 3: "Successful Mission"

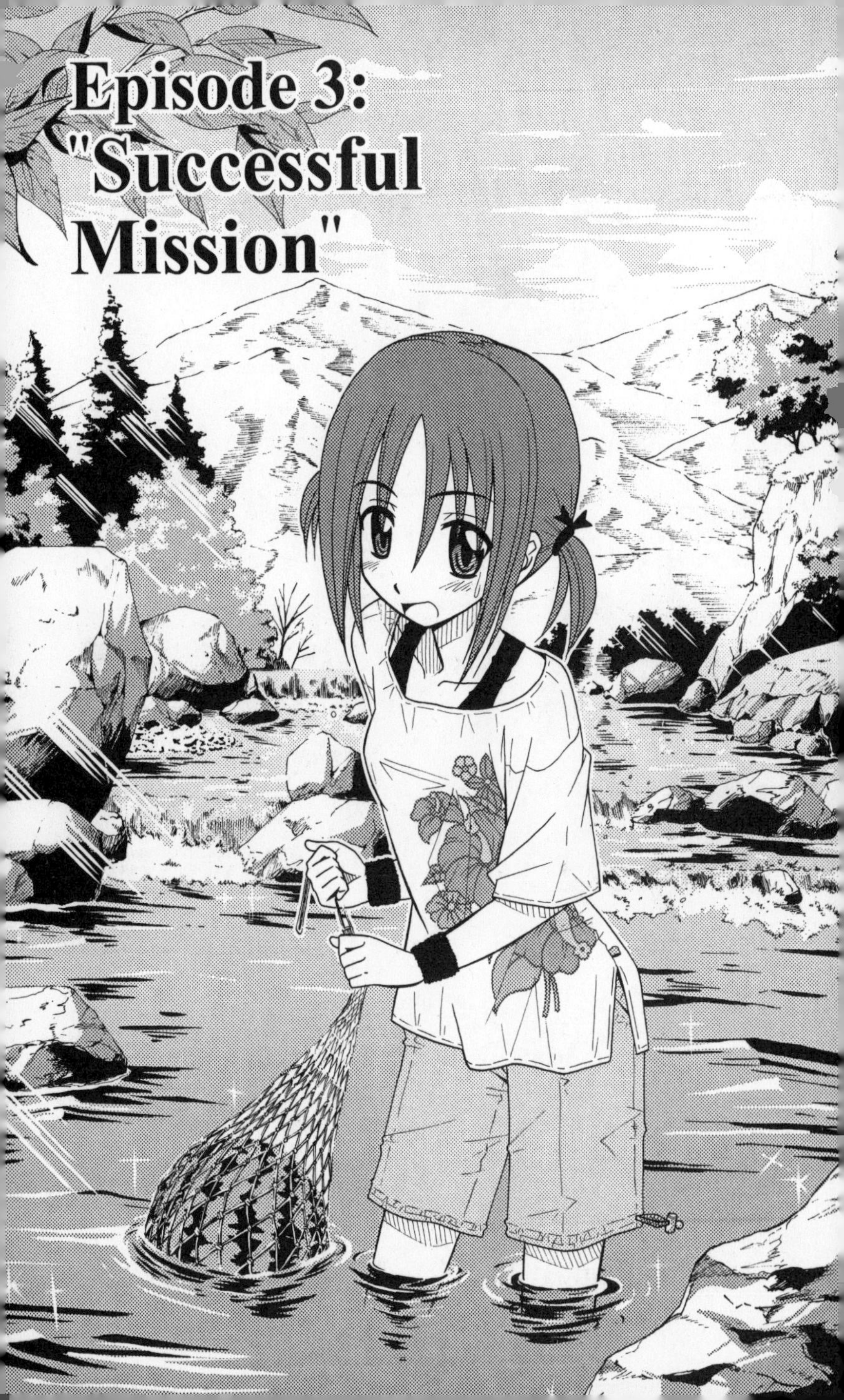

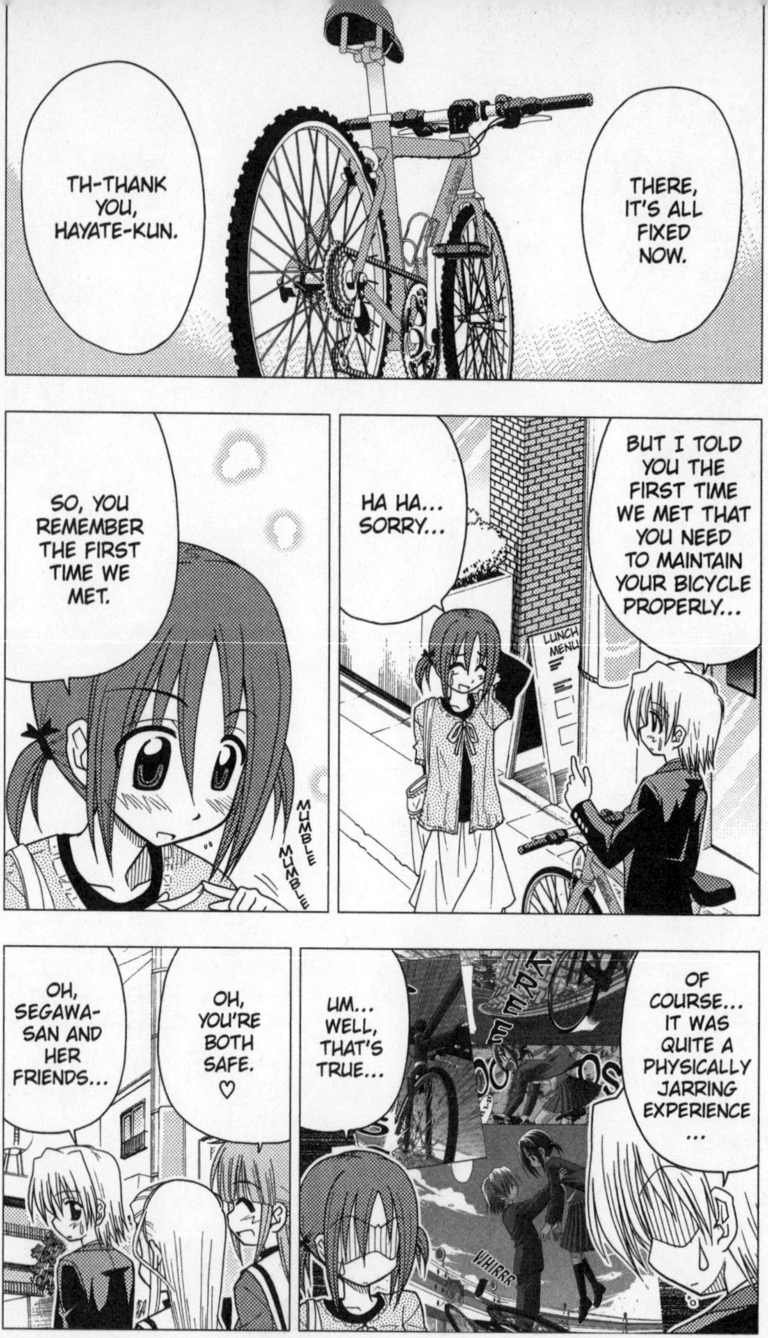
THERE, IT'S ALL FIXED NOW.
TH-THANK YOU, HAYATE-KUN.
BUT I TOLD YOU THE FIRST TIME WE MET THAT YOU NEED TO MAINTAIN YOUR BICYCLE PROPERLY...
HA HA... SORRY...
LUNCH MENU
SO, YOU REMEMBER THE FIRST TIME WE MET.
MUMBLE MUMBLE
OF COURSE... IT WAS QUITE A PHYSICALLY JARRING EXPERIENCE ...
UM... WELL, THAT'S TRUE...
WHIRRR
OH, YOU'RE BOTH SAFE. ♡
OH, SEGAWA-SAN AND HER FRIENDS...

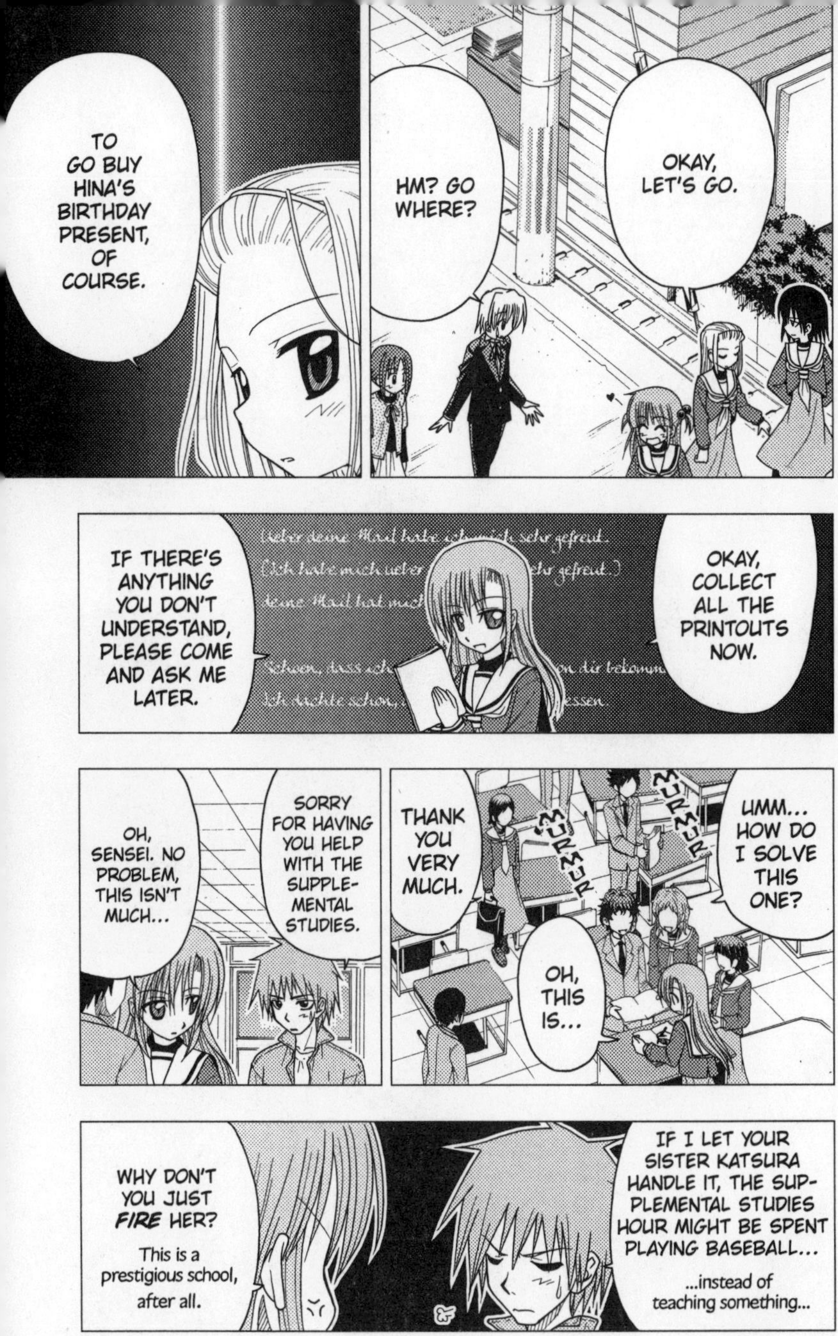
OKAY, LET'S GO.
HM? GO WHERE?
TO GO BUY HINA'S BIRTHDAY PRESENT, OF COURSE.
OKAY, COLLECT ALL THE PRINTOUTS NOW.
IF THERE'S ANYTHING YOU DON'T UNDERSTAND, PLEASE COME AND ASK ME LATER.
UMM... HOW DO I SOLVE THIS ONE?
MURMUR
MURMUR
THANK YOU VERY MUCH.
OH, THIS IS...
SORRY FOR HAVING YOU HELP WITH THE SUPPLE-MENTAL STUDIES.
OH, SENSEI. NO PROBLEM, THIS ISN'T MUCH...
IF I LET YOUR SISTER KATSURA HANDLE IT, THE SUP-PLEMENTAL STUDIES HOUR MIGHT BE SPENT PLAYING BASEBALL...
...instead of teaching something...
WHY DON'T YOU JUST *FIRE* HER?
This is a prestigious school, after all.

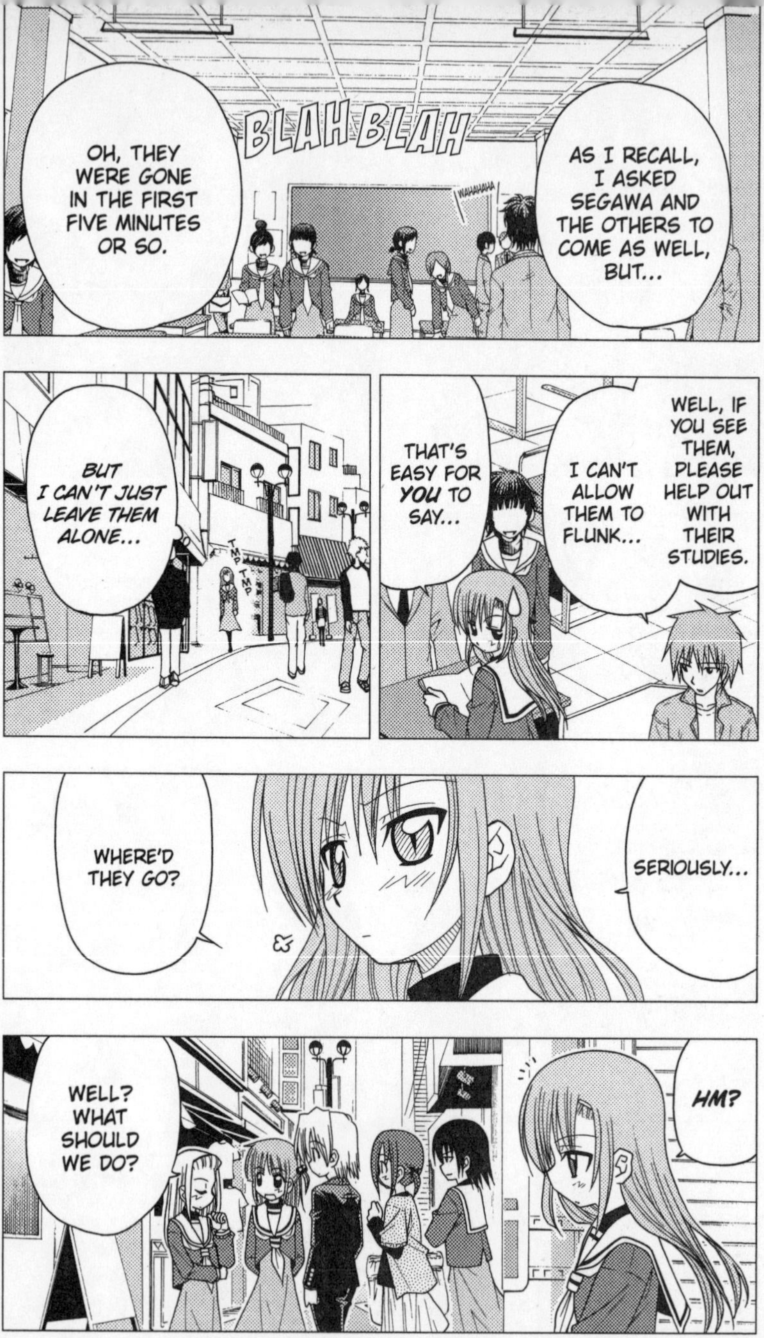
AS I RECALL, I ASKED SEGAWA AND THE OTHERS TO COME AS WELL, BUT...
BLAH BLAH
WAHAHAHA
OH, THEY WERE GONE IN THE FIRST FIVE MINUTES OR SO.
WELL, IF YOU SEE THEM, PLEASE HELP OUT WITH THEIR STUDIES.
I CAN'T ALLOW THEM TO FLUNK...
THAT'S EASY FOR *YOU* TO SAY...
BUT I CAN'T JUST LEAVE THEM ALONE...
TMP TMP
SERIOUSLY...
WHERE'D THEY GO?
HM?
WELL? WHAT SHOULD WE DO?

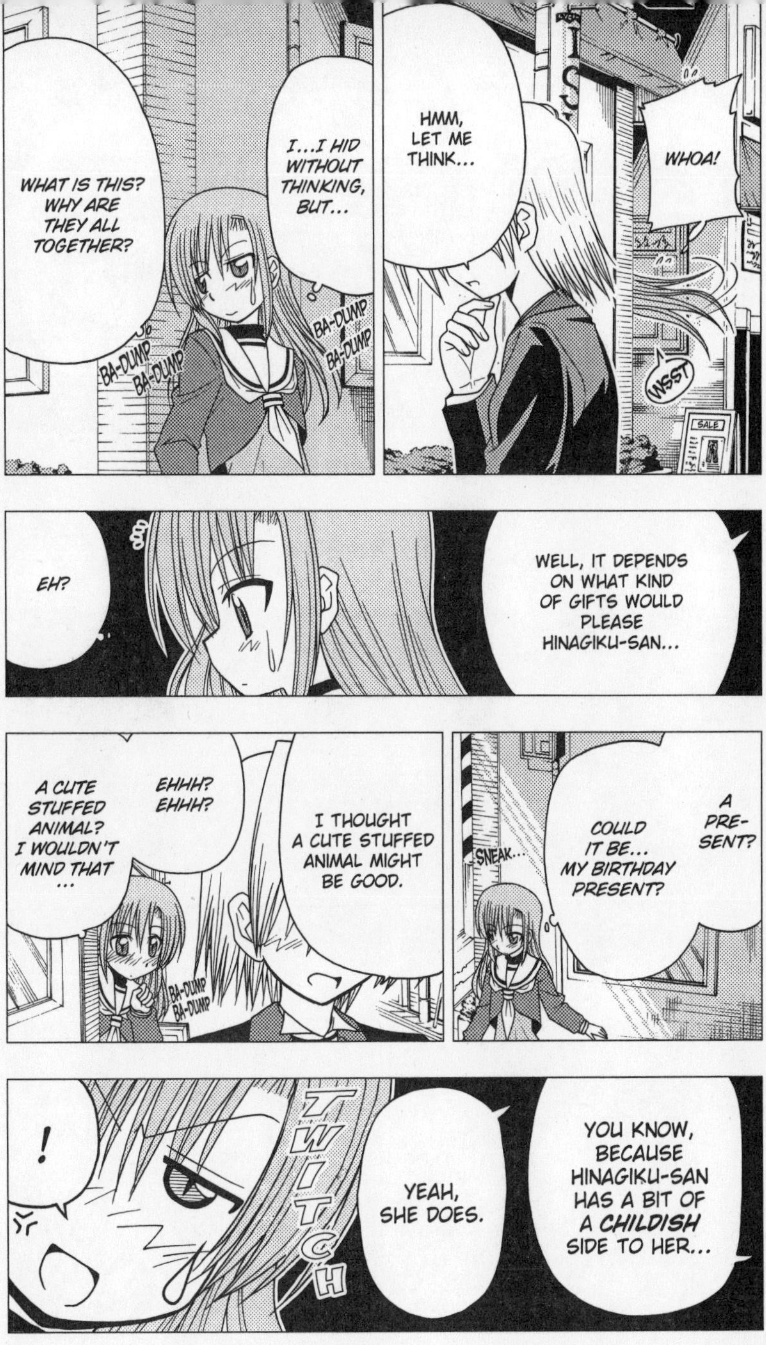
WHOA!
HMM, LET ME THINK...
WSST
I...I HID WITHOUT THINKING, BUT...
BA-DUMP BA-DUMP
WHAT IS THIS? WHY ARE THEY ALL TOGETHER?
BA-DUMP BA-DUMP
WELL, IT DEPENDS ON WHAT KIND OF GIFTS WOULD PLEASE HINAGIKU-SAN...
EH?
A PRESENT?
COULD IT BE... MY BIRTHDAY PRESENT?
SNEAK...
I THOUGHT A CUTE STUFFED ANIMAL MIGHT BE GOOD.
EHHH? EHHH?
A CUTE STUFFED ANIMAL? I WOULDN'T MIND THAT...
BA-DUMP BA-DUMP
YOU KNOW, BECAUSE HINAGIKU-SAN HAS A BIT OF A **CHILDISH** SIDE TO HER...
YEAH, SHE DOES.
TWITCH
!

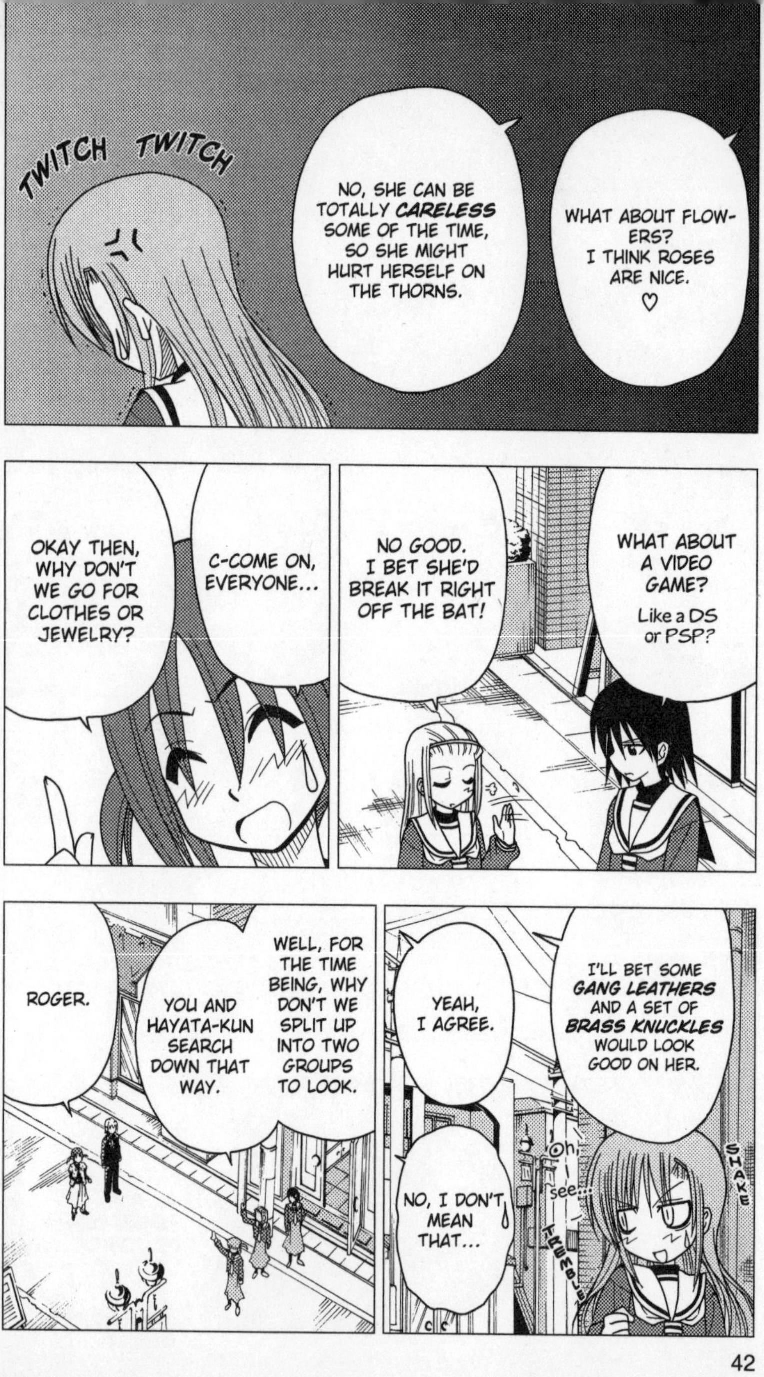
WHAT ABOUT FLOWERS? I THINK ROSES ARE NICE. ♡
NO, SHE CAN BE TOTALLY *CARELESS* SOME OF THE TIME, SO SHE MIGHT HURT HERSELF ON THE THORNS.
TWITCH TWITCH
WHAT ABOUT A VIDEO GAME? Like a DS or PSP?
NO GOOD. I BET SHE'D BREAK IT RIGHT OFF THE BAT!
C-COME ON, EVERYONE...
OKAY THEN, WHY DON'T WE GO FOR CLOTHES OR JEWELRY?
I'LL BET SOME *GANG LEATHERS* AND A SET OF *BRASS KNUCKLES* WOULD LOOK GOOD ON HER.
SHAKE
YEAH, I AGREE.
Oh, I see...
TREMBLE
NO, I DON'T MEAN THAT...
WELL, FOR THE TIME BEING, WHY DON'T WE SPLIT UP INTO TWO GROUPS TO LOOK.
YOU AND HAYATA-KUN SEARCH DOWN THAT WAY.
ROGER.

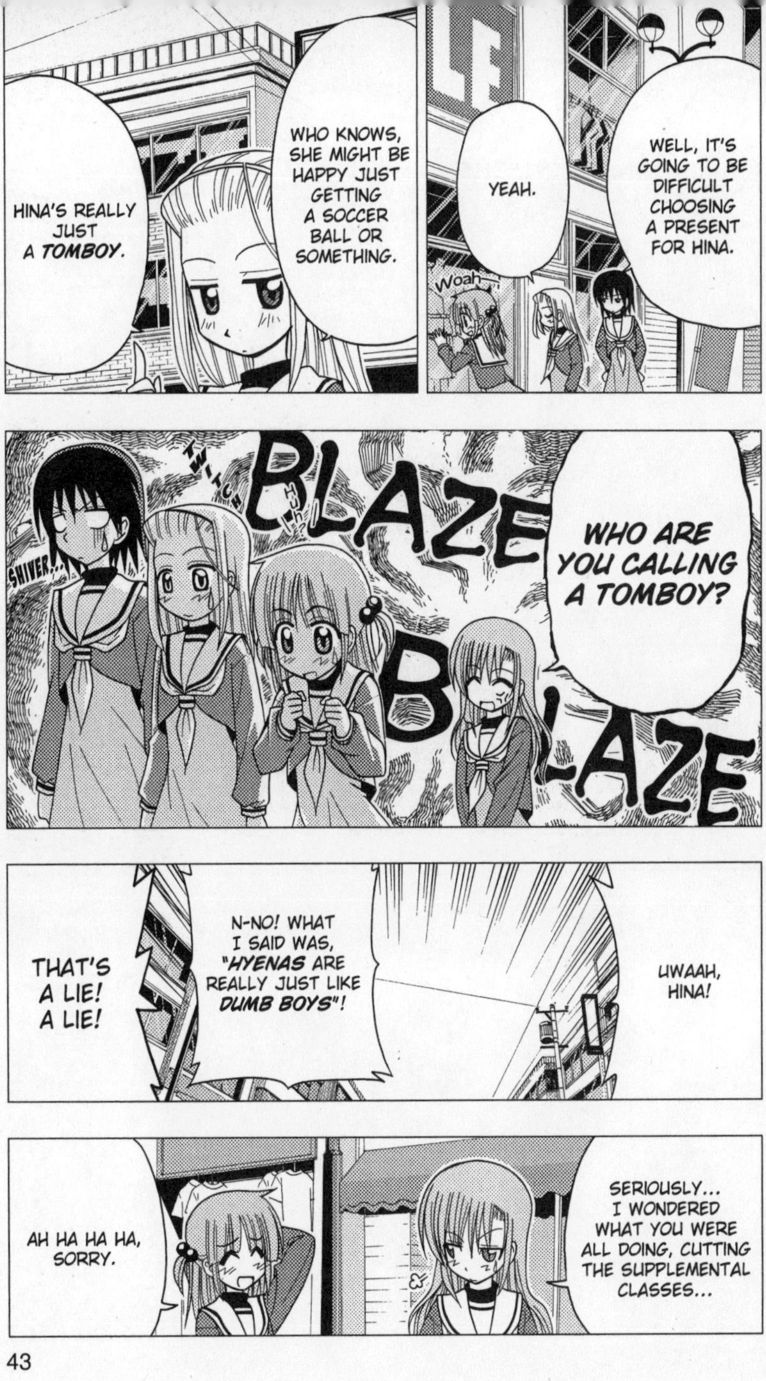
WELL, IT'S GOING TO BE DIFFICULT CHOOSING A PRESENT FOR HINA.
YEAH.
Woah...
WHO KNOWS, SHE MIGHT BE HAPPY JUST GETTING A SOCCER BALL OR SOMETHING.
HINA'S REALLY JUST A *TOMBOY*.
WHO ARE YOU CALLING A TOMBOY?
BLAZE
BLAZE
HUH?
TWITCH
SHIVER...
UWAAH, HINA!
N-NO! WHAT I SAID WAS, "*HYENAS* ARE REALLY JUST LIKE *DUMB BOYS*"!
THAT'S A LIE! A LIE!
SERIOUSLY... I WONDERED WHAT YOU WERE ALL DOING, CUTTING THE SUPPLEMENTAL CLASSES...
AH HA HA HA, SORRY.

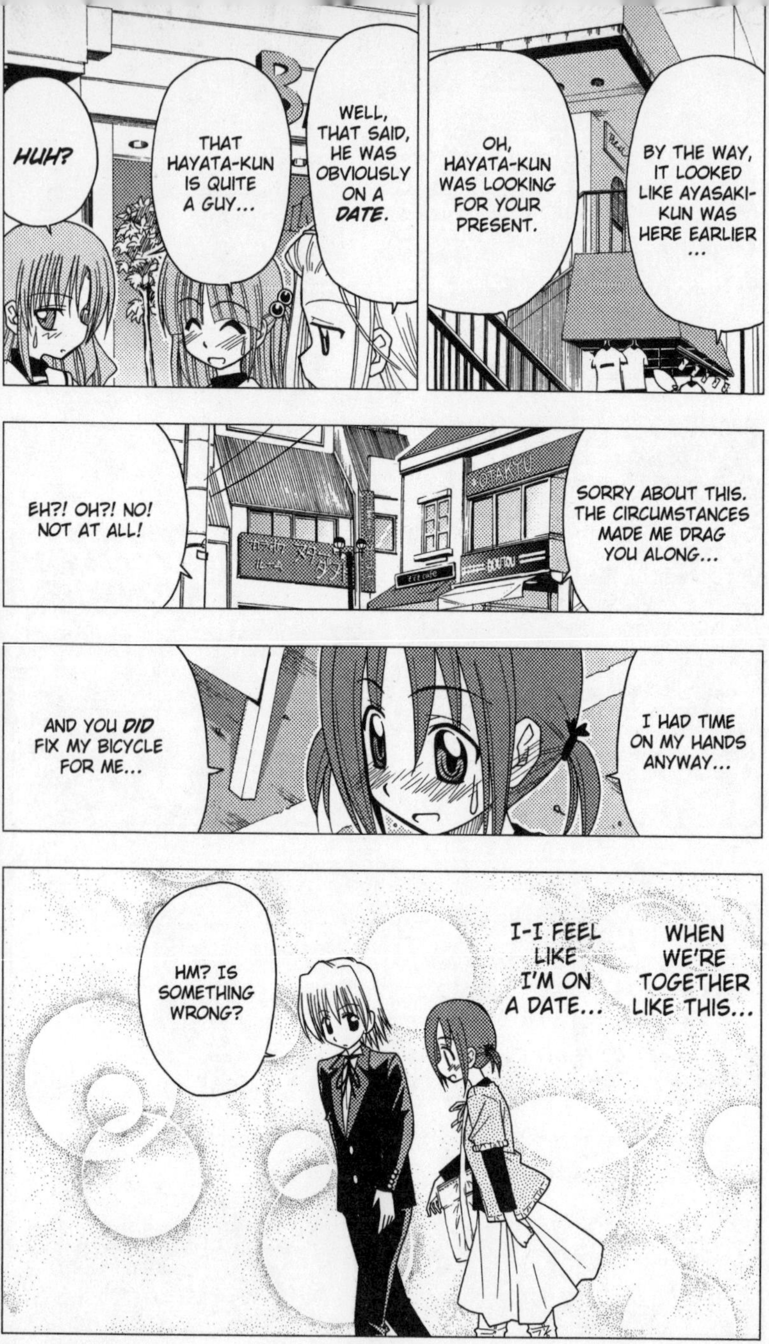
BY THE WAY, IT LOOKED LIKE AYASAKI-KUN WAS HERE EARLIER ...
OH, HAYATA-KUN WAS LOOKING FOR YOUR PRESENT.
WELL, THAT SAID, HE WAS OBVIOUSLY ON A *DATE*.
THAT HAYATA-KUN IS QUITE A GUY...
HUH?
SORRY ABOUT THIS. THE CIRCUMSTANCES MADE ME DRAG YOU ALONG...
EH?! OH?! NO! NOT AT ALL!
I HAD TIME ON MY HANDS ANYWAY...
AND YOU *DID* FIX MY BICYCLE FOR ME...
WHEN WE'RE TOGETHER LIKE THIS...
I-I FEEL LIKE I'M ON A DATE...
HM? IS SOMETHING WRONG?

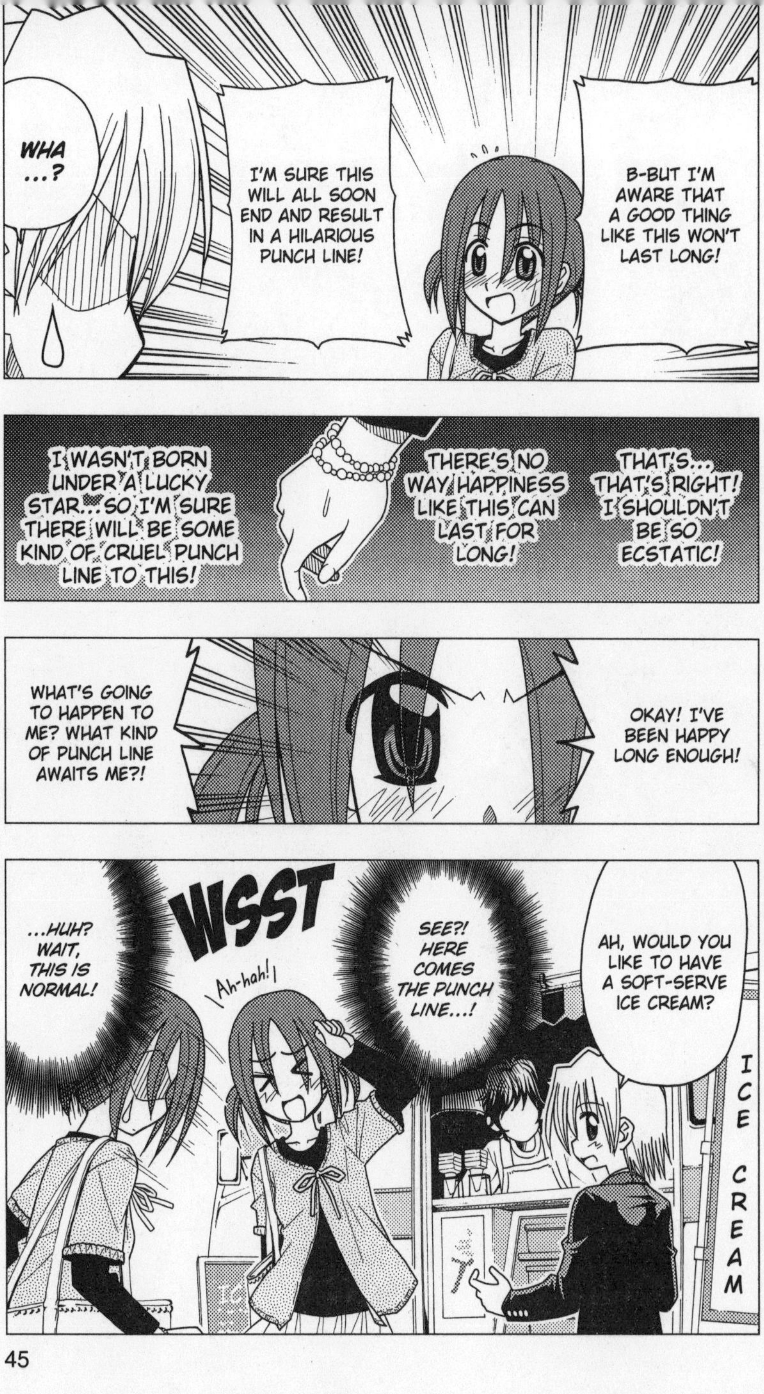
B-BUT I'M AWARE THAT A GOOD THING LIKE THIS WON'T LAST LONG!
I'M SURE THIS WILL ALL SOON END AND RESULT IN A HILARIOUS PUNCH LINE!
WHA ...?
THAT'S... THAT'S RIGHT! I SHOULDN'T BE SO ECSTATIC!
THERE'S NO WAY HAPPINESS LIKE THIS CAN LAST FOR LONG!
I WASN'T BORN UNDER A LUCKY STAR... SO I'M SURE THERE WILL BE SOME KIND OF CRUEL PUNCH LINE TO THIS!
OKAY! I'VE BEEN HAPPY LONG ENOUGH!
WHAT'S GOING TO HAPPEN TO ME? WHAT KIND OF PUNCH LINE AWAITS ME?!
AH, WOULD YOU LIKE TO HAVE A SOFT-SERVE ICE CREAM?
ICE CREAM
SEE?! HERE COMES THE PUNCH LINE...!
WSST
Ah-hah!
...HUH? WAIT, THIS IS NORMAL!

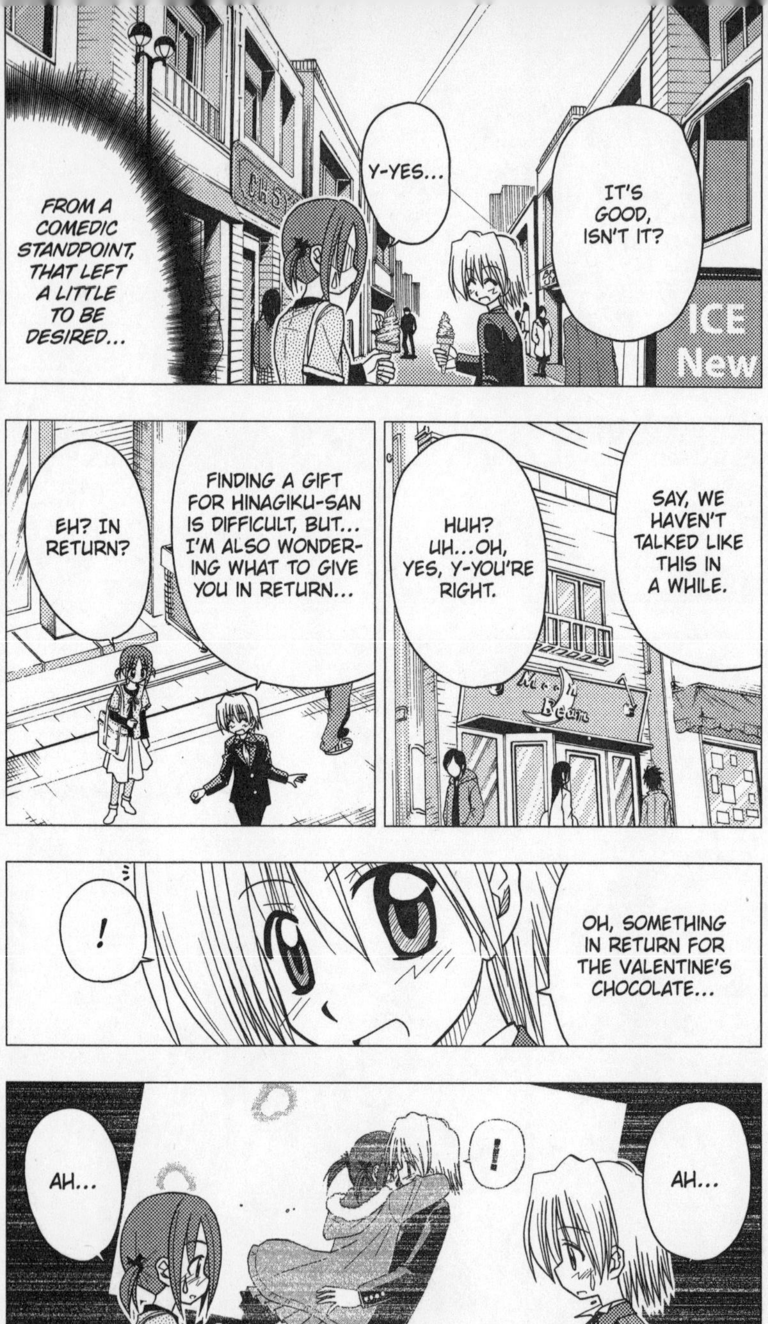
IT'S GOOD, ISN'T IT?
ICE New
Y-YES...
FROM A COMEDIC STANDPOINT, THAT LEFT A LITTLE TO BE DESIRED...
SAY, WE HAVEN'T TALKED LIKE THIS IN A WHILE.
HUH? UH...OH, YES, Y-YOU'RE RIGHT.
FINDING A GIFT FOR HINAGIKU-SAN IS DIFFICULT, BUT... I'M ALSO WONDERING WHAT TO GIVE YOU IN RETURN...
EH? IN RETURN?
OH, SOMETHING IN RETURN FOR THE VALENTINE'S CHOCOLATE...
!
AH...
!
AH...

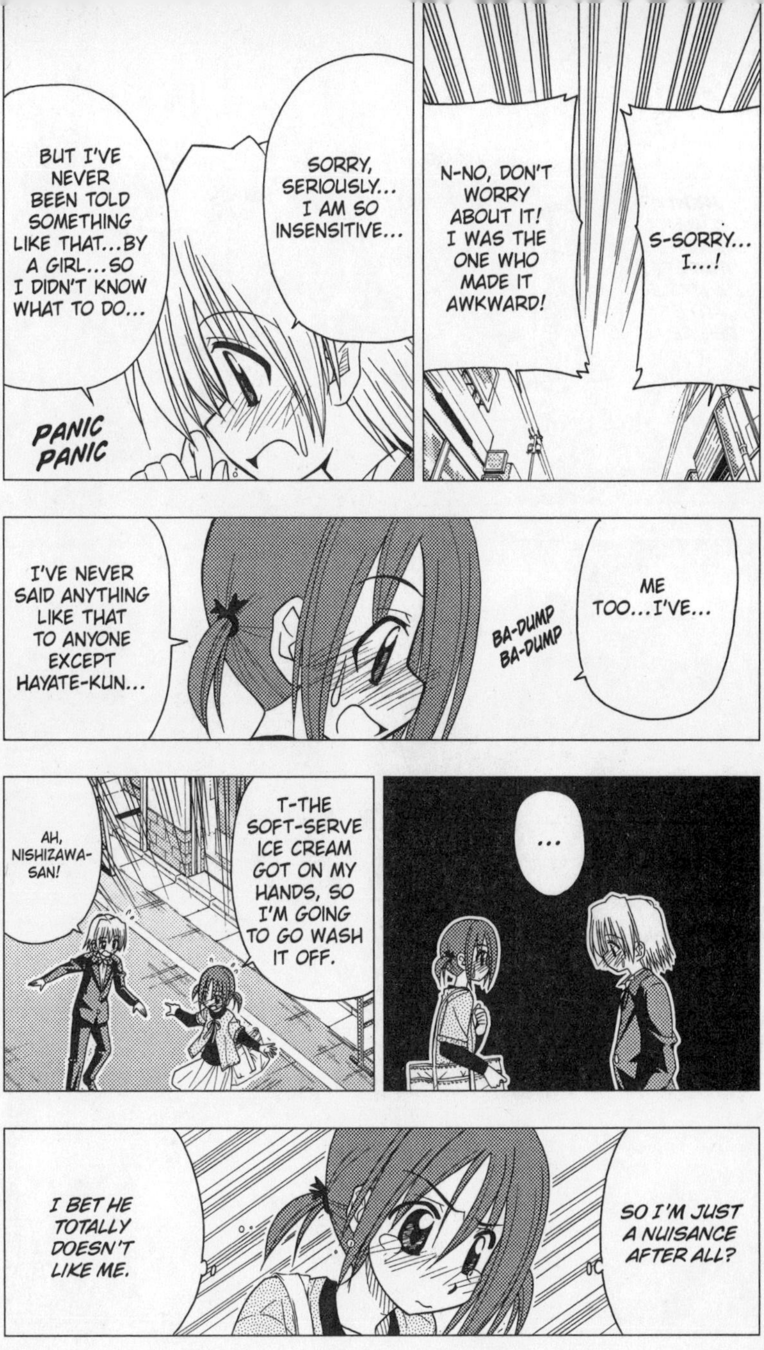
S-SORRY... I...!
N-NO, DON'T WORRY ABOUT IT! I WAS THE ONE WHO MADE IT AWKWARD!
SORRY, SERIOUSLY... I AM SO INSENSITIVE...
BUT I'VE NEVER BEEN TOLD SOMETHING LIKE THAT...BY A GIRL...SO I DIDN'T KNOW WHAT TO DO...
PANIC PANIC
ME TOO...I'VE...
BA-DUMP BA-DUMP
I'VE NEVER SAID ANYTHING LIKE THAT TO ANYONE EXCEPT HAYATE-KUN...
...
T-THE SOFT-SERVE ICE CREAM GOT ON MY HANDS, SO I'M GOING TO GO WASH IT OFF.
AH, NISHIZAWA-SAN!
SO I'M JUST A NUISANCE AFTER ALL?
I BET HE TOTALLY DOESN'T LIKE ME.

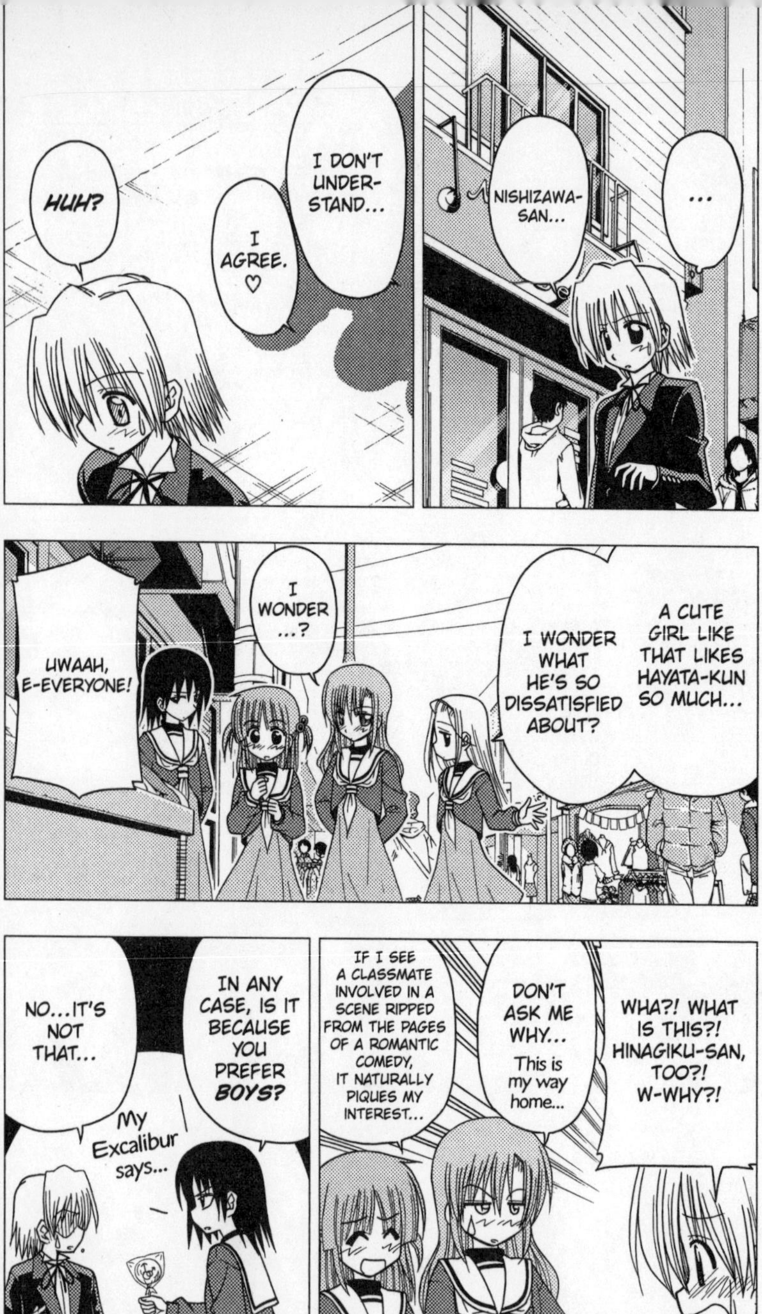
...
NISHIZAWA-SAN...
I DON'T UNDERSTAND...
I AGREE. ♡
HUH?
A CUTE GIRL LIKE THAT LIKES HAYATA-KUN SO MUCH...
I WONDER WHAT HE'S SO DISSATISFIED ABOUT?
I WONDER ...?
UWAAH, E-EVERYONE!
WHA?! WHAT IS THIS?! HINAGIKU-SAN, TOO?! W-WHY?!
DON'T ASK ME WHY...
This is my way home...
IF I SEE A CLASSMATE INVOLVED IN A SCENE RIPPED FROM THE PAGES OF A ROMANTIC COMEDY, IT NATURALLY PIQUES MY INTEREST...
IN ANY CASE, IS IT BECAUSE YOU PREFER *BOYS*?
NO...IT'S NOT THAT...
My Excalibur says...

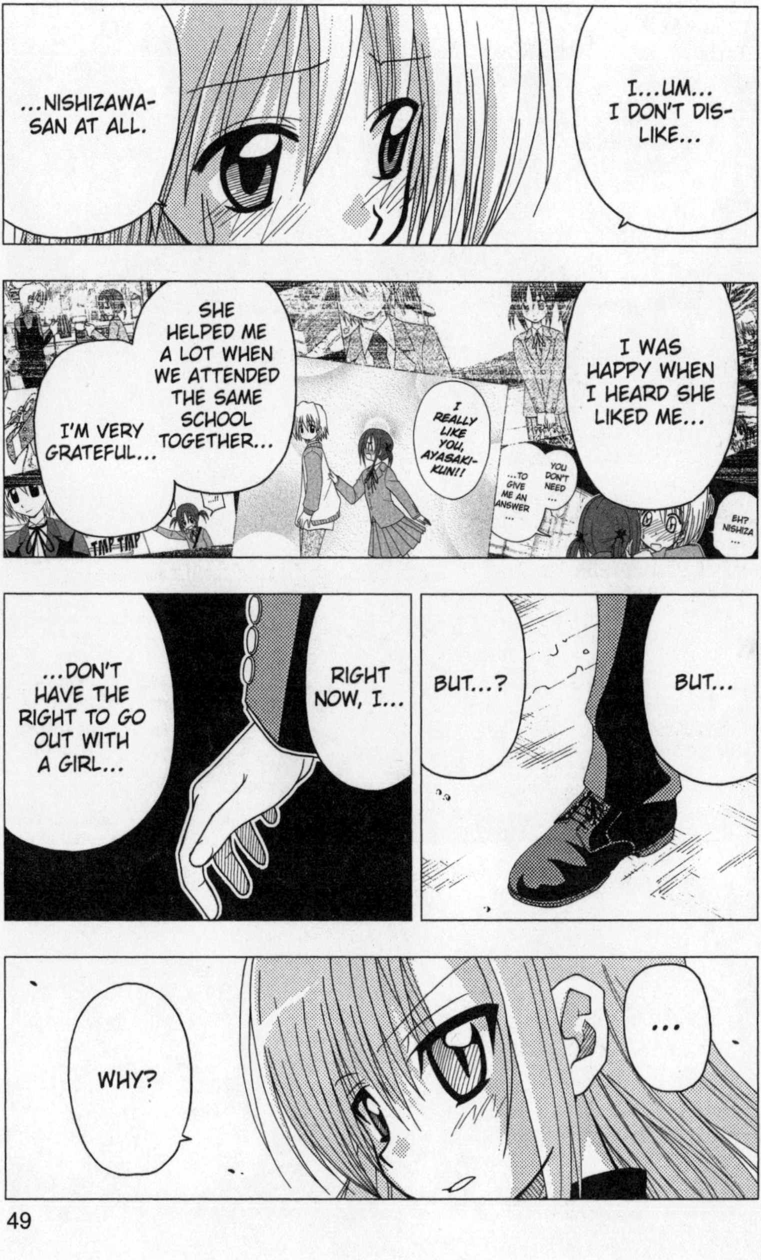
I...UM... I DON'T DIS-LIKE...
...NISHIZAWA-SAN AT ALL.
I WAS HAPPY WHEN I HEARD SHE LIKED ME...
EH? NISHIZA...
YOU DON'T NEED...
...TO GIVE ME AN ANSWER...
I REALLY LIKE YOU, AYASAKI-KUN!!
SHE HELPED ME A LOT WHEN WE ATTENDED THE SAME SCHOOL TOGETHER...
I'M VERY GRATEFUL...
...!!
TMP TMP
BUT...
BUT...?
RIGHT NOW, I...
...DON'T HAVE THE RIGHT TO GO OUT WITH A GIRL...
...
WHY?

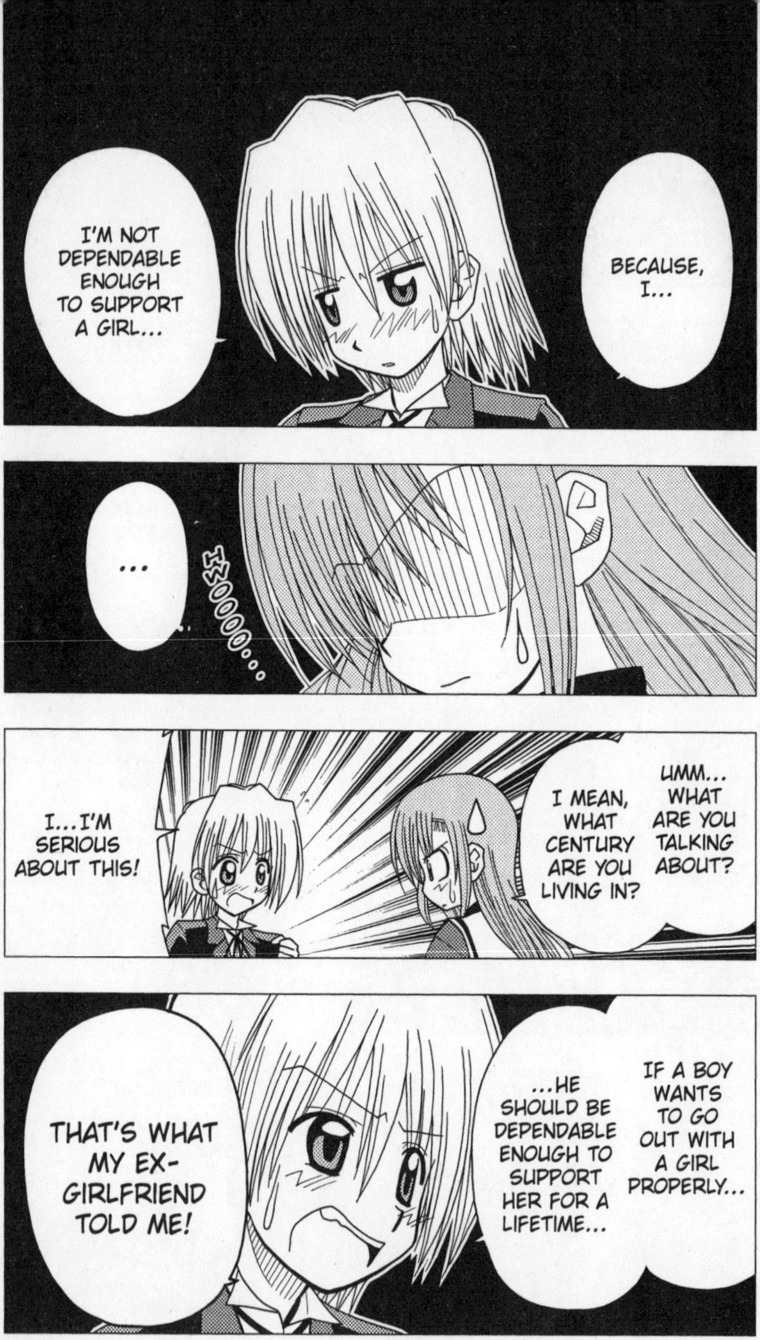
BECAUSE, I...
I'M NOT DEPENDABLE ENOUGH TO SUPPORT A GIRL...
HWOOOOO...
...
UMM... WHAT ARE YOU TALKING ABOUT?
I MEAN, WHAT CENTURY ARE YOU LIVING IN?
I...I'M SERIOUS ABOUT THIS!
IF A BOY WANTS TO GO OUT WITH A GIRL PROPERLY...
...HE SHOULD BE DEPENDABLE ENOUGH TO SUPPORT HER FOR A LIFETIME...
THAT'S WHAT MY EX-GIRLFRIEND TOLD ME!

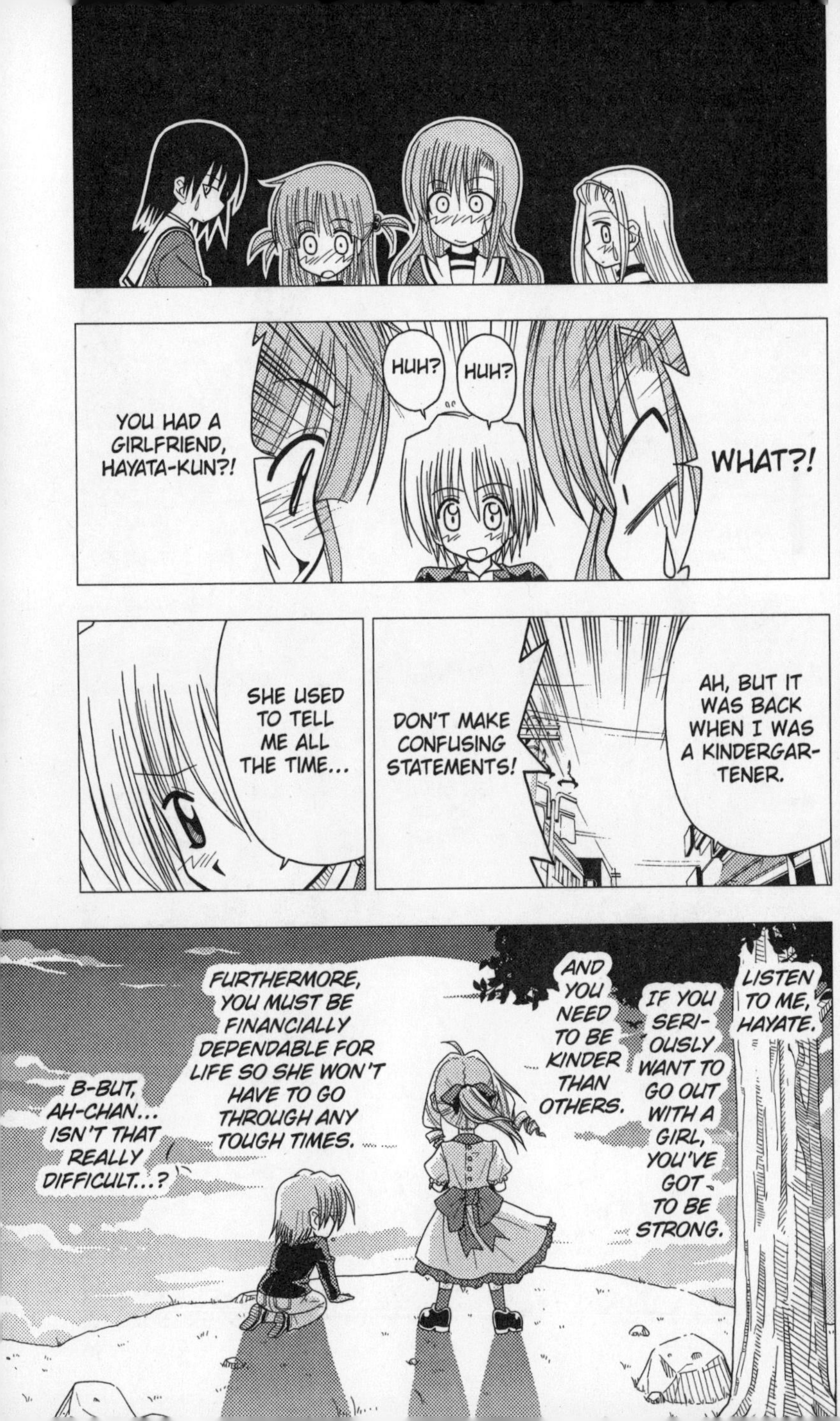
HUH?
HUH?
WHAT?!
YOU HAD A GIRLFRIEND, HAYATA-KUN?!
AH, BUT IT WAS BACK WHEN I WAS A KINDERGAR-TENER.
DON'T MAKE CONFUSING STATEMENTS!
SHE USED TO TELL ME ALL THE TIME...
LISTEN TO ME, HAYATE.
IF YOU SERI-OUSLY WANT TO GO OUT WITH A GIRL, YOU'VE GOT TO BE STRONG.
AND YOU NEED TO BE KINDER THAN OTHERS.
FURTHERMORE, YOU MUST BE FINANCIALLY DEPENDABLE FOR LIFE SO SHE WON'T HAVE TO GO THROUGH ANY TOUGH TIMES.
B-BUT, AH-CHAN... ISN'T THAT REALLY DIFFICULT...?

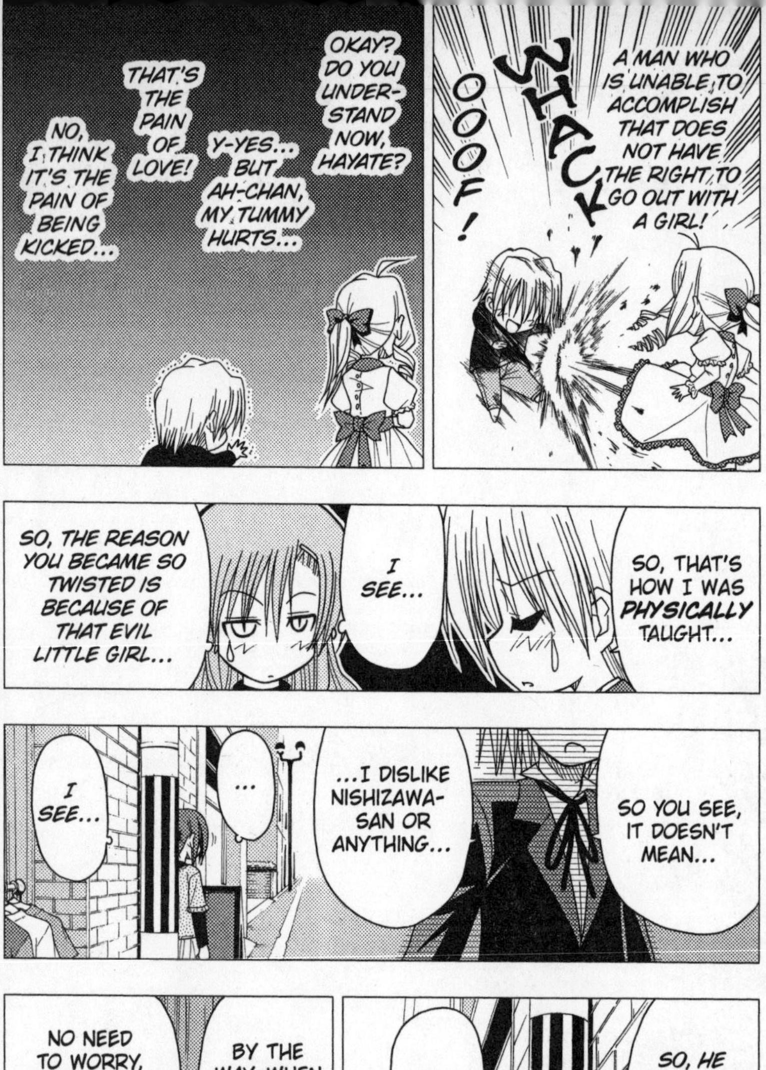
A MAN WHO IS UNABLE TO ACCOMPLISH THAT DOES NOT HAVE THE RIGHT TO GO OUT WITH A GIRL!
WHACK
OOOOF!
OKAY? DO YOU UNDER-STAND NOW, HAYATE?
Y-YES... BUT AH-CHAN, MY TUMMY HURTS...
THAT'S THE PAIN OF LOVE!
NO, I THINK IT'S THE PAIN OF BEING KICKED...
SO, THAT'S HOW I WAS **PHYSICALLY** TAUGHT...
I SEE...
SO, THE REASON YOU BECAME SO TWISTED IS BECAUSE OF THAT EVIL LITTLE GIRL...
SO YOU SEE, IT DOESN'T MEAN...
...I DISLIKE NISHIZAWA-SAN OR ANYTHING...
...
I SEE...
SO, HE DOESN'T DISLIKE ME AFTER ALL...
I'M GLAD...
BY THE WAY, WHEN IS HAYATE COMING BACK?
He's late ...
NO NEED TO WORRY, BECAUSE HE'S ONLY LATE WHEN HE'S INVOLVED IN SOME HUGE DEBACLE.

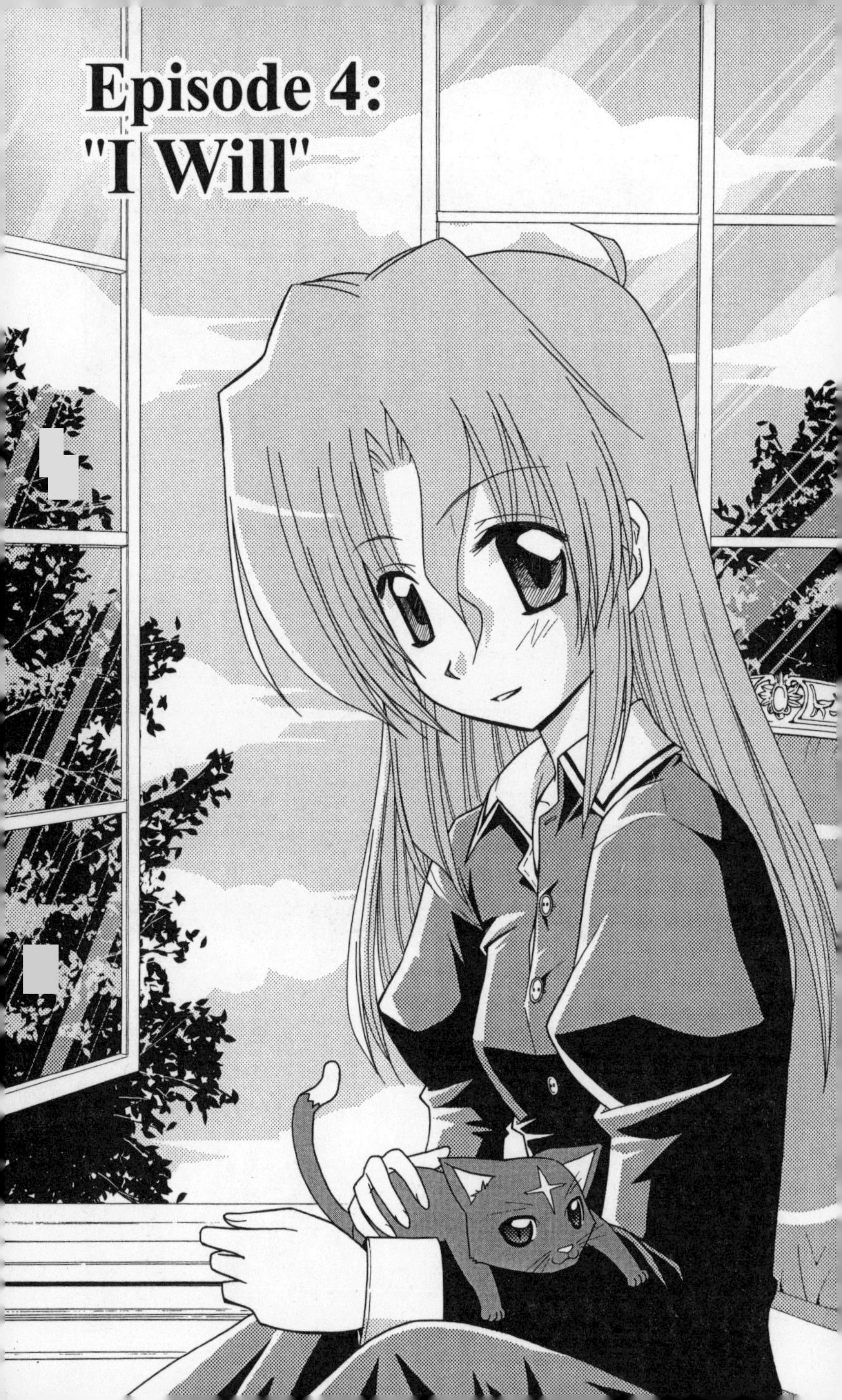
Episode 4:
"I Will"

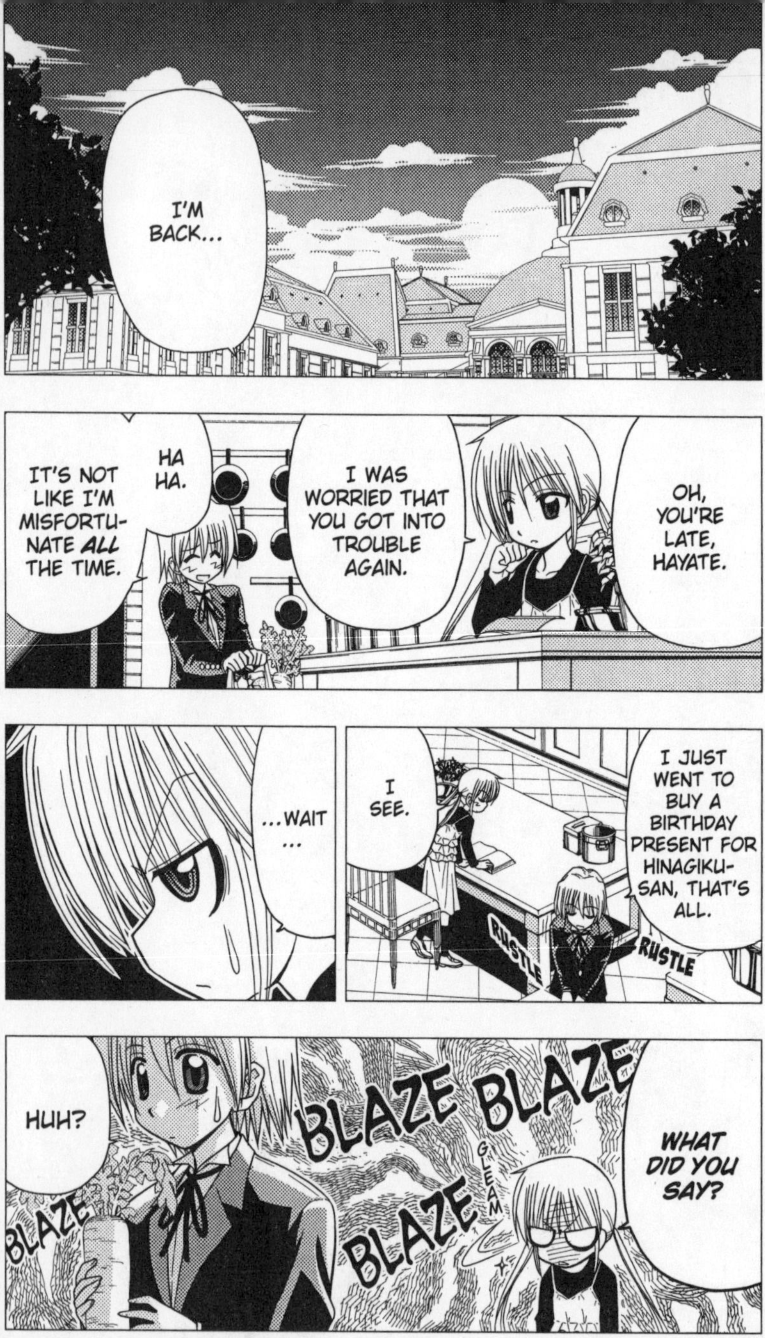
I'M BACK...
OH, YOU'RE LATE, HAYATE.
I WAS WORRIED THAT YOU GOT INTO TROUBLE AGAIN.
HA HA.
IT'S NOT LIKE I'M MISFORTUNATE *ALL* THE TIME.
I JUST WENT TO BUY A BIRTHDAY PRESENT FOR HINAGIKU-SAN, THAT'S ALL.
RUSTLE
RUSTLE
I SEE.
...WAIT ...
WHAT DID YOU SAY?
BLAZE BLAZE
GLEAM
BLAZE
BLAZE
BLAZE
HUH?

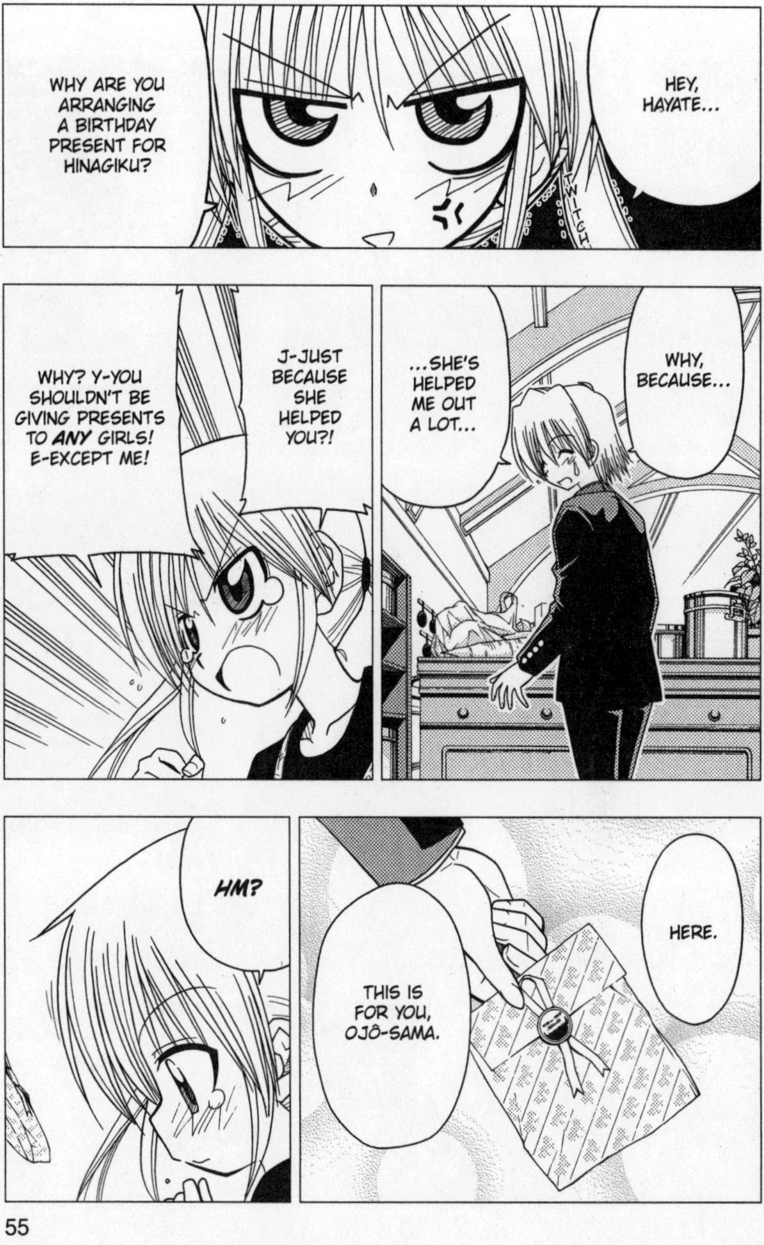
HEY, HAYATE...
WHY ARE YOU ARRANGING A BIRTHDAY PRESENT FOR HINAGIKU?
TWITCH
WHY, BECAUSE...
...SHE'S HELPED ME OUT A LOT...
J-JUST BECAUSE SHE HELPED YOU?!
WHY? Y-YOU SHOULDN'T BE GIVING PRESENTS TO *ANY* GIRLS! E-EXCEPT ME!
HERE.
THIS IS FOR YOU, OJÔ-SAMA.
HM?

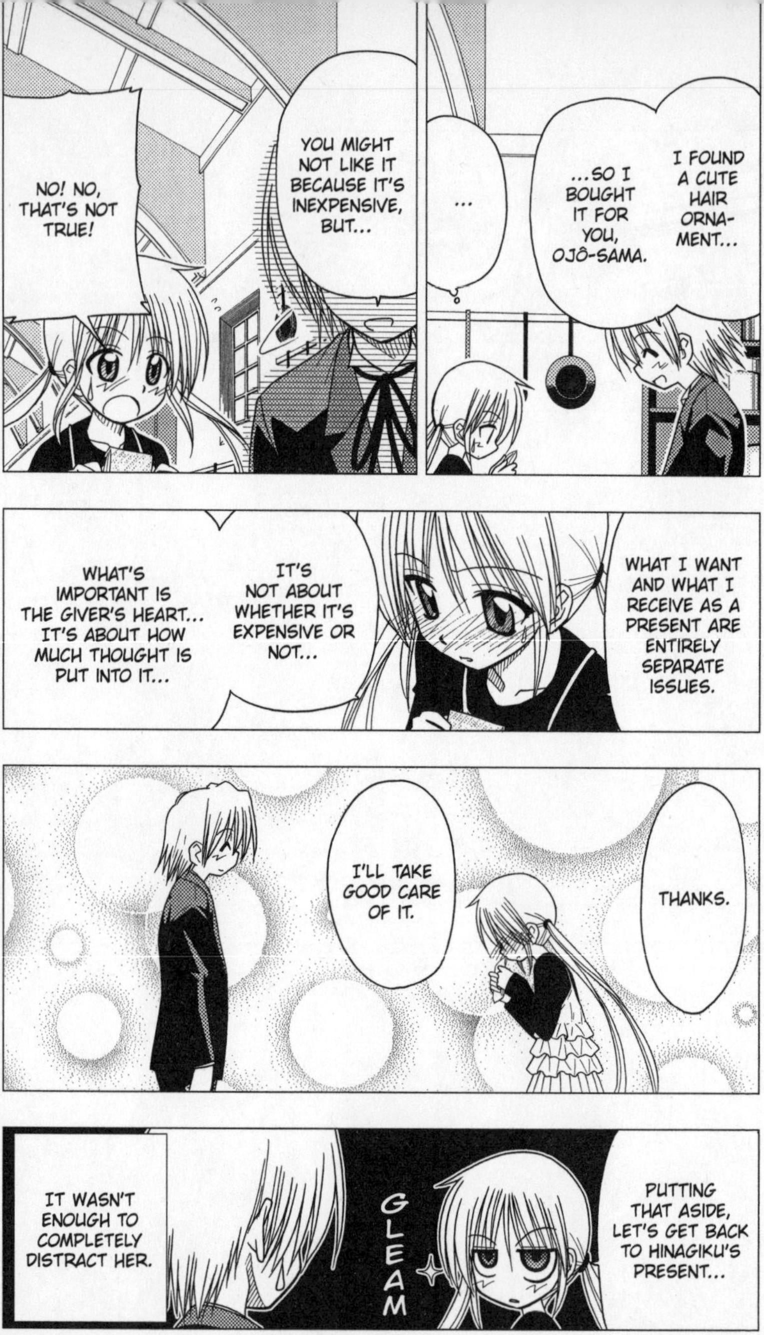
I FOUND A CUTE HAIR ORNA-MENT...
...SO I BOUGHT IT FOR YOU, OJÔ-SAMA.
...
YOU MIGHT NOT LIKE IT BECAUSE IT'S INEXPENSIVE, BUT...
NO! NO, THAT'S NOT TRUE!
WHAT I WANT AND WHAT I RECEIVE AS A PRESENT ARE ENTIRELY SEPARATE ISSUES.
IT'S NOT ABOUT WHETHER IT'S EXPENSIVE OR NOT...
WHAT'S IMPORTANT IS THE GIVER'S HEART... IT'S ABOUT HOW MUCH THOUGHT IS PUT INTO IT...
THANKS.
I'LL TAKE GOOD CARE OF IT.
PUTTING THAT ASIDE, LET'S GET BACK TO HINAGIKU'S PRESENT...
GLEAM
IT WASN'T ENOUGH TO COMPLETELY DISTRACT HER.

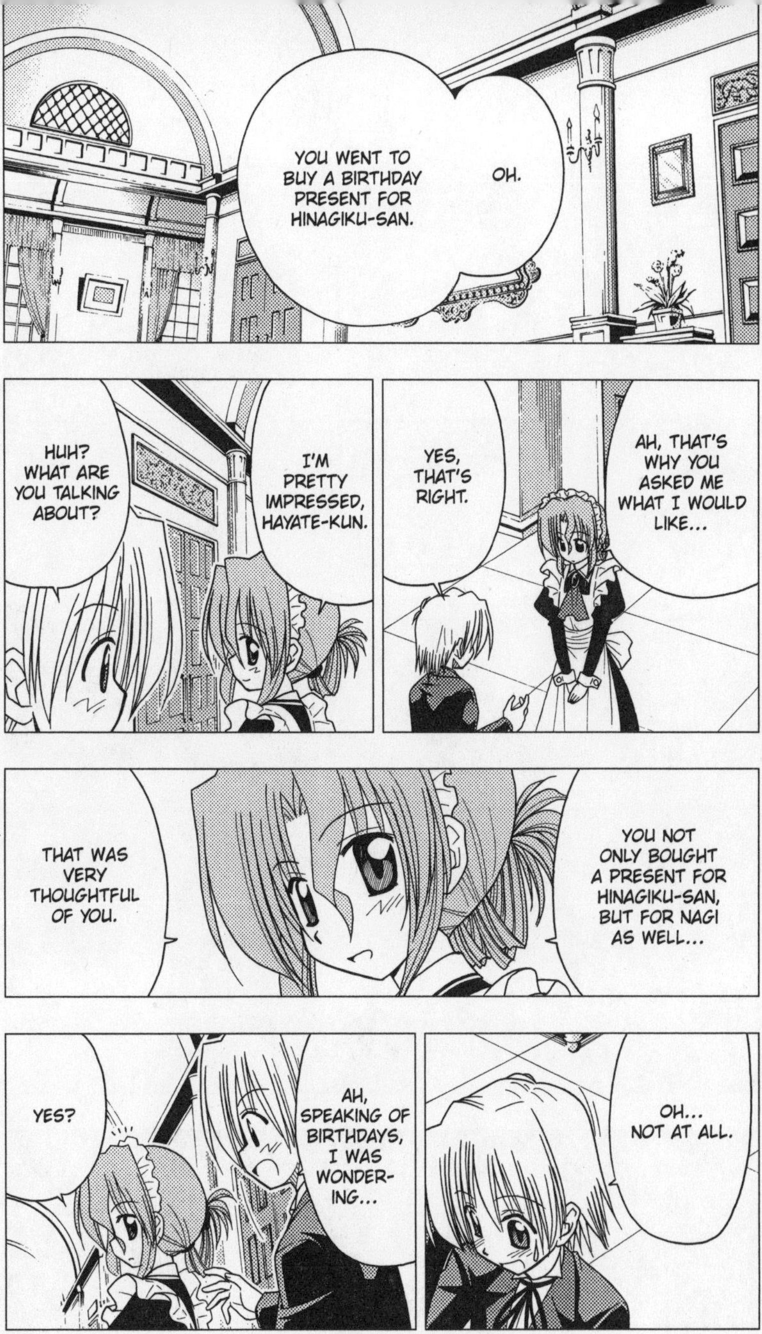
OH.
YOU WENT TO BUY A BIRTHDAY PRESENT FOR HINAGIKU-SAN.
AH, THAT'S WHY YOU ASKED ME WHAT I WOULD LIKE...
YES, THAT'S RIGHT.
I'M PRETTY IMPRESSED, HAYATE-KUN.
HUH? WHAT ARE YOU TALKING ABOUT?
YOU NOT ONLY BOUGHT A PRESENT FOR HINAGIKU-SAN, BUT FOR NAGI AS WELL...
THAT WAS VERY THOUGHTFUL OF YOU.
OH... NOT AT ALL.
AH, SPEAKING OF BIRTHDAYS, I WAS WONDER-ING...
YES?

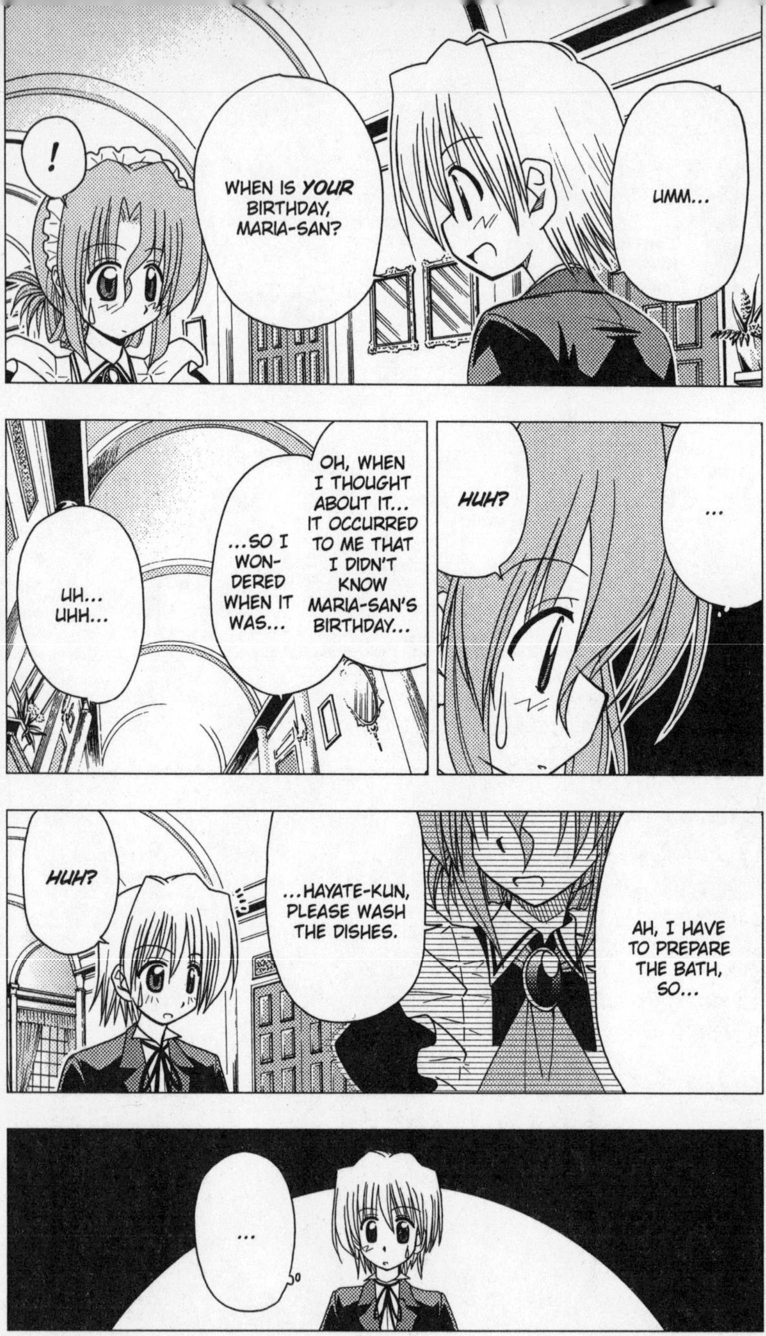

UMM...
WHEN IS *YOUR* BIRTHDAY, MARIA-SAN?
!
...
HUH?
OH, WHEN I THOUGHT ABOUT IT... IT OCCURRED TO ME THAT I DIDN'T KNOW MARIA-SAN'S BIRTHDAY...
...SO I WONDERED WHEN IT WAS...
UH... UHH...
AH, I HAVE TO PREPARE THE BATH, SO...
...HAYATE-KUN, PLEASE WASH THE DISHES.
HUH?
...

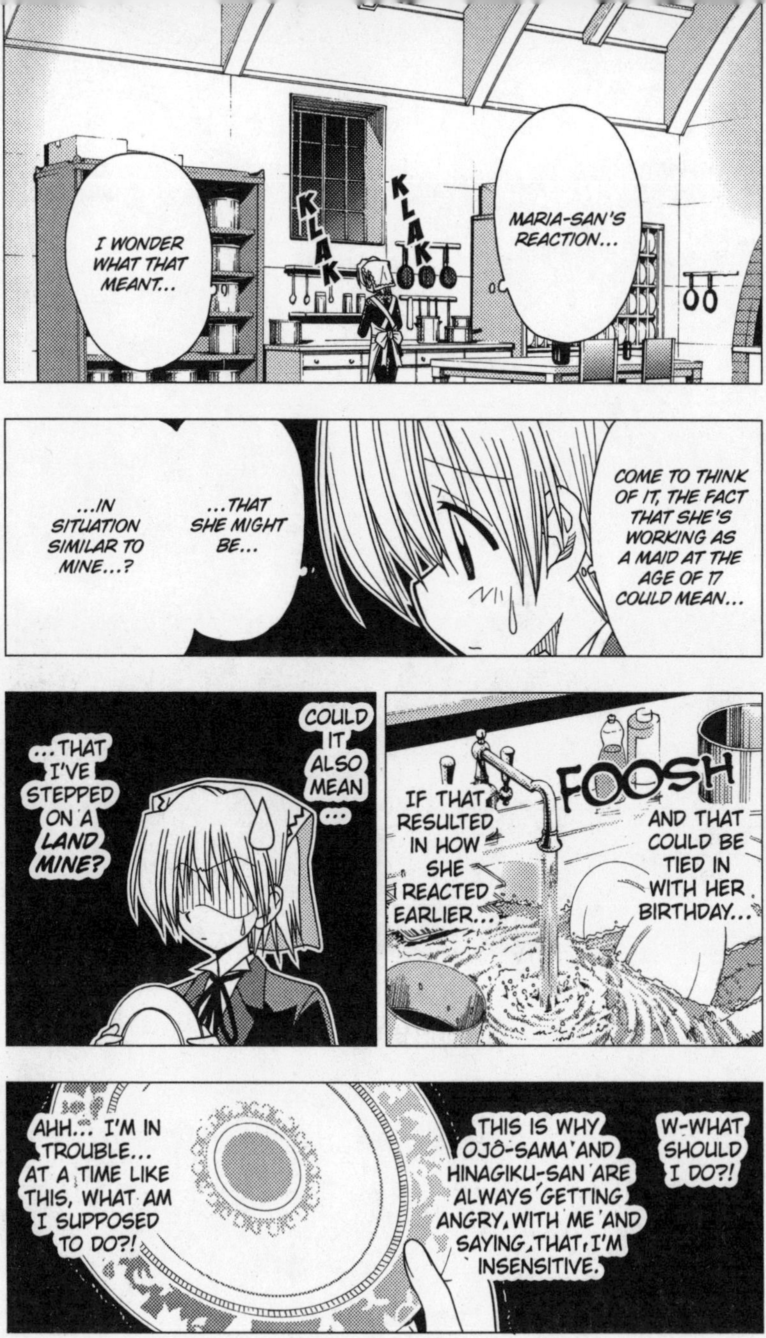
MARIA-SAN'S REACTION...
KLAK
KLAK
I WONDER WHAT THAT MEANT...
COME TO THINK OF IT, THE FACT THAT SHE'S WORKING AS A MAID AT THE AGE OF 17 COULD MEAN...
...THAT SHE MIGHT BE...
...IN SITUATION SIMILAR TO MINE...?
FOOSH
AND THAT COULD BE TIED IN WITH HER BIRTHDAY...
IF THAT RESULTED IN HOW SHE REACTED EARLIER...
COULD IT ALSO MEAN...
...THAT I'VE STEPPED ON A *LAND MINE?*
W-WHAT SHOULD I DO?!
THIS IS WHY OJÔ-SAMA AND HINAGIKU-SAN ARE ALWAYS GETTING ANGRY WITH ME AND SAYING THAT I'M INSENSITIVE.
AHH... I'M IN TROUBLE... AT A TIME LIKE THIS, WHAT AM I SUPPOSED TO DO?!

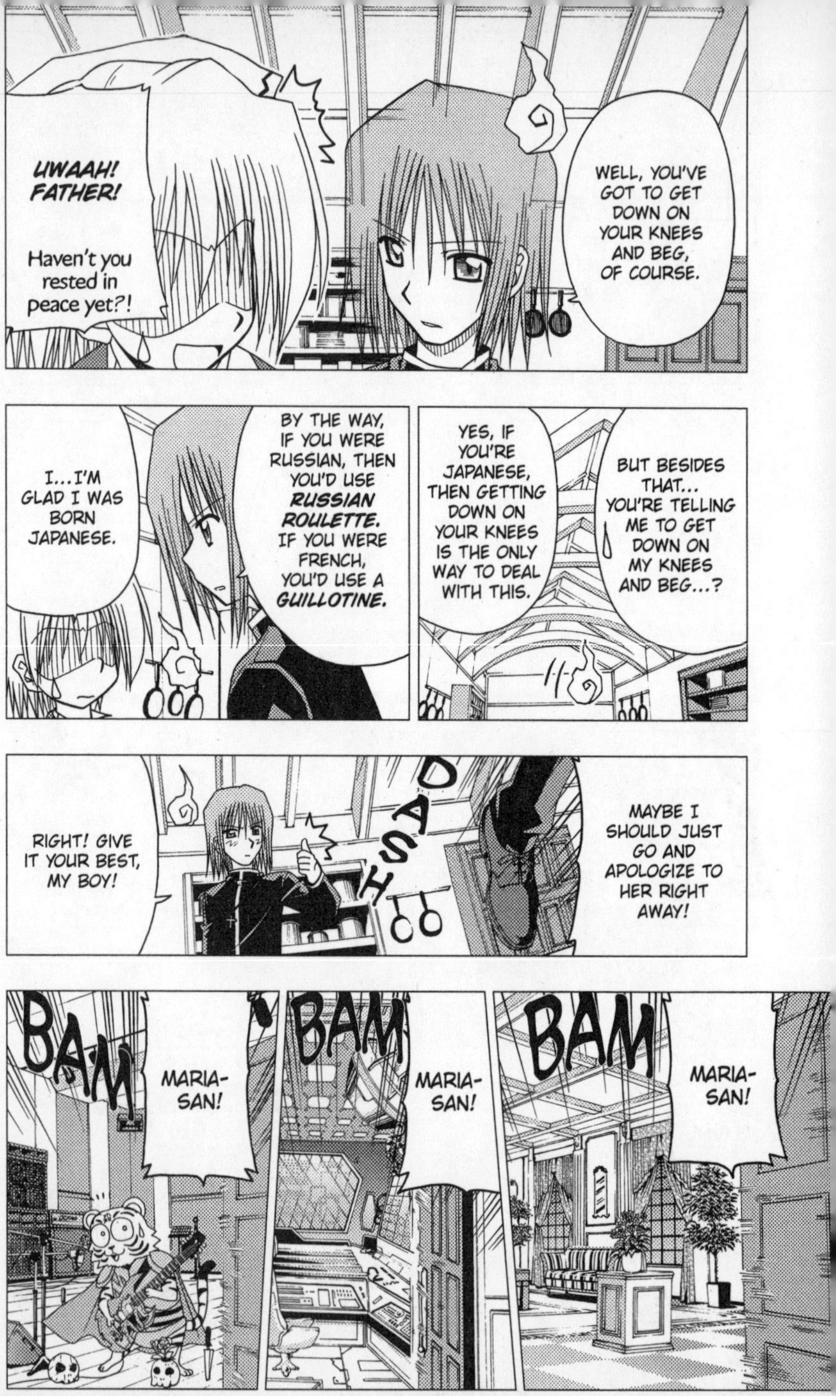
WELL, YOU'VE GOT TO GET DOWN ON YOUR KNEES AND BEG, OF COURSE.
UWAAH! FATHER!
Haven't you rested in peace yet?!
BUT BESIDES THAT... YOU'RE TELLING ME TO GET DOWN ON MY KNEES AND BEG...?
YES, IF YOU'RE JAPANESE, THEN GETTING DOWN ON YOUR KNEES IS THE ONLY WAY TO DEAL WITH THIS.
BY THE WAY, IF YOU WERE RUSSIAN, THEN YOU'D USE *RUSSIAN ROULETTE.* IF YOU WERE FRENCH, YOU'D USE A *GUILLOTINE.*
I...I'M GLAD I WAS BORN JAPANESE.
MAYBE I SHOULD JUST GO AND APOLOGIZE TO HER RIGHT AWAY!
DASH
RIGHT! GIVE IT YOUR BEST, MY BOY!
BAM
MARIA-SAN!
BAM
MARIA-SAN!
BAM
MARIA-SAN!

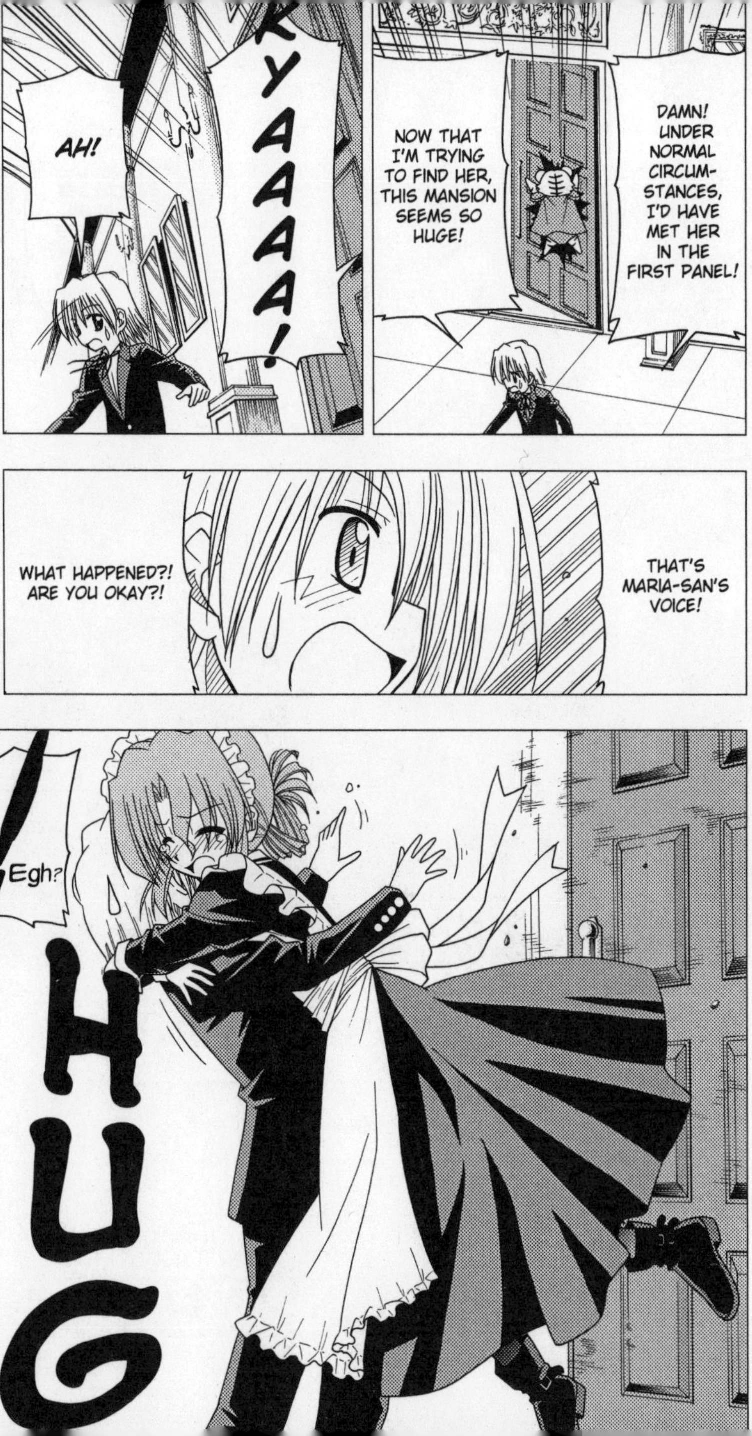
DAMN! UNDER NORMAL CIRCUM-STANCES, I'D HAVE MET HER IN THE FIRST PANEL!
NOW THAT I'M TRYING TO FIND HER, THIS MANSION SEEMS SO HUGE!
KYAAAAA!
AH!
THAT'S MARIA-SAN'S VOICE!
WHAT HAPPENED?! ARE YOU OKAY?!
Egh?
HUG

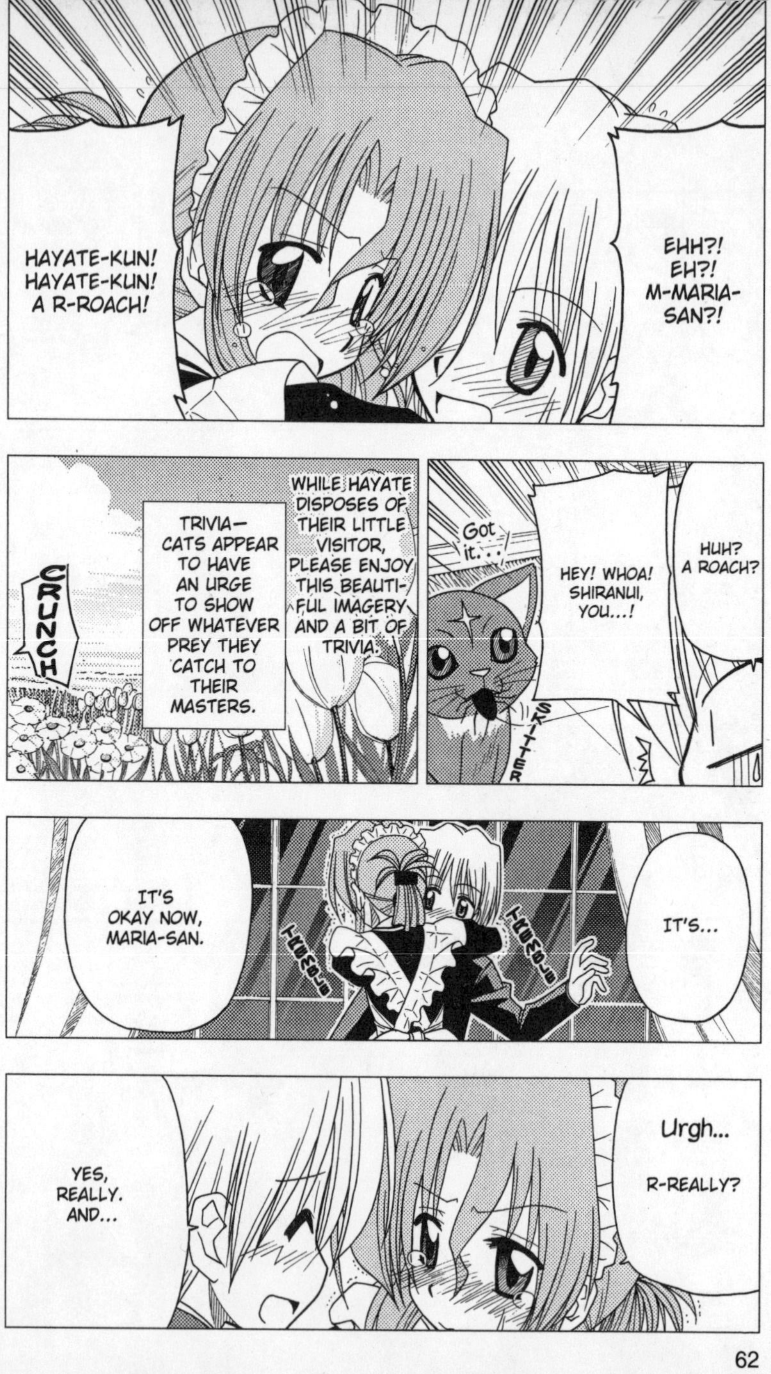
EHH?! EH?! M-MARIA-SAN?!
HAYATE-KUN! HAYATE-KUN! A R-ROACH!
HUH? A ROACH?
HEY! WHOA! SHIRANUI, YOU...!
Got it...
SKITTER
WHILE HAYATE DISPOSES OF THEIR LITTLE VISITOR, PLEASE ENJOY THIS BEAUTIFUL IMAGERY AND A BIT OF TRIVIA.
TRIVIA— CATS APPEAR TO HAVE AN URGE TO SHOW OFF WHATEVER PREY THEY CATCH TO THEIR MASTERS.
CRUNCH
IT'S...
TREMBLE
TREMBLE
IT'S OKAY NOW, MARIA-SAN.
Urgh...
R-REALLY?
YES, REALLY. AND...

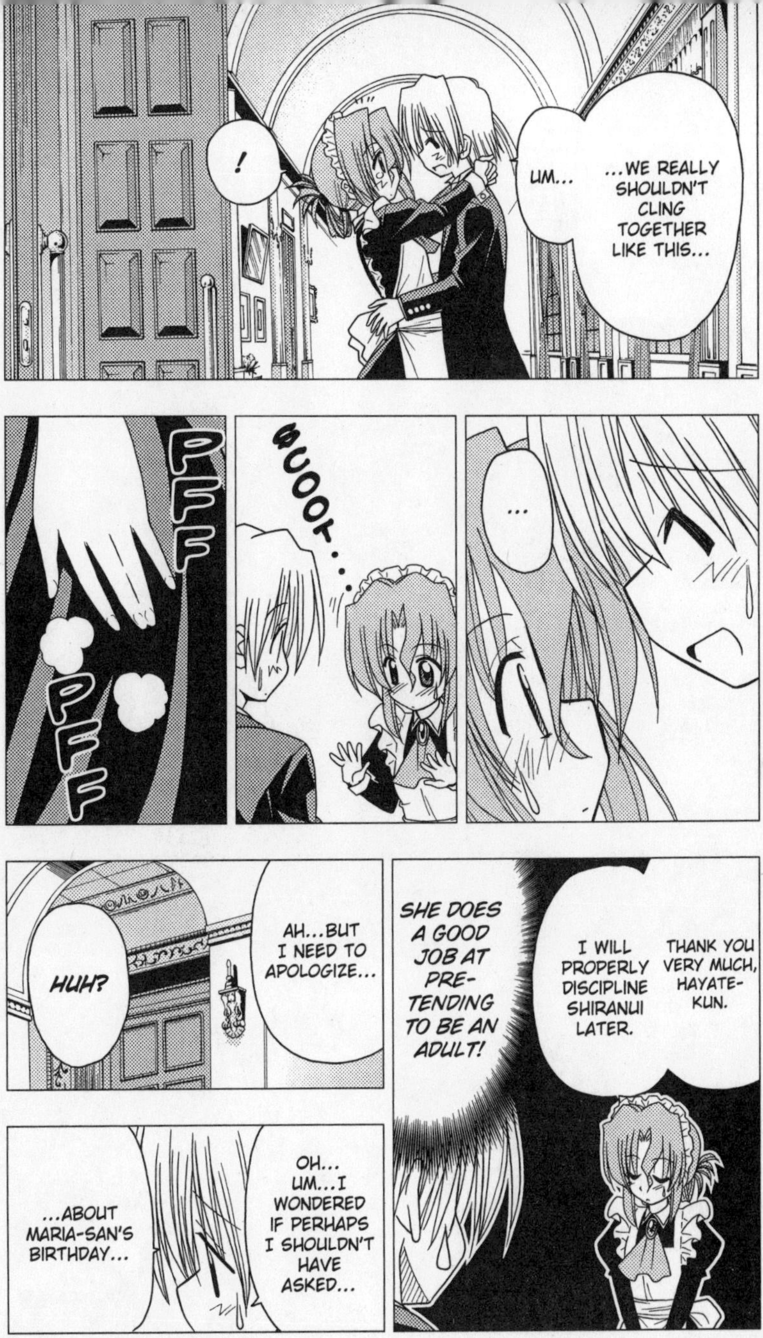
UM...
...WE REALLY SHOULDN'T CLING TOGETHER LIKE THIS...
!
...
SCOOT...
PFF
PFF
THANK YOU VERY MUCH, HAYATE-KUN.
I WILL PROPERLY DISCIPLINE SHIRANUI LATER.
SHE DOES A GOOD JOB AT PRE-TENDING TO BE AN ADULT!
AH...BUT I NEED TO APOLOGIZE...
HUH?
OH... UM...I WONDERED IF PERHAPS I SHOULDN'T HAVE ASKED...
...ABOUT MARIA-SAN'S BIRTHDAY...

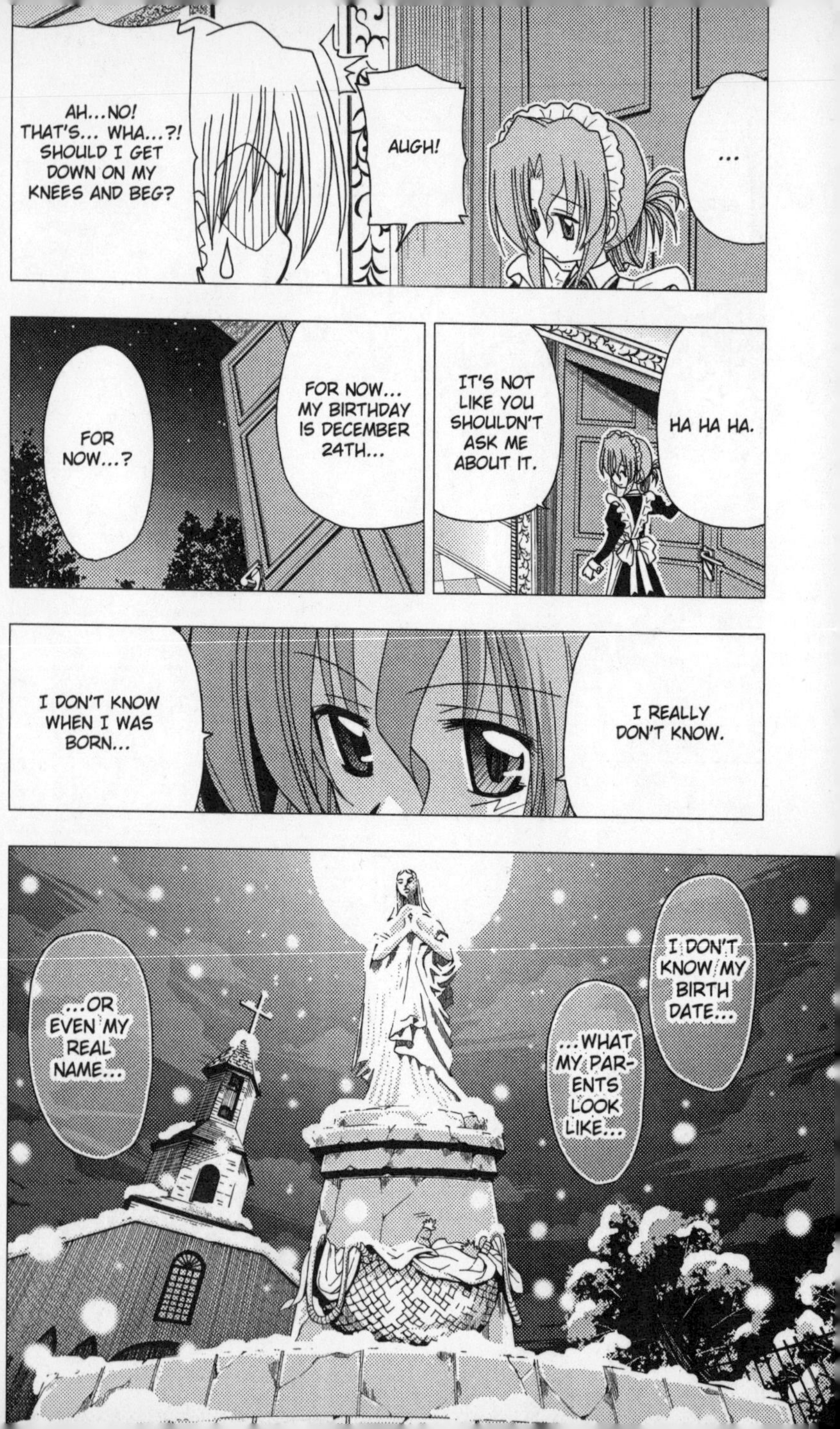
...
AUGH!
AH...NO! THAT'S... WHA...?! SHOULD I GET DOWN ON MY KNEES AND BEG?
HA HA HA.
IT'S NOT LIKE YOU SHOULDN'T ASK ME ABOUT IT.
FOR NOW... MY BIRTHDAY IS DECEMBER 24TH...
FOR NOW...?
I REALLY DON'T KNOW.
I DON'T KNOW WHEN I WAS BORN...
I DON'T KNOW MY BIRTH DATE...
...WHAT MY PAR-ENTS LOOK LIKE...
...OR EVEN MY REAL NAME...

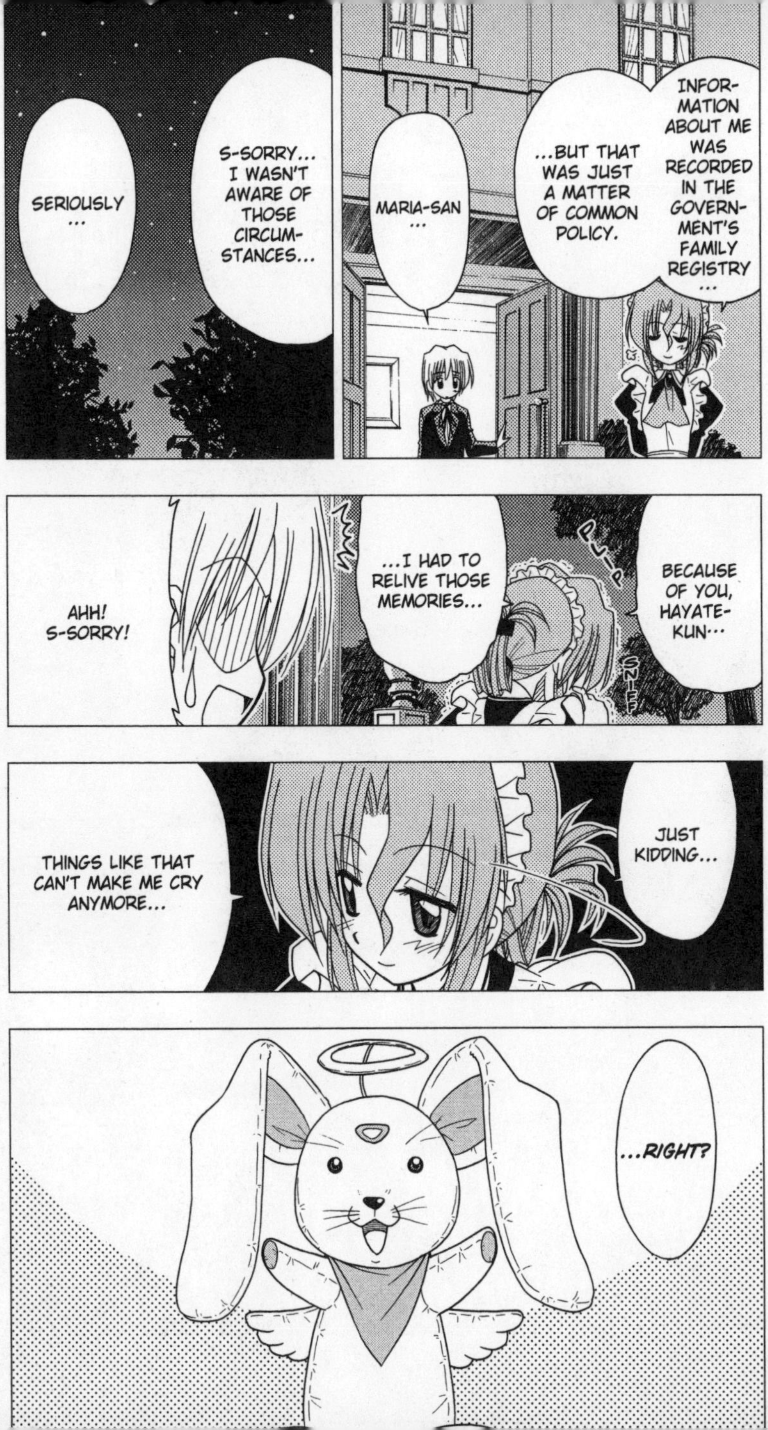
INFOR-MATION ABOUT ME WAS RECORDED IN THE GOVERN-MENT'S FAMILY REGISTRY...
...BUT THAT WAS JUST A MATTER OF COMMON POLICY.
MARIA-SAN...
S-SORRY... I WASN'T AWARE OF THOSE CIRCUM-STANCES...
SERIOUSLY...
BECAUSE OF YOU, HAYATE-KUN...
PU-P
SNIFF
...I HAD TO RELIVE THOSE MEMORIES...
AHH! S-SORRY!
JUST KIDDING...
THINGS LIKE THAT CAN'T MAKE ME CRY ANYMORE...
...RIGHT?

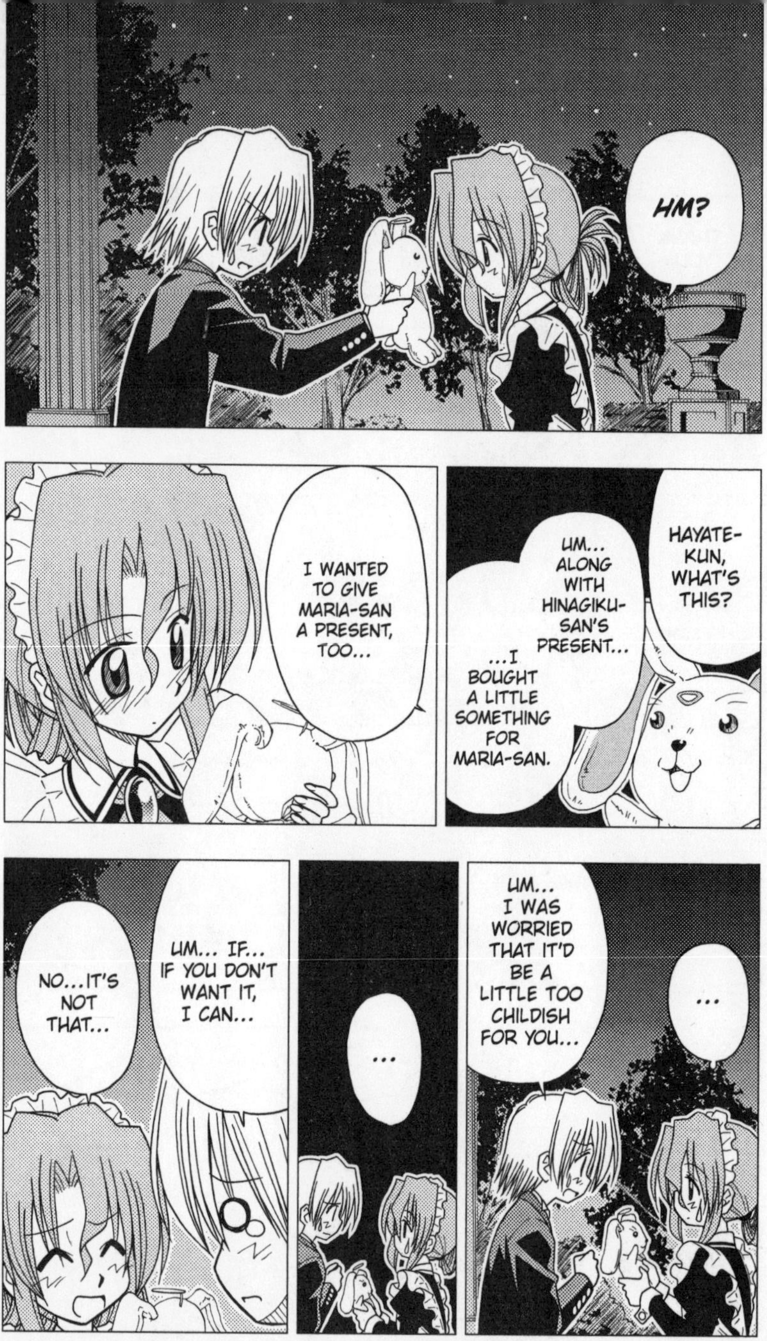
HM?
HAYATE-KUN, WHAT'S THIS?
UM... ALONG WITH HINAGIKU-SAN'S PRESENT...
...I BOUGHT A LITTLE SOMETHING FOR MARIA-SAN.
I WANTED TO GIVE MARIA-SAN A PRESENT, TOO...
UM... I WAS WORRIED THAT IT'D BE A LITTLE TOO CHILDISH FOR YOU...
...
...
UM... IF... IF YOU DON'T WANT IT, I CAN...
NO...IT'S NOT THAT...

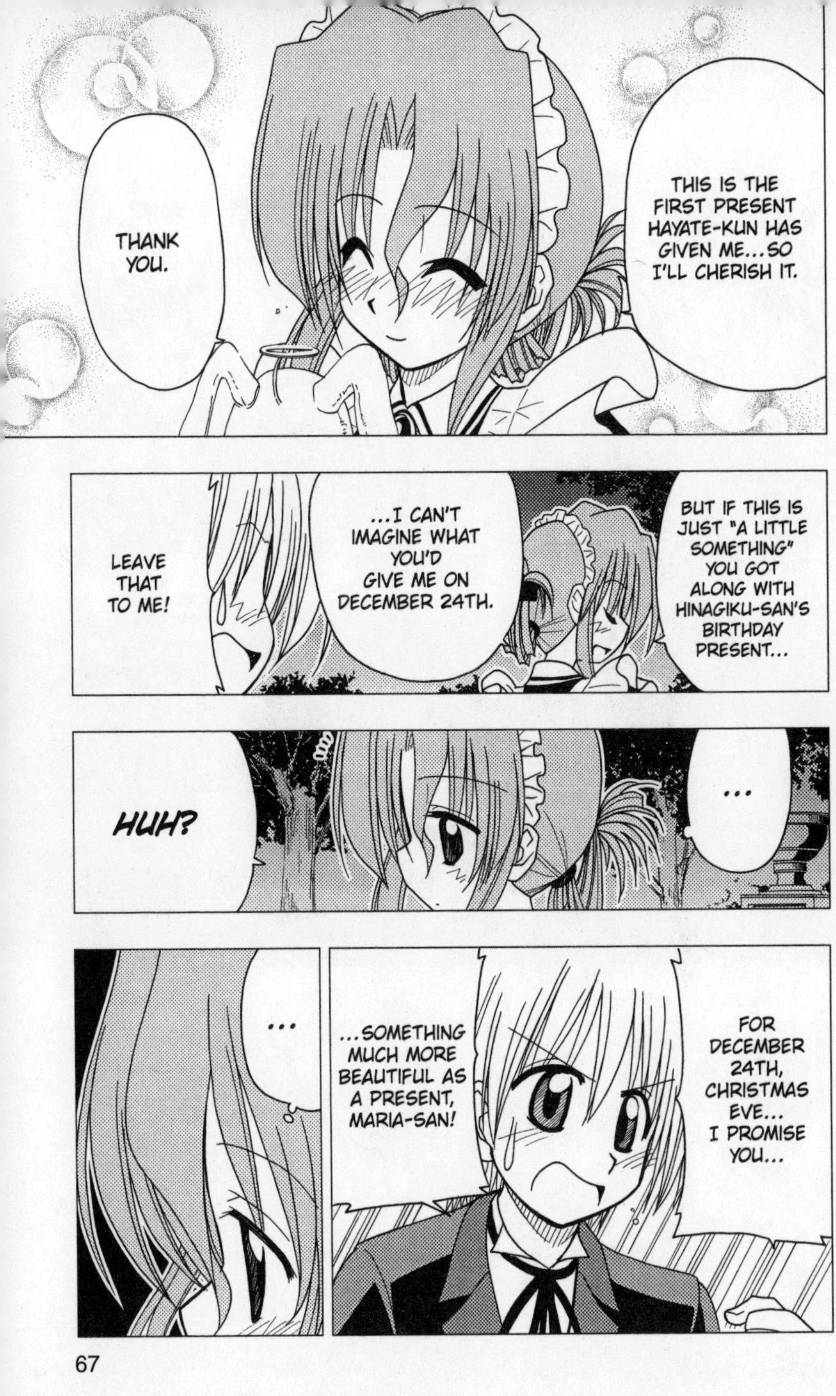
THIS IS THE FIRST PRESENT HAYATE-KUN HAS GIVEN ME...SO I'LL CHERISH IT.
THANK YOU.
BUT IF THIS IS JUST "A LITTLE SOMETHING" YOU GOT ALONG WITH HINAGIKU-SAN'S BIRTHDAY PRESENT...
...I CAN'T IMAGINE WHAT YOU'D GIVE ME ON DECEMBER 24TH.
LEAVE THAT TO ME!
...
HUH?
FOR DECEMBER 24TH, CHRISTMAS EVE... I PROMISE YOU...
...SOMETHING MUCH MORE BEAUTIFUL AS A PRESENT, MARIA-SAN!
...

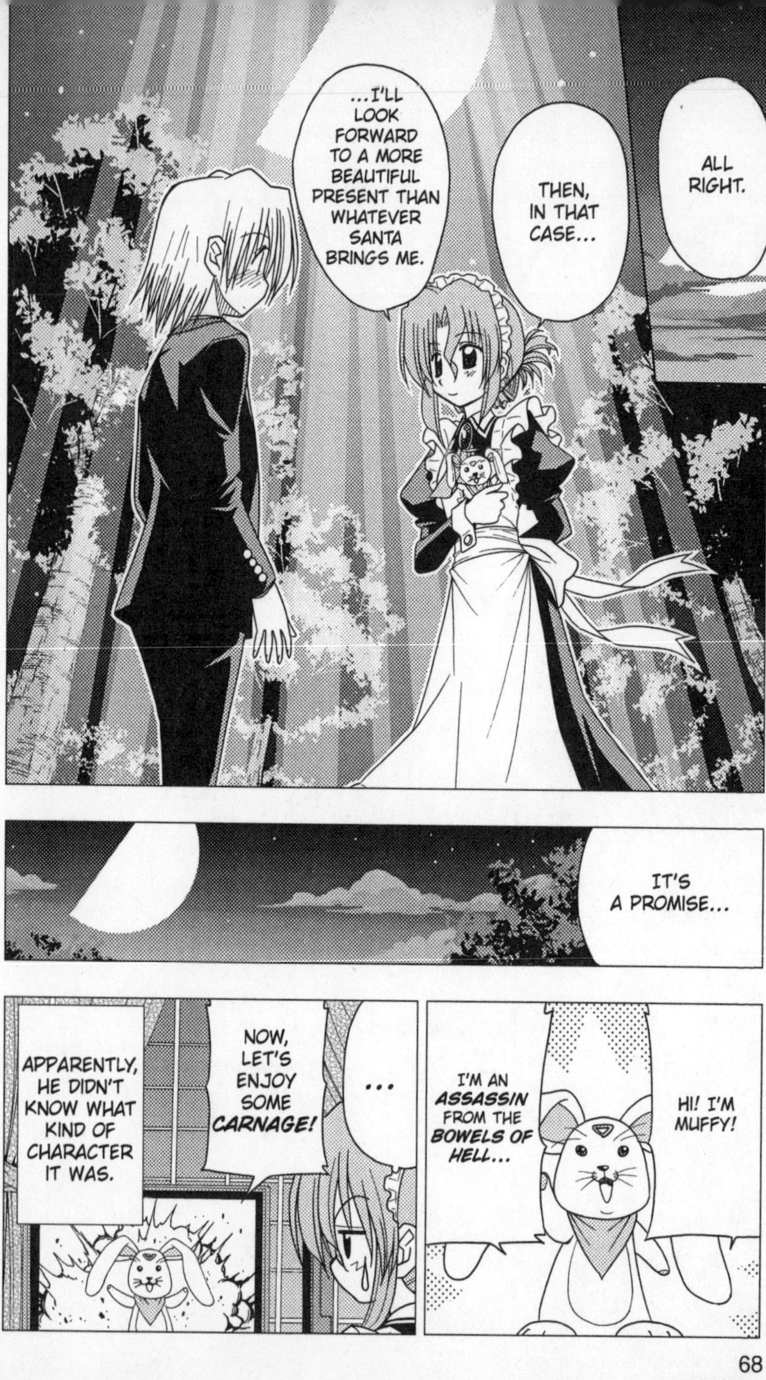
ALL RIGHT.
THEN, IN THAT CASE...
...I'LL LOOK FORWARD TO A MORE BEAUTIFUL PRESENT THAN WHATEVER SANTA BRINGS ME.
IT'S A PROMISE...
HI! I'M MUFFY!
I'M AN ASSASSIN FROM THE BOWELS OF HELL...
...
NOW, LET'S ENJOY SOME CARNAGE!
APPARENTLY, HE DIDN'T KNOW WHAT KIND OF CHARACTER IT WAS.

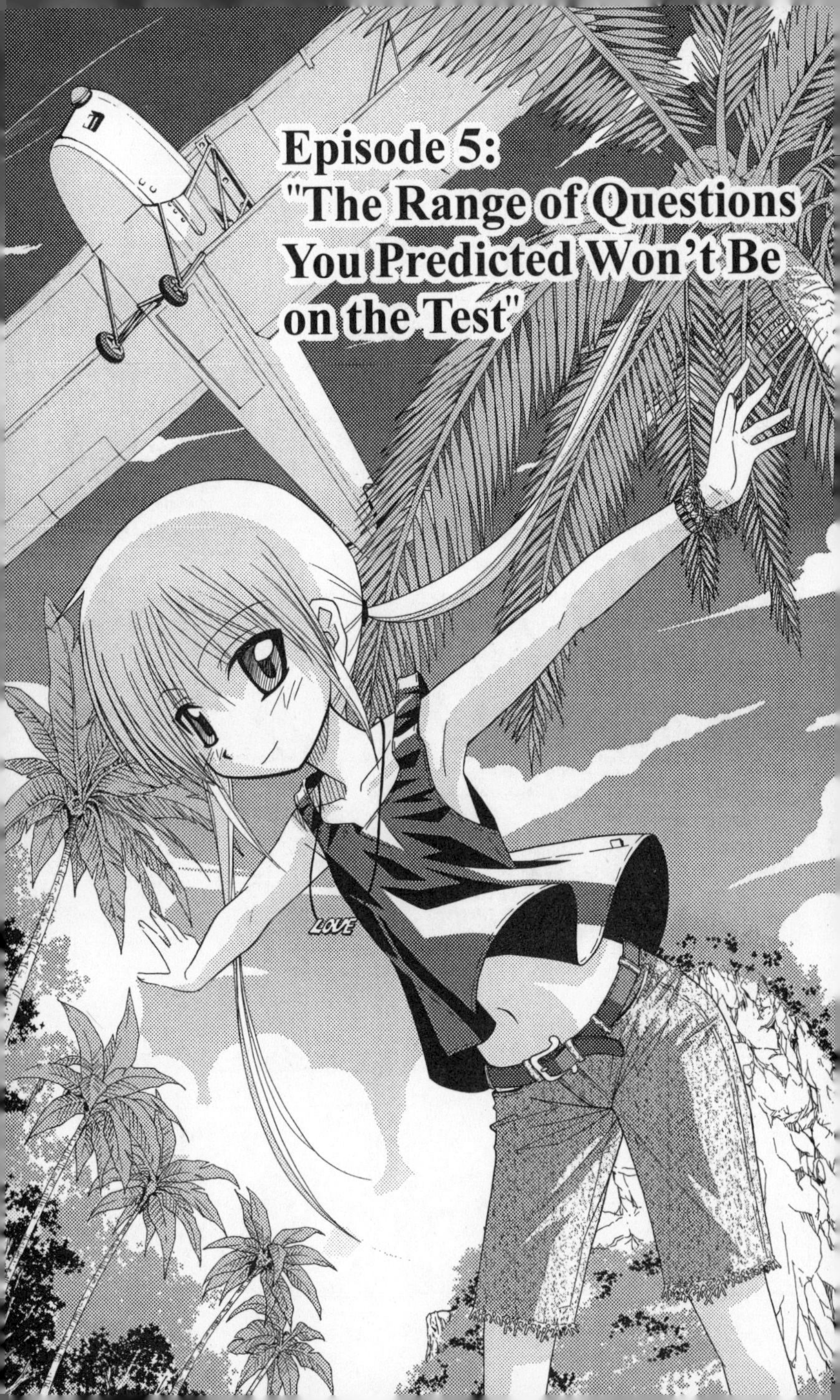
Episode 5:
"The Range of Questions You Predicted Won't Be on the Test"
LOVE

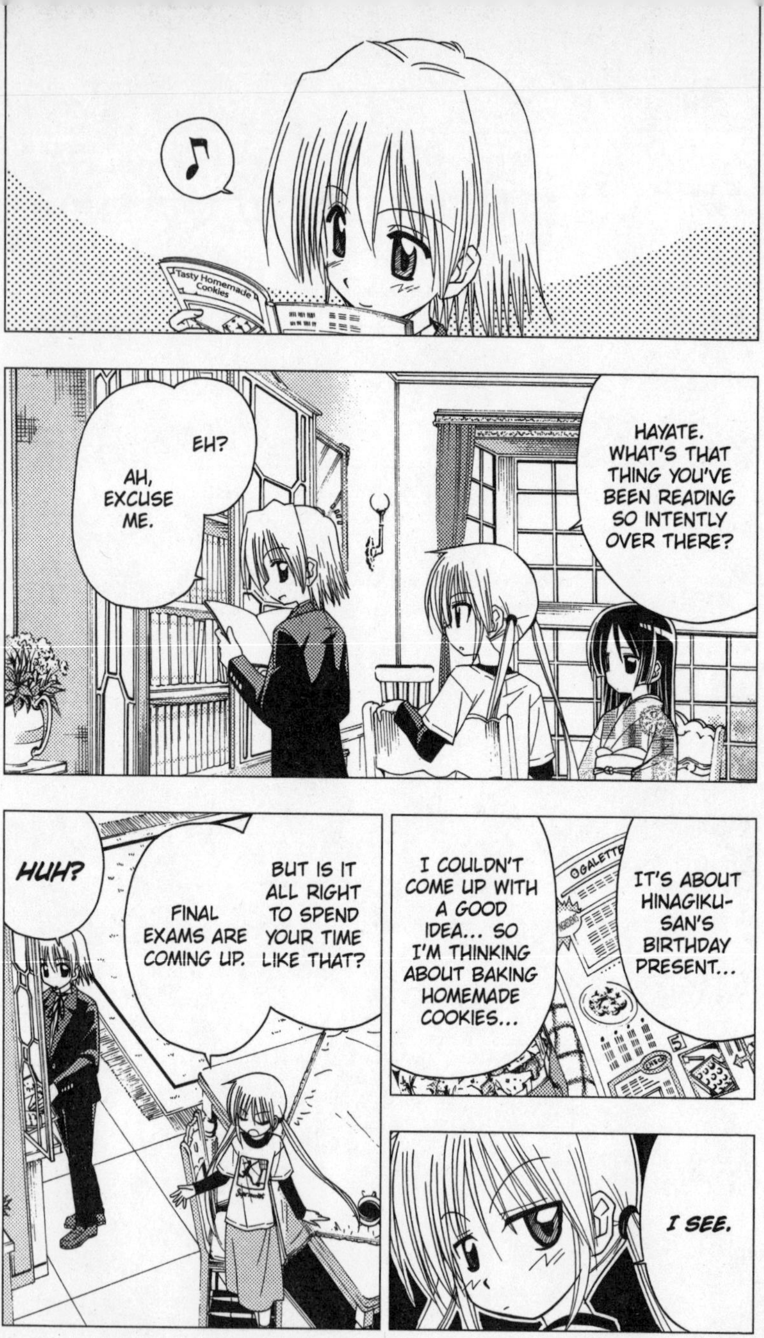
♪
Tasty Homemade Cookies
HAYATE. WHAT'S THAT THING YOU'VE BEEN READING SO INTENTLY OVER THERE?
EH?
AH, EXCUSE ME.
IT'S ABOUT HINAGIKU-SAN'S BIRTHDAY PRESENT...
GALETTE
I COULDN'T COME UP WITH A GOOD IDEA... SO I'M THINKING ABOUT BAKING HOMEMADE COOKIES...
I SEE.
BUT IS IT ALL RIGHT TO SPEND YOUR TIME LIKE THAT?
FINAL EXAMS ARE COMING UP.
HUH?

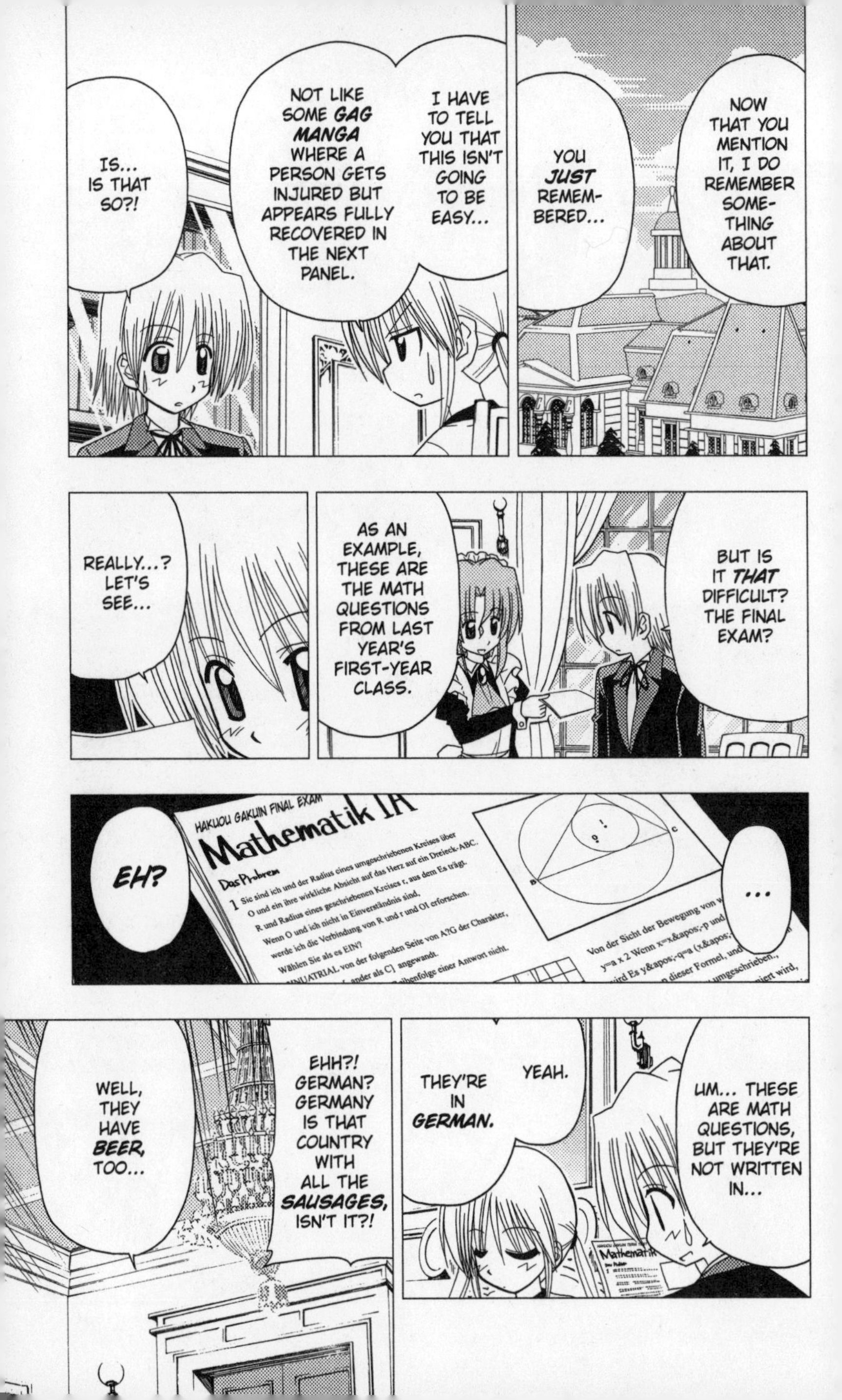
NOW THAT YOU MENTION IT, I DO REMEMBER SOMETHING ABOUT THAT.
YOU JUST REMEMBERED...
I HAVE TO TELL YOU THAT THIS ISN'T GOING TO BE EASY...
NOT LIKE SOME GAG MANGA WHERE A PERSON GETS INJURED BUT APPEARS FULLY RECOVERED IN THE NEXT PANEL.
IS... IS THAT SO?!
BUT IS IT THAT DIFFICULT? THE FINAL EXAM?
AS AN EXAMPLE, THESE ARE THE MATH QUESTIONS FROM LAST YEAR'S FIRST-YEAR CLASS.
REALLY...? LET'S SEE...
...
HAKUOU GAKUIN FINAL EXAM
Mathematik IA
Das Probrem
1 Sie sind ich und der Radius eines umgeschriebenen Kreises über
O und ein ihre wirkliche Absicht auf das Herz auf ein Dreieck-ABC.
R und Radius eines geschriebenen Kreises r, aus dem Es trägt.
Wenn O und ich nicht in Einverständnis sind,
werde ich die Verbindung von R und r und OI erforschen.
Wählen Sie als es EIN?
EH?
UM... THESE ARE MATH QUESTIONS, BUT THEY'RE NOT WRITTEN IN...
YEAH.
THEY'RE IN GERMAN.
EHH?! GERMAN? GERMANY IS THAT COUNTRY WITH ALL THE SAUSAGES, ISN'T IT?!
WELL, THEY HAVE BEER, TOO...

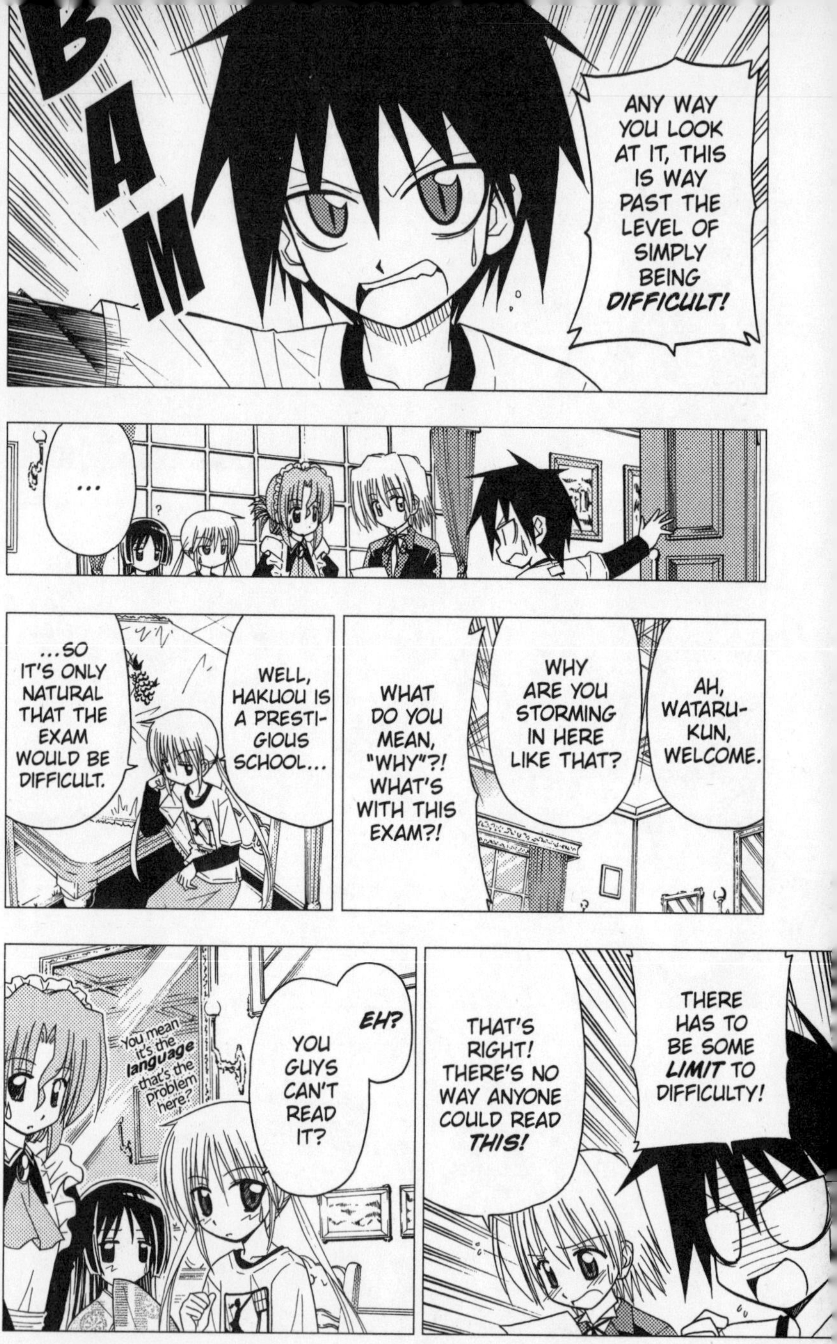
ANY WAY YOU LOOK AT IT, THIS IS WAY PAST THE LEVEL OF SIMPLY BEING *DIFFICULT!*
BAM
...
AH, WATARU-KUN, WELCOME.
WHY ARE YOU STORMING IN HERE LIKE THAT?
WHAT DO YOU MEAN, "WHY"?! WHAT'S WITH THIS EXAM?!
WELL, HAKUOU IS A PRESTI-GIOUS SCHOOL...
...SO IT'S ONLY NATURAL THAT THE EXAM WOULD BE DIFFICULT.
THERE HAS TO BE SOME *LIMIT* TO DIFFICULTY!
THAT'S RIGHT! THERE'S NO WAY ANYONE COULD READ *THIS!*
EH?
YOU GUYS CAN'T READ IT?
You mean it's the ***language*** that's the problem here?

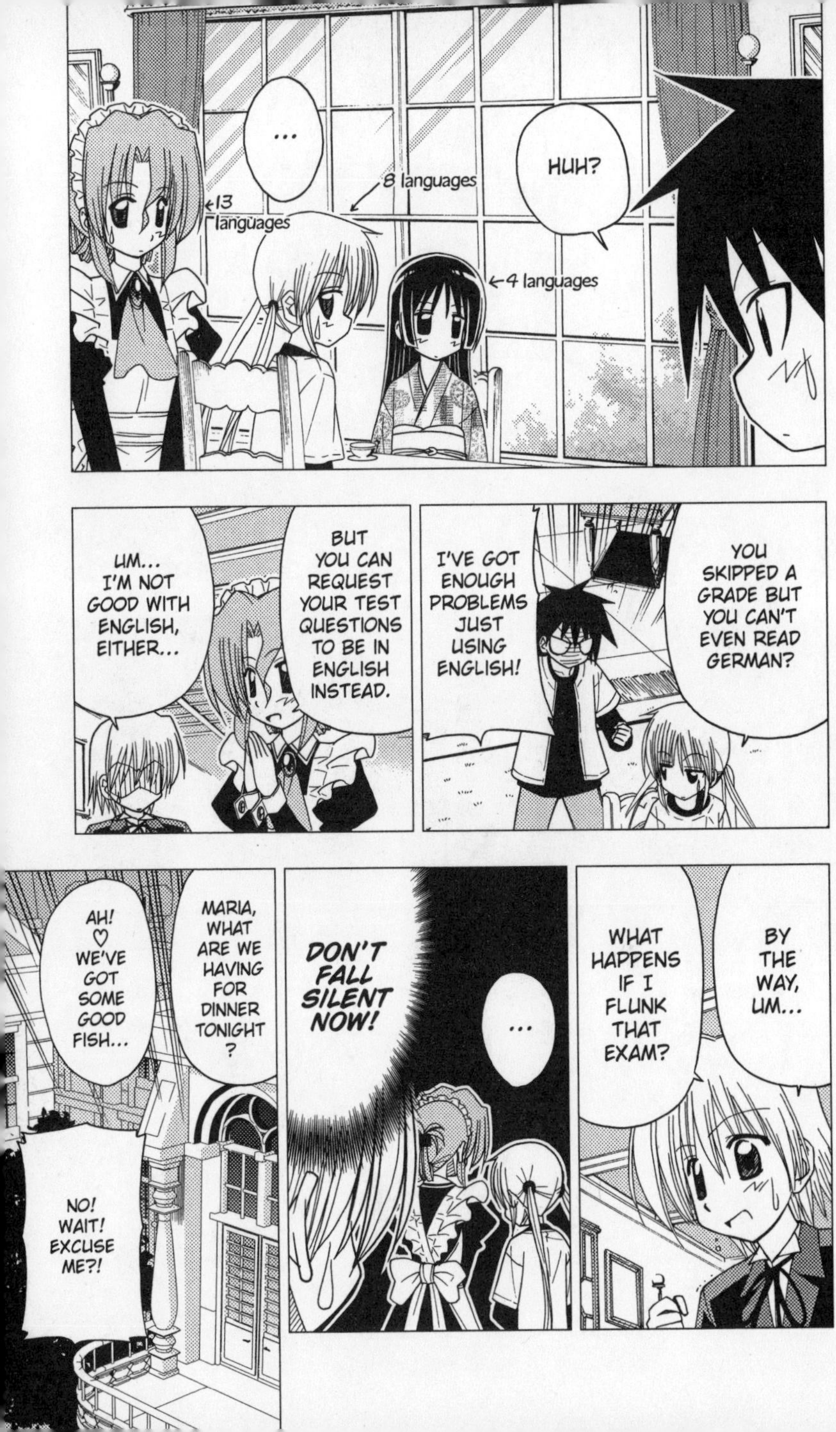
HUH?
...
8 languages
13 languages
4 languages
YOU SKIPPED A GRADE BUT YOU CAN'T EVEN READ GERMAN?
I'VE GOT ENOUGH PROBLEMS JUST USING ENGLISH!
BUT YOU CAN REQUEST YOUR TEST QUESTIONS TO BE IN ENGLISH INSTEAD.
UM... I'M NOT GOOD WITH ENGLISH, EITHER...
BY THE WAY, UM...
WHAT HAPPENS IF I FLUNK THAT EXAM?
...
DON'T FALL SILENT NOW!
MARIA, WHAT ARE WE HAVING FOR DINNER TONIGHT?
AH! ♡ WE'VE GOT SOME GOOD FISH...
NO! WAIT! EXCUSE ME?!

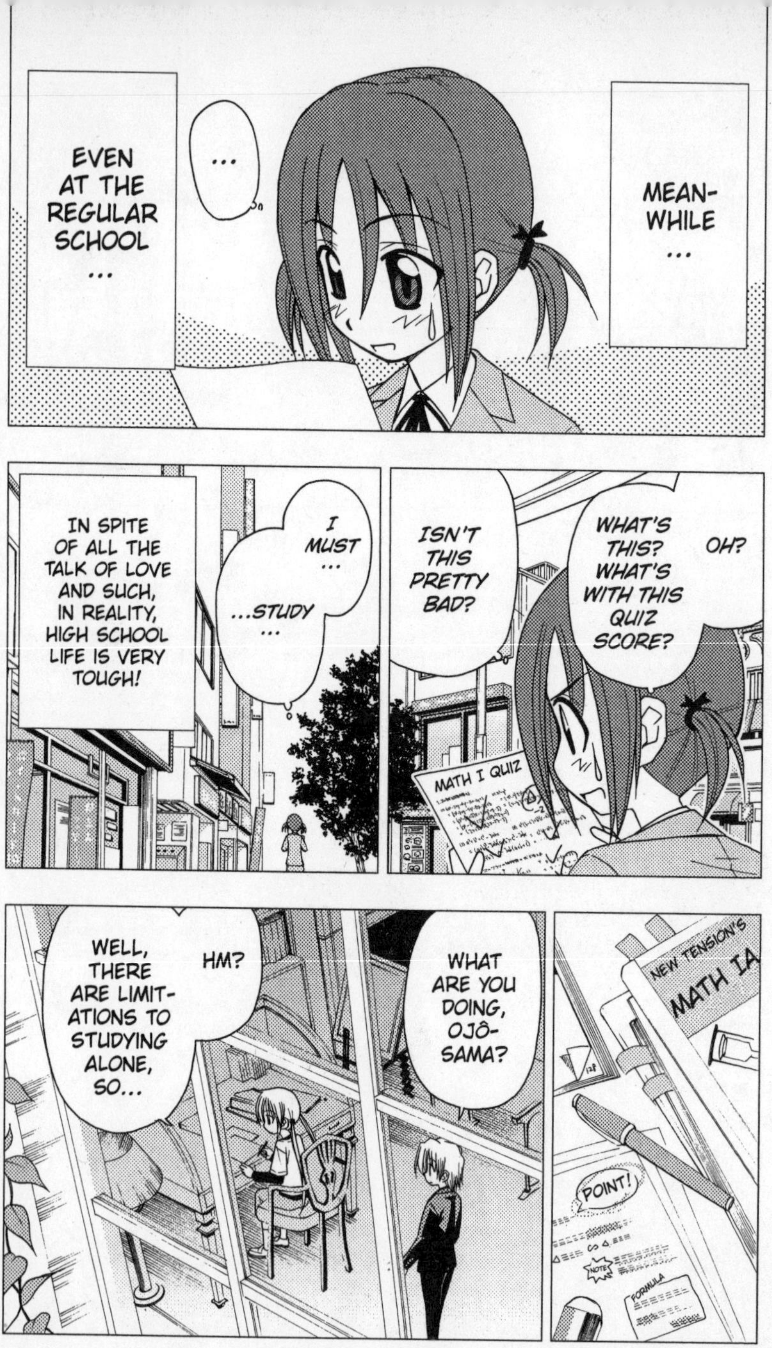
MEAN-WHILE ...
...
EVEN AT THE REGULAR SCHOOL ...
OH?
WHAT'S THIS? WHAT'S WITH THIS QUIZ SCORE?
ISN'T THIS PRETTY BAD?
MATH I QUIZ
I MUST ...
...STUDY ...
IN SPITE OF ALL THE TALK OF LOVE AND SUCH, IN REALITY, HIGH SCHOOL LIFE IS VERY TOUGH!
NEW TENSION'S
MATH IA
POINT!
NOTE
FORMULA
WHAT ARE YOU DOING, OJÔ-SAMA?
HM?
WELL, THERE ARE LIMIT-ATIONS TO STUDYING ALONE, SO...

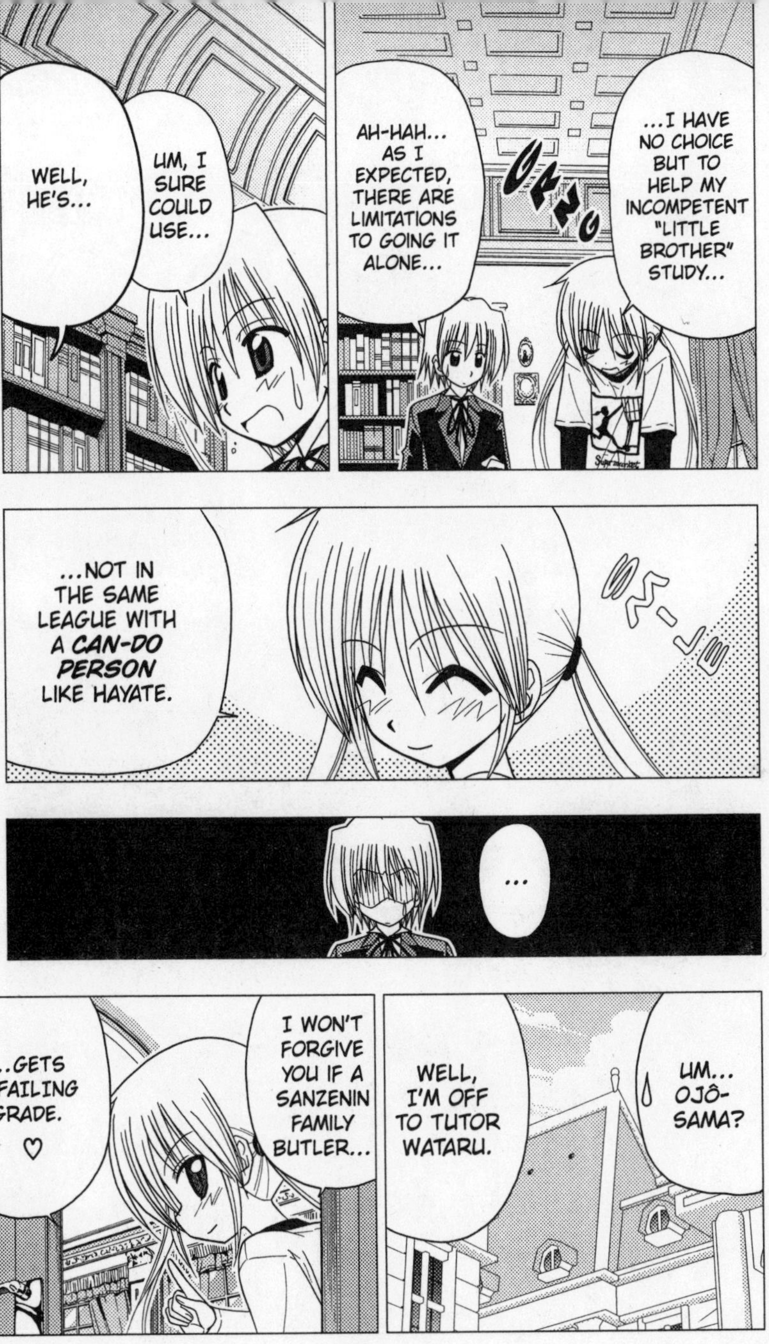
...I HAVE NO CHOICE BUT TO HELP MY INCOMPETENT "LITTLE BROTHER" STUDY...
AH-HAH... AS I EXPECTED, THERE ARE LIMITATIONS TO GOING IT ALONE...
UM, I SURE COULD USE...
WELL, HE'S...
...NOT IN THE SAME LEAGUE WITH A CAN-DO PERSON LIKE HAYATE.
...
UM... OJÔ-SAMA?
WELL, I'M OFF TO TUTOR WATARU.
I WON'T FORGIVE YOU IF A SANZENIN FAMILY BUTLER...
...GETS A FAILING GRADE. ♡

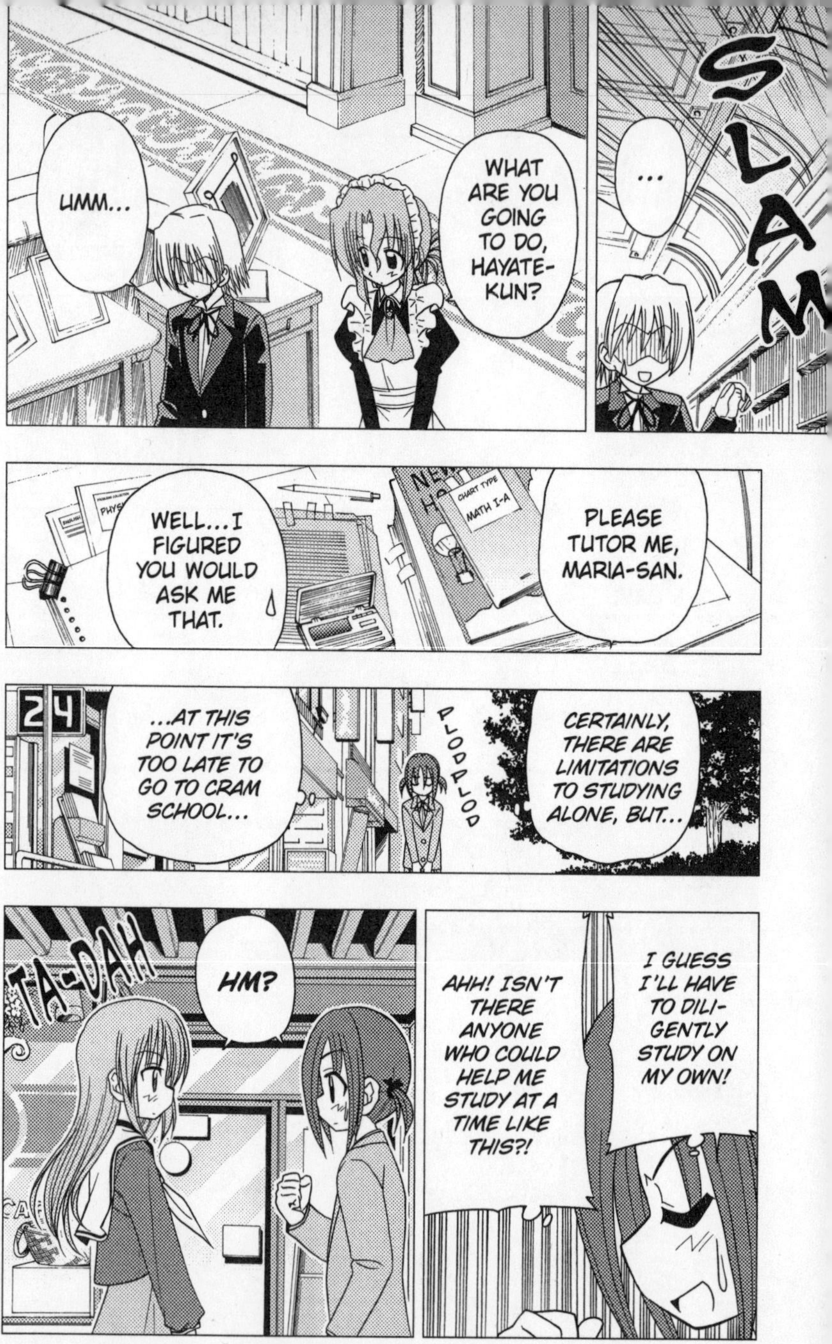
SLAM
...
WHAT ARE YOU GOING TO DO, HAYATE-KUN?
UMM...
PLEASE TUTOR ME, MARIA-SAN.
CHART TYPE
MATH I-A
WELL...I FIGURED YOU WOULD ASK ME THAT.
CERTAINLY, THERE ARE LIMITATIONS TO STUDYING ALONE, BUT...
PLODPLOD
...AT THIS POINT IT'S TOO LATE TO GO TO CRAM SCHOOL...
24
I GUESS I'LL HAVE TO DILI-GENTLY STUDY ON MY OWN!
AHH! ISN'T THERE ANYONE WHO COULD HELP ME STUDY AT A TIME LIKE THIS?!
HM?
TA-DAH

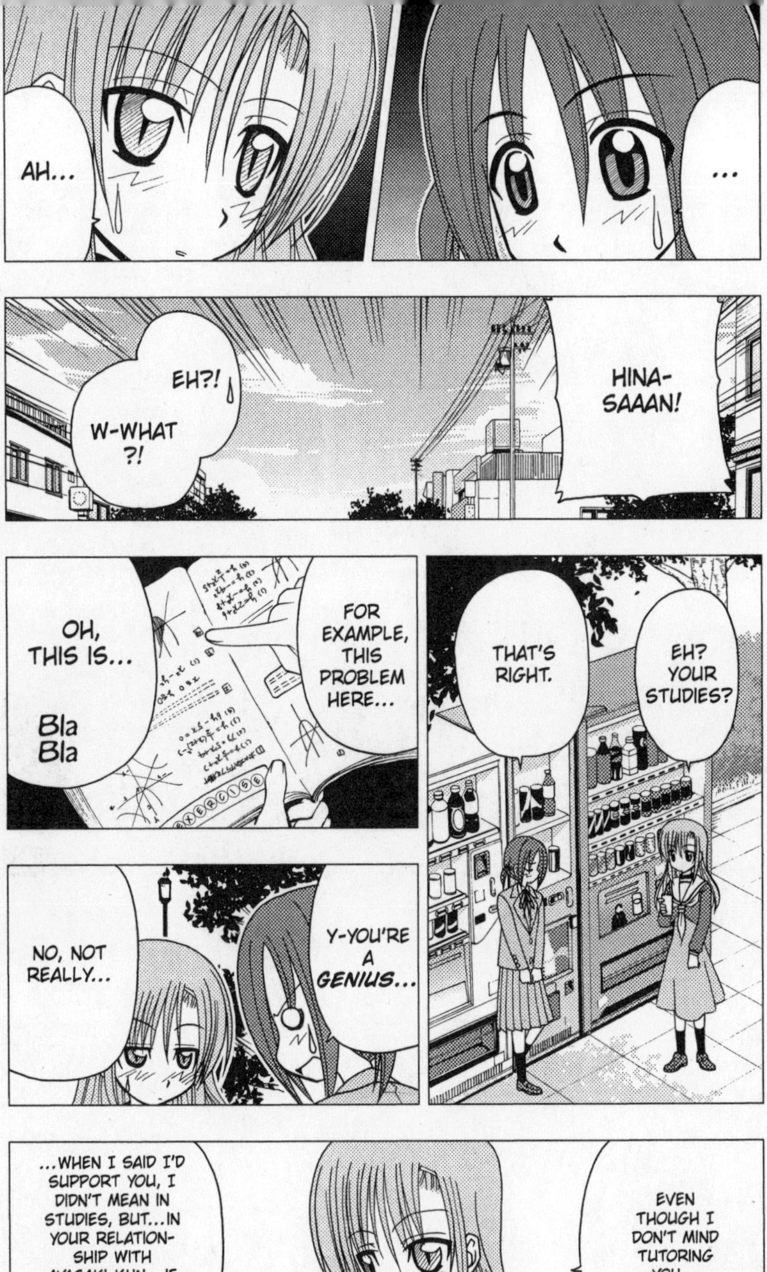
...
AH...
HINA-SAAAN!
EH?!
W-WHAT?!
EH? YOUR STUDIES?
THAT'S RIGHT.
FOR EXAMPLE, THIS PROBLEM HERE...
OH, THIS IS...
Bla Bla
Y-YOU'RE A GENIUS...
NO, NOT REALLY...
EVEN THOUGH I DON'T MIND TUTORING YOU...
...WHEN I SAID I'D SUPPORT YOU, I DIDN'T MEAN IN STUDIES, BUT...IN YOUR RELATIONSHIP WITH AYASAKI-KUN...IF YOU KNOW WHAT I MEAN...

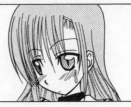

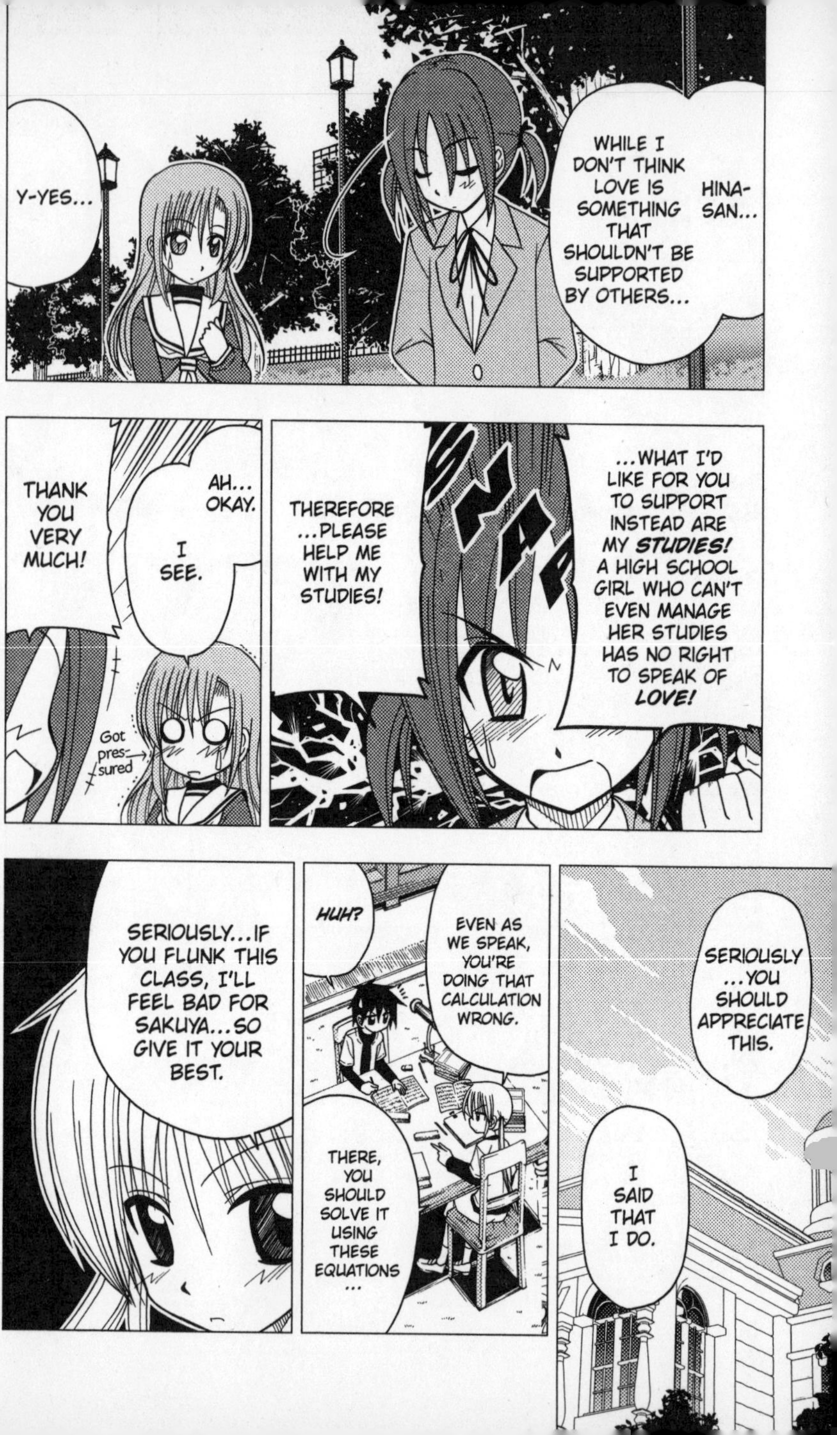
HINA-SAN...
WHILE I DON'T THINK LOVE IS SOMETHING THAT SHOULDN'T BE SUPPORTED BY OTHERS...
Y-YES...
...WHAT I'D LIKE FOR YOU TO SUPPORT INSTEAD ARE MY STUDIES! A HIGH SCHOOL GIRL WHO CAN'T EVEN MANAGE HER STUDIES HAS NO RIGHT TO SPEAK OF LOVE!
SNAP
THEREFORE ...PLEASE HELP ME WITH MY STUDIES!
AH... OKAY.
I SEE.
THANK YOU VERY MUCH!
Got pressured
SERIOUSLY ...YOU SHOULD APPRECIATE THIS.
I SAID THAT I DO.
EVEN AS WE SPEAK, YOU'RE DOING THAT CALCULATION WRONG.
HUH?
THERE, YOU SHOULD SOLVE IT USING THESE EQUATIONS...
SERIOUSLY...IF YOU FLUNK THIS CLASS, I'LL FEEL BAD FOR SAKUYA...SO GIVE IT YOUR BEST.

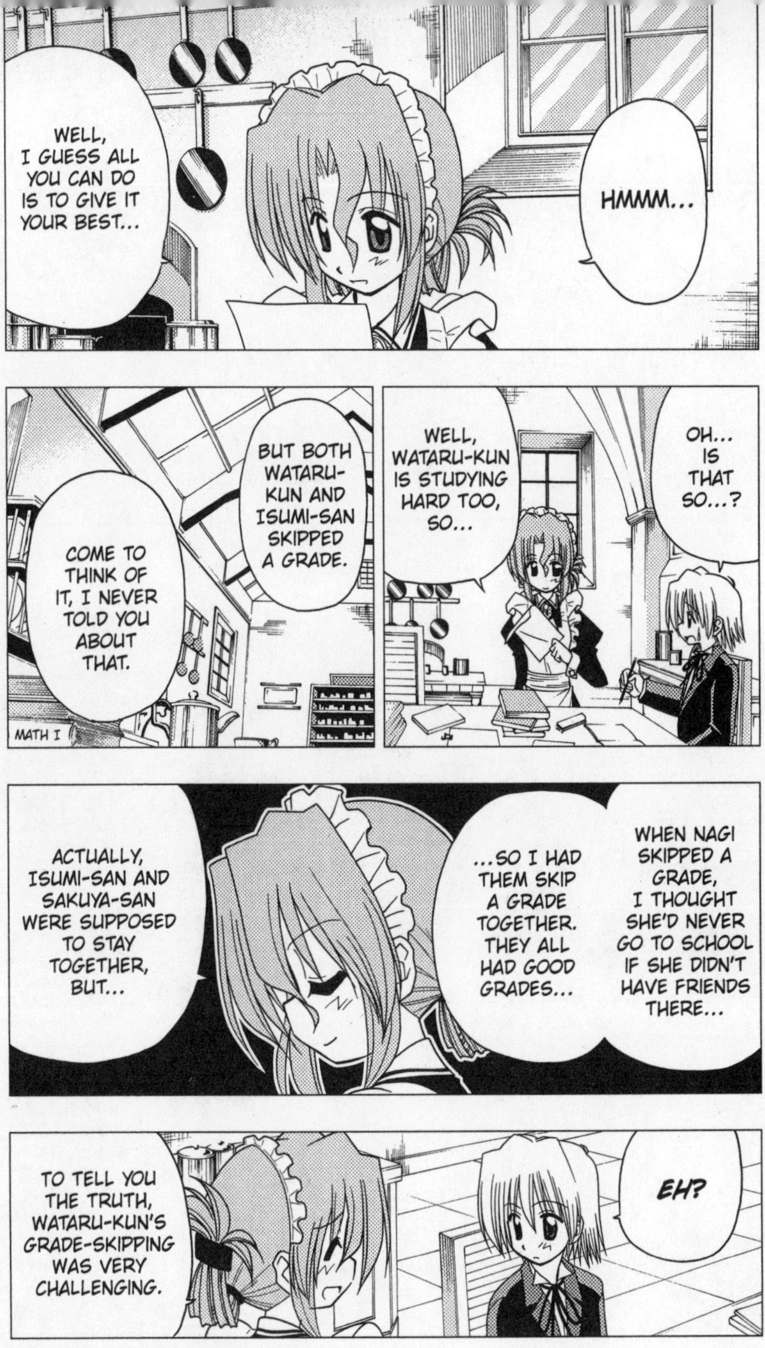
HMMM...
WELL, I GUESS ALL YOU CAN DO IS TO GIVE IT YOUR BEST...
OH... IS THAT SO...?
WELL, WATARU-KUN IS STUDYING HARD TOO, SO...
BUT BOTH WATARU-KUN AND ISUMI-SAN SKIPPED A GRADE.
COME TO THINK OF IT, I NEVER TOLD YOU ABOUT THAT.
MATH I
WHEN NAGI SKIPPED A GRADE, I THOUGHT SHE'D NEVER GO TO SCHOOL IF SHE DIDN'T HAVE FRIENDS THERE...
...SO I HAD THEM SKIP A GRADE TOGETHER. THEY ALL HAD GOOD GRADES...
ACTUALLY, ISUMI-SAN AND SAKUYA-SAN WERE SUPPOSED TO STAY TOGETHER, BUT...
EH?
TO TELL YOU THE TRUTH, WATARU-KUN'S GRADE-SKIPPING WAS VERY CHALLENGING.

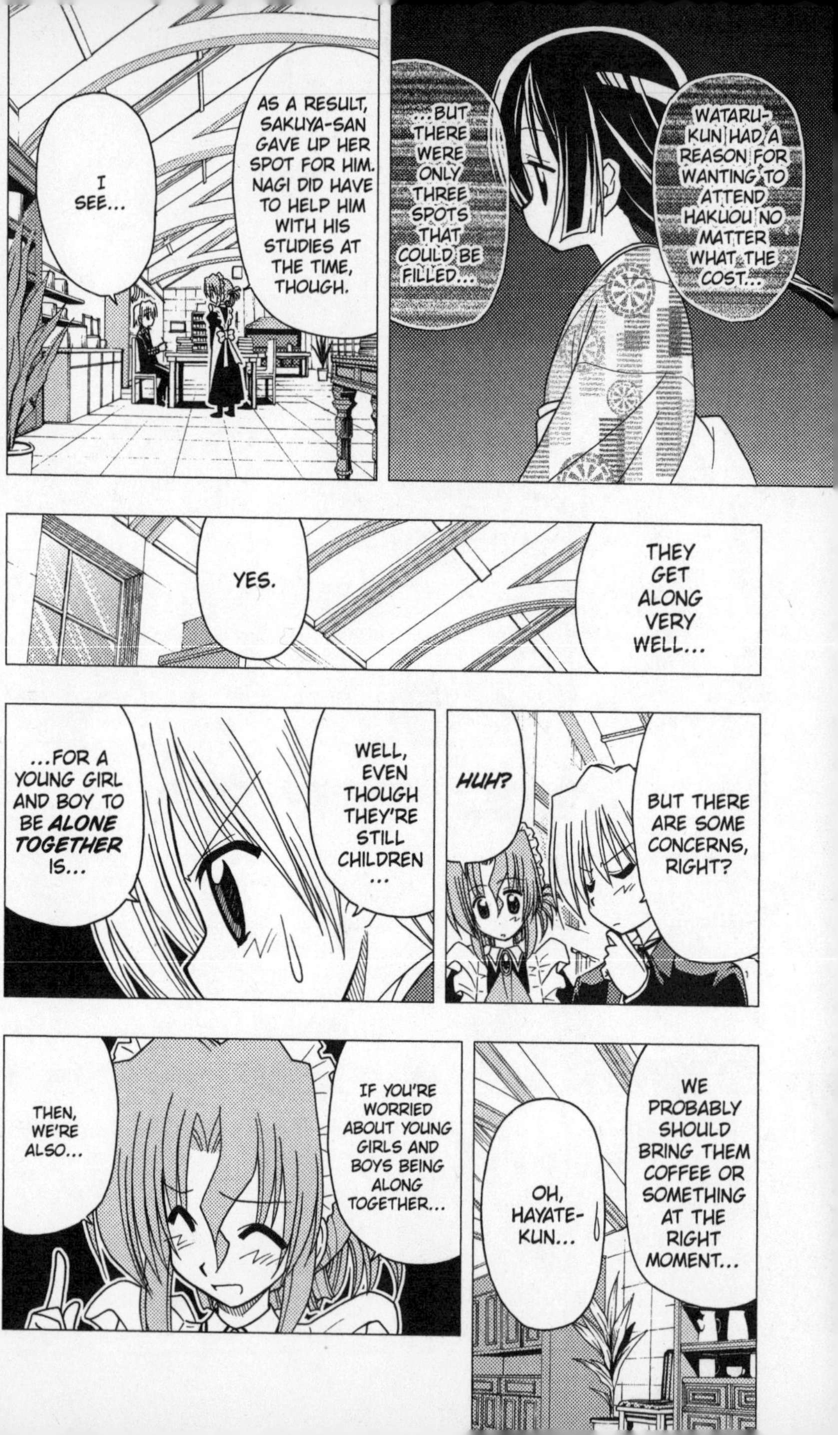
WATARU-KUN HAD A REASON FOR WANTING TO ATTEND HAKUOU NO MATTER WHAT THE COST...
...BUT THERE WERE ONLY THREE SPOTS THAT COULD BE FILLED...
AS A RESULT, SAKUYA-SAN GAVE UP HER SPOT FOR HIM. NAGI DID HAVE TO HELP HIM WITH HIS STUDIES AT THE TIME, THOUGH.
I SEE...
THEY GET ALONG VERY WELL...
YES.
BUT THERE ARE SOME CONCERNS, RIGHT?
HUH?
WELL, EVEN THOUGH THEY'RE STILL CHILDREN...
...FOR A YOUNG GIRL AND BOY TO BE ALONE TOGETHER IS...
WE PROBABLY SHOULD BRING THEM COFFEE OR SOMETHING AT THE RIGHT MOMENT...
OH, HAYATE-KUN...
IF YOU'RE WORRIED ABOUT YOUNG GIRLS AND BOYS BEING ALONG TOGETHER...
THEN, WE'RE ALSO...

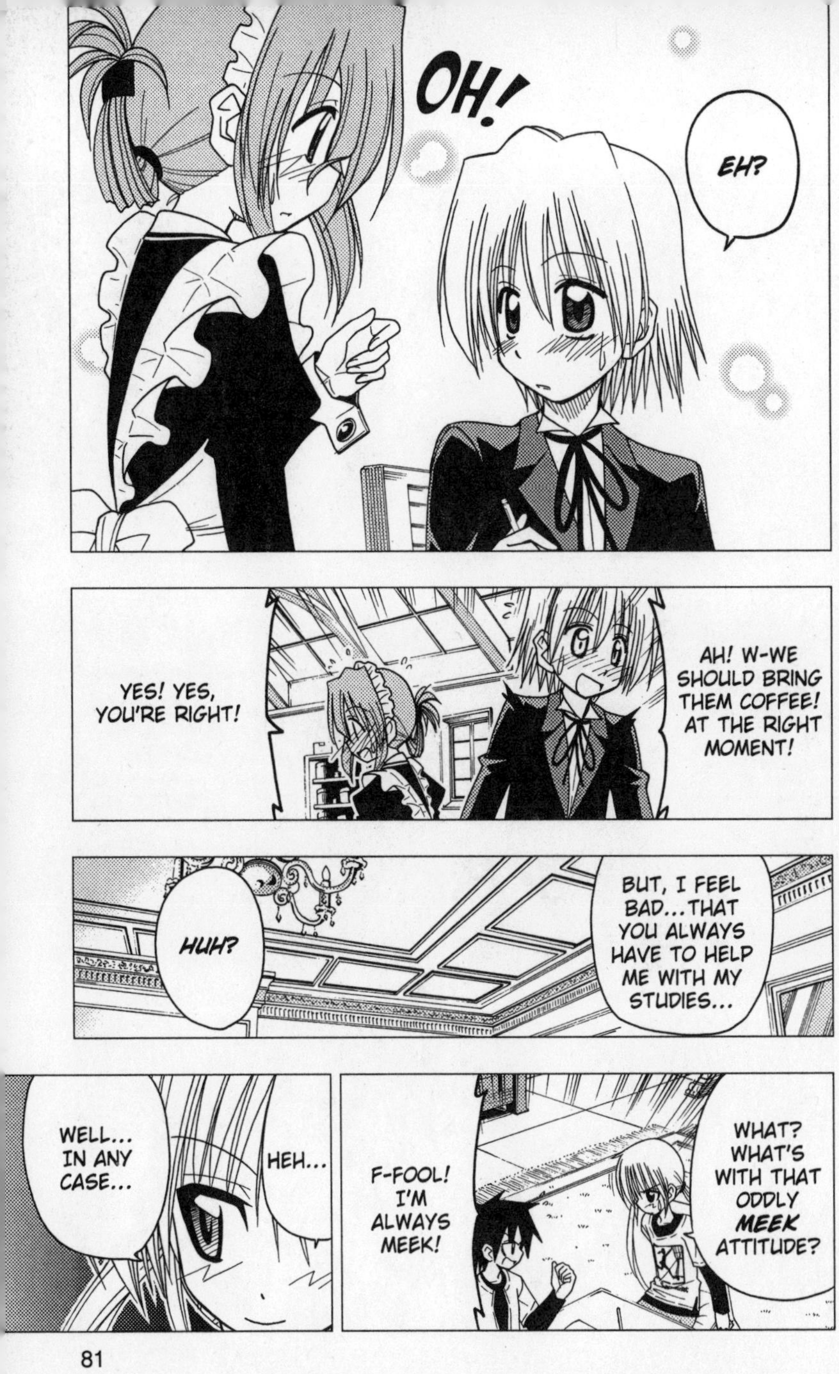
EH?
OH!
AH! W-WE SHOULD BRING THEM COFFEE! AT THE RIGHT MOMENT!
YES! YES, YOU'RE RIGHT!
BUT, I FEEL BAD...THAT YOU ALWAYS HAVE TO HELP ME WITH MY STUDIES...
HUH?
WHAT? WHAT'S WITH THAT ODDLY MEEK ATTITUDE?
F-FOOL! I'M ALWAYS MEEK!
HEH...
WELL... IN ANY CASE...

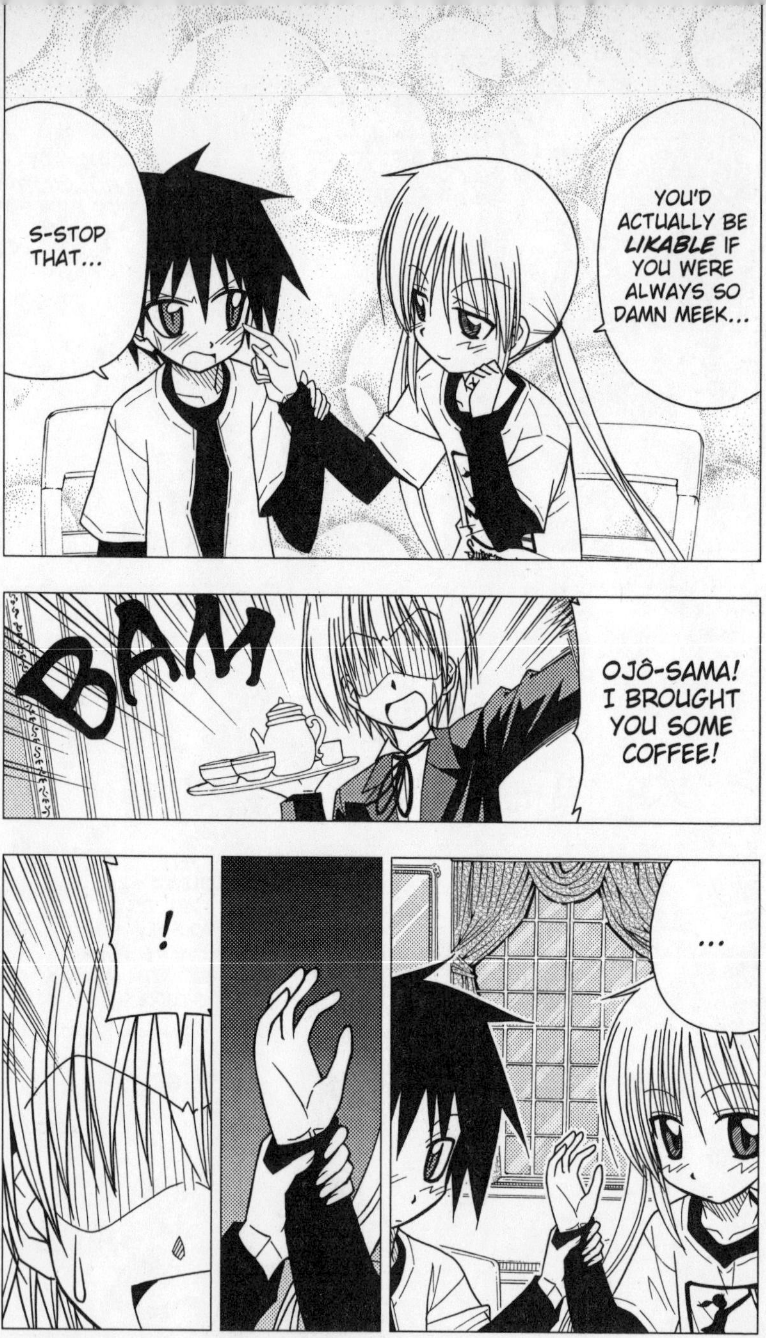
YOU'D ACTUALLY BE LIKABLE IF YOU WERE ALWAYS SO DAMN MEEK...
S-STOP THAT...
OJÔ-SAMA! I BROUGHT YOU SOME COFFEE!
BAM
...
!

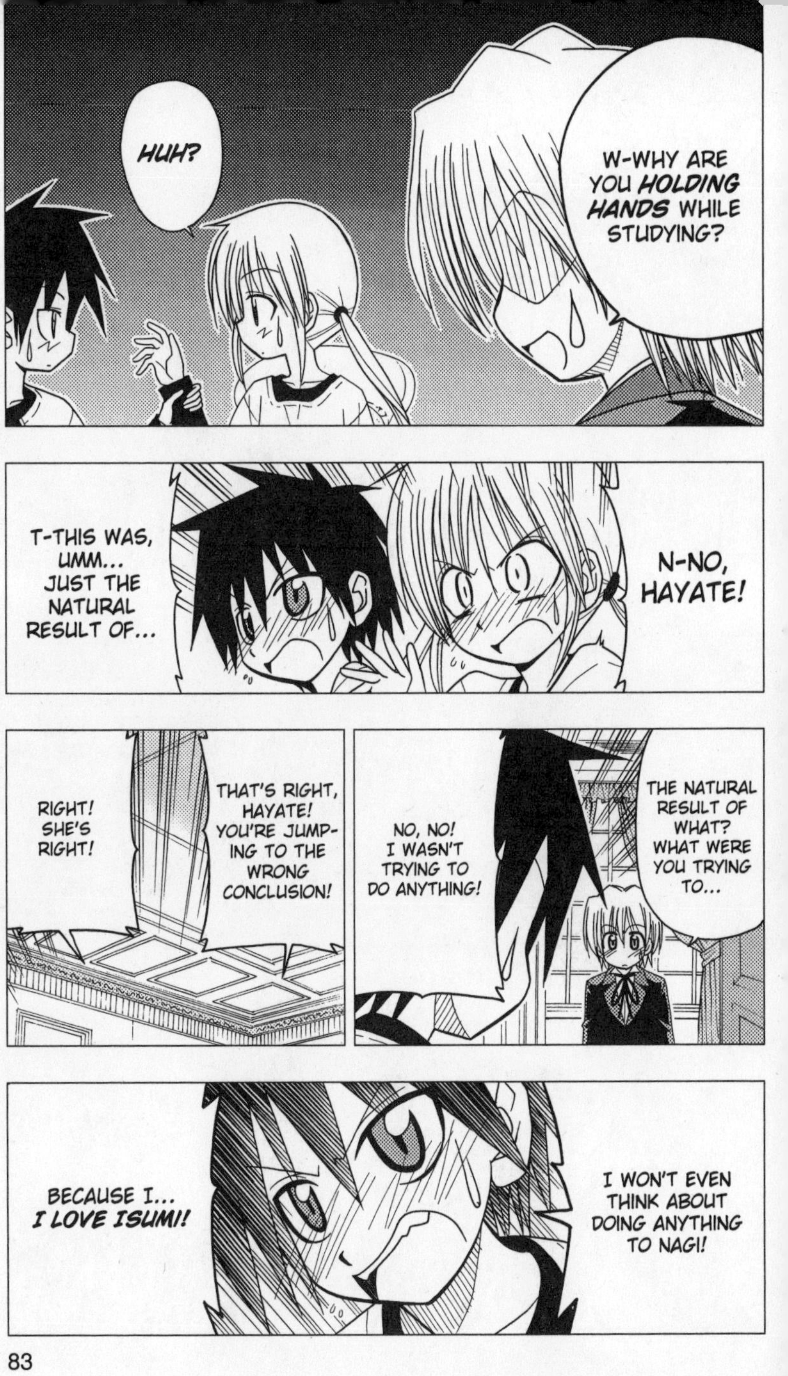
W-WHY ARE YOU **HOLDING HANDS** WHILE STUDYING?
HUH?
N-NO, HAYATE!
T-THIS WAS, UMM... JUST THE NATURAL RESULT OF...
THE NATURAL RESULT OF WHAT? WHAT WERE YOU TRYING TO...
NO, NO! I WASN'T TRYING TO DO ANYTHING!
THAT'S RIGHT, HAYATE! YOU'RE JUMP-ING TO THE WRONG CONCLUSION!
RIGHT! SHE'S RIGHT!
I WON'T EVEN THINK ABOUT DOING ANYTHING TO NAGI!
BECAUSE I... *I LOVE ISUMI!*

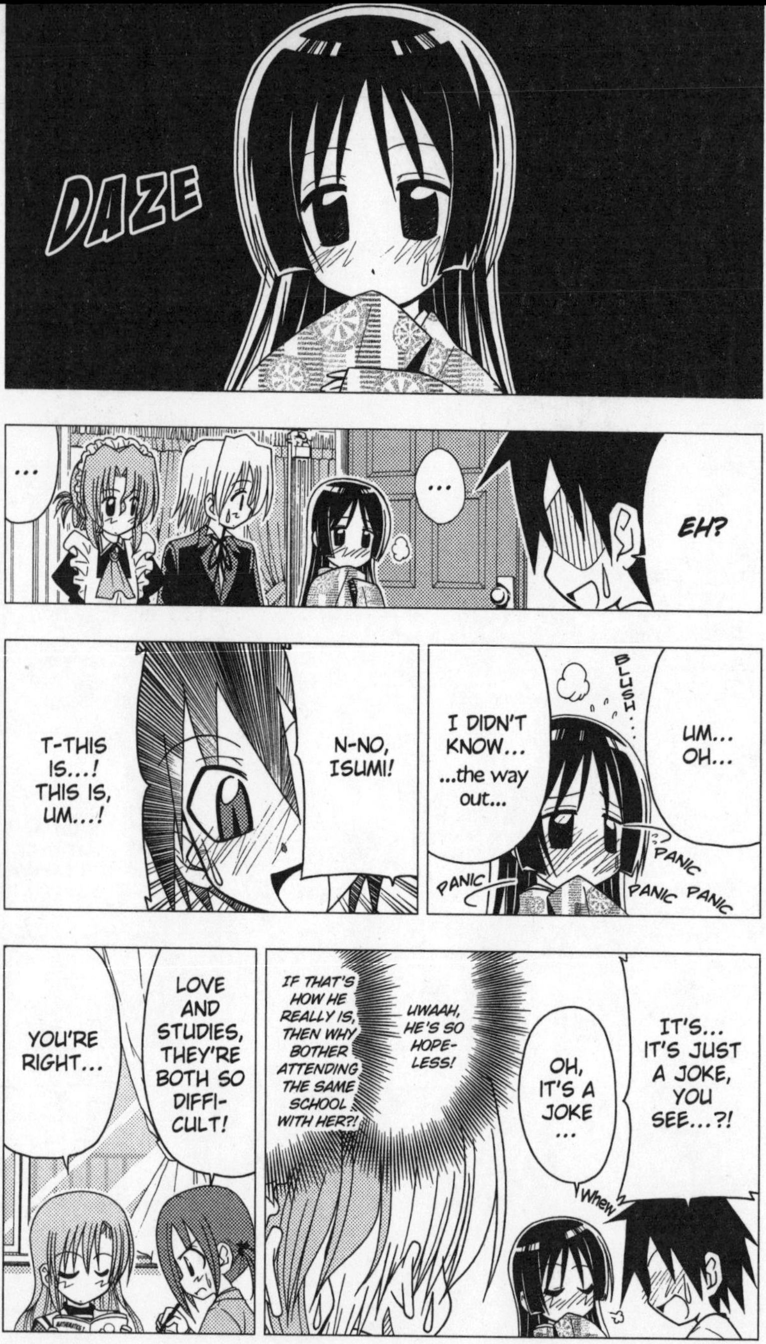
DAZE
EH?
...
...
UM... OH...
BLUSH...
I DIDN'T KNOW... ...the way out...
PANIC PANIC PANIC PANIC
N-NO, ISUMI!
T-THIS IS...! THIS IS, UM...!
IT'S... IT'S JUST A JOKE, YOU SEE...?!
OH, IT'S A JOKE ...
Whew
UWAAH, HE'S SO HOPE-LESS!
IF THAT'S HOW HE REALLY IS, THEN WHY BOTHER ATTENDING THE SAME SCHOOL WITH HER?!
LOVE AND STUDIES, THEY'RE BOTH SO DIFFI-CULT!
YOU'RE RIGHT...

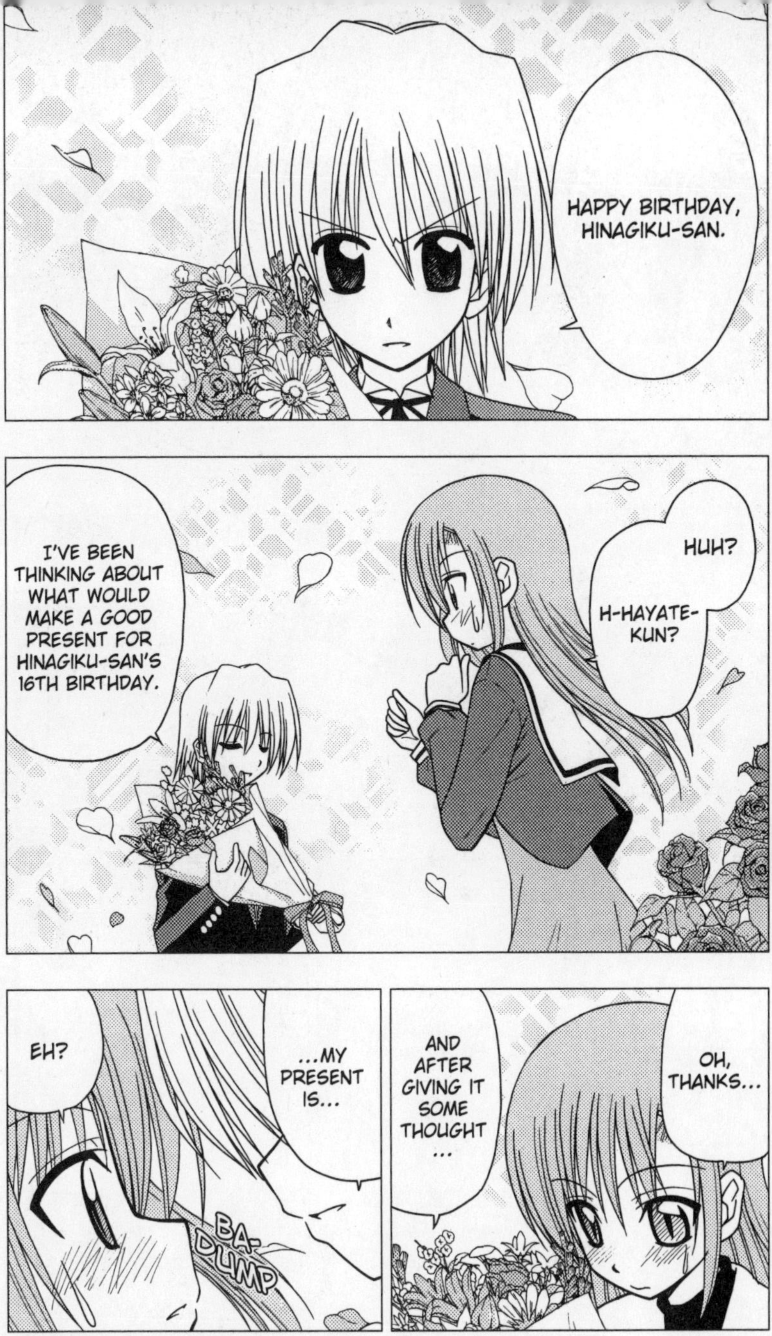
HAPPY BIRTHDAY, HINAGIKU-SAN.
HUH?
H-HAYATE-KUN?
I'VE BEEN THINKING ABOUT WHAT WOULD MAKE A GOOD PRESENT FOR HINAGIKU-SAN'S 16TH BIRTHDAY.
OH, THANKS...
AND AFTER GIVING IT SOME THOUGHT...
...MY PRESENT IS...
EH?
BA-DUMP

Episode 6: "Moment"

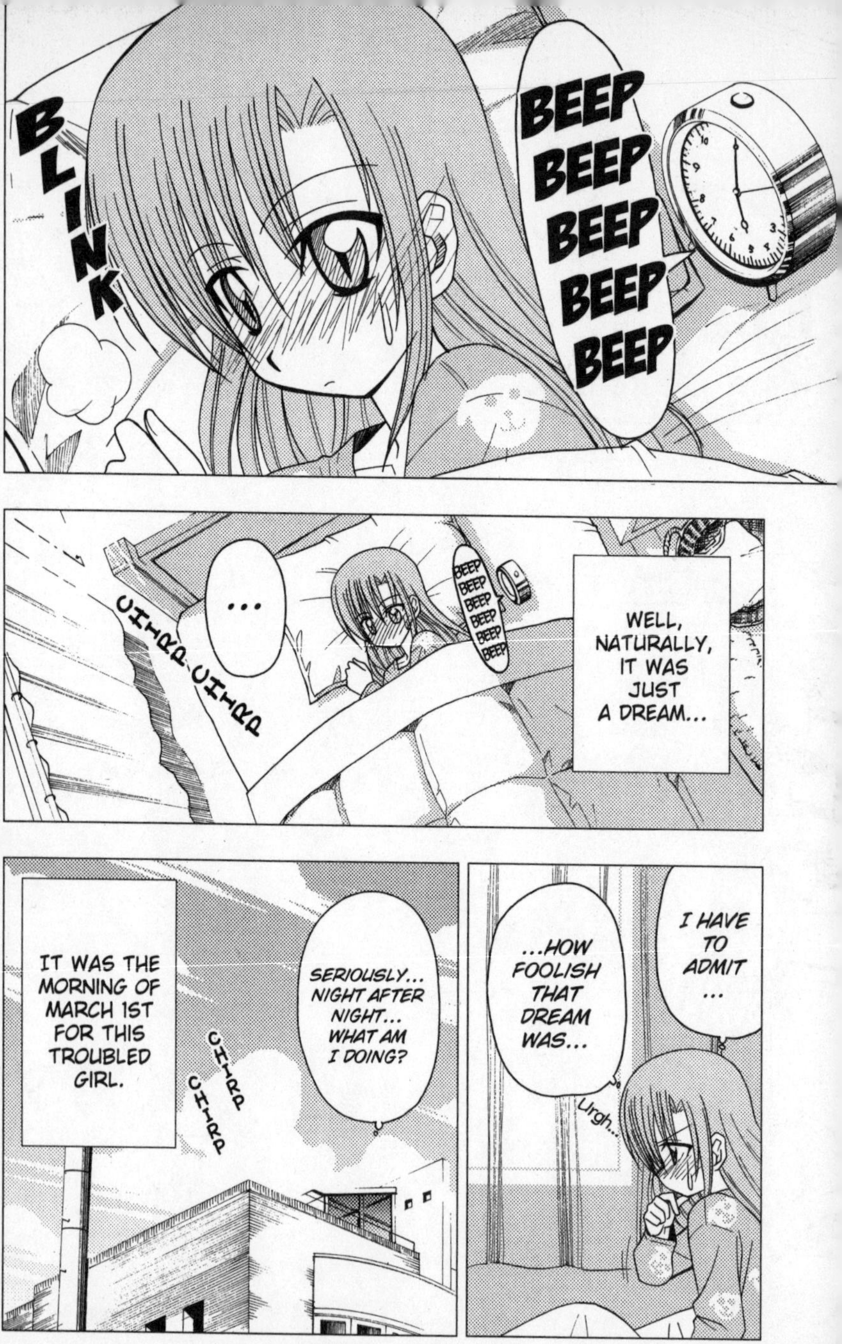
BEEP BEEP BEEP BEEP BEEP
BLINK
WELL, NATURALLY, IT WAS JUST A DREAM...
BEEP BEEP BEEP BEEP BEEP BEEP
...
CHIRP CHIRP
I HAVE TO ADMIT ...
...HOW FOOLISH THAT DREAM WAS...
Urgh...
SERIOUSLY... NIGHT AFTER NIGHT... WHAT AM I DOING?
CHIRP CHIRP
IT WAS THE MORNING OF MARCH 1ST FOR THIS TROUBLED GIRL.

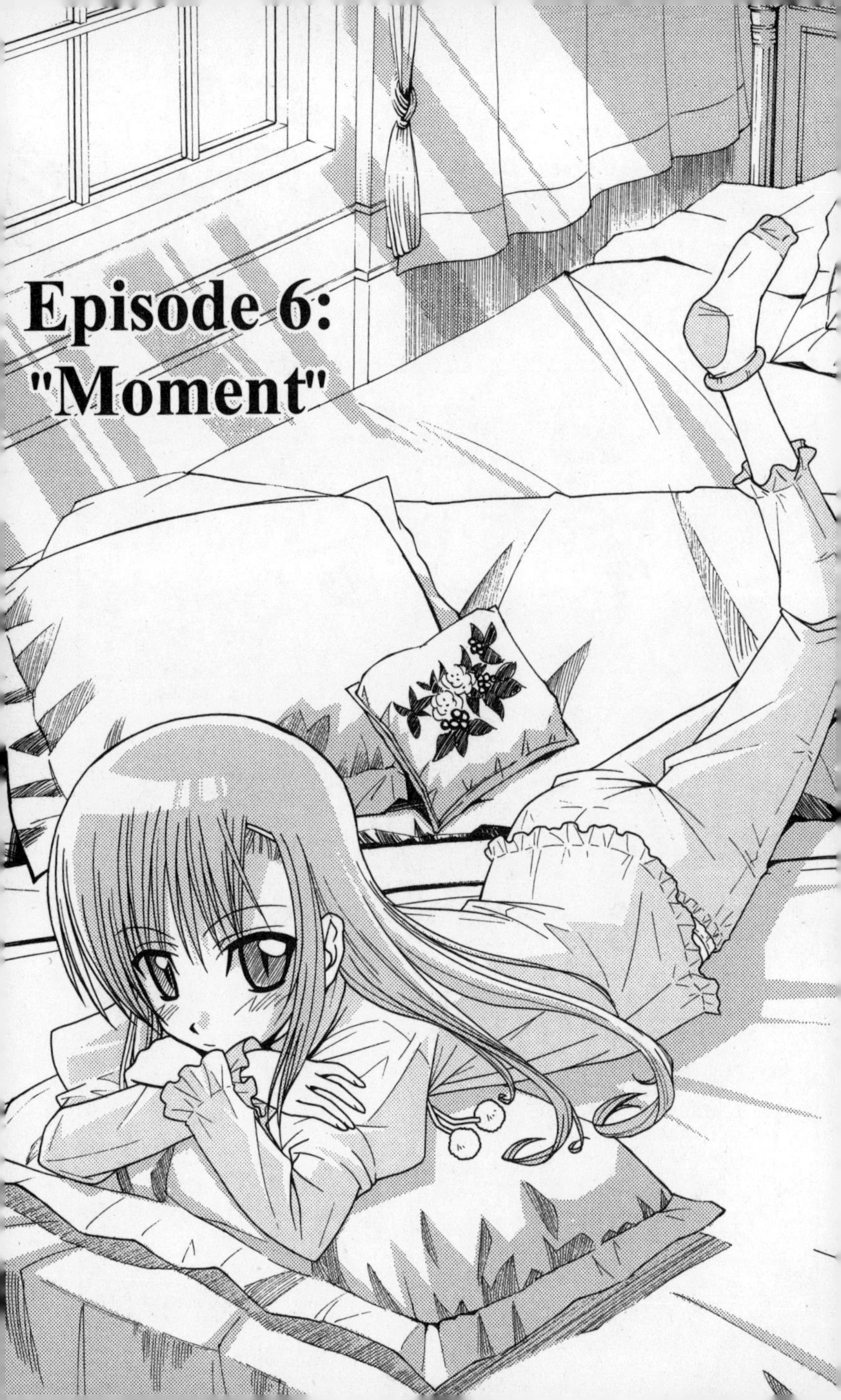
Episode 6:
"Moment"

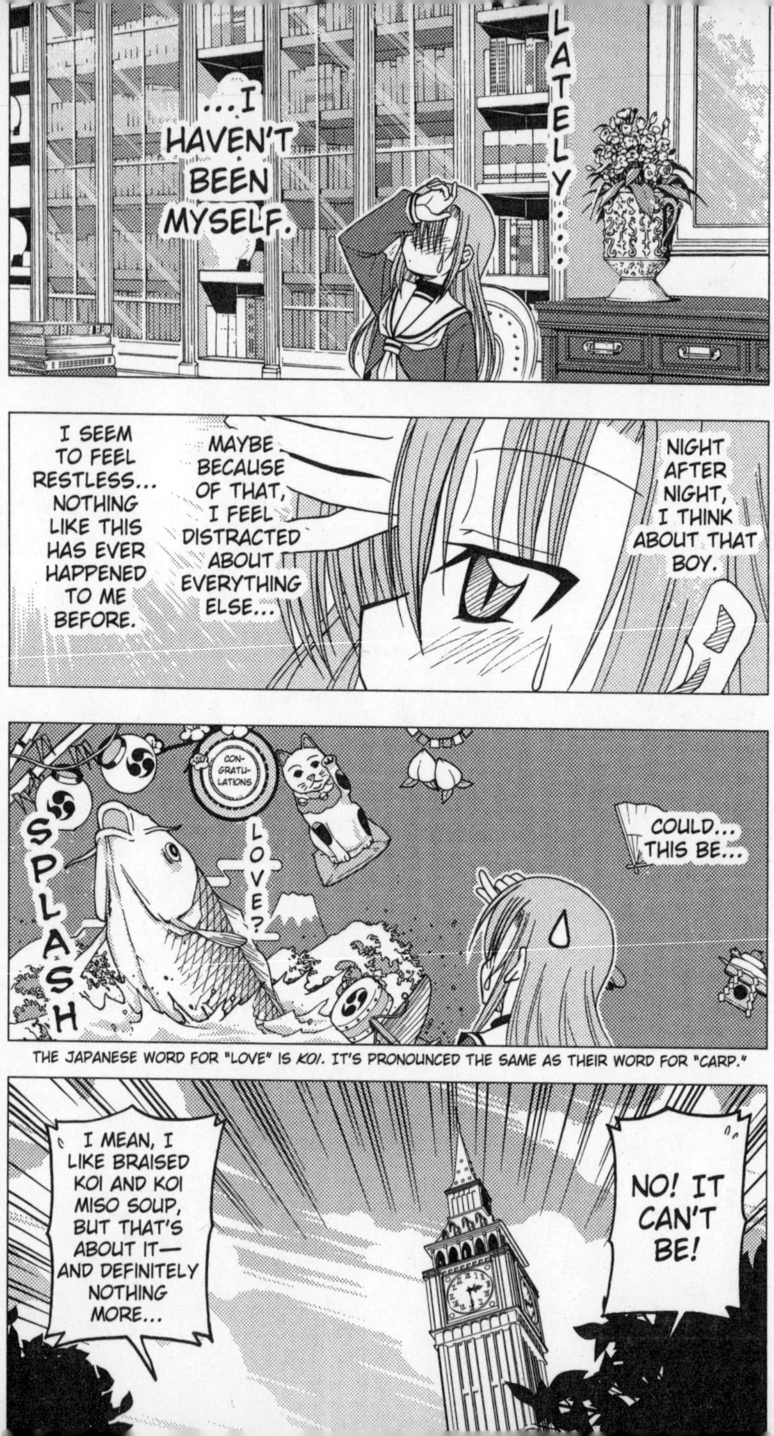
LATELY...
...I HAVEN'T BEEN MYSELF.
NIGHT AFTER NIGHT, I THINK ABOUT THAT BOY.
MAYBE BECAUSE OF THAT, I FEEL DISTRACTED ABOUT EVERYTHING ELSE...
I SEEM TO FEEL RESTLESS... NOTHING LIKE THIS HAS EVER HAPPENED TO ME BEFORE.
COULD... THIS BE...
CONGRATULATIONS
LOVE?
SPLASH
NO! IT CAN'T BE!
I MEAN, I LIKE BRAISED KOI AND KOI MISO SOUP, BUT THAT'S ABOUT IT—AND DEFINITELY NOTHING MORE...
THE JAPANESE WORD FOR "LOVE" IS *KOI*. IT'S PRONOUNCED THE SAME AS THEIR WORD FOR "CARP."

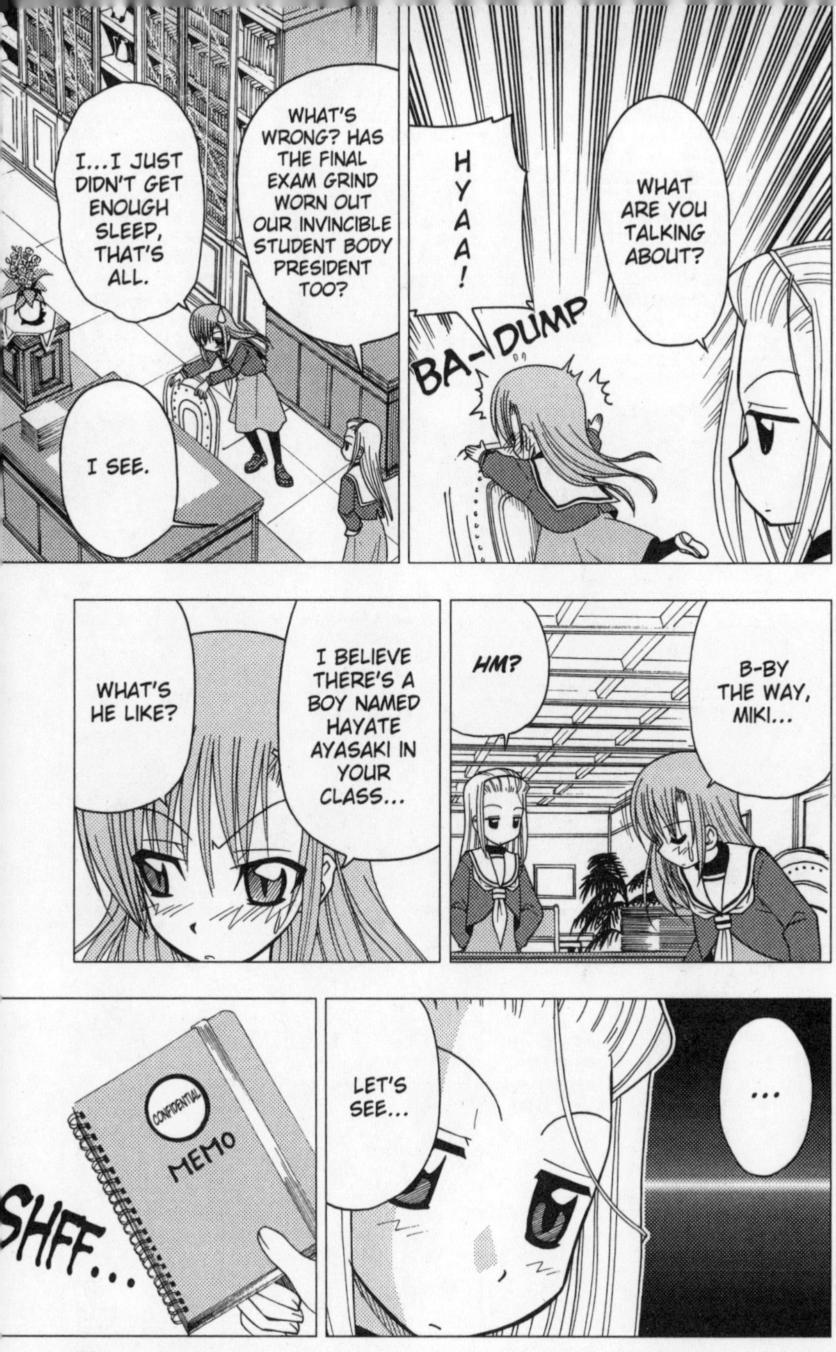

WHAT ARE YOU TALKING ABOUT?
HYAA!
BA-DUMP
WHAT'S WRONG? HAS THE FINAL EXAM GRIND WORN OUT OUR INVINCIBLE STUDENT BODY PRESIDENT TOO?
I...I JUST DIDN'T GET ENOUGH SLEEP, THAT'S ALL.
I SEE.
B-BY THE WAY, MIKI...
HM?
I BELIEVE THERE'S A BOY NAMED HAYATE AYASAKI IN YOUR CLASS...
WHAT'S HE LIKE?
...
LET'S SEE...
CONFIDENTIAL
MEMO
SHFF...

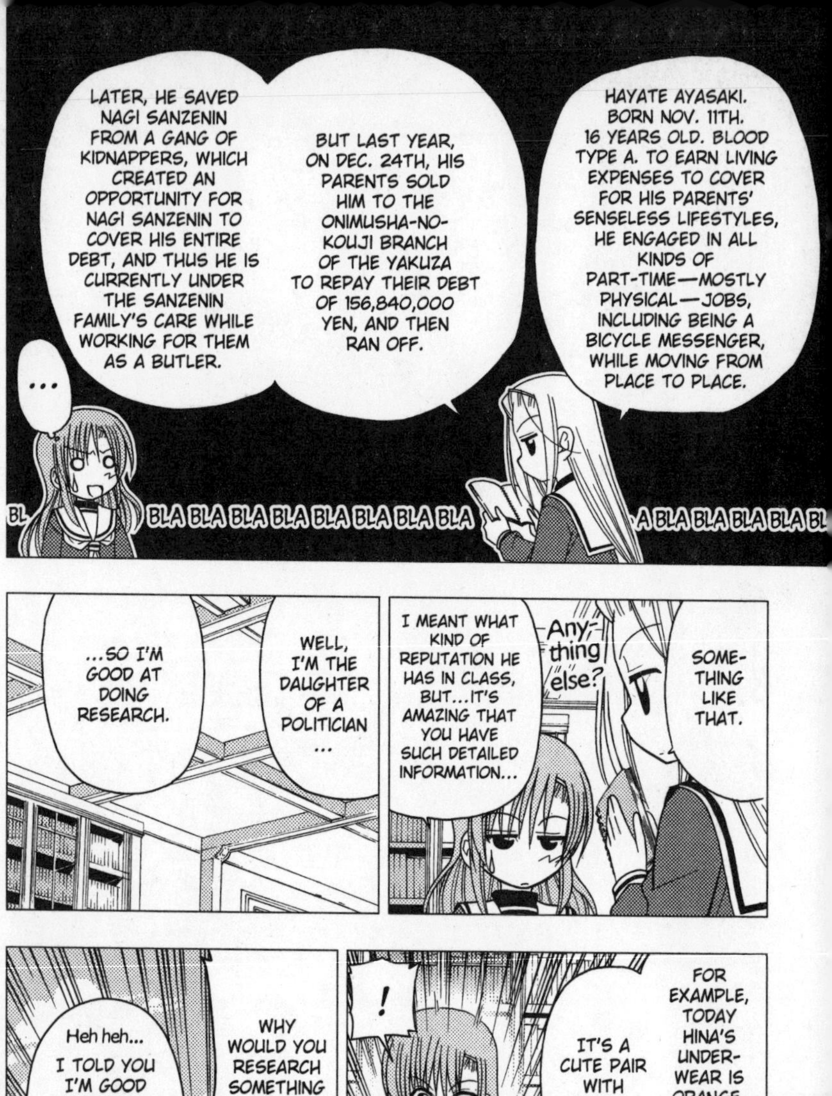

HAYATE AYASAKI. BORN NOV. 11TH. 16 YEARS OLD. BLOOD TYPE A. TO EARN LIVING EXPENSES TO COVER FOR HIS PARENTS' SENSELESS LIFESTYLES, HE ENGAGED IN ALL KINDS OF PART-TIME—MOSTLY PHYSICAL—JOBS, INCLUDING BEING A BICYCLE MESSENGER, WHILE MOVING FROM PLACE TO PLACE.
BUT LAST YEAR, ON DEC. 24TH, HIS PARENTS SOLD HIM TO THE ONIMUSHA-NO-KOUJI BRANCH OF THE YAKUZA TO REPAY THEIR DEBT OF 156,840,000 YEN, AND THEN RAN OFF.
LATER, HE SAVED NAGI SANZENIN FROM A GANG OF KIDNAPPERS, WHICH CREATED AN OPPORTUNITY FOR NAGI SANZENIN TO COVER HIS ENTIRE DEBT, AND THUS HE IS CURRENTLY UNDER THE SANZENIN FAMILY'S CARE WHILE WORKING FOR THEM AS A BUTLER.
...
BLA BLA BLA BLA BLA BLA BLA BLA BLA BLA BLA BLA BLA
SOME-THING LIKE THAT.
Any-thing else?
I MEANT WHAT KIND OF REPUTATION HE HAS IN CLASS, BUT...IT'S AMAZING THAT YOU HAVE SUCH DETAILED INFORMATION...
WELL, I'M THE DAUGHTER OF A POLITICIAN...
...SO I'M GOOD AT DOING RESEARCH.
FOR EXAMPLE, TODAY HINA'S UNDER-WEAR IS ORANGE.
IT'S A CUTE PAIR WITH FRILLS.
WSST
!
WHY WOULD YOU RESEARCH SOMETHING LIKE THAT ?!
Heh heh... I TOLD YOU I'M GOOD AT DOING RESEARCH. ACTUALLY, I SAW YOU CHANGING EARLIER.

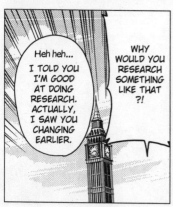

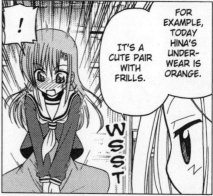

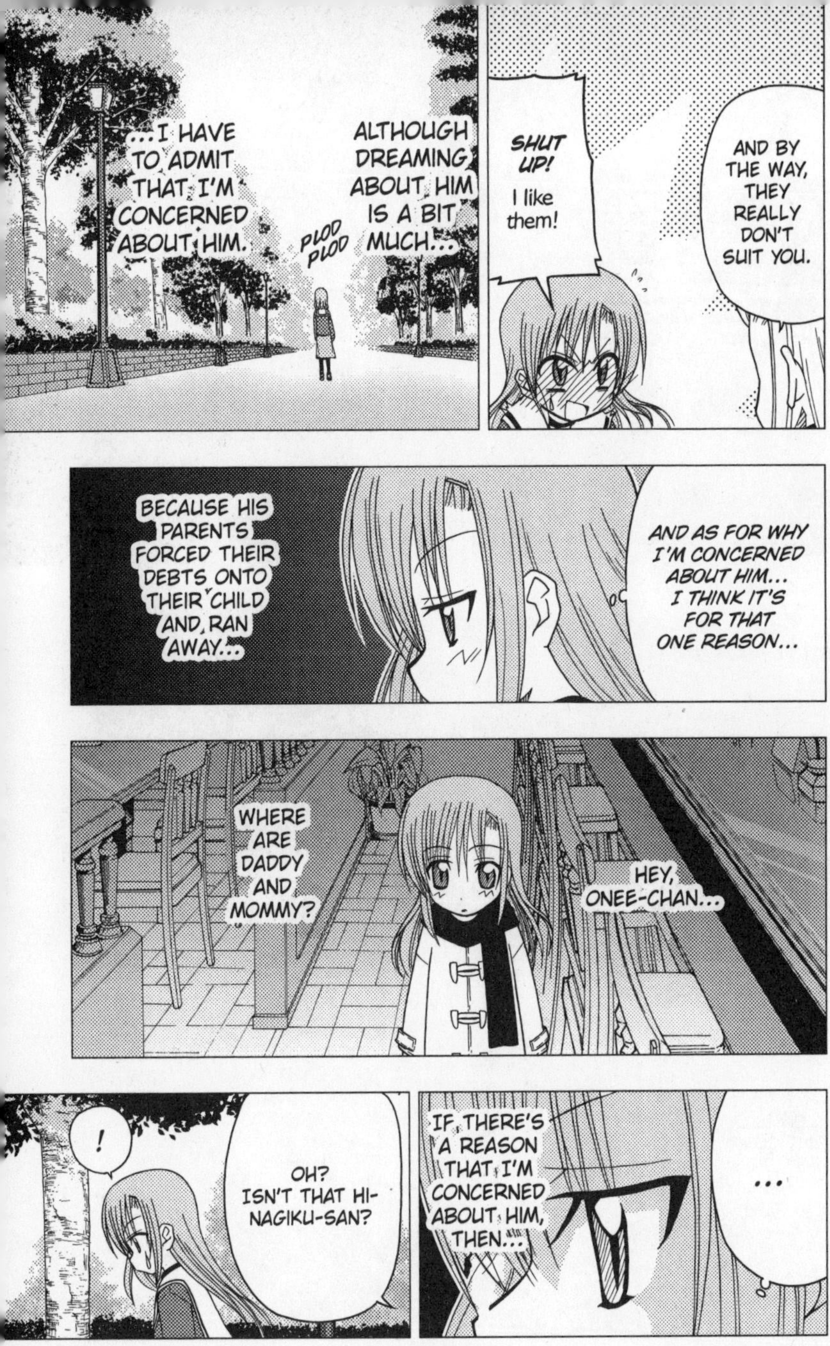
AND BY THE WAY, THEY REALLY DON'T SUIT YOU.
SHUT UP!
I like them!
ALTHOUGH DREAMING ABOUT HIM IS A BIT MUCH...
PLOD PLOD
...I HAVE TO ADMIT THAT I'M CONCERNED ABOUT HIM.
AND AS FOR WHY I'M CONCERNED ABOUT HIM... I THINK IT'S FOR THAT ONE REASON...
BECAUSE HIS PARENTS FORCED THEIR DEBTS ONTO THEIR CHILD AND RAN AWAY...
HEY, ONEE-CHAN...
WHERE ARE DADDY AND MOMMY?
...
IF THERE'S A REASON THAT I'M CONCERNED ABOUT HIM, THEN...
OH? ISN'T THAT HI-NAGIKU-SAN?
!

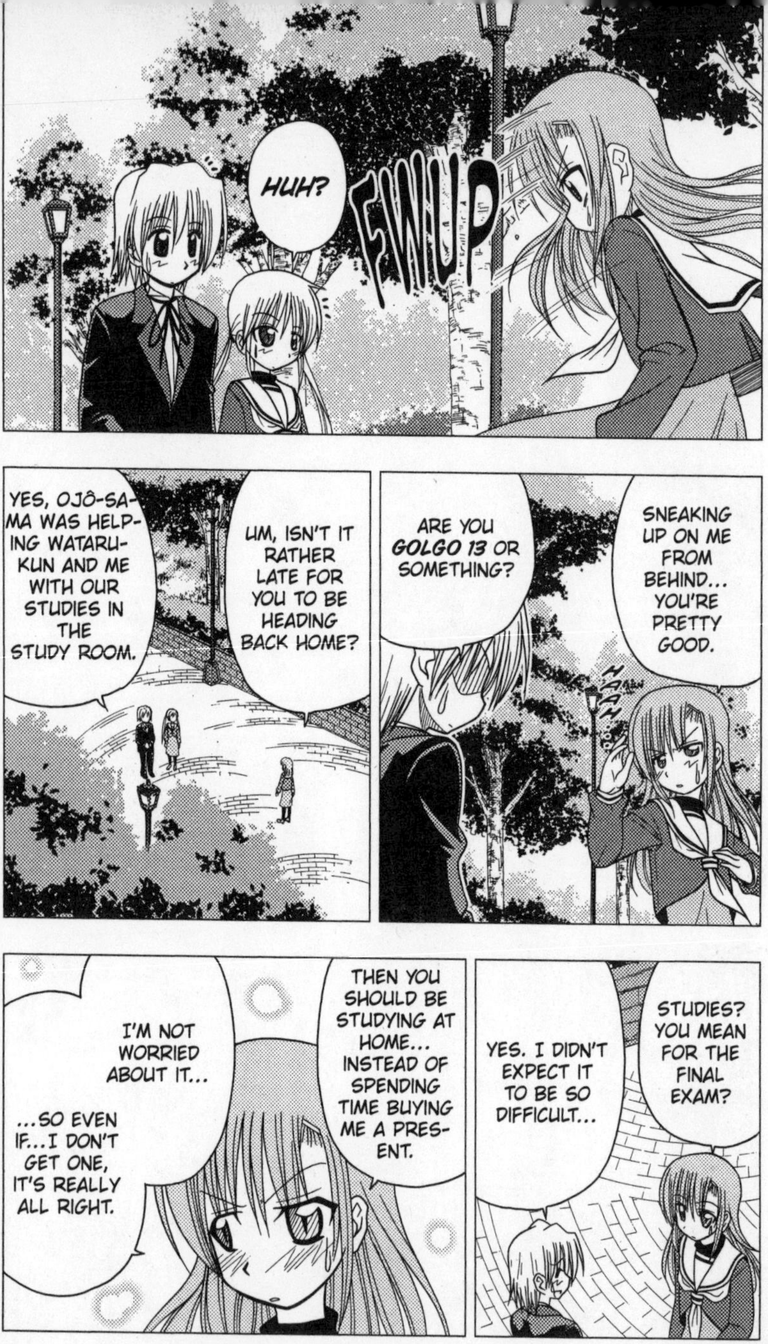
FWUP
HUH?
SNEAKING UP ON ME FROM BEHIND... YOU'RE PRETTY GOOD.
HAAH...
ARE YOU *GOLGO 13* OR SOMETHING?
UM, ISN'T IT RATHER LATE FOR YOU TO BE HEADING BACK HOME?
YES, OJÔ-SAMA WAS HELPING WATARU-KUN AND ME WITH OUR STUDIES IN THE STUDY ROOM.
STUDIES? YOU MEAN FOR THE FINAL EXAM?
YES. I DIDN'T EXPECT IT TO BE SO DIFFICULT...
THEN YOU SHOULD BE STUDYING AT HOME... INSTEAD OF SPENDING TIME BUYING ME A PRESENT.
I'M NOT WORRIED ABOUT IT...
...SO EVEN IF...I DON'T GET ONE, IT'S REALLY ALL RIGHT.

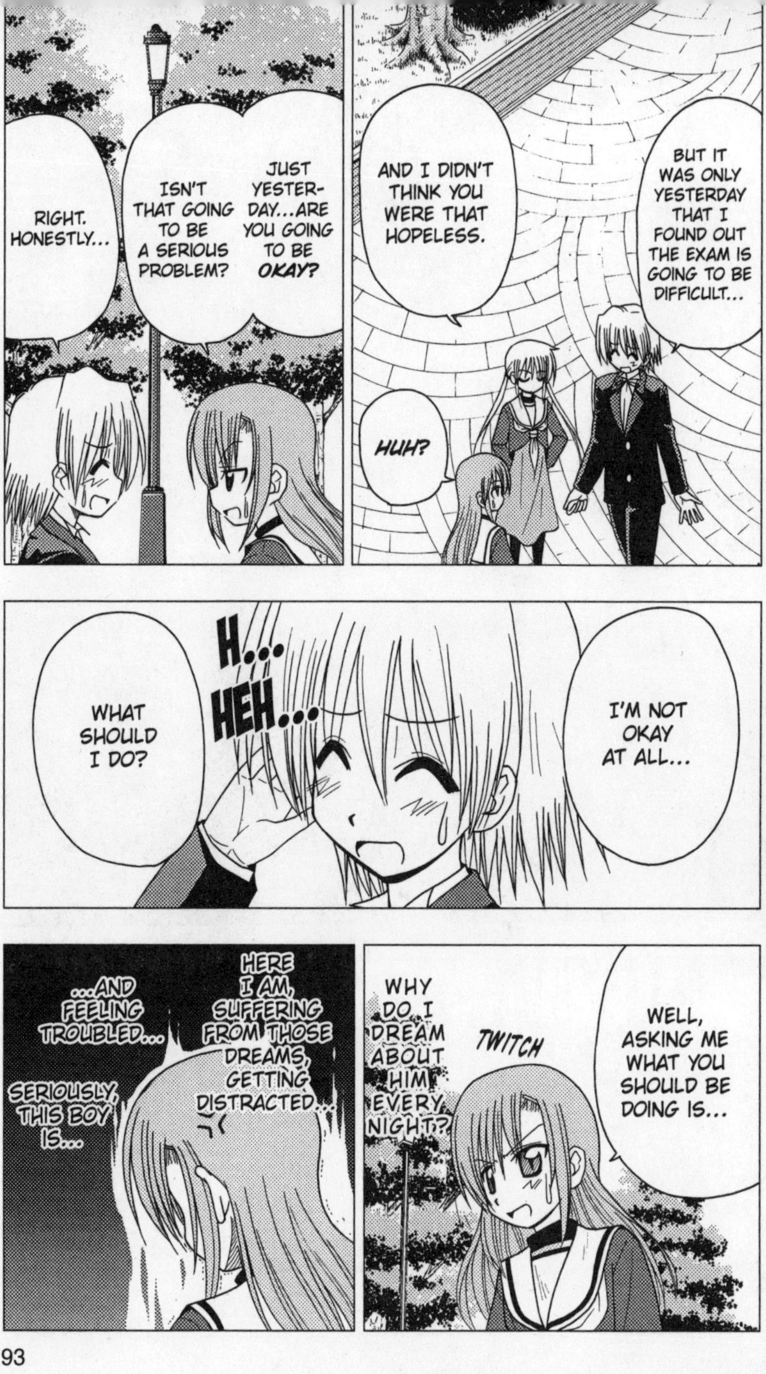
BUT IT WAS ONLY YESTERDAY THAT I FOUND OUT THE EXAM IS GOING TO BE DIFFICULT...
AND I DIDN'T THINK YOU WERE THAT HOPELESS.
HUH?
JUST YESTER-DAY...ARE YOU GOING TO BE *OKAY?*
ISN'T THAT GOING TO BE A SERIOUS PROBLEM?
RIGHT. HONESTLY...
I'M NOT OKAY AT ALL...
H... HEH...
WHAT SHOULD I DO?
WELL, ASKING ME WHAT YOU SHOULD BE DOING IS...
TWITCH
WHY DO I DREAM ABOUT HIM EVERY NIGHT?
HERE I AM, SUFFERING FROM THOSE DREAMS, GETTING DISTRACTED...
...AND FEELING TROUBLED...
SERIOUSLY, THIS BOY IS...

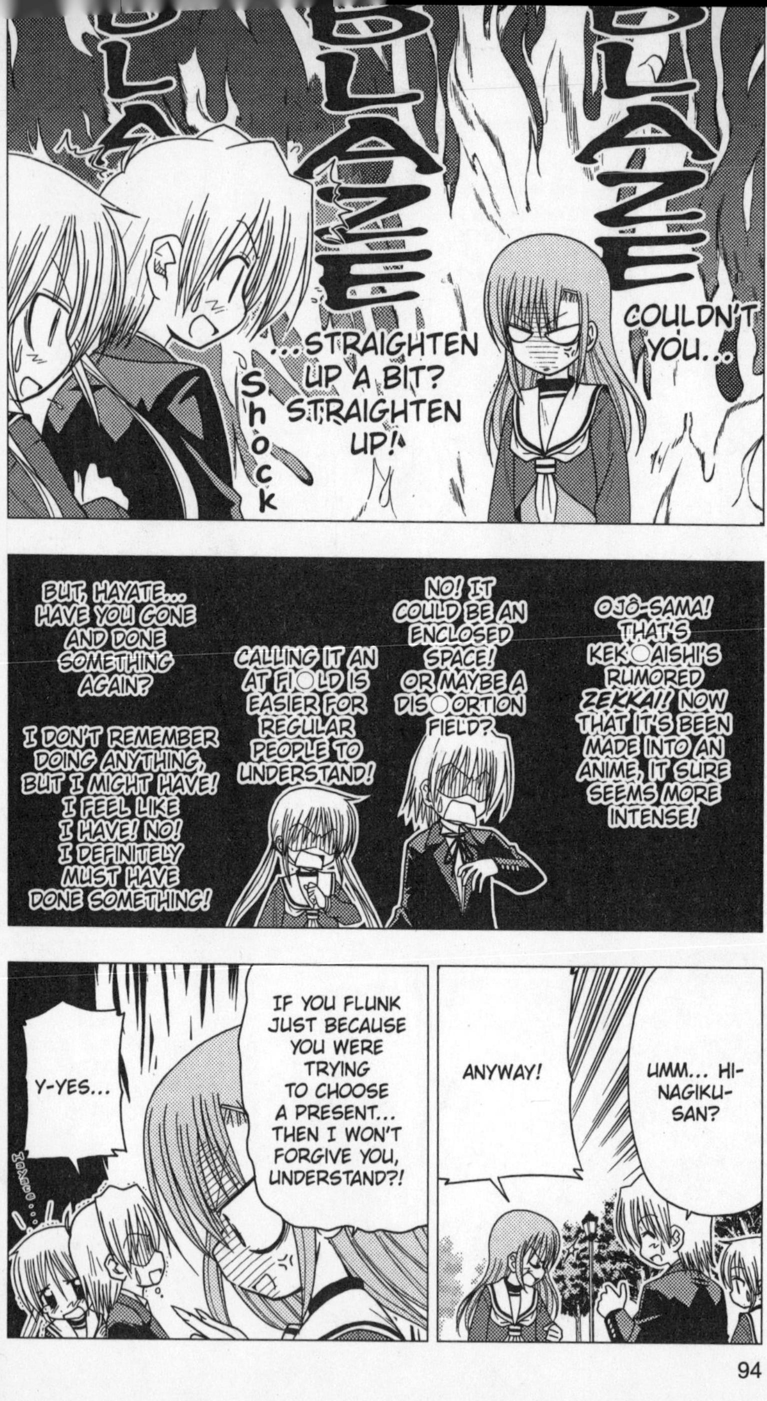

BLAZE
BLAZE
BLA
COULDN'T YOU...
...STRAIGHTEN UP A BIT? STRAIGHTEN UP!
Shock
OJÔ-SAMA! THAT'S KEK◯AISHI'S RUMORED ZEKKAI!! NOW THAT IT'S BEEN MADE INTO AN ANIME, IT SURE SEEMS MORE INTENSE!
NO! IT COULD BE AN ENCLOSED SPACE! OR MAYBE A DIS◯ORTION FIELD?
CALLING IT AN AT FI◯LD IS EASIER FOR REGULAR PEOPLE TO UNDERSTAND!
BUT, HAYATE... HAVE YOU GONE AND DONE SOMETHING AGAIN?
I DON'T REMEMBER DOING ANYTHING, BUT I MIGHT HAVE! I FEEL LIKE I HAVE! NO! I DEFINITELY MUST HAVE DONE SOMETHING!
UMM... HI-NAGIKU-SAN?
ANYWAY!
IF YOU FLUNK JUST BECAUSE YOU WERE TRYING TO CHOOSE A PRESENT... THEN I WON'T FORGIVE YOU, UNDERSTAND?!
Y-YES...

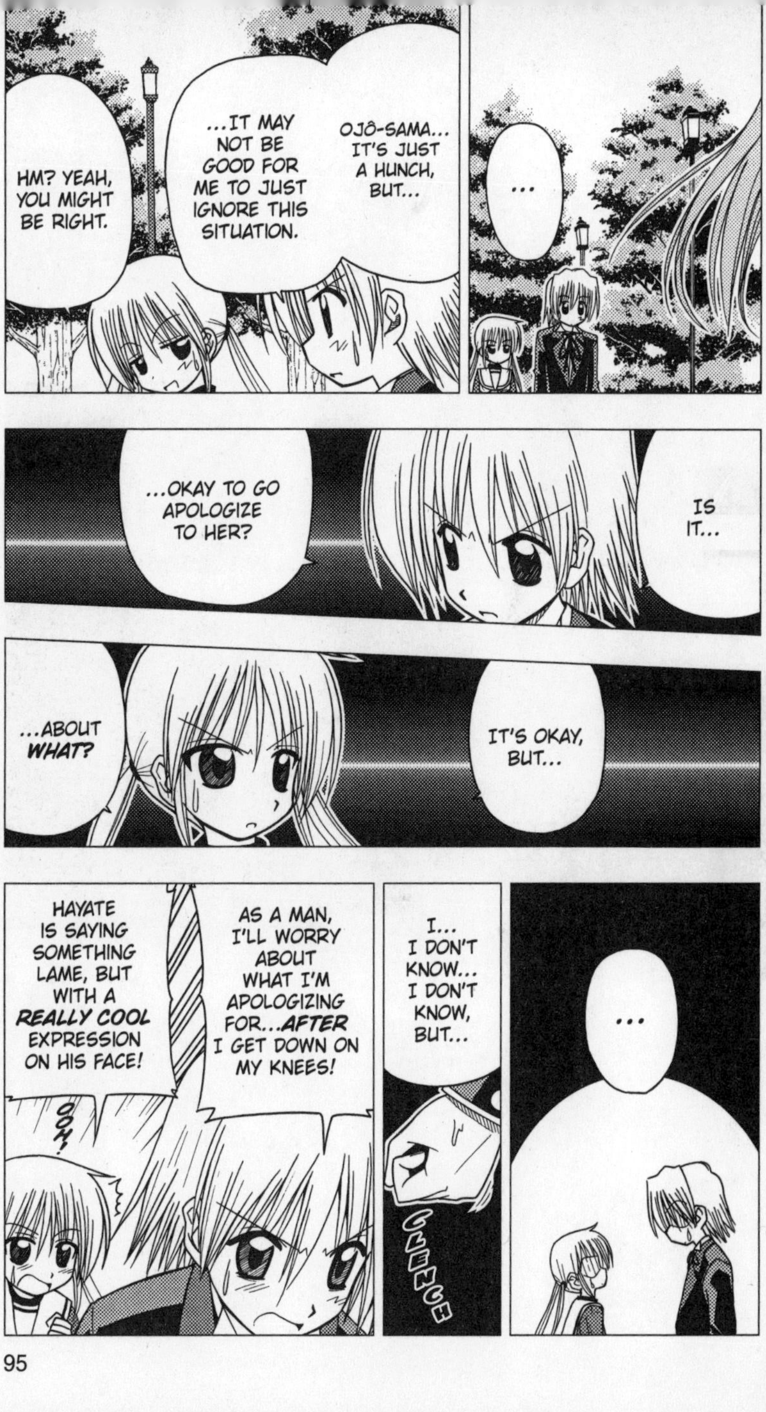
...
OJÔ-SAMA... IT'S JUST A HUNCH, BUT...
...IT MAY NOT BE GOOD FOR ME TO JUST IGNORE THIS SITUATION.
HM? YEAH, YOU MIGHT BE RIGHT.
IS IT...
...OKAY TO GO APOLOGIZE TO HER?
IT'S OKAY, BUT...
...ABOUT *WHAT?*
...
I... I DON'T KNOW... I DON'T KNOW, BUT...
CLENCH
AS A MAN, I'LL WORRY ABOUT WHAT I'M APOLOGIZING FOR...*AFTER* I GET DOWN ON MY KNEES!
OOH!
HAYATE IS SAYING SOMETHING LAME, BUT WITH A *REALLY COOL* EXPRESSION ON HIS FACE!

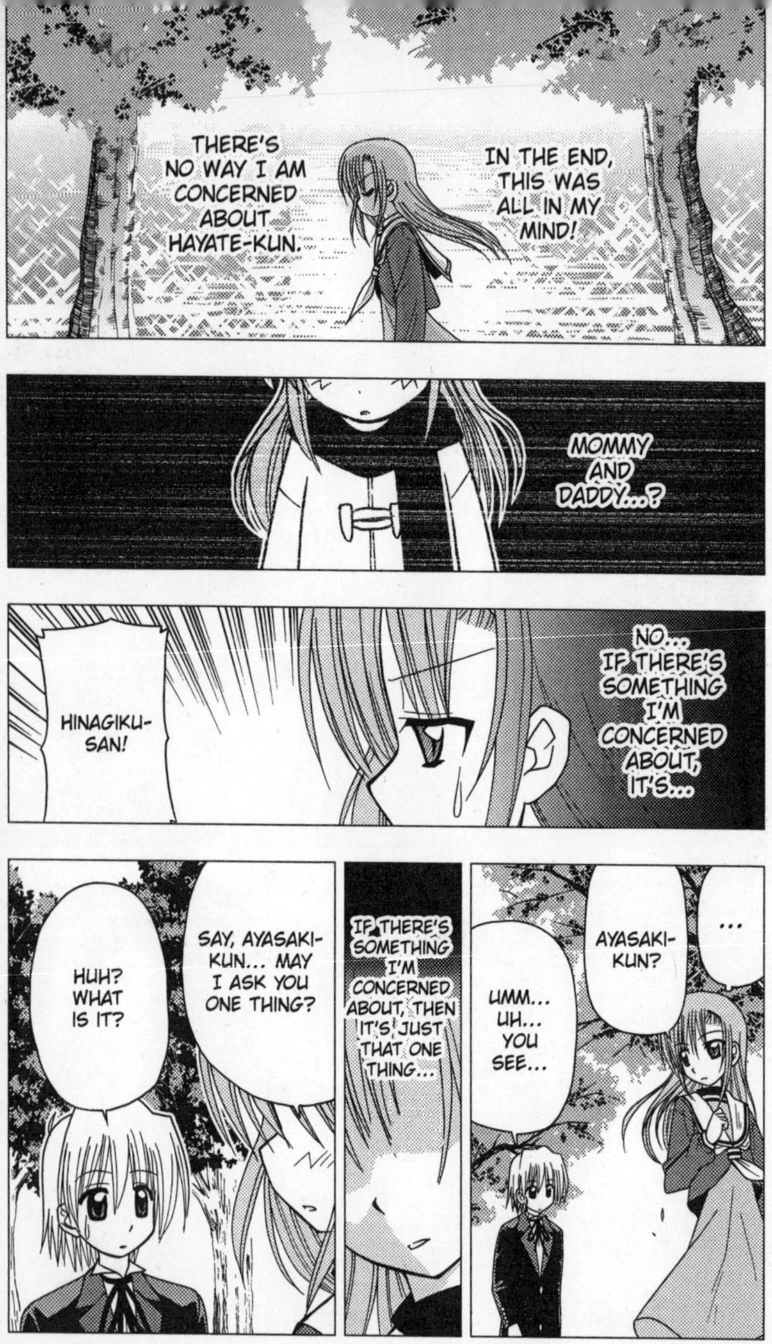
IN THE END, THIS WAS ALL IN MY MIND!
THERE'S NO WAY I AM CONCERNED ABOUT HAYATE-KUN.
MOMMY AND DADDY...?
NO... IF THERE'S SOMETHING I'M CONCERNED ABOUT, IT'S...
HINAGIKU-SAN!
...
AYASAKI-KUN?
UMM... UH... YOU SEE...
IF THERE'S SOMETHING I'M CONCERNED ABOUT, THEN IT'S JUST THAT ONE THING...
SAY, AYASAKI-KUN... MAY I ASK YOU ONE THING?
HUH? WHAT IS IT?

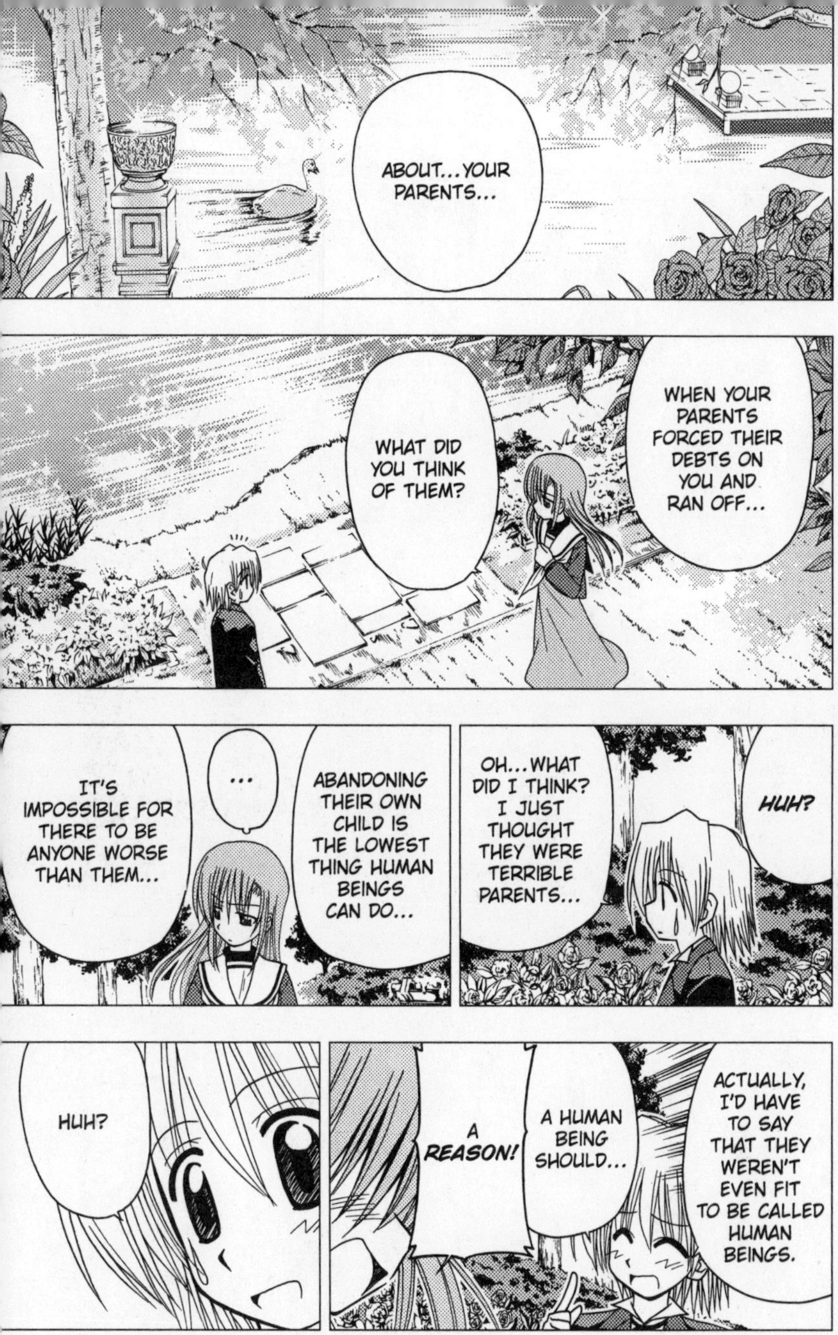
ABOUT...YOUR PARENTS...
WHEN YOUR PARENTS FORCED THEIR DEBTS ON YOU AND RAN OFF...
WHAT DID YOU THINK OF THEM?
HUH?
OH...WHAT DID I THINK? I JUST THOUGHT THEY WERE TERRIBLE PARENTS...
ABANDONING THEIR OWN CHILD IS THE LOWEST THING HUMAN BEINGS CAN DO...
...
IT'S IMPOSSIBLE FOR THERE TO BE ANYONE WORSE THAN THEM...
ACTUALLY, I'D HAVE TO SAY THAT THEY WEREN'T EVEN FIT TO BE CALLED HUMAN BEINGS.
A HUMAN BEING SHOULD...
A *REASON!*
HUH?

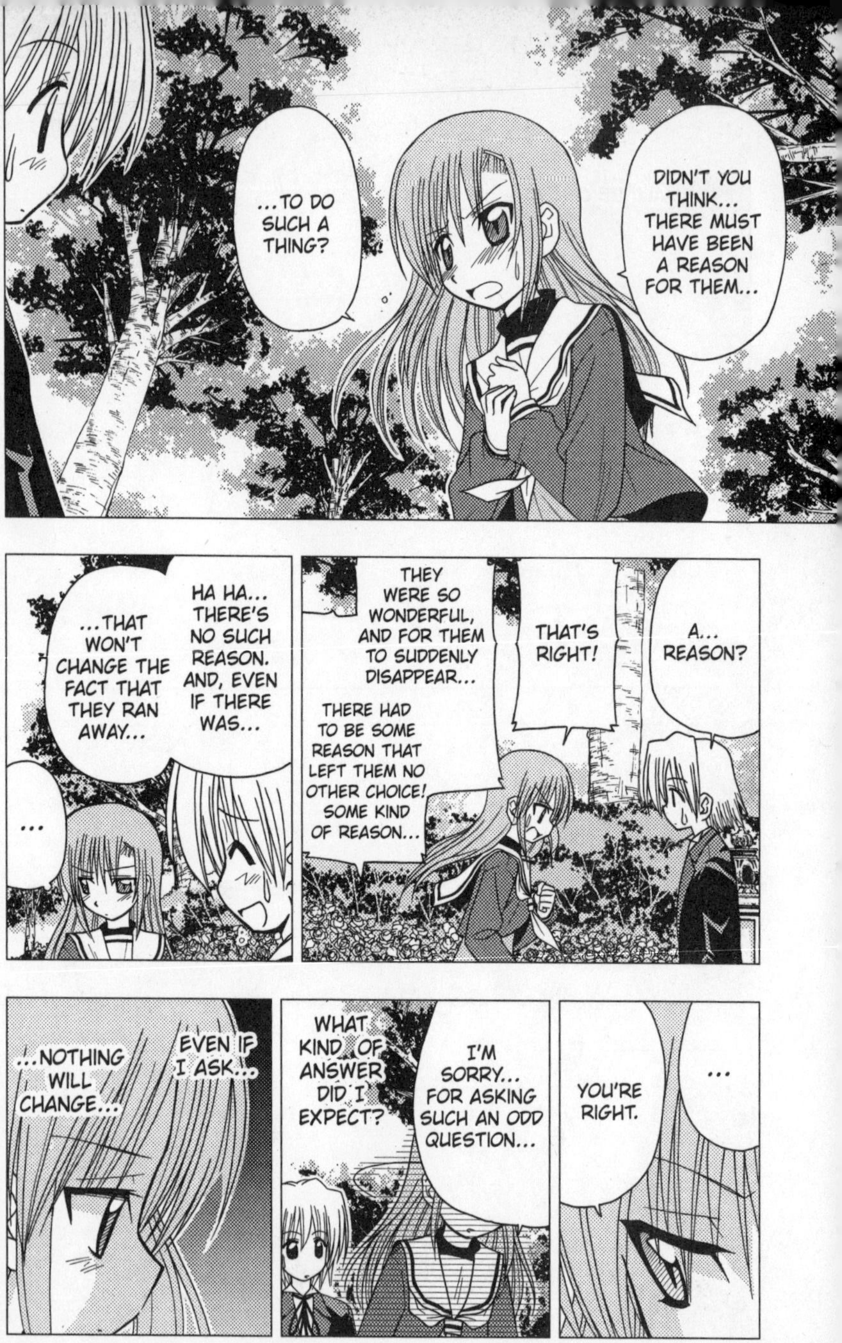
DIDN'T YOU THINK... THERE MUST HAVE BEEN A REASON FOR THEM...
...TO DO SUCH A THING?
A... REASON?
THAT'S RIGHT!
THEY WERE SO WONDERFUL, AND FOR THEM TO SUDDENLY DISAPPEAR...
THERE HAD TO BE SOME REASON THAT LEFT THEM NO OTHER CHOICE! SOME KIND OF REASON...
HA HA... THERE'S NO SUCH REASON. AND, EVEN IF THERE WAS...
...THAT WON'T CHANGE THE FACT THAT THEY RAN AWAY...
...
...
YOU'RE RIGHT.
I'M SORRY... FOR ASKING SUCH AN ODD QUESTION...
WHAT KIND OF ANSWER DID I EXPECT?
EVEN IF I ASK...
...NOTHING WILL CHANGE...

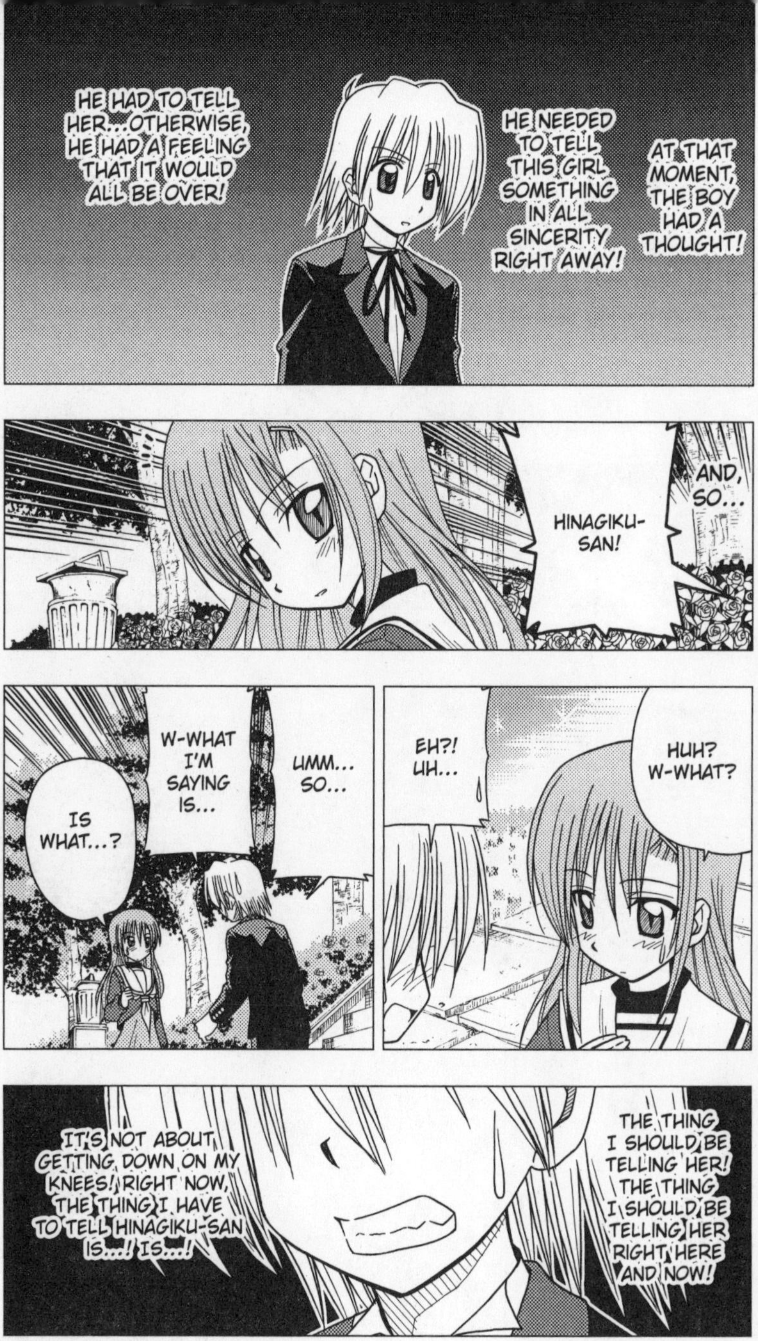
AT THAT MOMENT, THE BOY HAD A THOUGHT!
HE NEEDED TO TELL THIS GIRL SOMETHING IN ALL SINCERITY RIGHT AWAY!
HE HAD TO TELL HER...OTHERWISE, HE HAD A FEELING THAT IT WOULD ALL BE OVER!
AND, SO...
HINAGIKU-SAN!
HUH? W-WHAT?
EH?! UH...
UMM... SO...
W-WHAT I'M SAYING IS...
IS WHAT...?
THE THING I SHOULD BE TELLING HER! THE THING I SHOULD BE TELLING HER RIGHT HERE AND NOW!
IT'S NOT ABOUT GETTING DOWN ON MY KNEES! RIGHT NOW, THE THING I HAVE TO TELL HINAGIKU-SAN IS...! IS...!

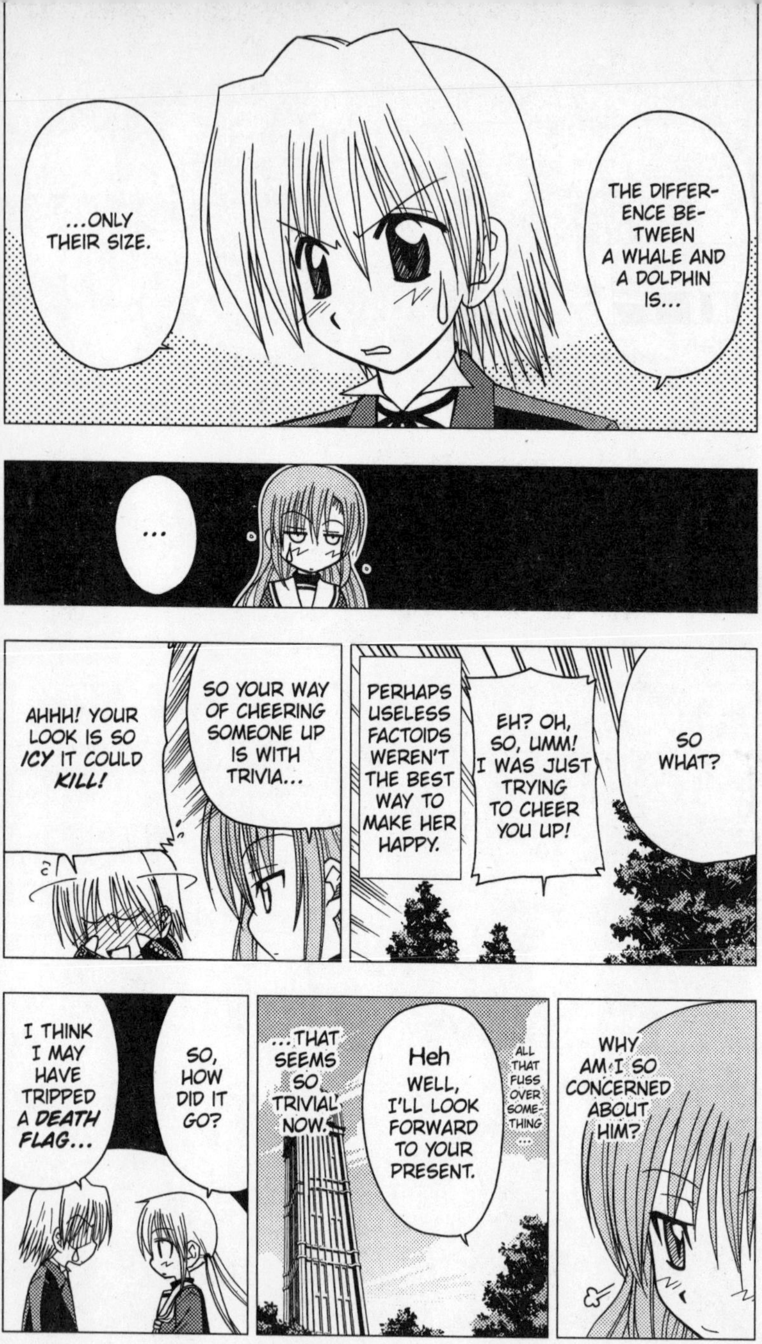
THE DIFFERENCE BETWEEN A WHALE AND A DOLPHIN IS...
...ONLY THEIR SIZE.
...
SO WHAT?
EH? OH, SO, UMM! I WAS JUST TRYING TO CHEER YOU UP!
PERHAPS USELESS FACTOIDS WEREN'T THE BEST WAY TO MAKE HER HAPPY.
SO YOUR WAY OF CHEERING SOMEONE UP IS WITH TRIVIA...
AHHH! YOUR LOOK IS SO *ICY* IT COULD ***KILL!***
WHY AM I SO CONCERNED ABOUT HIM?
ALL THAT FUSS OVER SOME-THING ...
Heh WELL, I'LL LOOK FORWARD TO YOUR PRESENT.
...THAT SEEMS SO TRIVIAL NOW.
SO, HOW DID IT GO?
I THINK I MAY HAVE TRIPPED A ***DEATH FLAG...***

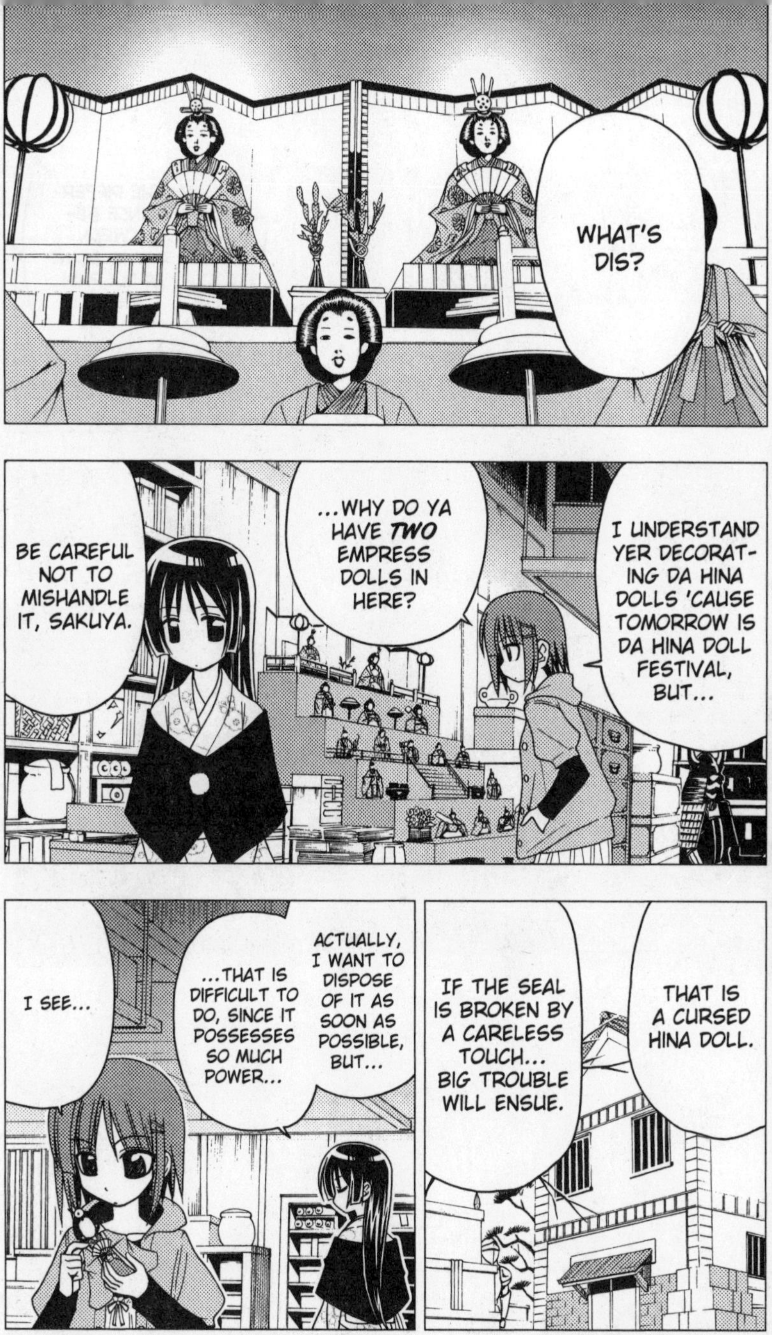
WHAT'S DIS?
I UNDERSTAND YER DECORATING DA HINA DOLLS 'CAUSE TOMORROW IS DA HINA DOLL FESTIVAL, BUT...
...WHY DO YA HAVE *TWO* EMPRESS DOLLS IN HERE?
BE CAREFUL NOT TO MISHANDLE IT, SAKUYA.
THAT IS A CURSED HINA DOLL.
IF THE SEAL IS BROKEN BY A CARELESS TOUCH... BIG TROUBLE WILL ENSUE.
ACTUALLY, I WANT TO DISPOSE OF IT AS SOON AS POSSIBLE, BUT...
...THAT IS DIFFICULT TO DO, SINCE IT POSSESSES SO MUCH POWER...
I SEE...

Episode 7: "Around the Time of the Hina Doll Festival ~ Spirited Away by the Demon ~"

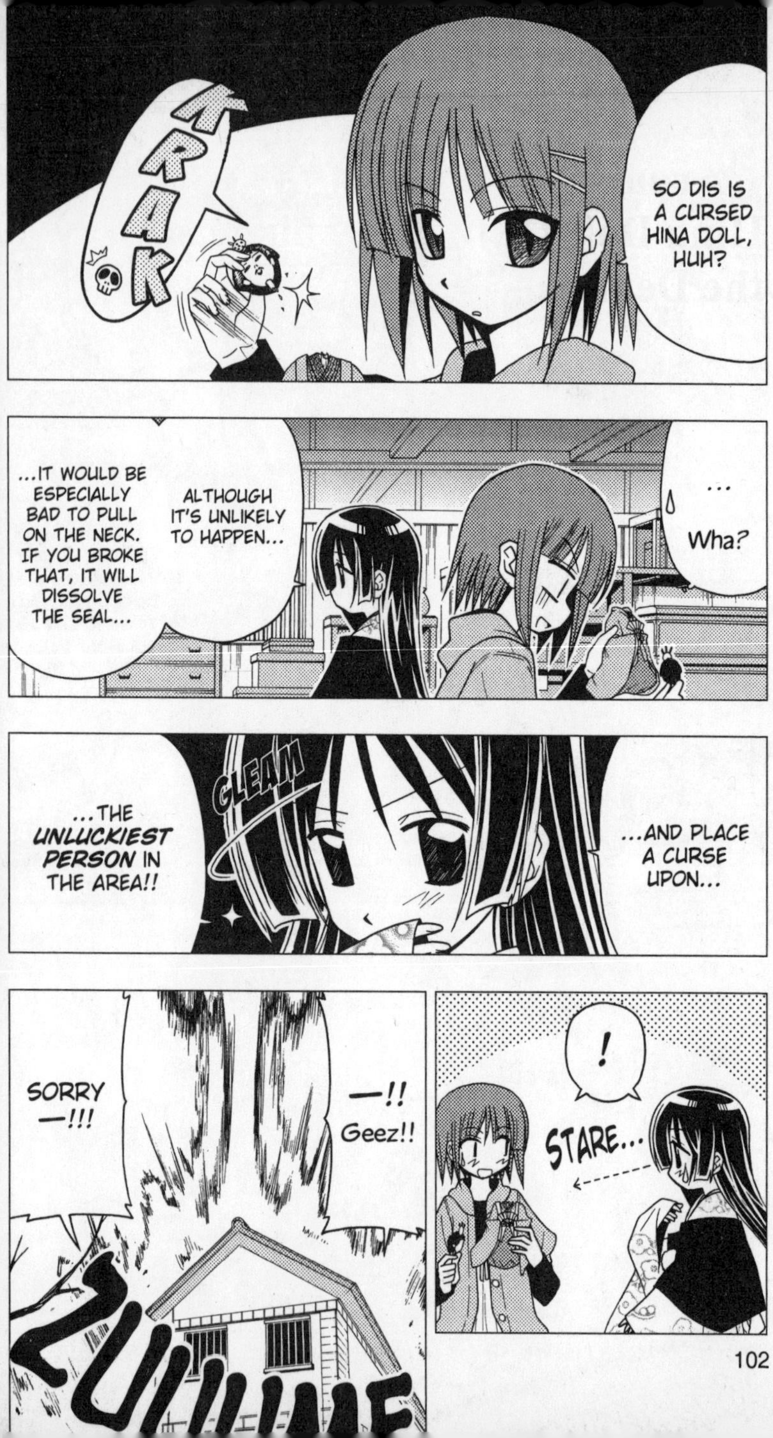
SO DIS IS A CURSED HINA DOLL, HUH?
KRAK
... Wha?
ALTHOUGH IT'S UNLIKELY TO HAPPEN...
...IT WOULD BE ESPECIALLY BAD TO PULL ON THE NECK. IF YOU BROKE THAT, IT WILL DISSOLVE THE SEAL...
...AND PLACE A CURSE UPON...
GLEAM
...THE UNLUCKIEST PERSON IN THE AREA!!
!
STARE...
—!! Geez!!
SORRY —!!!

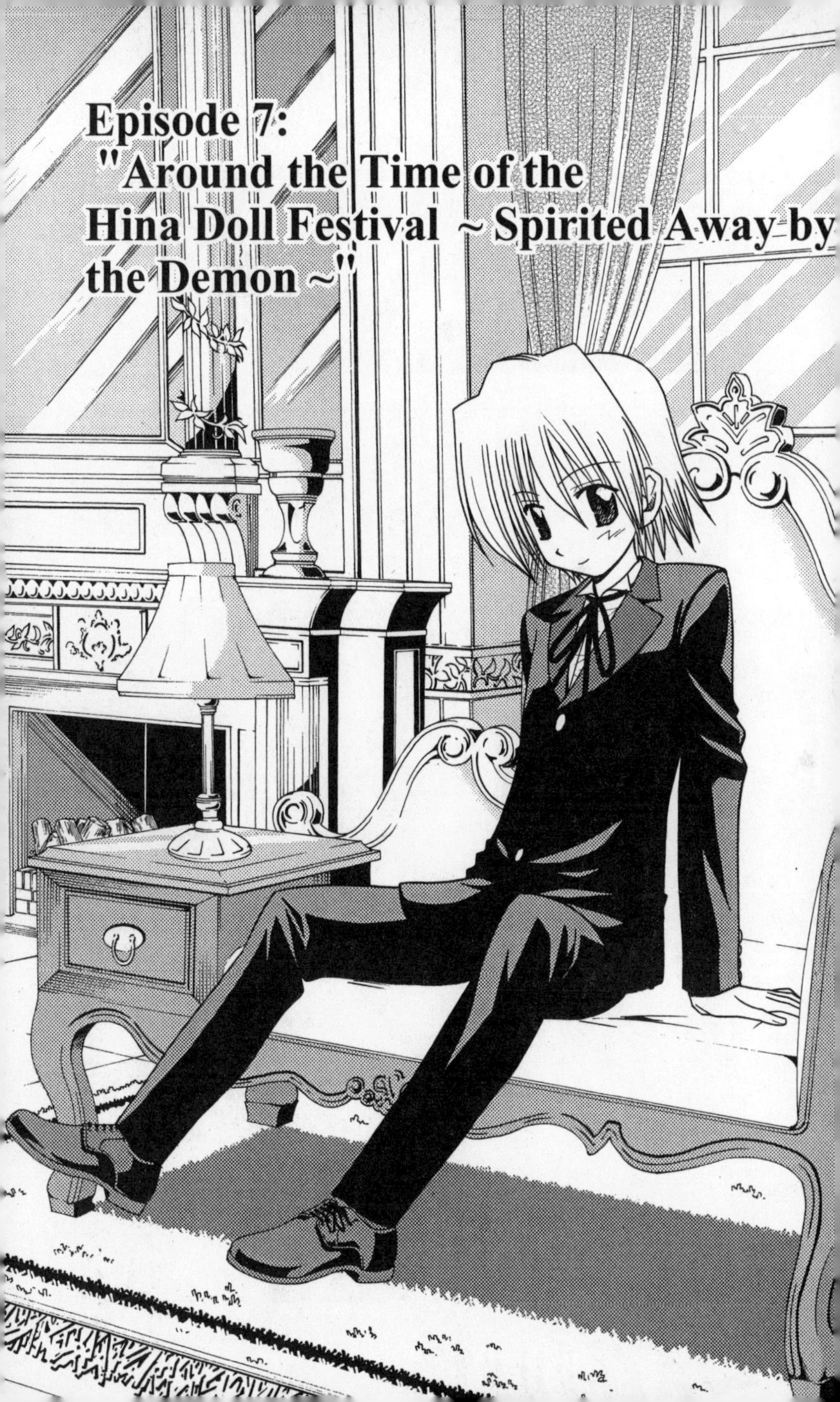
Episode 7:
"Around the Time of the Hina Doll Festival ~ Spirited Away by the Demon ~"

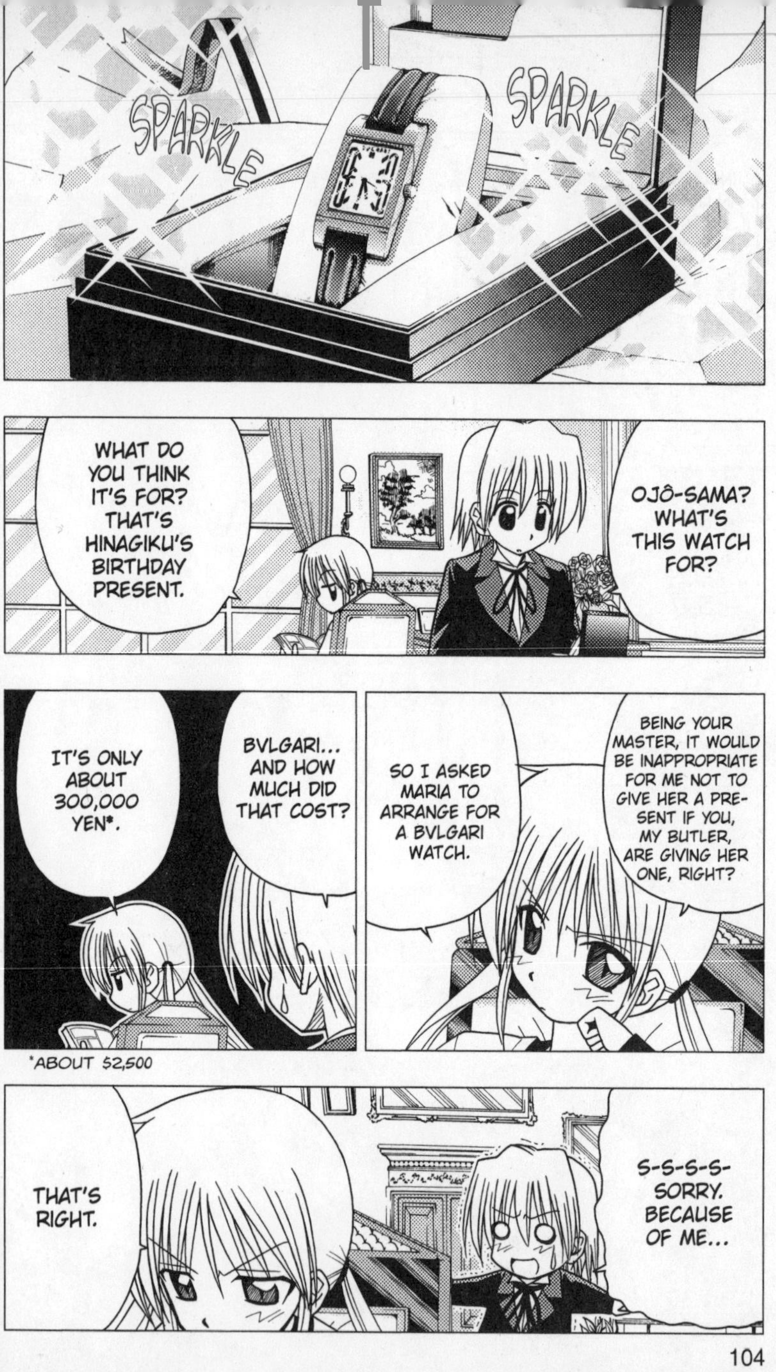
SPARKLE
SPARKLE
OJÔ-SAMA? WHAT'S THIS WATCH FOR?
WHAT DO YOU THINK IT'S FOR? THAT'S HINAGIKU'S BIRTHDAY PRESENT.
BEING YOUR MASTER, IT WOULD BE INAPPROPRIATE FOR ME NOT TO GIVE HER A PRE-SENT IF YOU, MY BUTLER, ARE GIVING HER ONE, RIGHT?
SO I ASKED MARIA TO ARRANGE FOR A BVLGARI WATCH.
BVLGARI... AND HOW MUCH DID THAT COST?
IT'S ONLY ABOUT 300,000 YEN*.
S-S-S-S-SORRY. BECAUSE OF ME...
THAT'S RIGHT.

*ABOUT $2,500

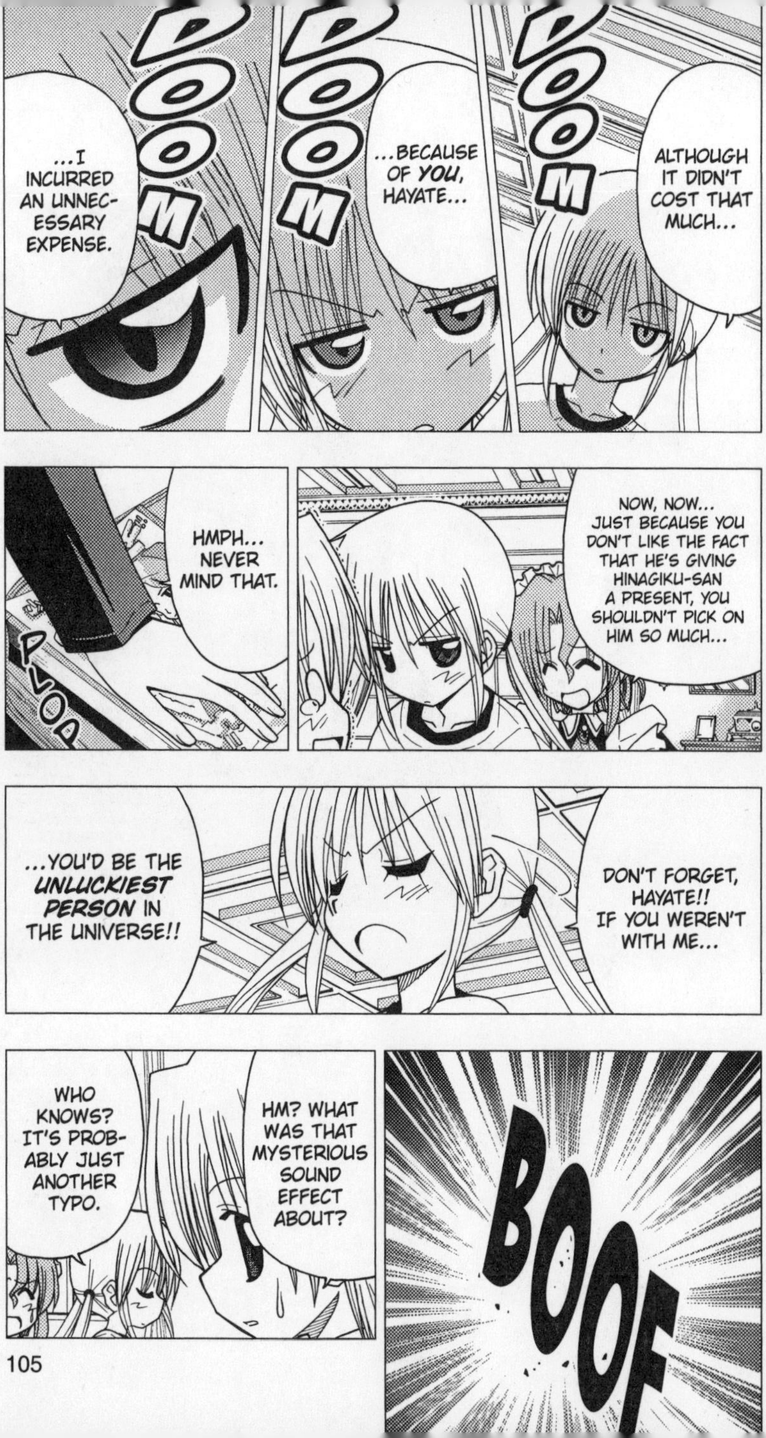
ALTHOUGH IT DIDN'T COST THAT MUCH...
DOOOM
...BECAUSE OF *YOU*, HAYATE...
DOOOM
...I INCURRED AN UNNEC-ESSARY EXPENSE.
DOOOM
NOW, NOW... JUST BECAUSE YOU DON'T LIKE THE FACT THAT HE'S GIVING HINAGIKU-SAN A PRESENT, YOU SHOULDN'T PICK ON HIM SO MUCH...
HMPH... NEVER MIND THAT.
DON'T FORGET, HAYATE!! IF YOU WEREN'T WITH ME...
...YOU'D BE THE ***UNLUCKIEST PERSON*** IN THE UNIVERSE!!
BOOF
HM? WHAT WAS THAT MYSTERIOUS SOUND EFFECT ABOUT?
WHO KNOWS? IT'S PROB-ABLY JUST ANOTHER TYPO.

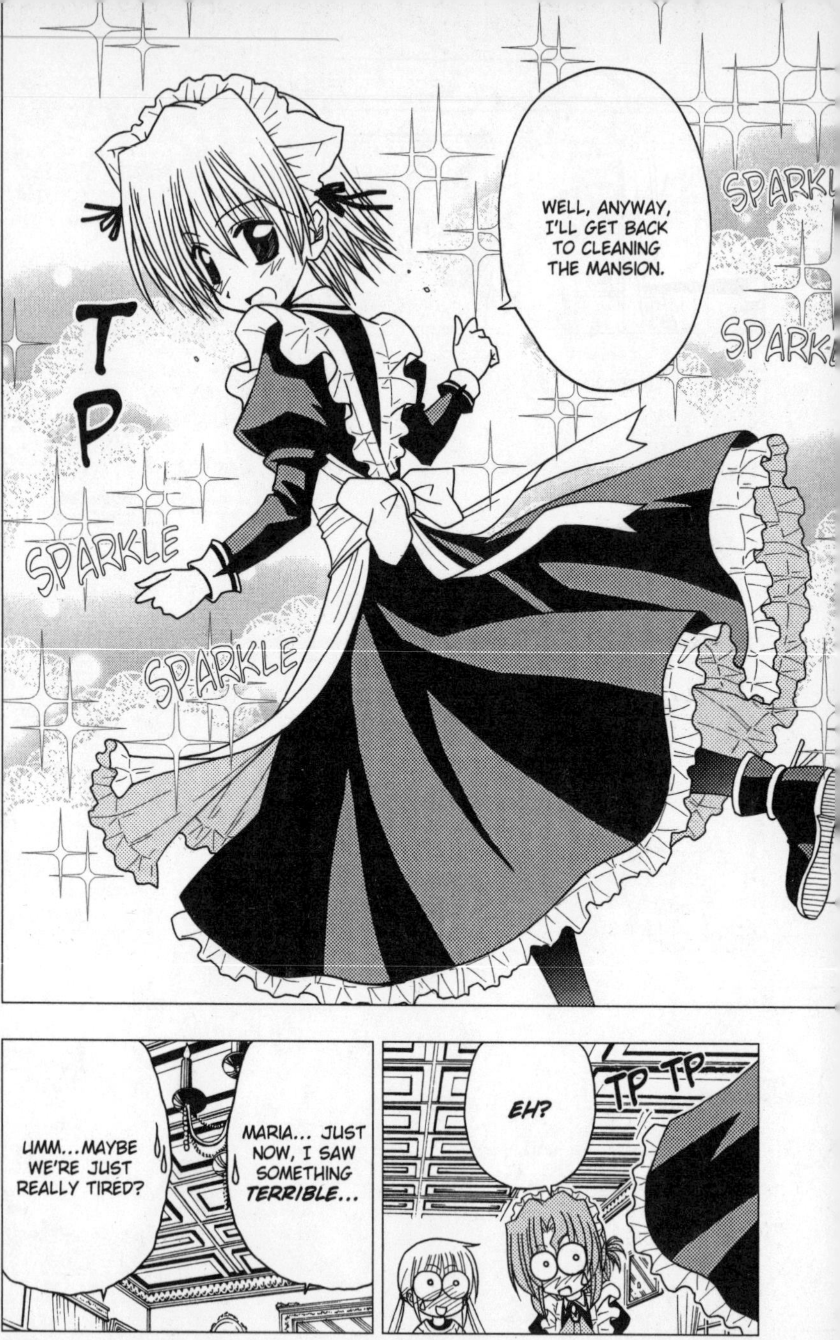
SPARKL
WELL, ANYWAY, I'LL GET BACK TO CLEANING THE MANSION.
SPARK
TP
SPARKLE
SPARKLE
TP TP
EH?
MARIA... JUST NOW, I SAW SOMETHING TERRIBLE...
UMM...MAYBE WE'RE JUST REALLY TIRED?

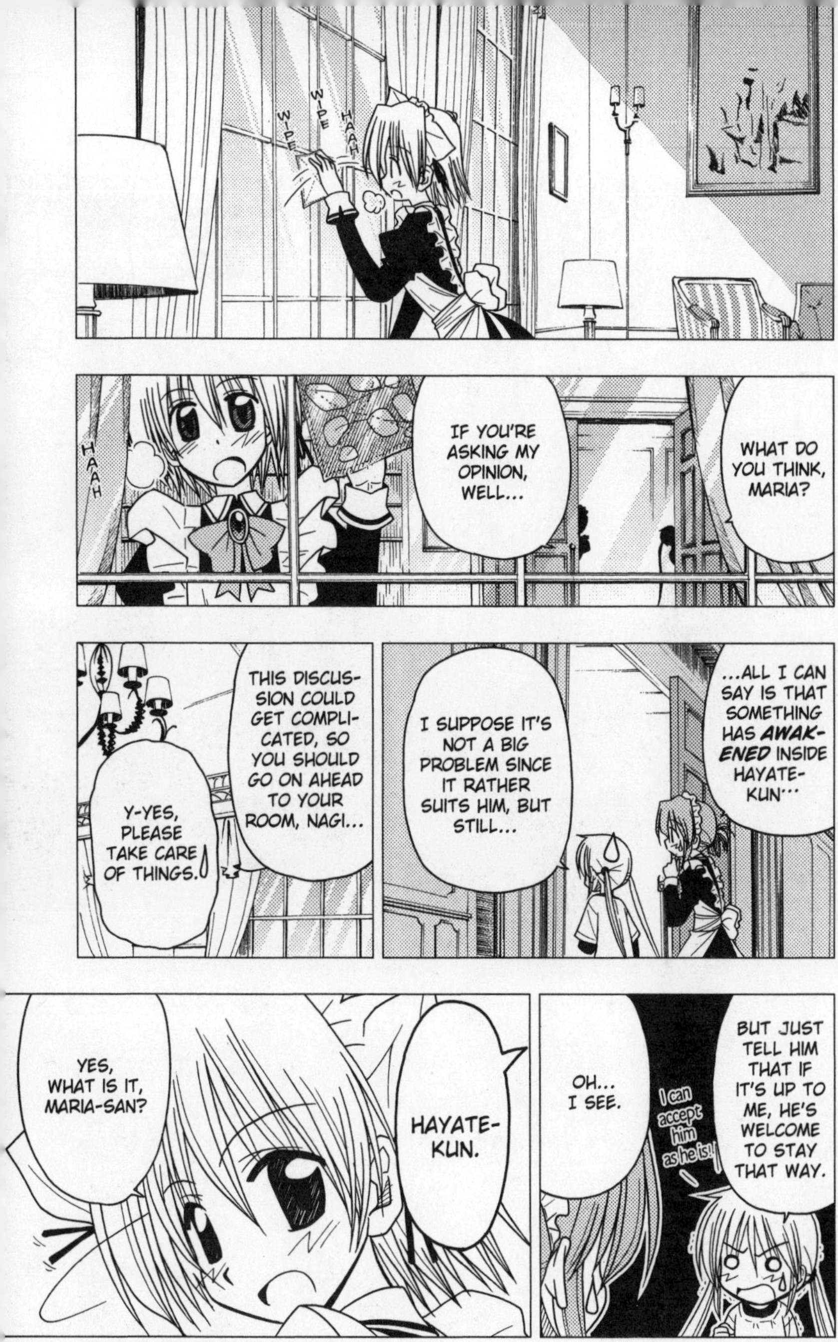
HAAH
WIPE
WIPE
WHAT DO YOU THINK, MARIA?
IF YOU'RE ASKING MY OPINION, WELL...
HAAH
...ALL I CAN SAY IS THAT SOMETHING HAS *AWAKENED* INSIDE HAYATE-KUN...
I SUPPOSE IT'S NOT A BIG PROBLEM SINCE IT RATHER SUITS HIM, BUT STILL...
THIS DISCUSSION COULD GET COMPLICATED, SO YOU SHOULD GO ON AHEAD TO YOUR ROOM, NAGI...
Y-YES, PLEASE TAKE CARE OF THINGS.
BUT JUST TELL HIM THAT IF IT'S UP TO ME, HE'S WELCOME TO STAY THAT WAY.
I can accept him as he is!
OH... I SEE.
HAYATE-KUN.
YES, WHAT IS IT, MARIA-SAN?

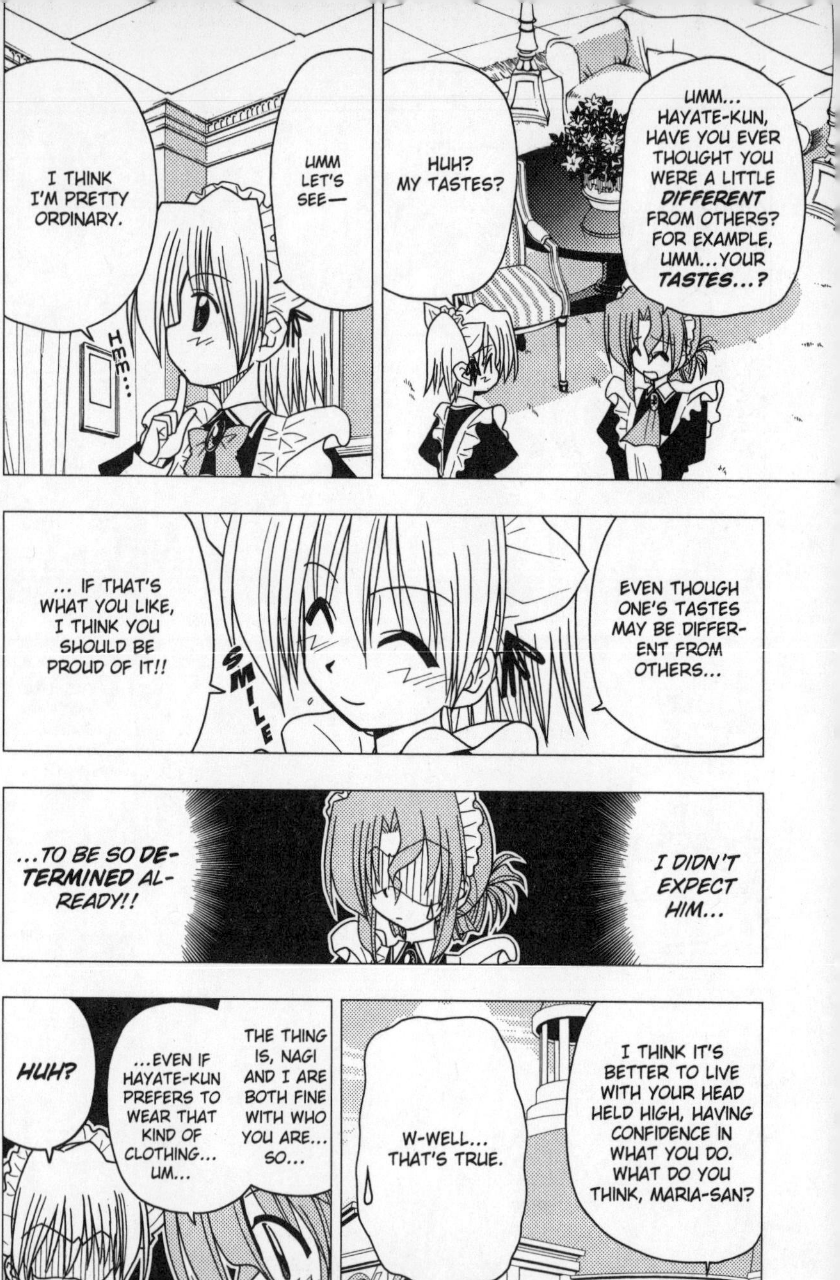
UMM... HAYATE-KUN, HAVE YOU EVER THOUGHT YOU WERE A LITTLE DIFFERENT FROM OTHERS? FOR EXAMPLE, UMM...YOUR TASTES...?
HUH? MY TASTES?
UMM LET'S SEE—
HMM...
I THINK I'M PRETTY ORDINARY.
EVEN THOUGH ONE'S TASTES MAY BE DIFFERENT FROM OTHERS...
SMILE
... IF THAT'S WHAT YOU LIKE, I THINK YOU SHOULD BE PROUD OF IT!!
I DIDN'T EXPECT HIM...
...TO BE SO DETERMINED ALREADY!!
I THINK IT'S BETTER TO LIVE WITH YOUR HEAD HELD HIGH, HAVING CONFIDENCE IN WHAT YOU DO. WHAT DO YOU THINK, MARIA-SAN?
W-WELL... THAT'S TRUE.
THE THING IS, NAGI AND I ARE BOTH FINE WITH WHO YOU ARE... SO...
...EVEN IF HAYATE-KUN PREFERS TO WEAR THAT KIND OF CLOTHING... UM...
HUH?

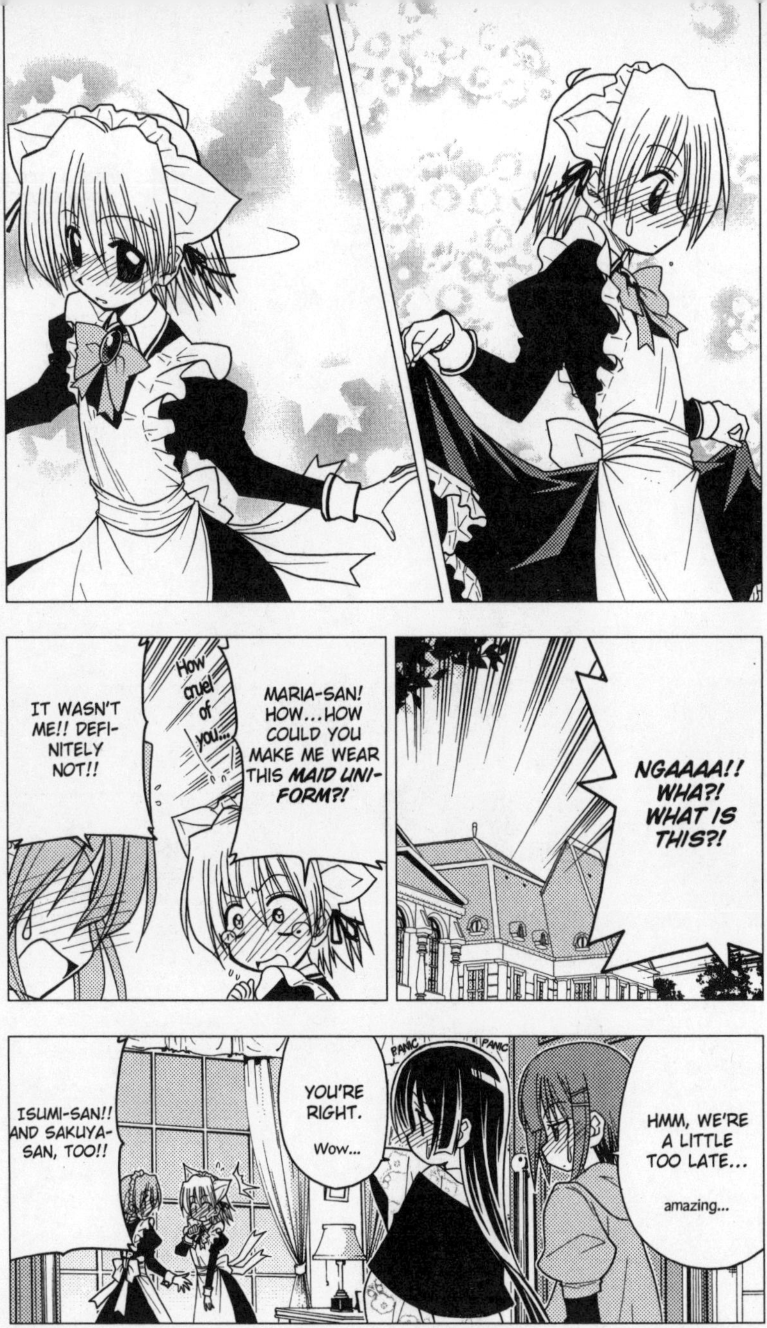
NGAAAA!! WHA?! WHAT IS THIS?!
MARIA-SAN! HOW...HOW COULD YOU MAKE ME WEAR THIS MAID UNIFORM?!
How cruel of you...
IT WASN'T ME!! DEFINITELY NOT!!
HMM, WE'RE A LITTLE TOO LATE...
amazing...
PANIC
PANIC
YOU'RE RIGHT.
Wow...
ISUMI-SAN!! AND SAKUYA-SAN, TOO!!

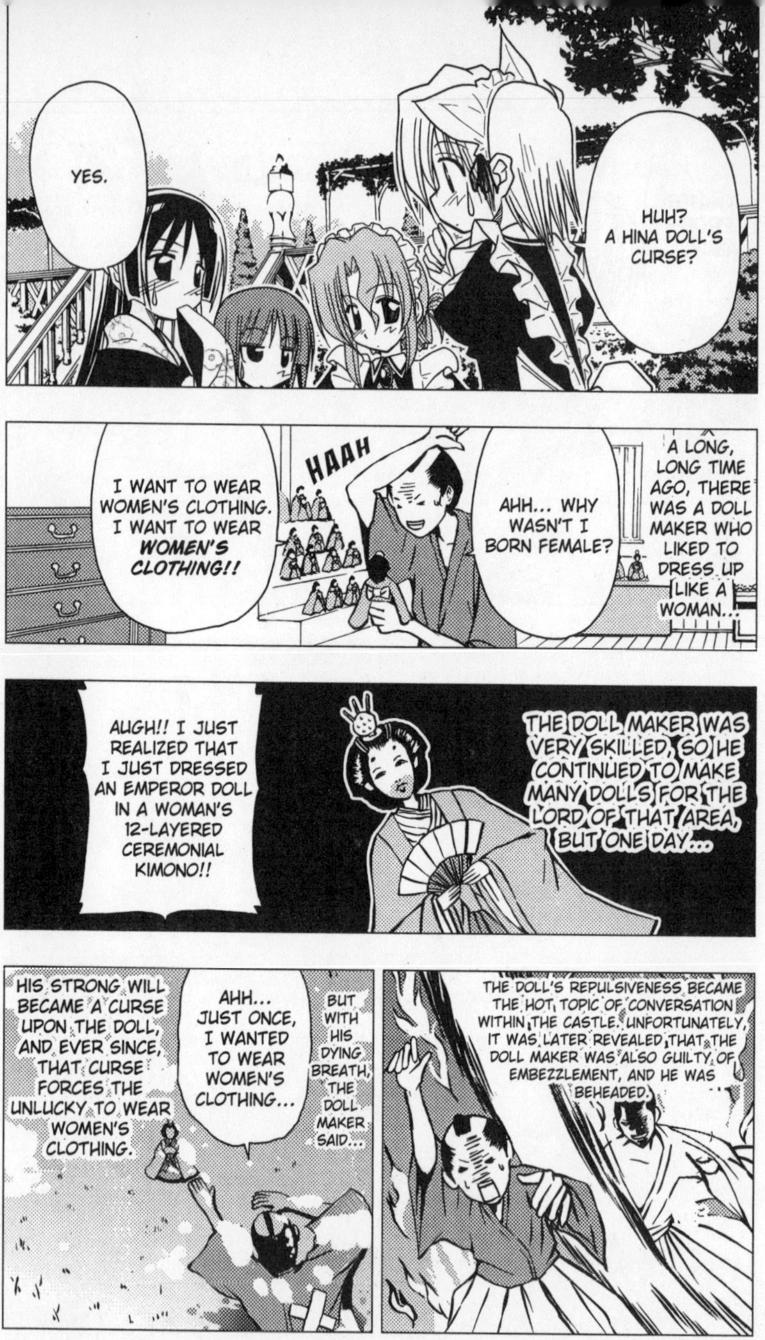
HUH? A HINA DOLL'S CURSE?
YES.
A LONG, LONG TIME AGO, THERE WAS A DOLL MAKER WHO LIKED TO DRESS UP LIKE A WOMAN...
AHH... WHY WASN'T I BORN FEMALE?
HAAH
I WANT TO WEAR WOMEN'S CLOTHING. I WANT TO WEAR *WOMEN'S CLOTHING!!*
THE DOLL MAKER WAS VERY SKILLED, SO HE CONTINUED TO MAKE MANY DOLLS FOR THE LORD OF THAT AREA, BUT ONE DAY...
AUGH!! I JUST REALIZED THAT I JUST DRESSED AN EMPEROR DOLL IN A WOMAN'S 12-LAYERED CEREMONIAL KIMONO!!
THE DOLL'S REPULSIVENESS BECAME THE HOT TOPIC OF CONVERSATION WITHIN THE CASTLE. UNFORTUNATELY, IT WAS LATER REVEALED THAT THE DOLL MAKER WAS ALSO GUILTY OF EMBEZZLEMENT, AND HE WAS BEHEADED.
BUT WITH HIS DYING BREATH, THE DOLL MAKER SAID...
AHH... JUST ONCE, I WANTED TO WEAR WOMEN'S CLOTHING...
HIS STRONG WILL BECAME A CURSE UPON THE DOLL, AND EVER SINCE, THAT CURSE FORCES THE UNLUCKY TO WEAR WOMEN'S CLOTHING.

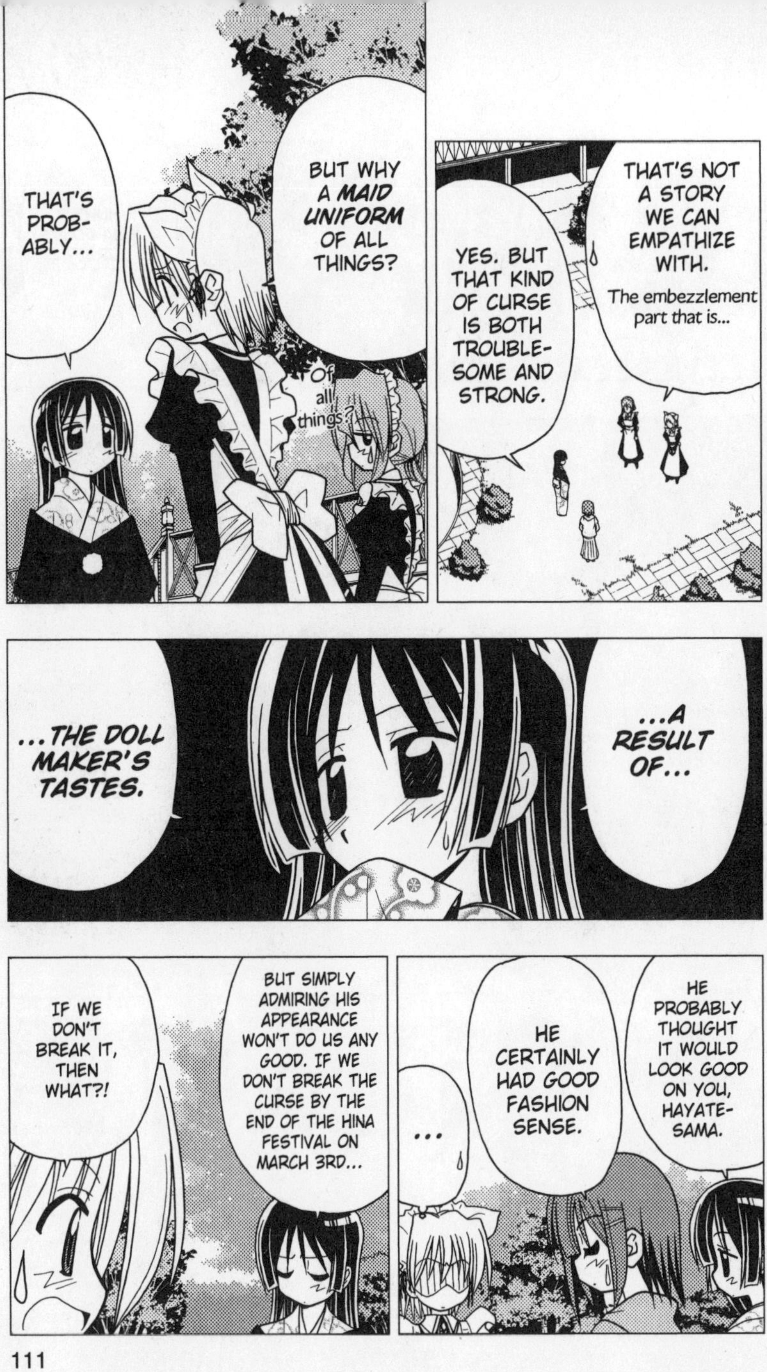
THAT'S NOT A STORY WE CAN EMPATHIZE WITH.
The embezzlement part that is...
YES. BUT THAT KIND OF CURSE IS BOTH TROUBLESOME AND STRONG.
BUT WHY A MAID UNIFORM OF ALL THINGS?
Of all things?
THAT'S PROBABLY...
...A RESULT OF...
...THE DOLL MAKER'S TASTES.
HE PROBABLY THOUGHT IT WOULD LOOK GOOD ON YOU, HAYATE-SAMA.
HE CERTAINLY HAD GOOD FASHION SENSE.
...
BUT SIMPLY ADMIRING HIS APPEARANCE WON'T DO US ANY GOOD. IF WE DON'T BREAK THE CURSE BY THE END OF THE HINA FESTIVAL ON MARCH 3RD...
IF WE DON'T BREAK IT, THEN WHAT?!

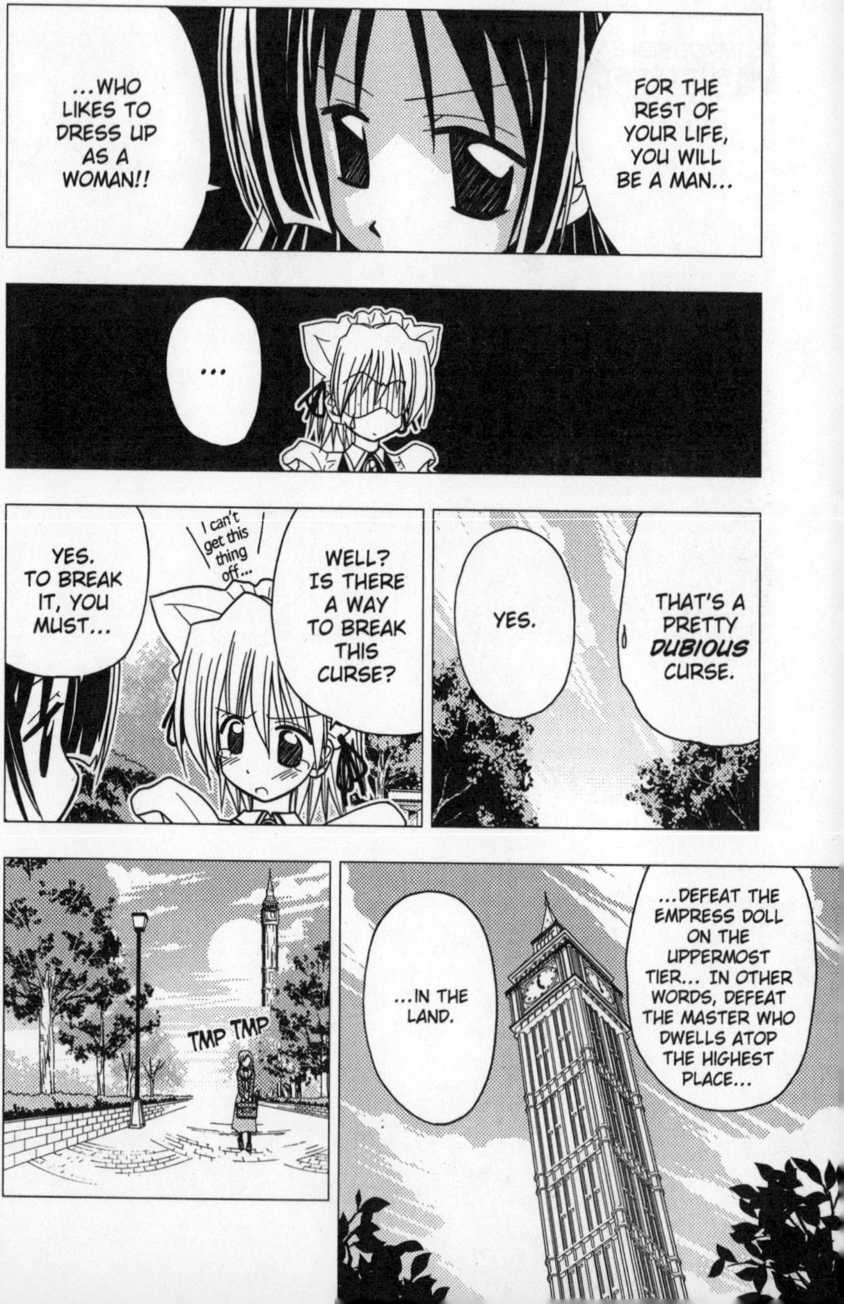
FOR THE REST OF YOUR LIFE, YOU WILL BE A MAN...
...WHO LIKES TO DRESS UP AS A WOMAN!!
...
THAT'S A PRETTY DUBIOUS CURSE.
YES.
WELL? IS THERE A WAY TO BREAK THIS CURSE?
I can't get this thing off...
YES. TO BREAK IT, YOU MUST...
...DEFEAT THE EMPRESS DOLL ON THE UPPERMOST TIER... IN OTHER WORDS, DEFEAT THE MASTER WHO DWELLS ATOP THE HIGHEST PLACE...
...IN THE LAND.
TMP TMP

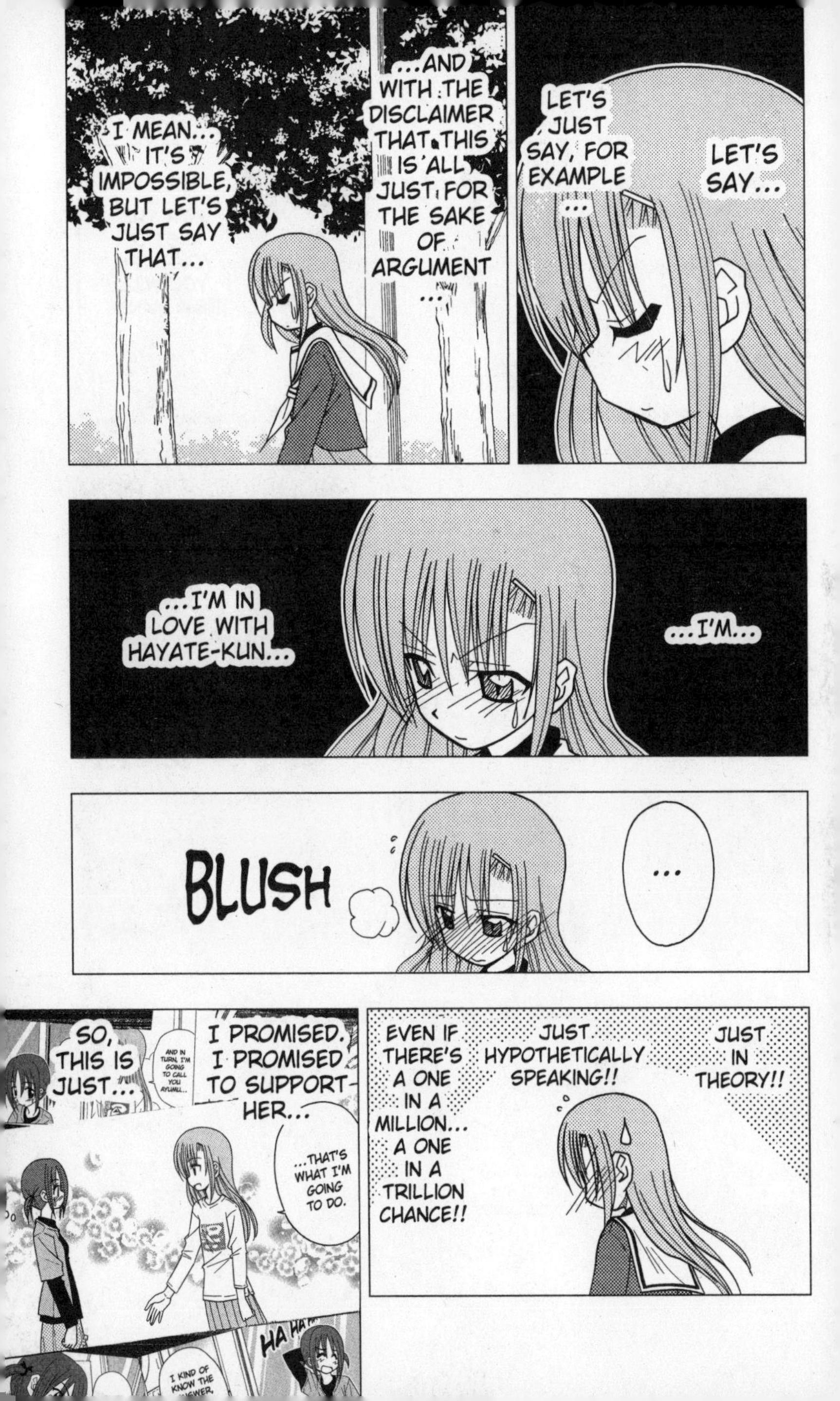
LET'S SAY...
LET'S JUST SAY, FOR EXAMPLE ...
...AND WITH THE DISCLAIMER THAT THIS IS ALL JUST FOR THE SAKE OF ARGUMENT ...
I MEAN... IT'S IMPOSSIBLE, BUT LET'S JUST SAY THAT...
...I'M...
...I'M IN LOVE WITH HAYATE-KUN...
...
BLUSH
JUST IN THEORY!!
JUST HYPOTHETICALLY SPEAKING!!
EVEN IF THERE'S A ONE IN A MILLION... A ONE IN A TRILLION CHANCE!!
I PROMISED. I PROMISED TO SUPPORT HER...
AND IN TURN, I'M GOING TO CALL YOU AYUMU...
SO, THIS IS JUST...
...THAT'S WHAT I'M GOING TO DO.
HA HA
I KIND OF KNOW THE

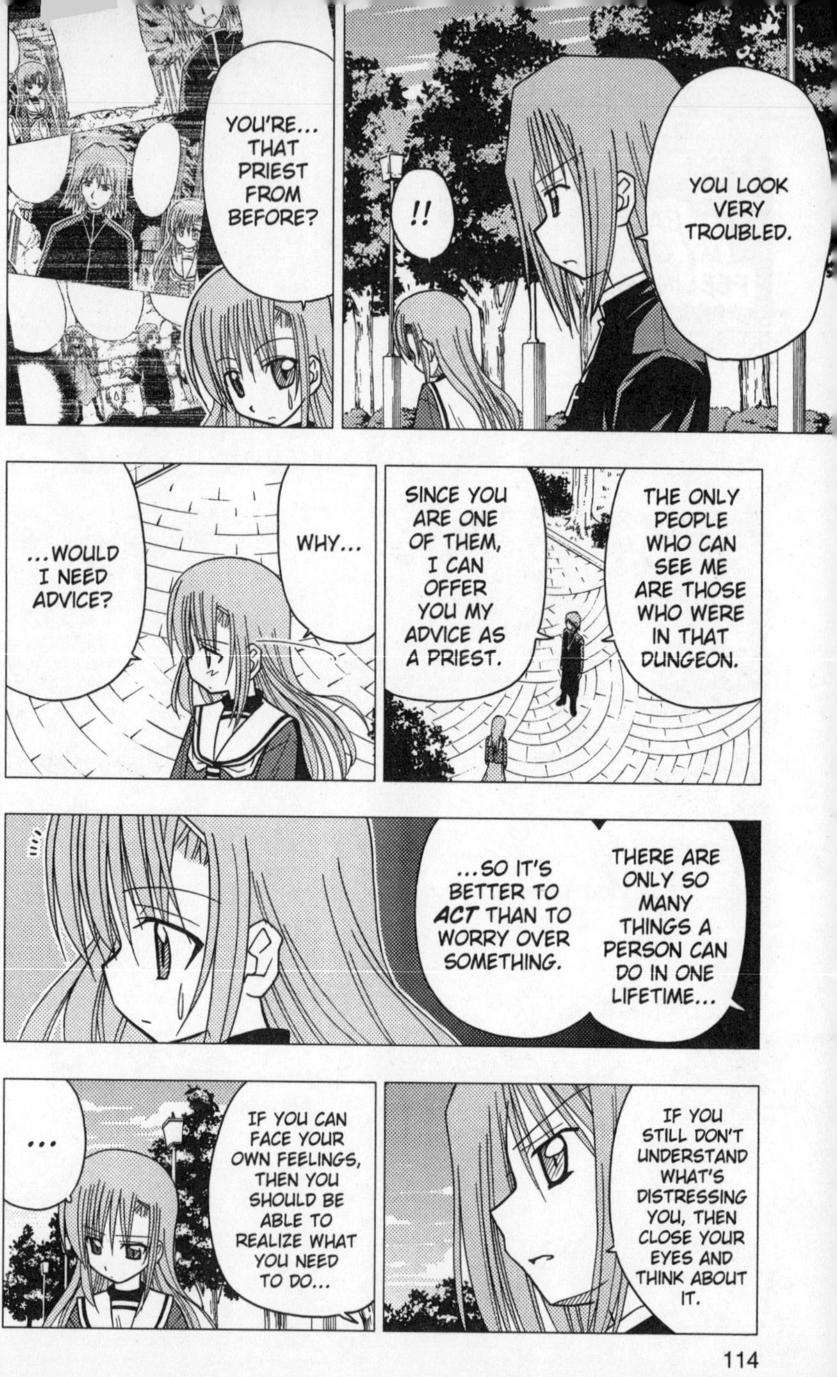
YOU LOOK VERY TROUBLED.
!!
YOU'RE... THAT PRIEST FROM BEFORE?
THE ONLY PEOPLE WHO CAN SEE ME ARE THOSE WHO WERE IN THAT DUNGEON.
SINCE YOU ARE ONE OF THEM, I CAN OFFER YOU MY ADVICE AS A PRIEST.
WHY...
...WOULD I NEED ADVICE?
THERE ARE ONLY SO MANY THINGS A PERSON CAN DO IN ONE LIFETIME...
...SO IT'S BETTER TO *ACT* THAN TO WORRY OVER SOMETHING.
IF YOU STILL DON'T UNDERSTAND WHAT'S DISTRESSING YOU, THEN CLOSE YOUR EYES AND THINK ABOUT IT.
IF YOU CAN FACE YOUR OWN FEELINGS, THEN YOU SHOULD BE ABLE TO REALIZE WHAT YOU NEED TO DO...
...

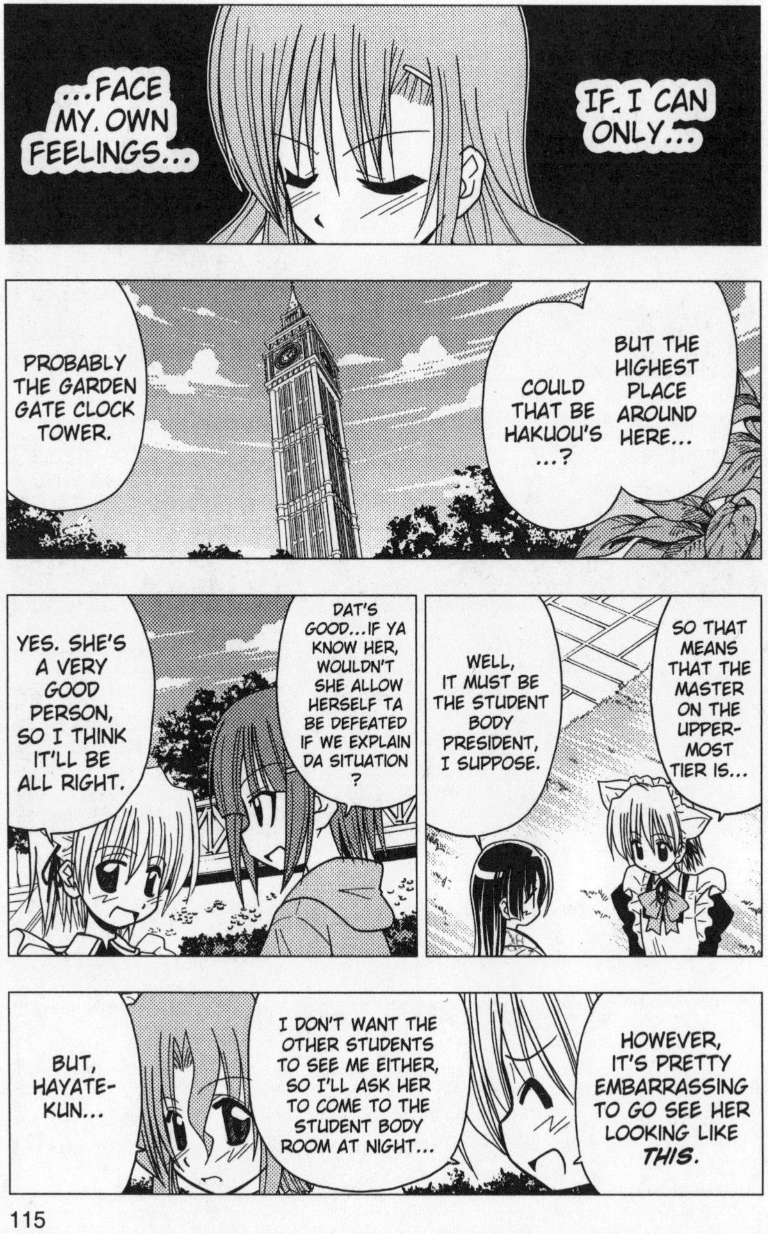
IF I CAN ONLY...
...FACE MY OWN FEELINGS...
BUT THE HIGHEST PLACE AROUND HERE...
COULD THAT BE HAKUOU'S ...?
PROBABLY THE GARDEN GATE CLOCK TOWER.
SO THAT MEANS THAT THE MASTER ON THE UPPER-MOST TIER IS...
WELL, IT MUST BE THE STUDENT BODY PRESIDENT, I SUPPOSE.
DAT'S GOOD...IF YA KNOW HER, WOULDN'T SHE ALLOW HERSELF TA BE DEFEATED IF WE EXPLAIN DA SITUATION ?
YES. SHE'S A VERY GOOD PERSON, SO I THINK IT'LL BE ALL RIGHT.
HOWEVER, IT'S PRETTY EMBARRASSING TO GO SEE HER LOOKING LIKE *THIS*.
I DON'T WANT THE OTHER STUDENTS TO SEE ME EITHER, SO I'LL ASK HER TO COME TO THE STUDENT BODY ROOM AT NIGHT...
BUT, HAYATE-KUN...

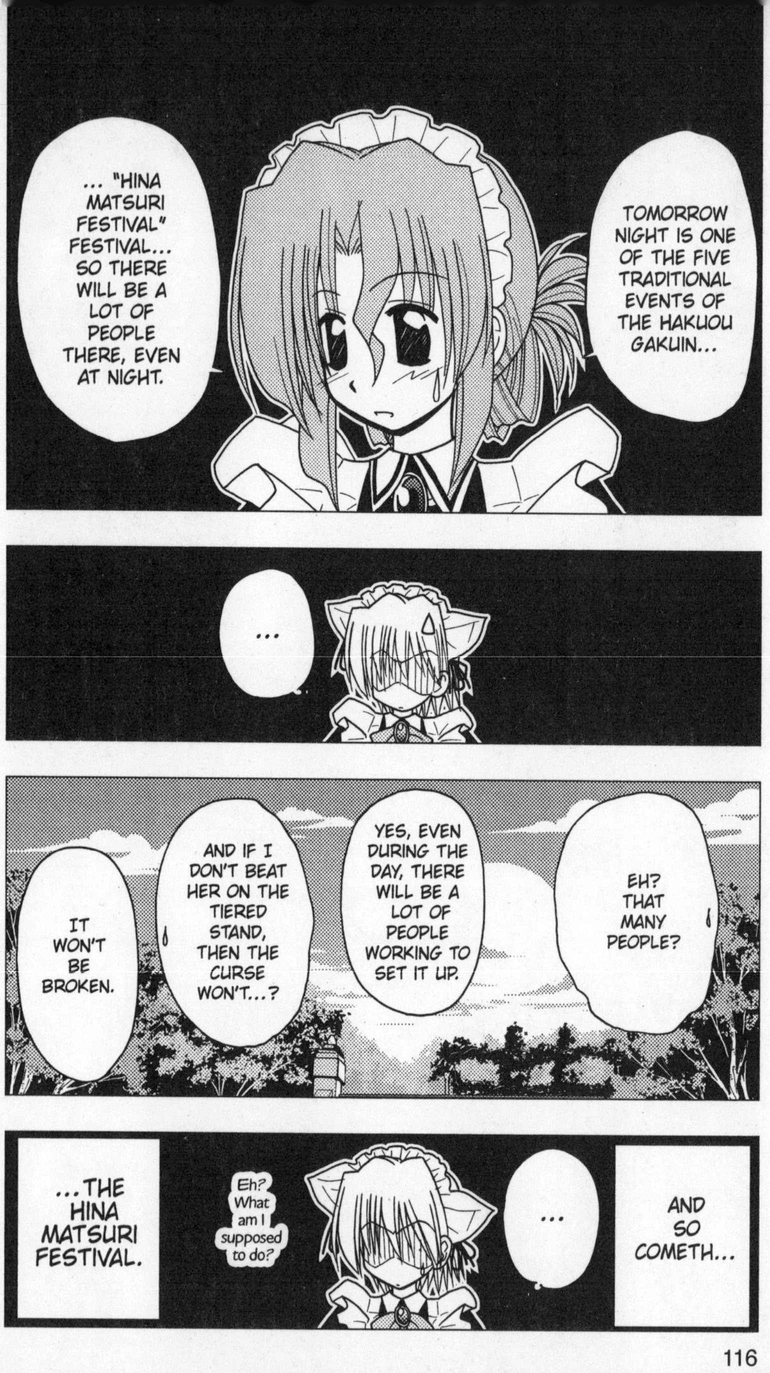
TOMORROW NIGHT IS ONE OF THE FIVE TRADITIONAL EVENTS OF THE HAKUOU GAKUIN...
... "HINA MATSURI FESTIVAL" FESTIVAL... SO THERE WILL BE A LOT OF PEOPLE THERE, EVEN AT NIGHT.
...
EH? THAT MANY PEOPLE?
YES, EVEN DURING THE DAY, THERE WILL BE A LOT OF PEOPLE WORKING TO SET IT UP.
AND IF I DON'T BEAT HER ON THE TIERED STAND, THEN THE CURSE WON'T...?
IT WON'T BE BROKEN.
AND SO COMETH...
...
Eh? What am I supposed to do?
...THE HINA MATSURI FESTIVAL.

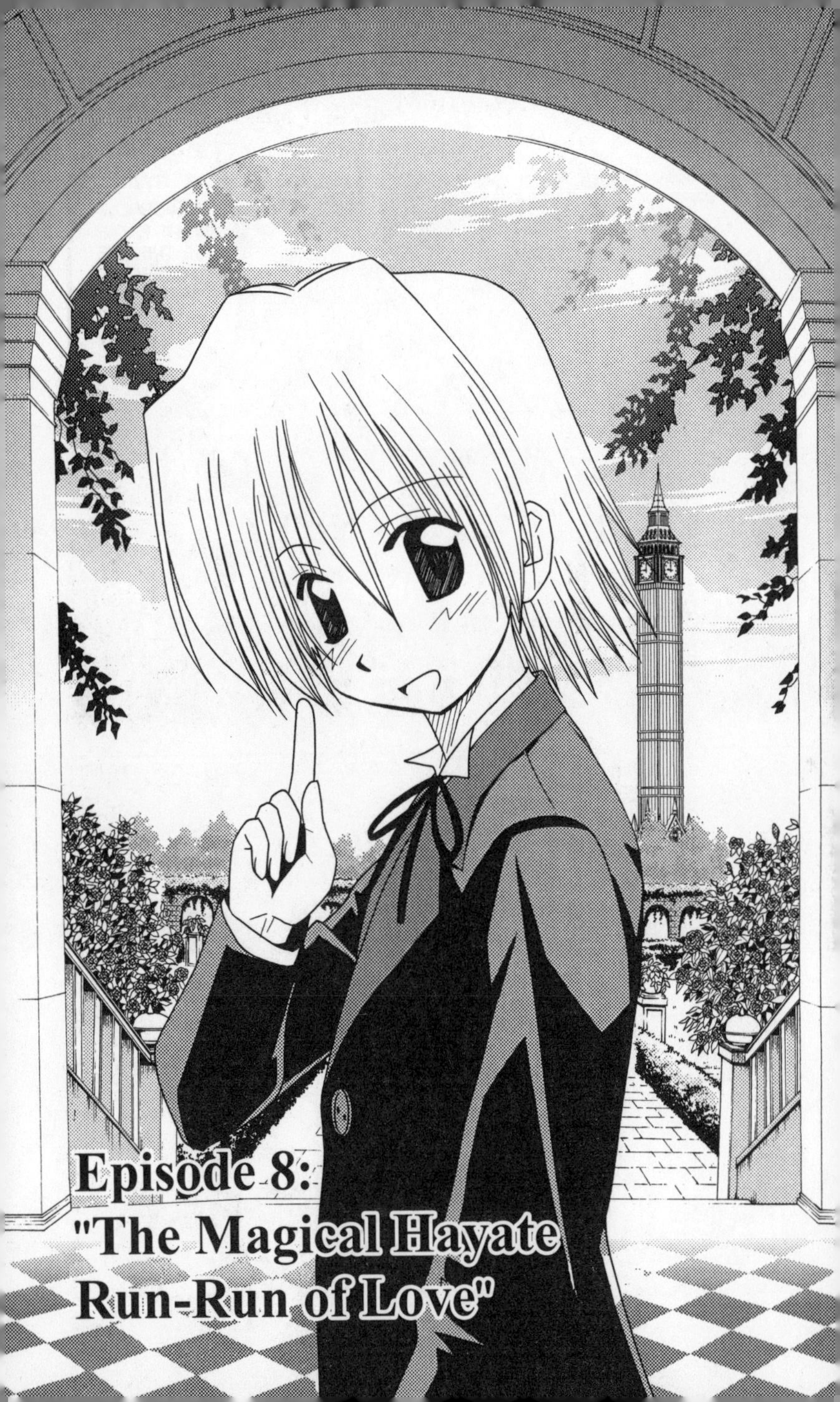
Episode 8:
"The Magical Hayate Run-Run of Love"

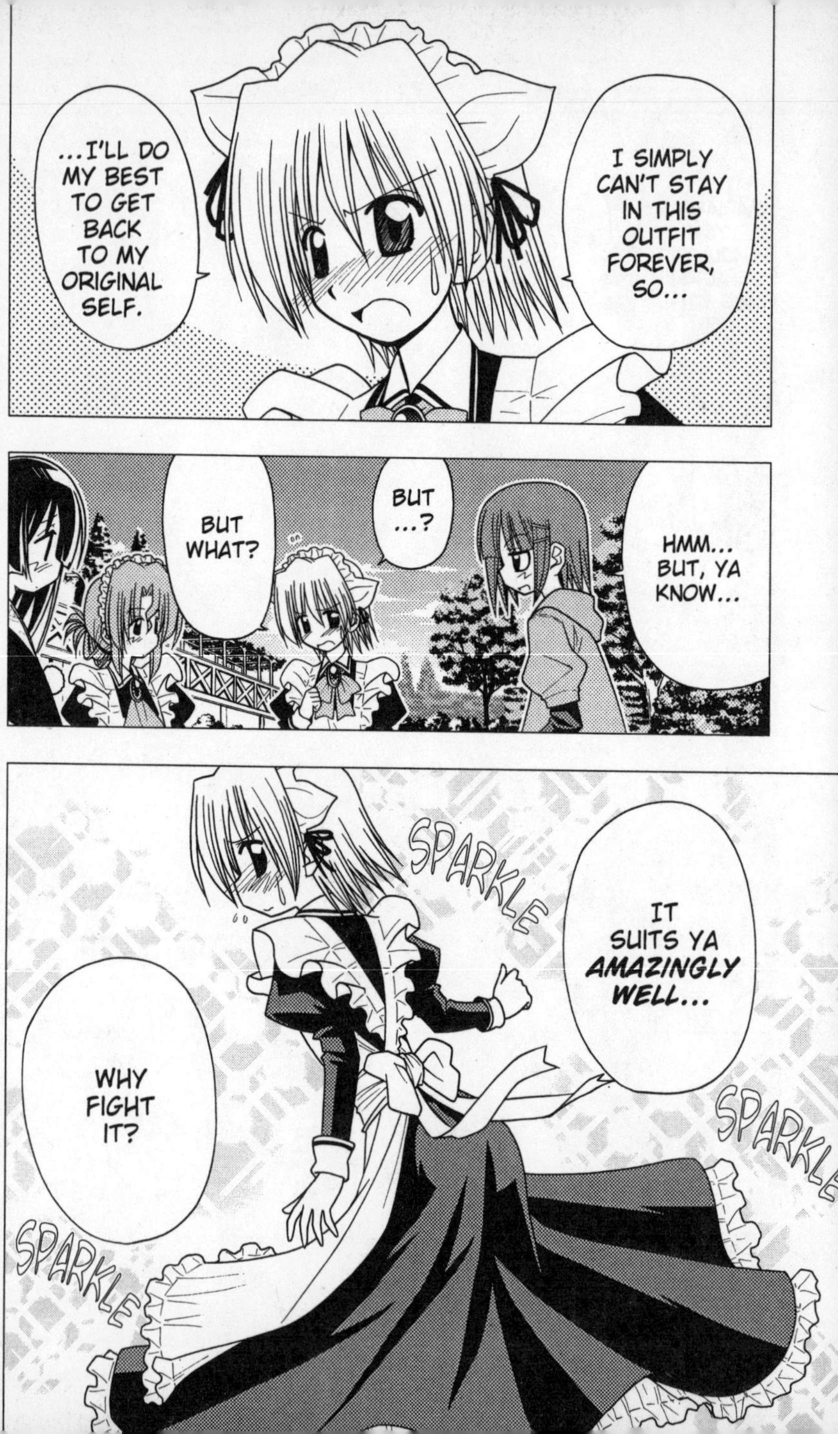
I SIMPLY CAN'T STAY IN THIS OUTFIT FOREVER, SO...
...I'LL DO MY BEST TO GET BACK TO MY ORIGINAL SELF.
HMM... BUT, YA KNOW...
BUT ...?
BUT WHAT?
IT SUITS YA AMAZINGLY WELL...
SPARKLE
SPARKLE
SPARKLE
WHY FIGHT IT?

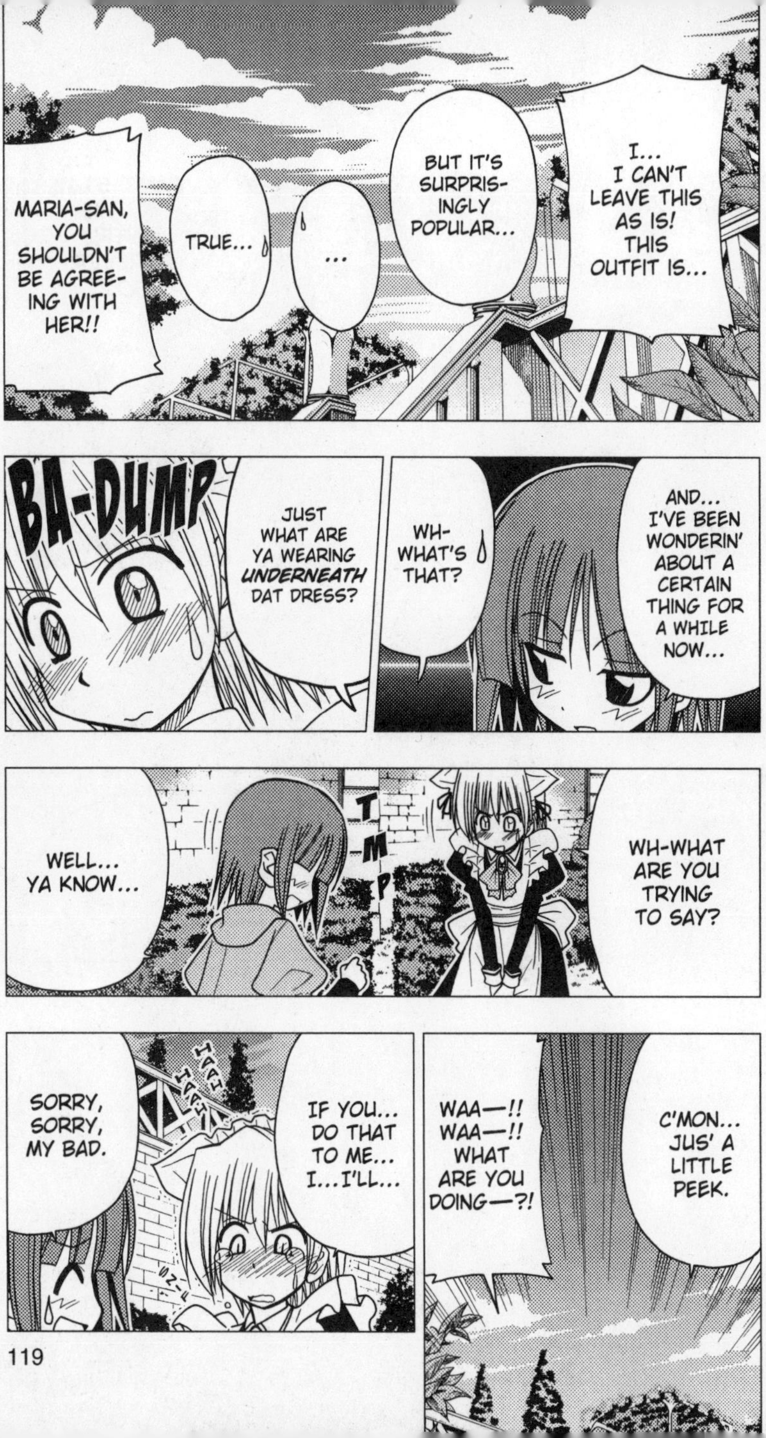
I... I CAN'T LEAVE THIS AS IS! THIS OUTFIT IS...
BUT IT'S SURPRISINGLY POPULAR...
...
TRUE...
MARIA-SAN, YOU SHOULDN'T BE AGREEING WITH HER!!
AND... I'VE BEEN WONDERIN' ABOUT A CERTAIN THING FOR A WHILE NOW...
WH-WHAT'S THAT?
JUST WHAT ARE YA WEARING *UNDERNEATH* DAT DRESS?
BA-DUMP
WH-WHAT ARE YOU TRYING TO SAY?
TMP
WELL... YA KNOW...
C'MON... JUS' A LITTLE PEEK.
WAA—!! WAA—!! WHAT ARE YOU DOING—?!
IF YOU... DO THAT TO ME... I...I'LL...
HAAH HAAH
SORRY, SORRY, MY BAD.

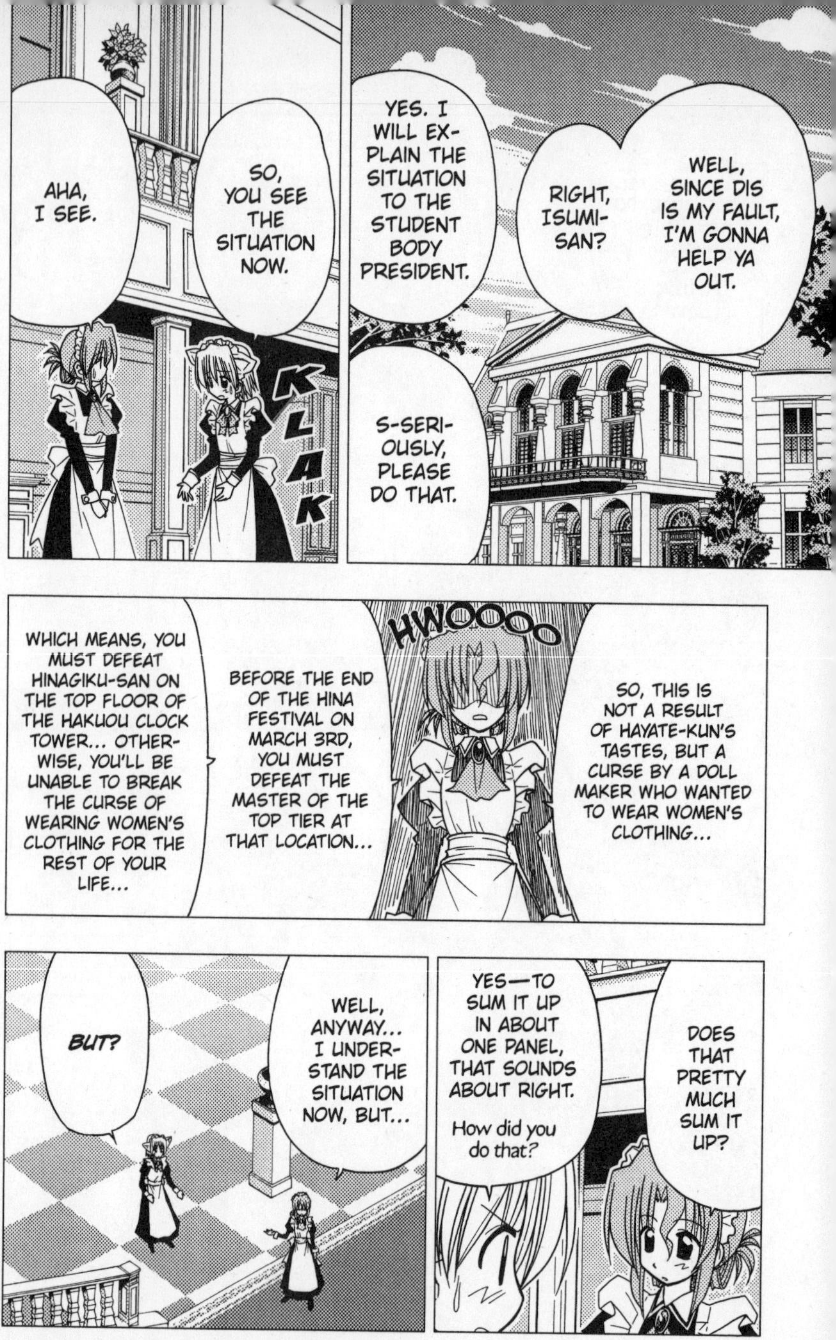
WELL, SINCE DIS IS MY FAULT, I'M GONNA HELP YA OUT.
RIGHT, ISUMI-SAN?
YES. I WILL EX-PLAIN THE SITUATION TO THE STUDENT BODY PRESIDENT.
S-SERI-OUSLY, PLEASE DO THAT.
SO, YOU SEE THE SITUATION NOW.
KLAK
AHA, I SEE.
SO, THIS IS NOT A RESULT OF HAYATE-KUN'S TASTES, BUT A CURSE BY A DOLL MAKER WHO WANTED TO WEAR WOMEN'S CLOTHING...
HWOOOO
BEFORE THE END OF THE HINA FESTIVAL ON MARCH 3RD, YOU MUST DEFEAT THE MASTER OF THE TOP TIER AT THAT LOCATION...
WHICH MEANS, YOU MUST DEFEAT HINAGIKU-SAN ON THE TOP FLOOR OF THE HAKUOU CLOCK TOWER... OTHER-WISE, YOU'LL BE UNABLE TO BREAK THE CURSE OF WEARING WOMEN'S CLOTHING FOR THE REST OF YOUR LIFE...
DOES THAT PRETTY MUCH SUM IT UP?
YES—TO SUM IT UP IN ABOUT ONE PANEL, THAT SOUNDS ABOUT RIGHT.
How did you do that?
WELL, ANYWAY... I UNDER-STAND THE SITUATION NOW, BUT...
BUT?

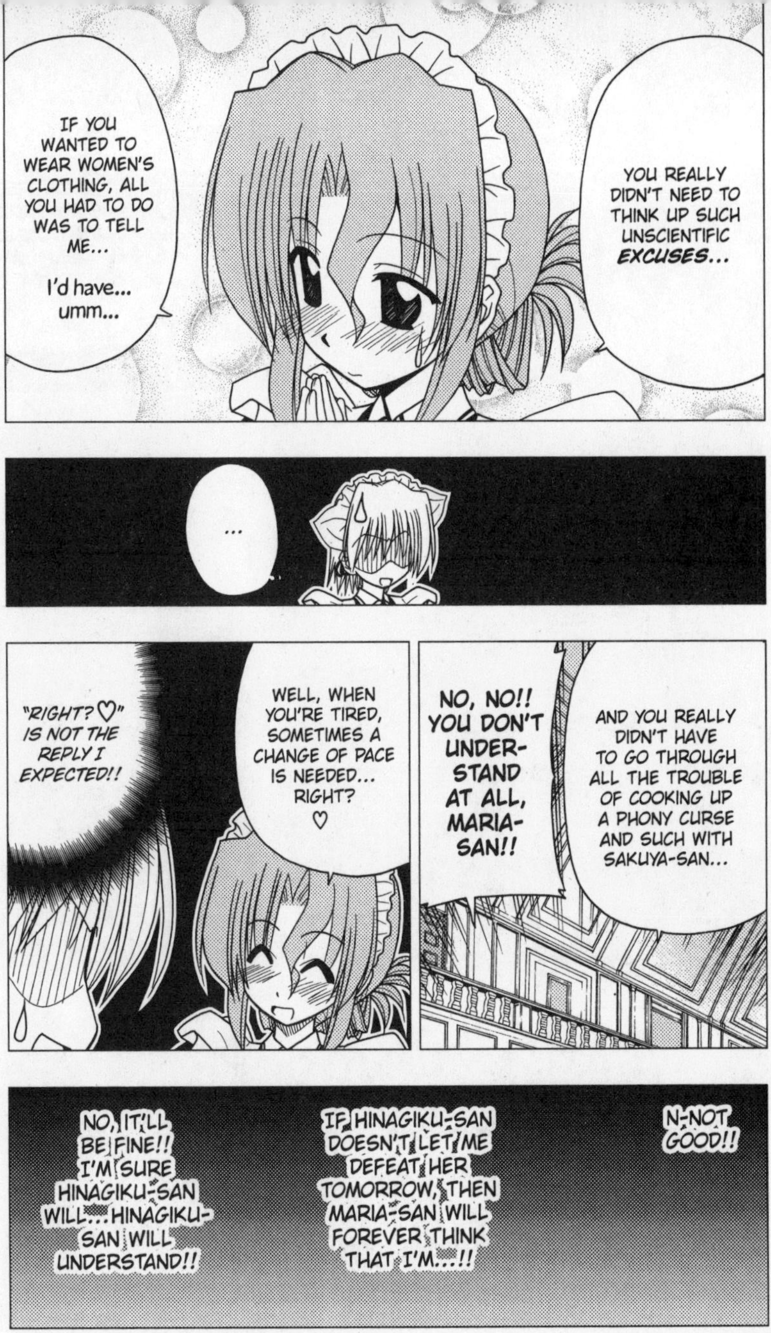
YOU REALLY DIDN'T NEED TO THINK UP SUCH UNSCIENTIFIC **EXCUSES...**
IF YOU WANTED TO WEAR WOMEN'S CLOTHING, ALL YOU HAD TO DO WAS TO TELL ME...
I'd have... umm...
...
AND YOU REALLY DIDN'T HAVE TO GO THROUGH ALL THE TROUBLE OF COOKING UP A PHONY CURSE AND SUCH WITH SAKUYA-SAN...
NO, NO!! YOU DON'T UNDERSTAND AT ALL, MARIA-SAN!!
WELL, WHEN YOU'RE TIRED, SOMETIMES A CHANGE OF PACE IS NEEDED... RIGHT? ♡
"RIGHT? ♡" IS NOT THE REPLY I EXPECTED!!
N-NOT GOOD!!
IF HINAGIKU-SAN DOESN'T LET ME DEFEAT HER TOMORROW, THEN MARIA-SAN WILL FOREVER THINK THAT I'M...!!
NO, IT'LL BE FINE!! I'M SURE HINAGIKU-SAN WILL... HINAGIKU-SAN WILL UNDERSTAND!!

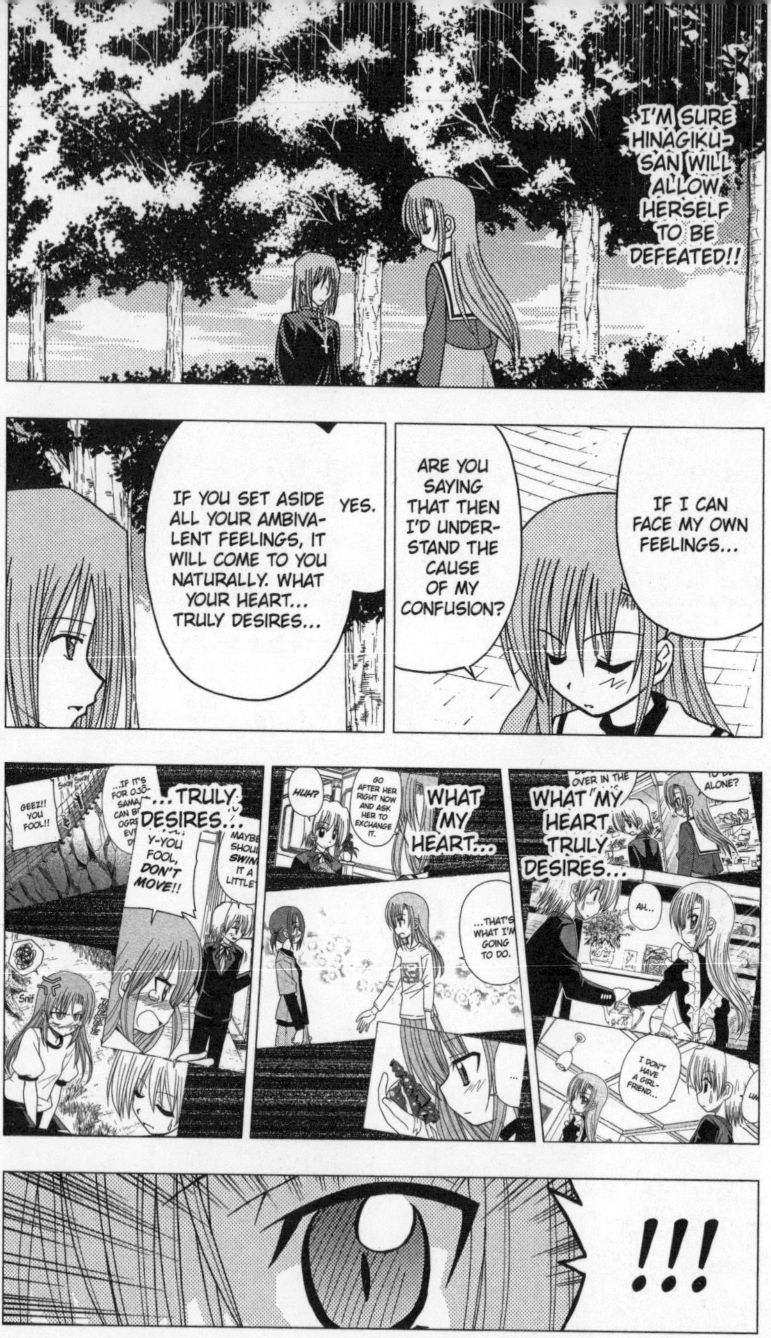
I'M SURE HINAGIKU-SAN WILL ALLOW HERSELF TO BE DEFEATED!!
IF I CAN FACE MY OWN FEELINGS...
ARE YOU SAYING THAT THEN I'D UNDERSTAND THE CAUSE OF MY CONFUSION?
YES.
IF YOU SET ASIDE ALL YOUR AMBIVALENT FEELINGS, IT WILL COME TO YOU NATURALLY. WHAT YOUR HEART... TRULY DESIRES...
WHAT MY HEART TRULY DESIRES...
AH...
I DON'T HAVE A GIRL-FRIEND...
WHAT MY HEART...
HUH?
GO AFTER HER RIGHT NOW AND ASK HER TO EXCHANGE IT.
...THAT'S WHAT I'M GOING TO DO.
...
...TRULY DESIRES...
GEEZ!! YOU FOOL!!
Y-YOU FOOL, DON'T MOVE!!
Snif
!!!

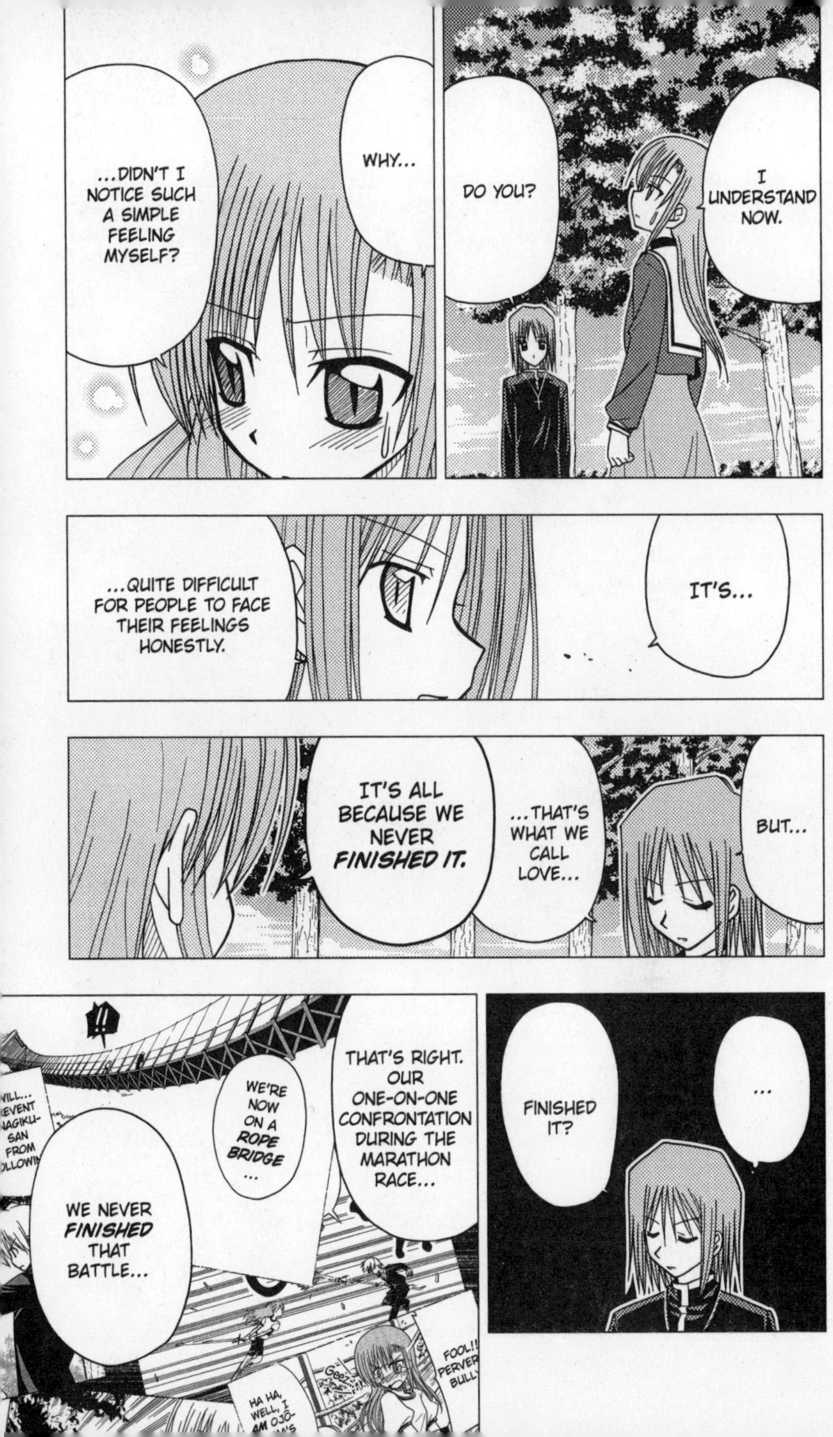
I UNDERSTAND NOW.
DO YOU?
WHY...
...DIDN'T I NOTICE SUCH A SIMPLE FEELING MYSELF?
IT'S...
...QUITE DIFFICULT FOR PEOPLE TO FACE THEIR FEELINGS HONESTLY.
BUT...
...THAT'S WHAT WE CALL LOVE...
IT'S ALL BECAUSE WE NEVER *FINISHED IT.*
...
FINISHED IT?
!!
THAT'S RIGHT. OUR ONE-ON-ONE CONFRONTATION DURING THE MARATHON RACE...
WE'RE NOW ON A *ROPE BRIDGE*...
WE NEVER *FINISHED* THAT BATTLE...

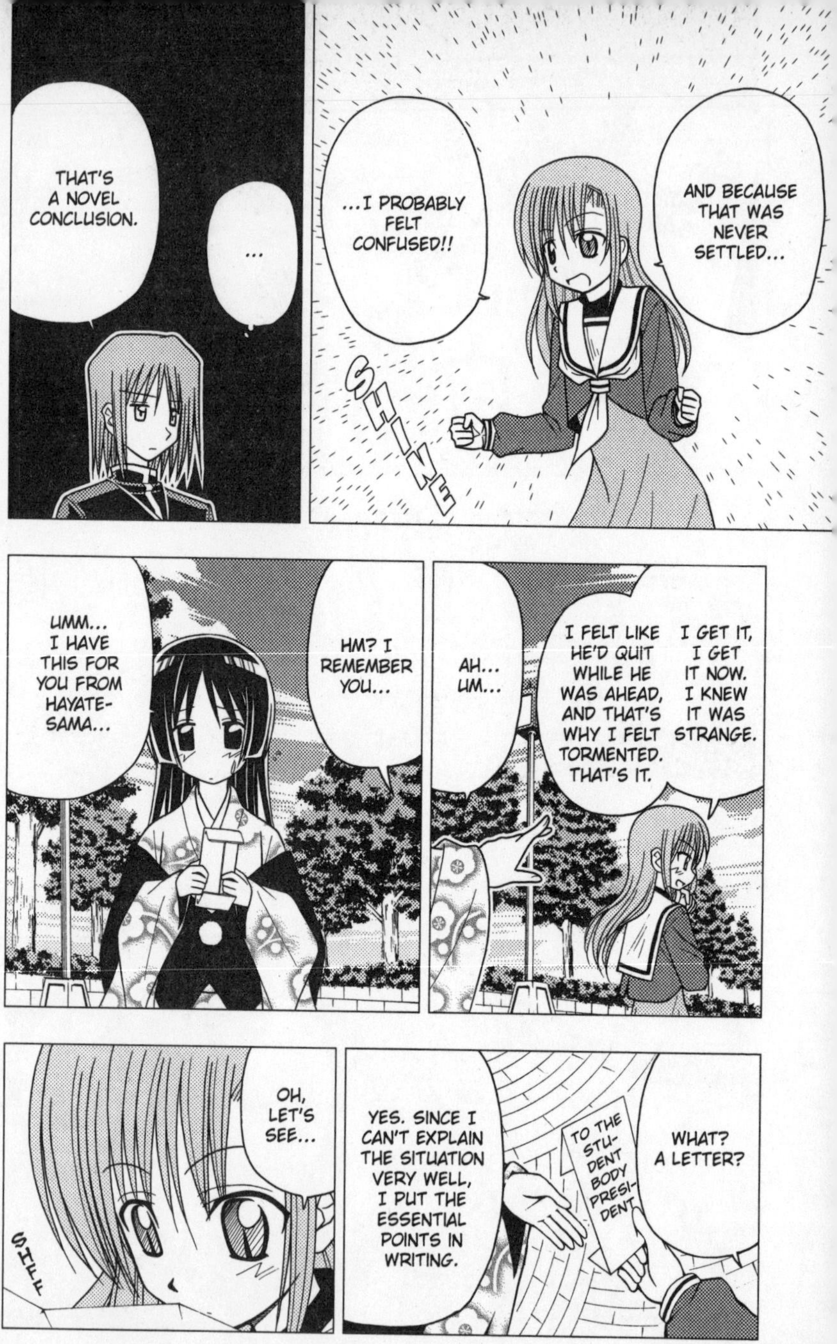
AND BECAUSE THAT WAS NEVER SETTLED...
...I PROBABLY FELT CONFUSED!!
SHINE
THAT'S A NOVEL CONCLUSION.
...
I GET IT, I GET IT NOW. I KNEW IT WAS STRANGE.
I FELT LIKE HE'D QUIT WHILE HE WAS AHEAD, AND THAT'S WHY I FELT TORMENTED. THAT'S IT.
AH... UM...
HM? I REMEMBER YOU...
UMM... I HAVE THIS FOR YOU FROM HAYATE-SAMA...
WHAT? A LETTER?
TO THE STUDENT BODY PRESIDENT
YES. SINCE I CAN'T EXPLAIN THE SITUATION VERY WELL, I PUT THE ESSENTIAL POINTS IN WRITING.
OH, LET'S SEE...
SHFF

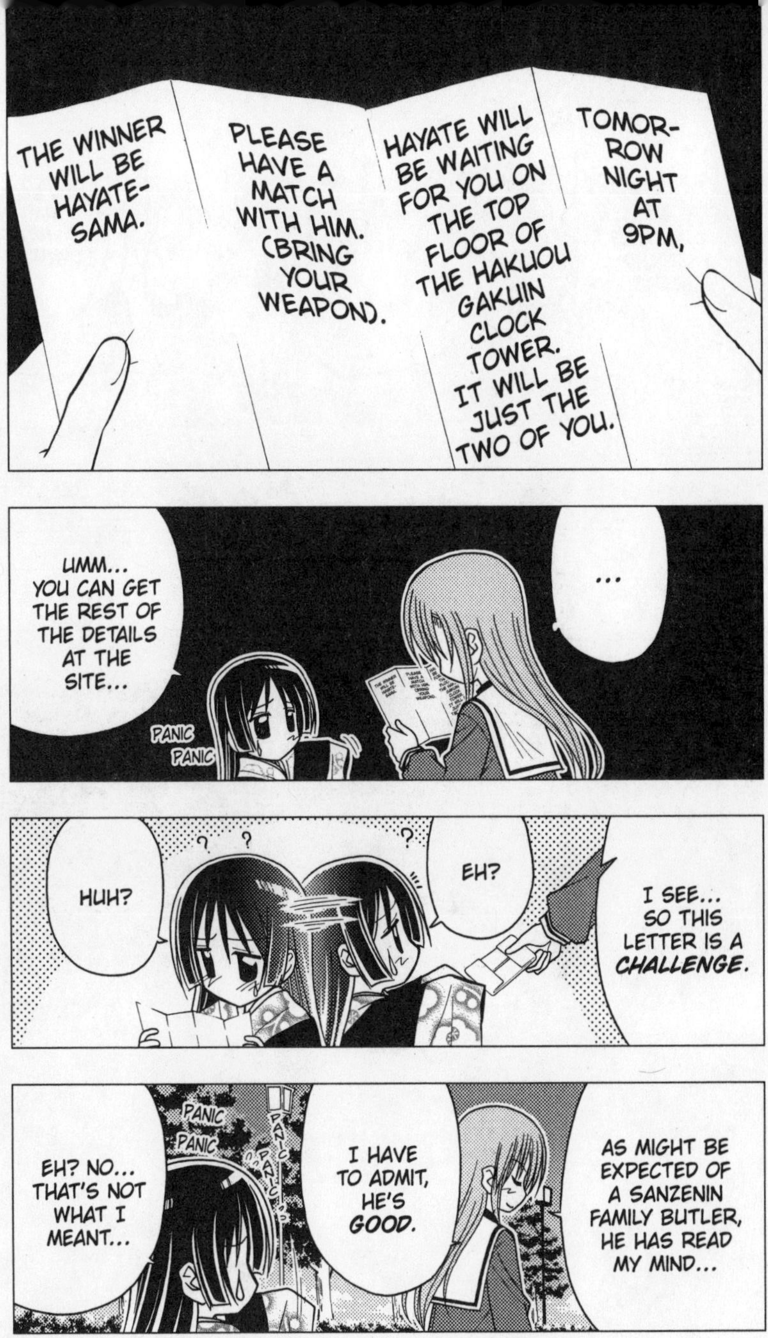
TOMORROW NIGHT AT 9PM,
HAYATE WILL BE WAITING FOR YOU ON THE TOP FLOOR OF THE HAKUOU GAKUIN CLOCK TOWER. IT WILL BE JUST THE TWO OF YOU.
PLEASE HAVE A MATCH WITH HIM. (BRING YOUR WEAPON).
THE WINNER WILL BE HAYATE-SAMA.
...
UMM... YOU CAN GET THE REST OF THE DETAILS AT THE SITE...
PANIC PANIC
I SEE... SO THIS LETTER IS A CHALLENGE.
EH?
HUH?
AS MIGHT BE EXPECTED OF A SANZENIN FAMILY BUTLER, HE HAS READ MY MIND...
I HAVE TO ADMIT, HE'S GOOD.
PANIC PANIC
PANIC PANIC
EH? NO... THAT'S NOT WHAT I MEANT...

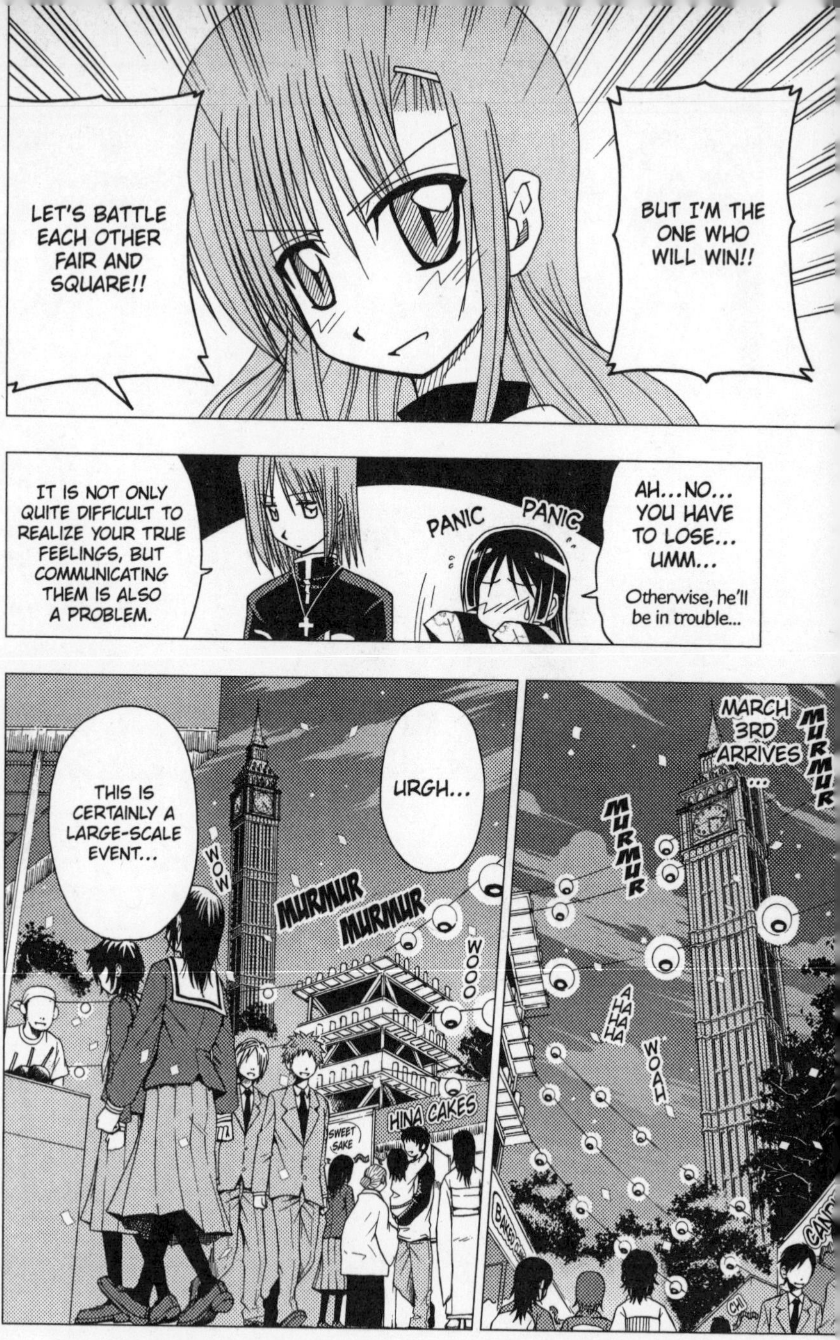
BUT I'M THE ONE WHO WILL WIN!!
LET'S BATTLE EACH OTHER FAIR AND SQUARE!!
AH...NO... YOU HAVE TO LOSE... UMM...
Otherwise, he'll be in trouble...
PANIC
PANIC
IT IS NOT ONLY QUITE DIFFICULT TO REALIZE YOUR TRUE FEELINGS, BUT COMMUNICATING THEM IS ALSO A PROBLEM.
MARCH 3RD ARRIVES...
MURMUR
MURMUR
MURMUR
AHAHAHA
WOAH
CHI
URGH...
THIS IS CERTAINLY A LARGE-SCALE EVENT...
WOW
MURMUR
MURMUR
WOOO
HINA CAKES
SWEET SAKE

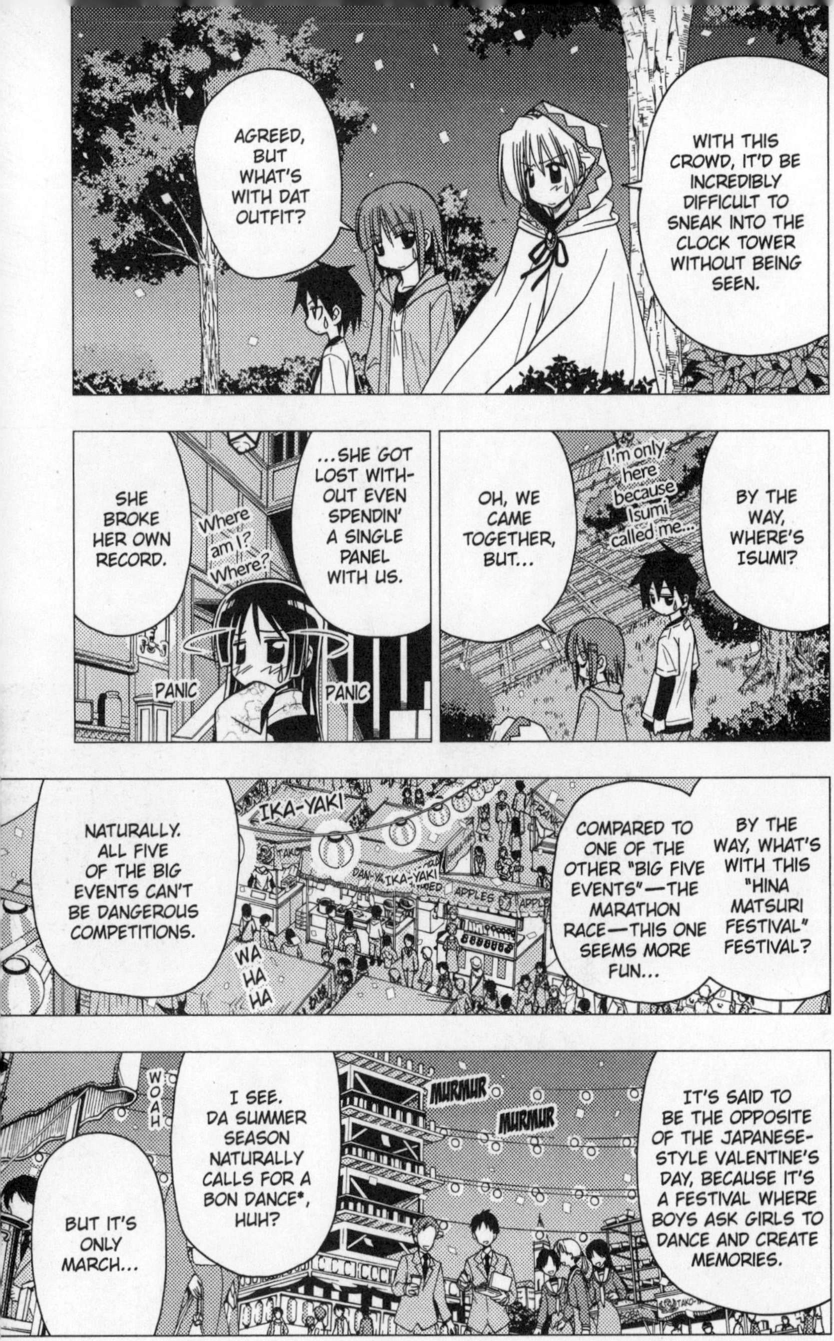
WITH THIS CROWD, IT'D BE INCREDIBLY DIFFICULT TO SNEAK INTO THE CLOCK TOWER WITHOUT BEING SEEN.
AGREED, BUT WHAT'S WITH DAT OUTFIT?
BY THE WAY, WHERE'S ISUMI?
I'm only here because Isumi called me...
OH, WE CAME TOGETHER, BUT...
...SHE GOT LOST WITHOUT EVEN SPENDIN' A SINGLE PANEL WITH US.
Where am I? Where?
SHE BROKE HER OWN RECORD.
PANIC
PANIC
BY THE WAY, WHAT'S WITH THIS "HINA MATSURI FESTIVAL" FESTIVAL?
COMPARED TO ONE OF THE OTHER "BIG FIVE EVENTS"—THE MARATHON RACE—THIS ONE SEEMS MORE FUN...
IKA-YAKI
APPLES
NATURALLY. ALL FIVE OF THE BIG EVENTS CAN'T BE DANGEROUS COMPETITIONS.
WA HA HA
IT'S SAID TO BE THE OPPOSITE OF THE JAPANESE-STYLE VALENTINE'S DAY, BECAUSE IT'S A FESTIVAL WHERE BOYS ASK GIRLS TO DANCE AND CREATE MEMORIES.
MURMUR
MURMUR
I SEE. DA SUMMER SEASON NATURALLY CALLS FOR A BON DANCE*, HUH?
WOAH
BUT IT'S ONLY MARCH...

* AN ANNUAL SUMMER CELEBRATION TO HONOR THE DEAD.

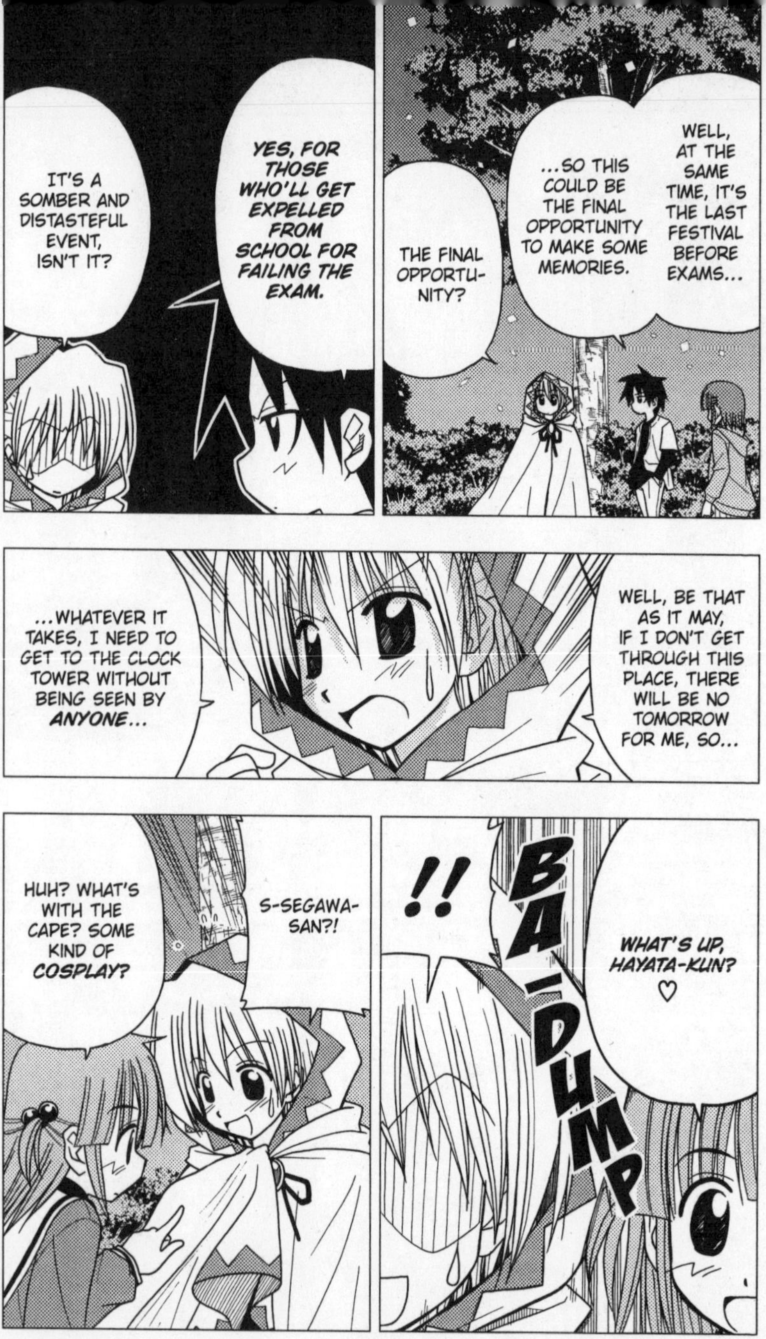
WELL, AT THE SAME TIME, IT'S THE LAST FESTIVAL BEFORE EXAMS...
...SO THIS COULD BE THE FINAL OPPORTUNITY TO MAKE SOME MEMORIES.
THE FINAL OPPORTU-NITY?
YES, FOR THOSE WHO'LL GET EXPELLED FROM SCHOOL FOR FAILING THE EXAM.
IT'S A SOMBER AND DISTASTEFUL EVENT, ISN'T IT?
WELL, BE THAT AS IT MAY, IF I DON'T GET THROUGH THIS PLACE, THERE WILL BE NO TOMORROW FOR ME, SO...
...WHATEVER IT TAKES, I NEED TO GET TO THE CLOCK TOWER WITHOUT BEING SEEN BY ANYONE...
WHAT'S UP, HAYATA-KUN? ♡
BA-DUMP
!!
S-SEGAWA-SAN?!
HUH? WHAT'S WITH THE CAPE? SOME KIND OF COSPLAY?

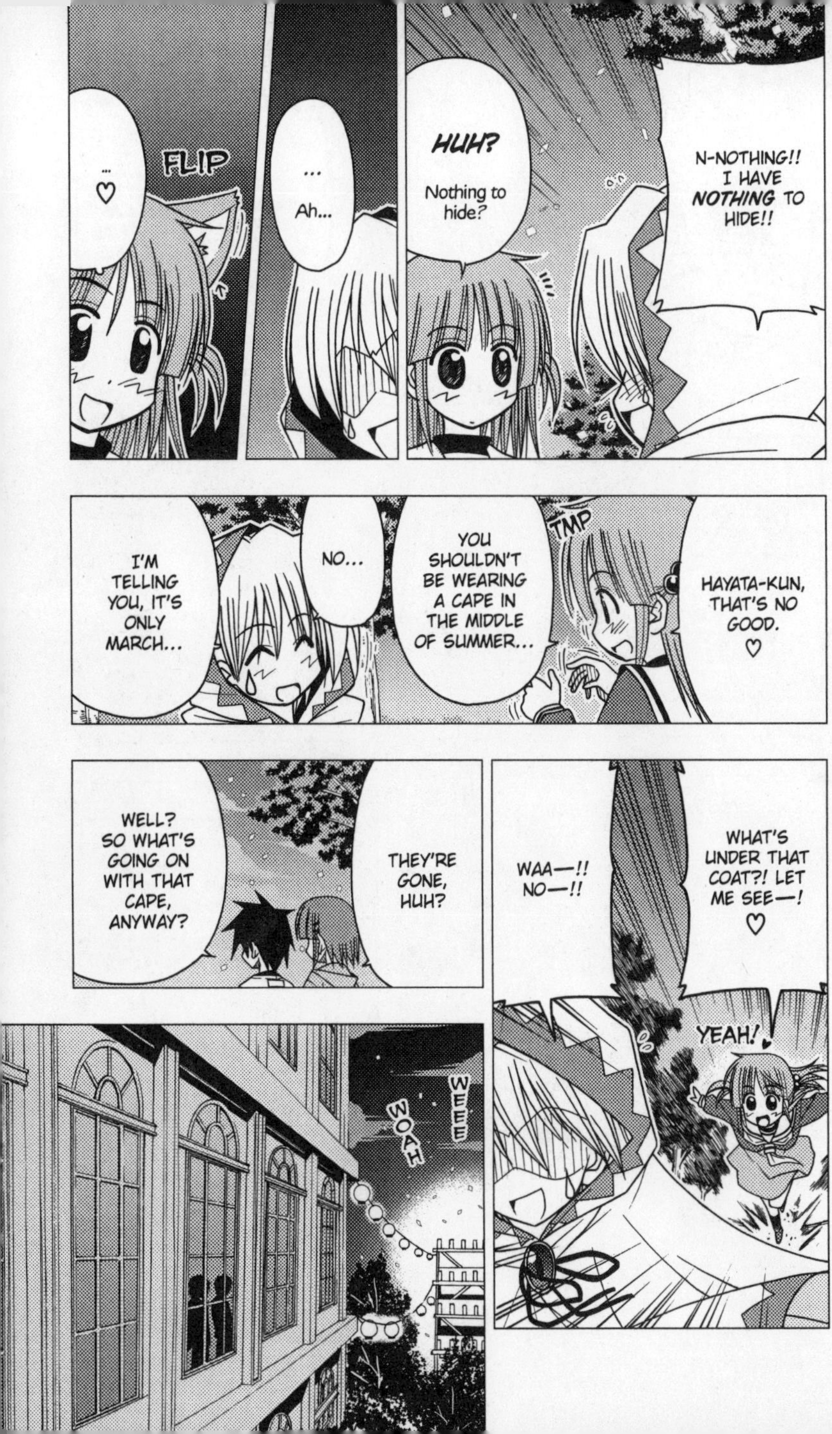
N-NOTHING!! I HAVE NOTHING TO HIDE!!
HUH? Nothing to hide?
...
Ah...
FLIP
... ♡
HAYATA-KUN, THAT'S NO GOOD. ♡
TMP
YOU SHOULDN'T BE WEARING A CAPE IN THE MIDDLE OF SUMMER...
NO...
I'M TELLING YOU, IT'S ONLY MARCH...
WHAT'S UNDER THAT COAT?! LET ME SEE—! ♡
WAA—!! NO—!!
YEAH!
THEY'RE GONE, HUH?
WELL? SO WHAT'S GOING ON WITH THAT CAPE, ANYWAY?
WEEE
WOAH

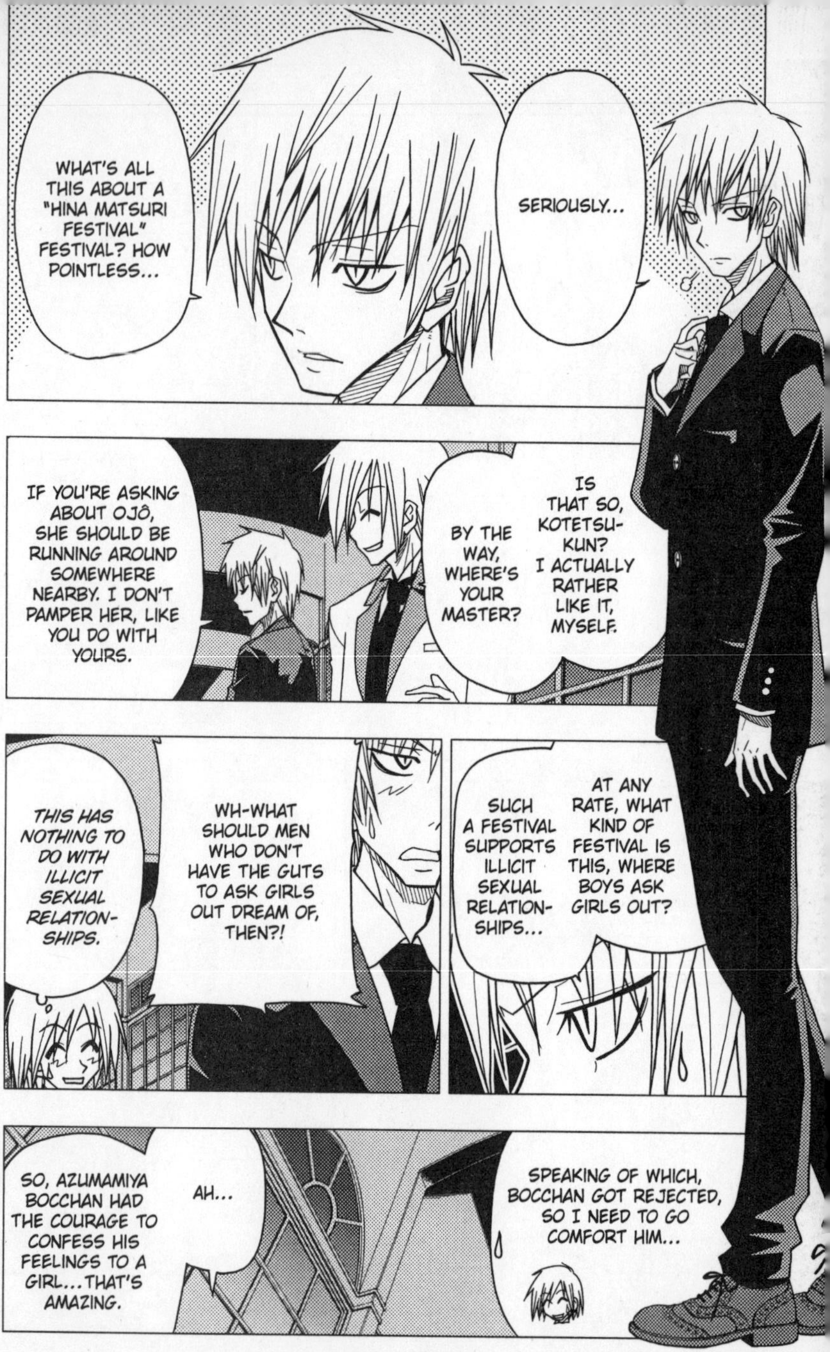
SERIOUSLY...
WHAT'S ALL THIS ABOUT A "HINA MATSURI FESTIVAL" FESTIVAL? HOW POINTLESS...
IS THAT SO, KOTETSU-KUN? I ACTUALLY RATHER LIKE IT, MYSELF.
BY THE WAY, WHERE'S YOUR MASTER?
IF YOU'RE ASKING ABOUT OJÔ, SHE SHOULD BE RUNNING AROUND SOMEWHERE NEARBY. I DON'T PAMPER HER, LIKE YOU DO WITH YOURS.
AT ANY RATE, WHAT KIND OF FESTIVAL IS THIS, WHERE BOYS ASK GIRLS OUT?
SUCH A FESTIVAL SUPPORTS ILLICIT SEXUAL RELATION-SHIPS...
WH-WHAT SHOULD MEN WHO DON'T HAVE THE GUTS TO ASK GIRLS OUT DREAM OF, THEN?!
THIS HAS NOTHING TO DO WITH ILLICIT SEXUAL RELATION-SHIPS.
SPEAKING OF WHICH, BOCCHAN GOT REJECTED, SO I NEED TO GO COMFORT HIM...
AH...
SO, AZUMAMIYA BOCCHAN HAD THE COURAGE TO CONFESS HIS FEELINGS TO A GIRL...THAT'S AMAZING.

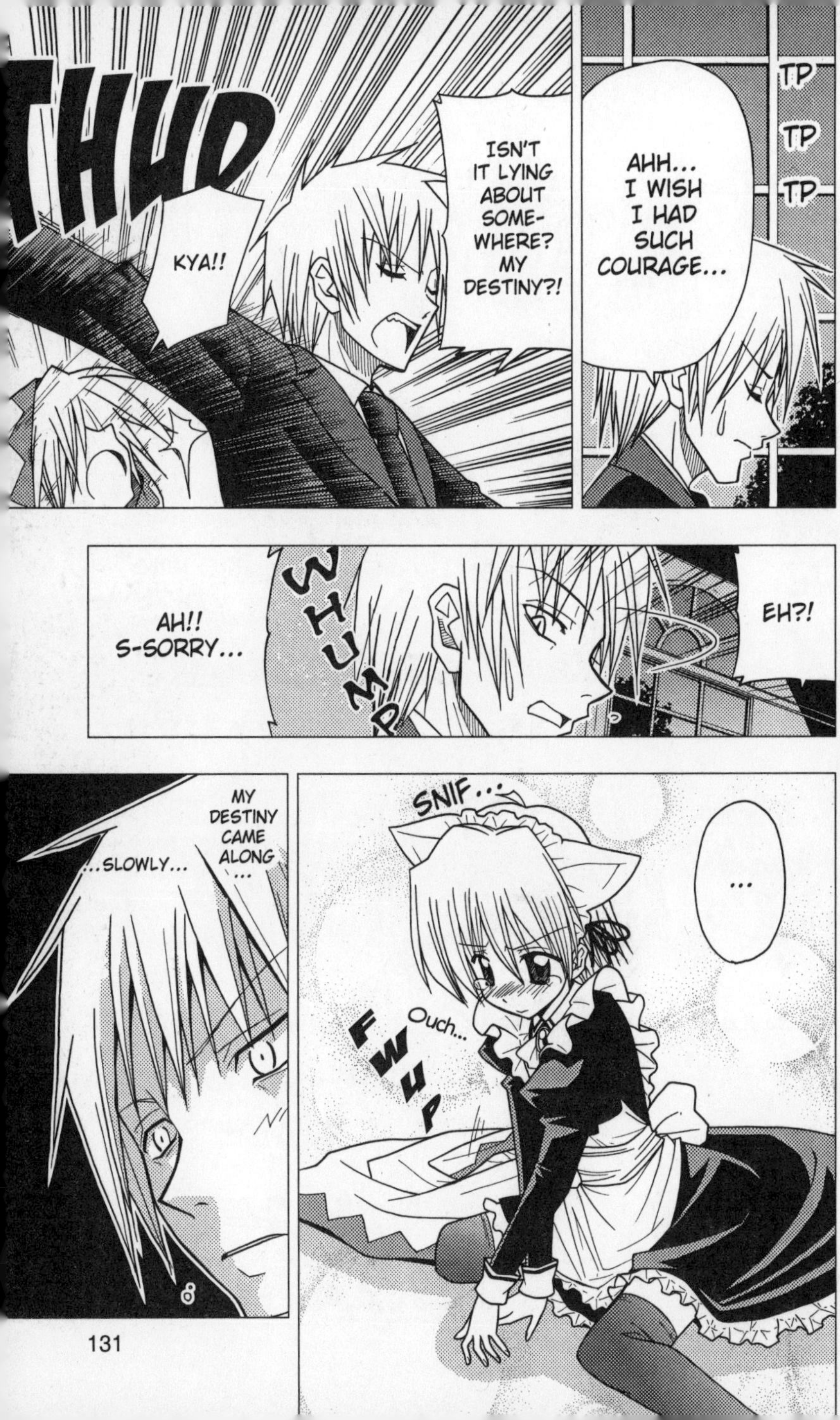
TP
TP
TP
AHH... I WISH I HAD SUCH COURAGE...
THUD
ISN'T IT LYING ABOUT SOME-WHERE? MY DESTINY?!
KYA!!
EH?!
WHUMP
AH!! S-SORRY...
SNIF...
...
Ouch...
FWUP
MY DESTINY CAME ALONG...
...SLOWLY...

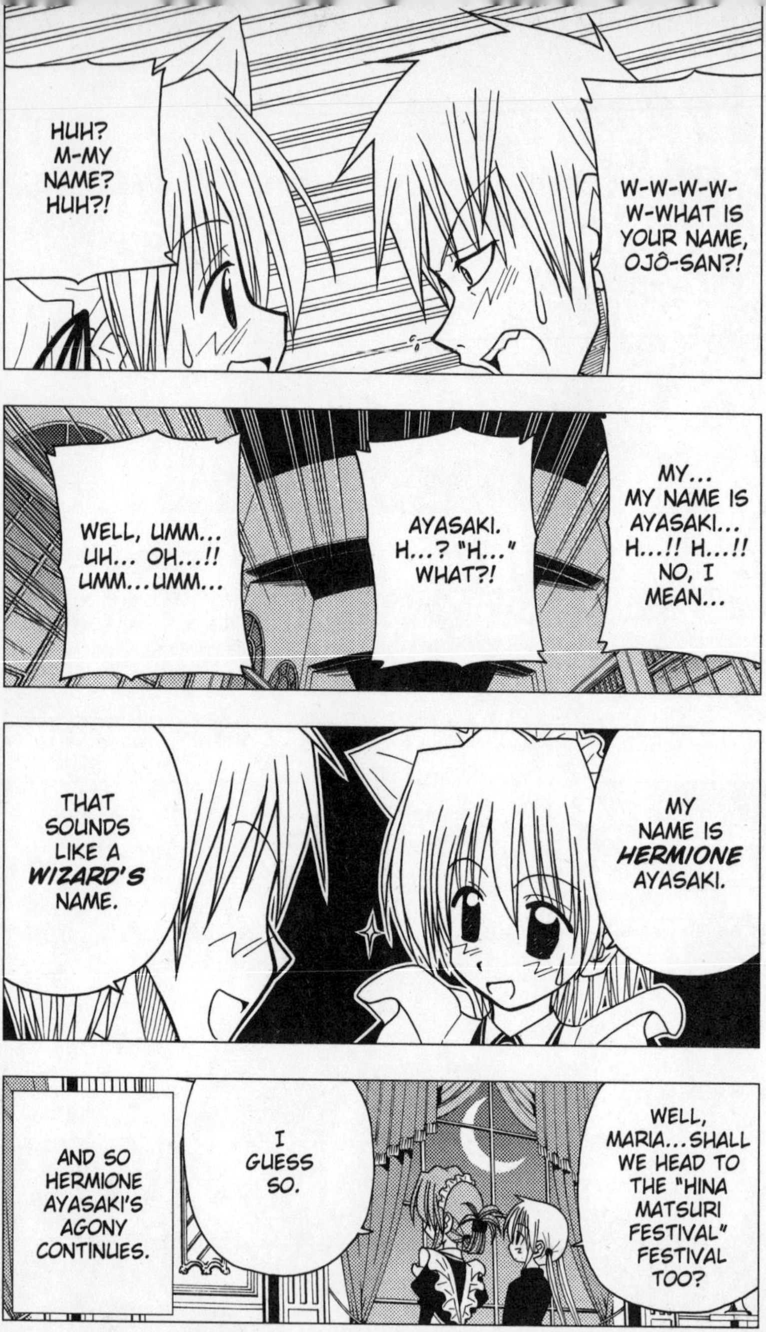
W-W-W-W-W-WHAT IS YOUR NAME, OJÔ-SAN?!
HUH? M-MY NAME? HUH?!
MY... MY NAME IS AYASAKI... H...!! H...!! NO, I MEAN...
AYASAKI. H...? "H..." WHAT?!
WELL, UMM... UH... OH...!! UMM...UMM...
MY NAME IS HERMIONE AYASAKI.
THAT SOUNDS LIKE A WIZARD'S NAME.
WELL, MARIA...SHALL WE HEAD TO THE "HINA MATSURI FESTIVAL" FESTIVAL TOO?
I GUESS SO.
AND SO HERMIONE AYASAKI'S AGONY CONTINUES.

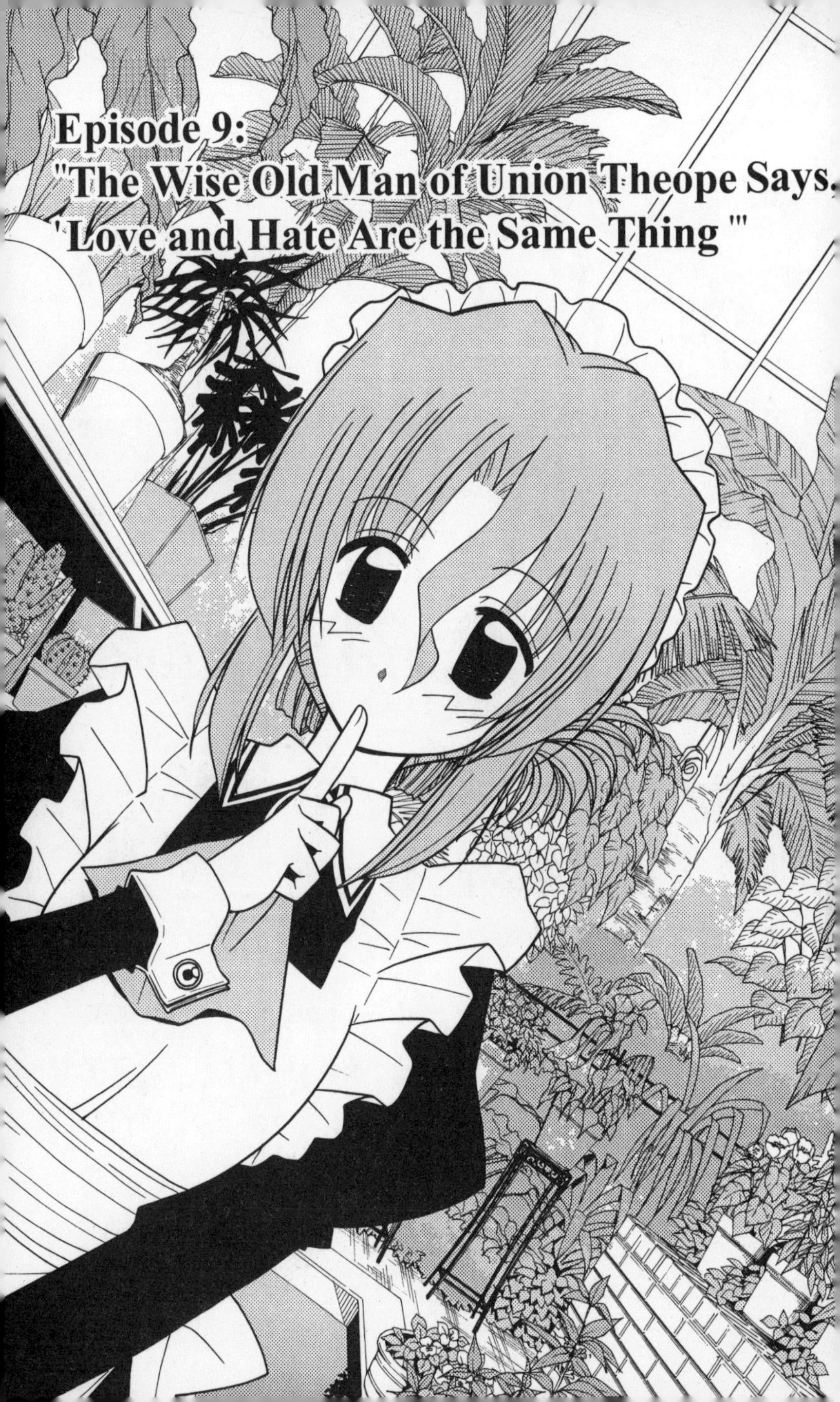
Episode 9:
"The Wise Old Man of Union Theope Says,
'Love and Hate Are the Same Thing'"

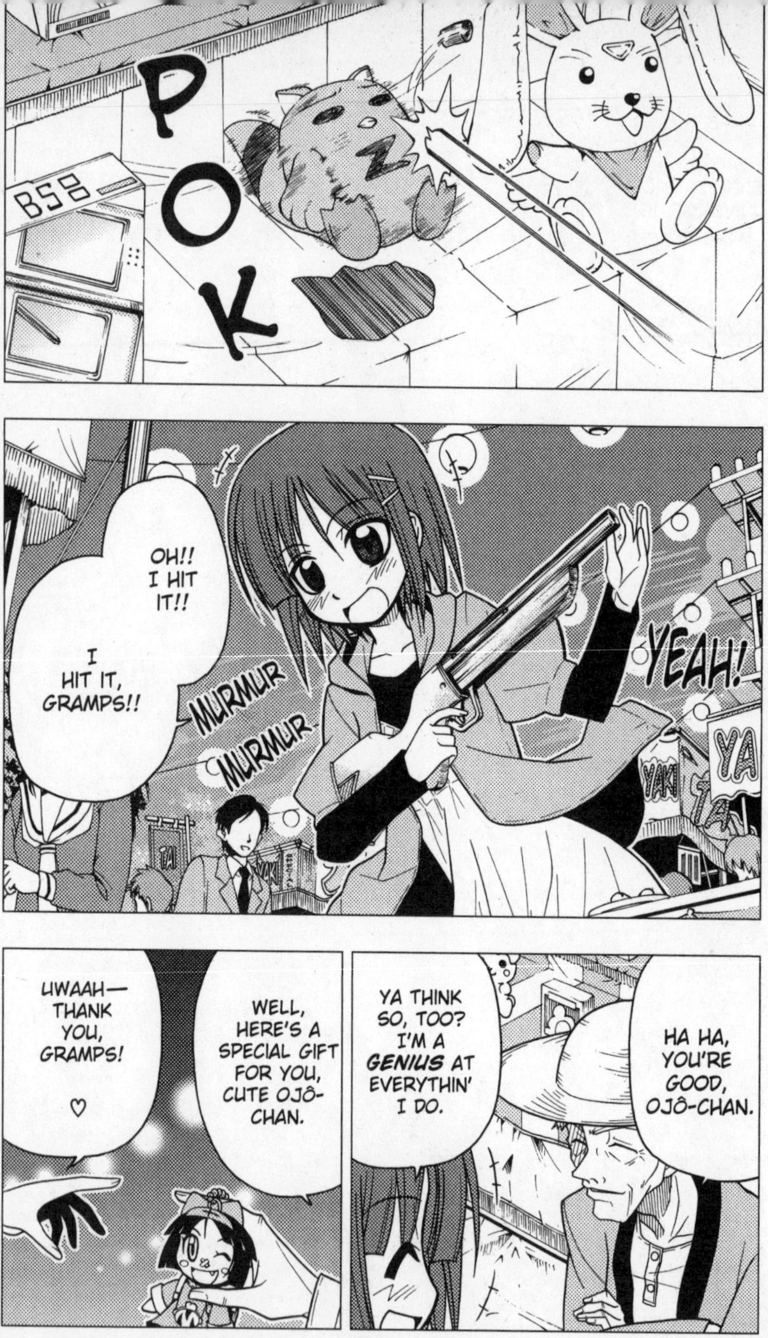
POK
YEAH!
OH!! I HIT IT!!
I HIT IT, GRAMPS!!
MURMUR
MURMUR
HA HA, YOU'RE GOOD, OJÔ-CHAN.
YA THINK SO, TOO? I'M A **GENIUS** AT EVERYTHIN' I DO.
WELL, HERE'S A SPECIAL GIFT FOR YOU, CUTE OJÔ-CHAN.
UWAAH— THANK YOU, GRAMPS!
♡

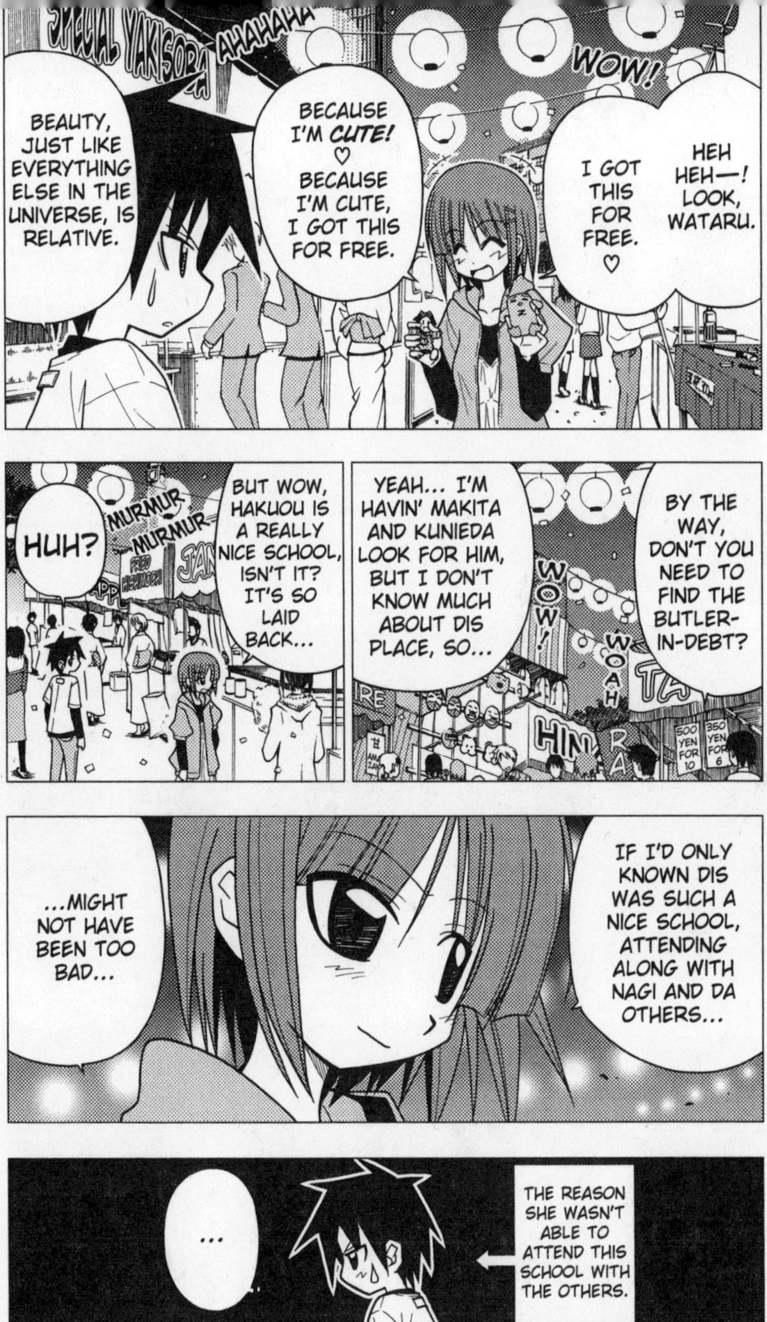
WOW!
HEH HEH—! LOOK, WATARU.
I GOT THIS FOR FREE. ♡
BECAUSE I'M ***CUTE!*** ♡ BECAUSE I'M CUTE, I GOT THIS FOR FREE.
AHAHAHA
SPECIAL YAKISOBA
BEAUTY, JUST LIKE EVERYTHING ELSE IN THE UNIVERSE, IS RELATIVE.
BY THE WAY, DON'T YOU NEED TO FIND THE BUTLER-IN-DEBT?
WOW!
WOAH
500 YEN FOR 10
350 YEN FOR 6
YEAH... I'M HAVIN' MAKITA AND KUNIEDA LOOK FOR HIM, BUT I DON'T KNOW MUCH ABOUT DIS PLACE, SO...
BUT WOW, HAKUOU IS A REALLY NICE SCHOOL, ISN'T IT? IT'S SO LAID BACK...
MURMUR
MURMUR
FRIED HISHIMOCHI
HUH?
IF I'D ONLY KNOWN DIS WAS SUCH A NICE SCHOOL, ATTENDING ALONG WITH NAGI AND DA OTHERS...
...MIGHT NOT HAVE BEEN TOO BAD...
THE REASON SHE WASN'T ABLE TO ATTEND THIS SCHOOL WITH THE OTHERS.
...

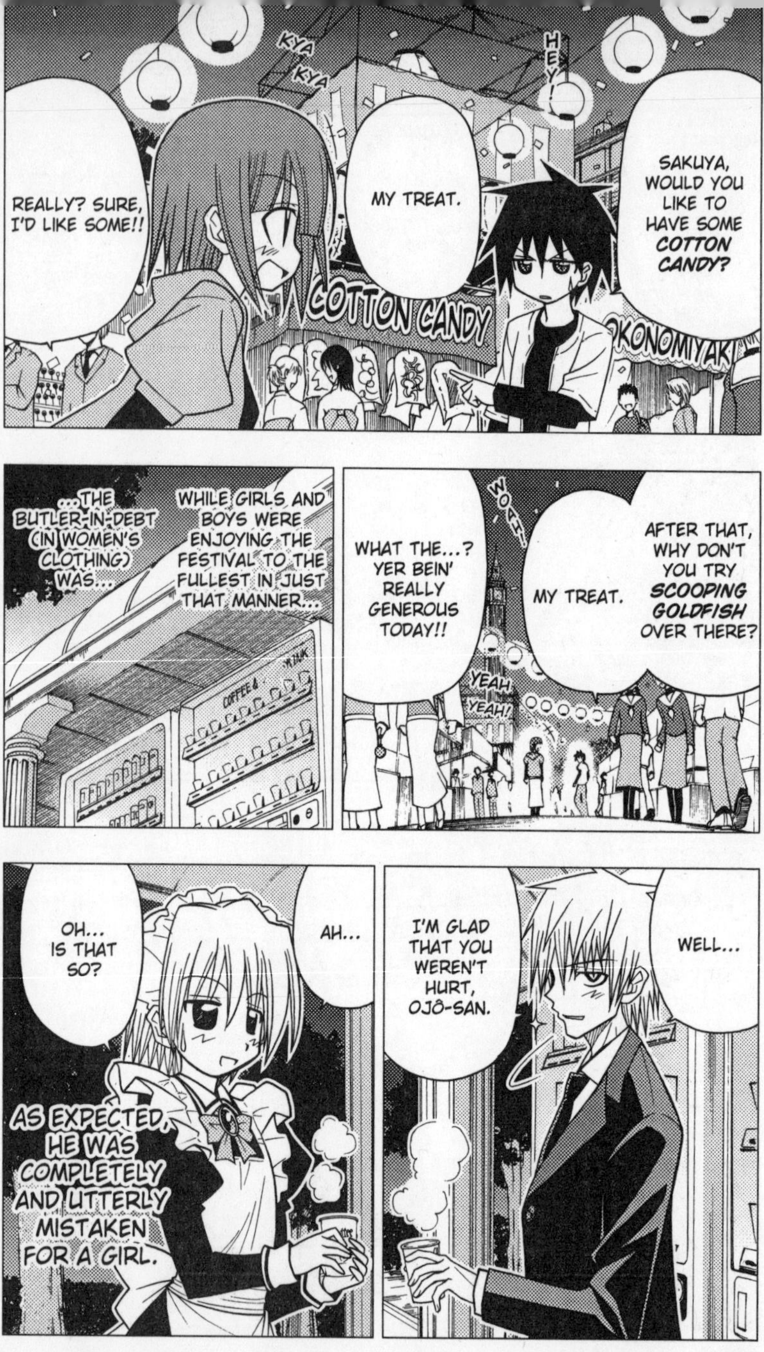
SAKUYA, WOULD YOU LIKE TO HAVE SOME ***COTTON CANDY?***
HEY!
KYA KYA
MY TREAT.
REALLY? SURE, I'D LIKE SOME!!
COTTON CANDY
OKONOMIYAK
AFTER THAT, WHY DON'T YOU TRY ***SCOOPING GOLDFISH*** OVER THERE?
MY TREAT.
WOAH
WHAT THE...? YER BEIN' REALLY GENEROUS TODAY!!
YEAH YEAH!
WHILE GIRLS AND BOYS WERE ENJOYING THE FESTIVAL TO THE FULLEST IN JUST THAT MANNER...
...THE BUTLER-IN-DEBT (IN WOMEN'S CLOTHING) WAS...
WELL...
I'M GLAD THAT YOU WEREN'T HURT, OJÔ-SAN.
AH...
OH... IS THAT SO?
AS EXPECTED, HE WAS COMPLETELY AND UTTERLY MISTAKEN FOR A GIRL.

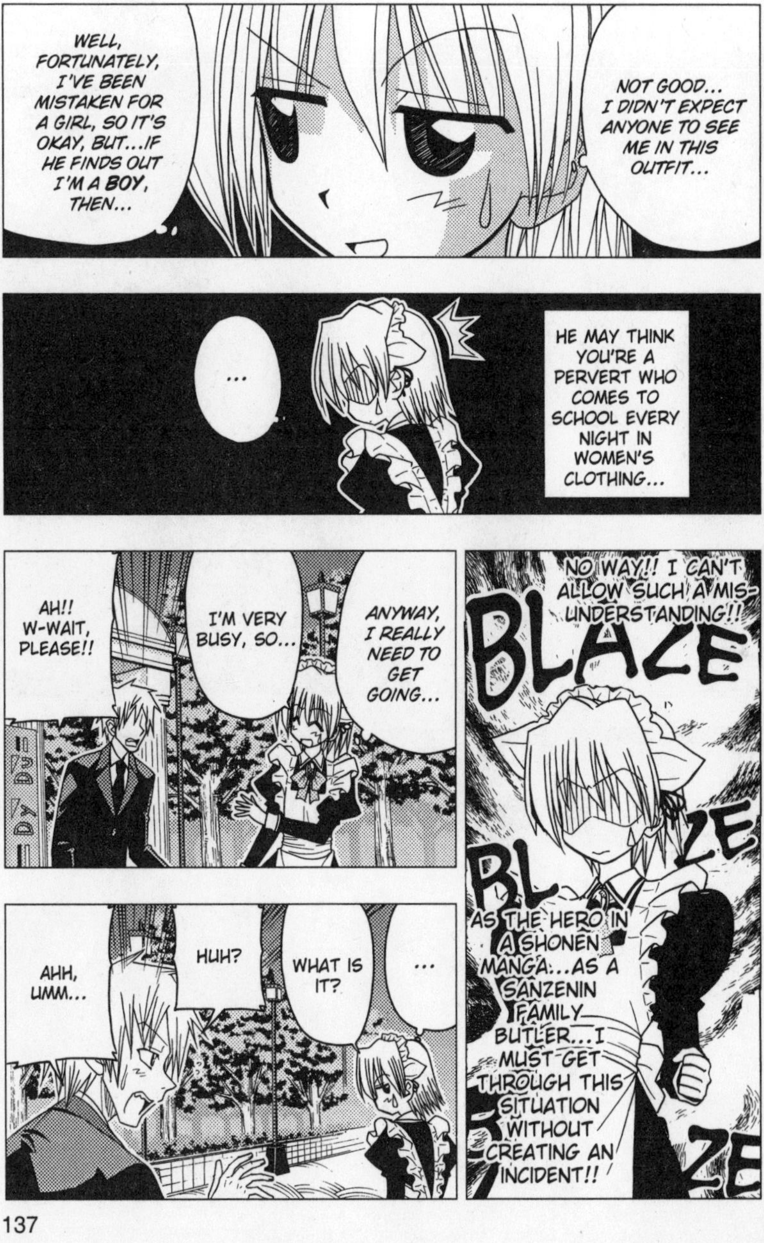
NOT GOOD... I DIDN'T EXPECT ANYONE TO SEE ME IN THIS OUTFIT...
WELL, FORTUNATELY, I'VE BEEN MISTAKEN FOR A GIRL, SO IT'S OKAY, BUT...IF HE FINDS OUT I'M A BOY, THEN...
HE MAY THINK YOU'RE A PERVERT WHO COMES TO SCHOOL EVERY NIGHT IN WOMEN'S CLOTHING...
...
NO WAY!! I CAN'T ALLOW SUCH A MIS-UNDERSTANDING!!
BLAZE
BL ZE
AS THE HERO IN A SHONEN MANGA...AS A SANZENIN FAMILY BUTLER...I MUST GET THROUGH THIS SITUATION WITHOUT CREATING AN INCIDENT!!
ZE
ANYWAY, I REALLY NEED TO GET GOING...
I'M VERY BUSY, SO...
AH!! W-WAIT, PLEASE!!
...
WHAT IS IT?
HUH?
AHH, UMM...

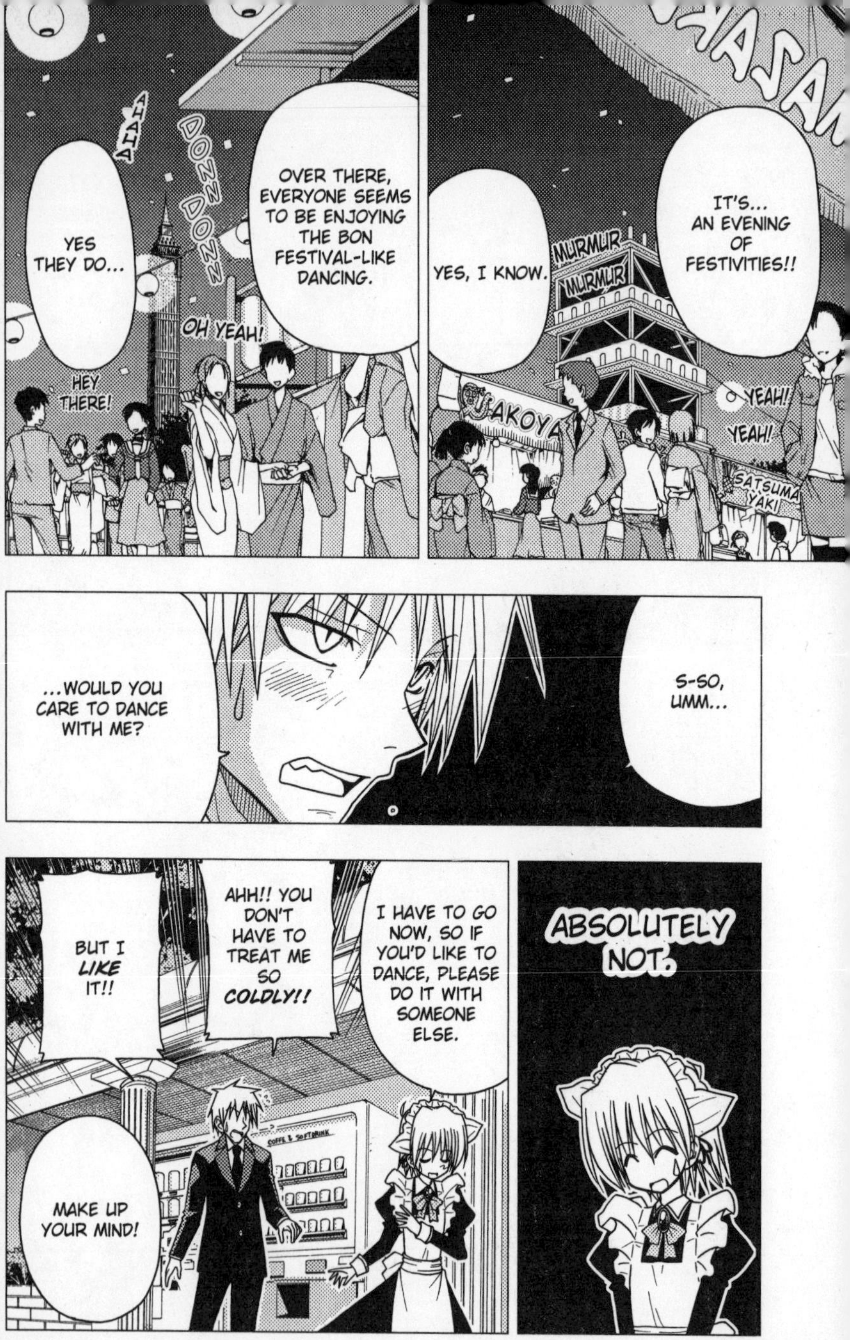
IT'S... AN EVENING OF FESTIVITIES!!
YES, I KNOW.
MURMUR
MURMUR
YEAH!
YEAH!
SATSUMA YAKI
OVER THERE, EVERYONE SEEMS TO BE ENJOYING THE BON FESTIVAL-LIKE DANCING.
YES THEY DO...
DONN DONN DONN
AHAHA
OH YEAH!
HEY THERE!
S-SO, UMM...
...WOULD YOU CARE TO DANCE WITH ME?
ABSOLUTELY NOT.
I HAVE TO GO NOW, SO IF YOU'D LIKE TO DANCE, PLEASE DO IT WITH SOMEONE ELSE.
AHH!! YOU DON'T HAVE TO TREAT ME SO *COLDLY!!*
BUT I *LIKE* IT!!
MAKE UP YOUR MIND!

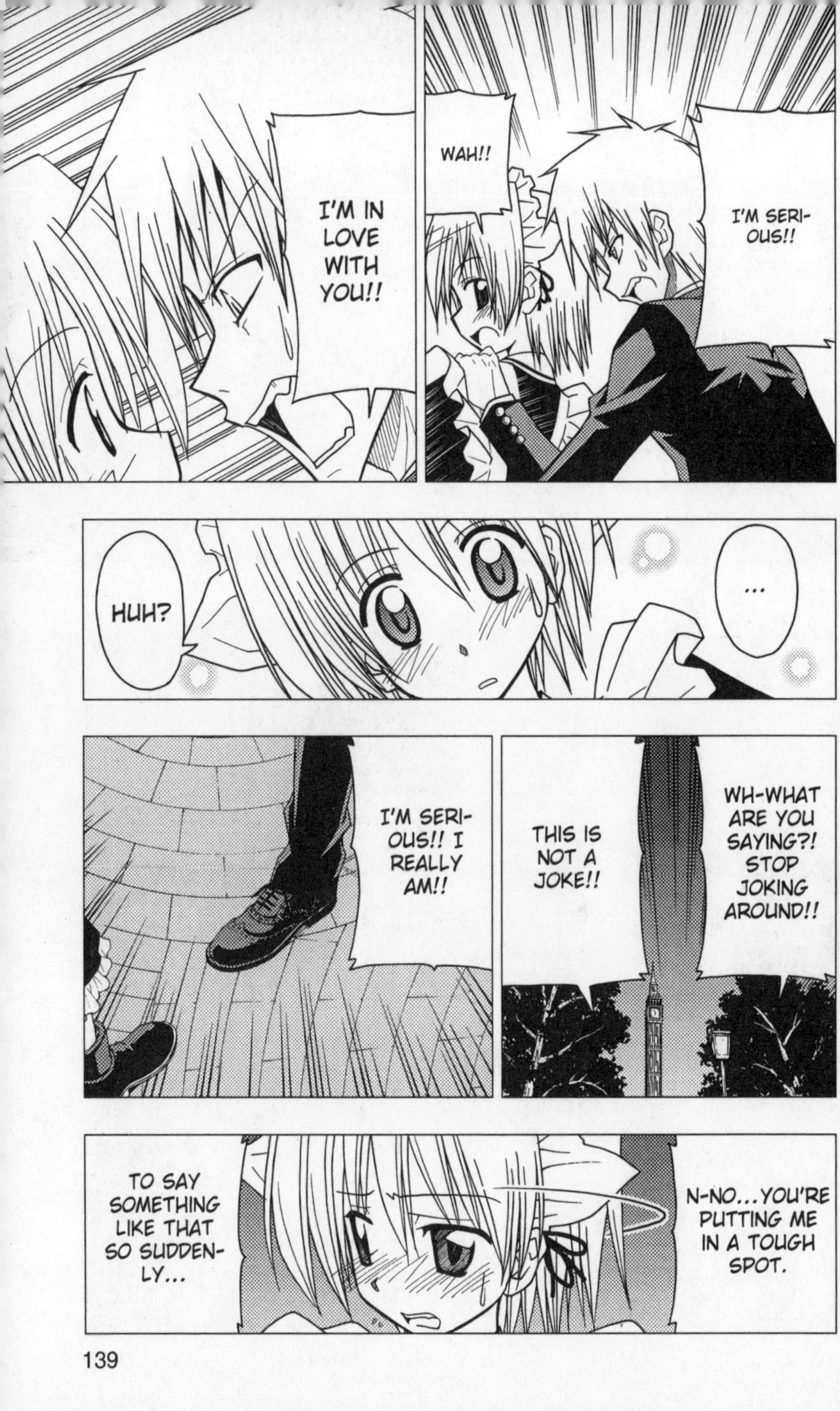
I'M SERIOUS!!
WAH!!
I'M IN LOVE WITH YOU!!
...
HUH?
WH-WHAT ARE YOU SAYING?! STOP JOKING AROUND!!
THIS IS NOT A JOKE!!
I'M SERIOUS!! I REALLY AM!!
N-NO...YOU'RE PUTTING ME IN A TOUGH SPOT.
TO SAY SOMETHING LIKE THAT SO SUDDENLY...

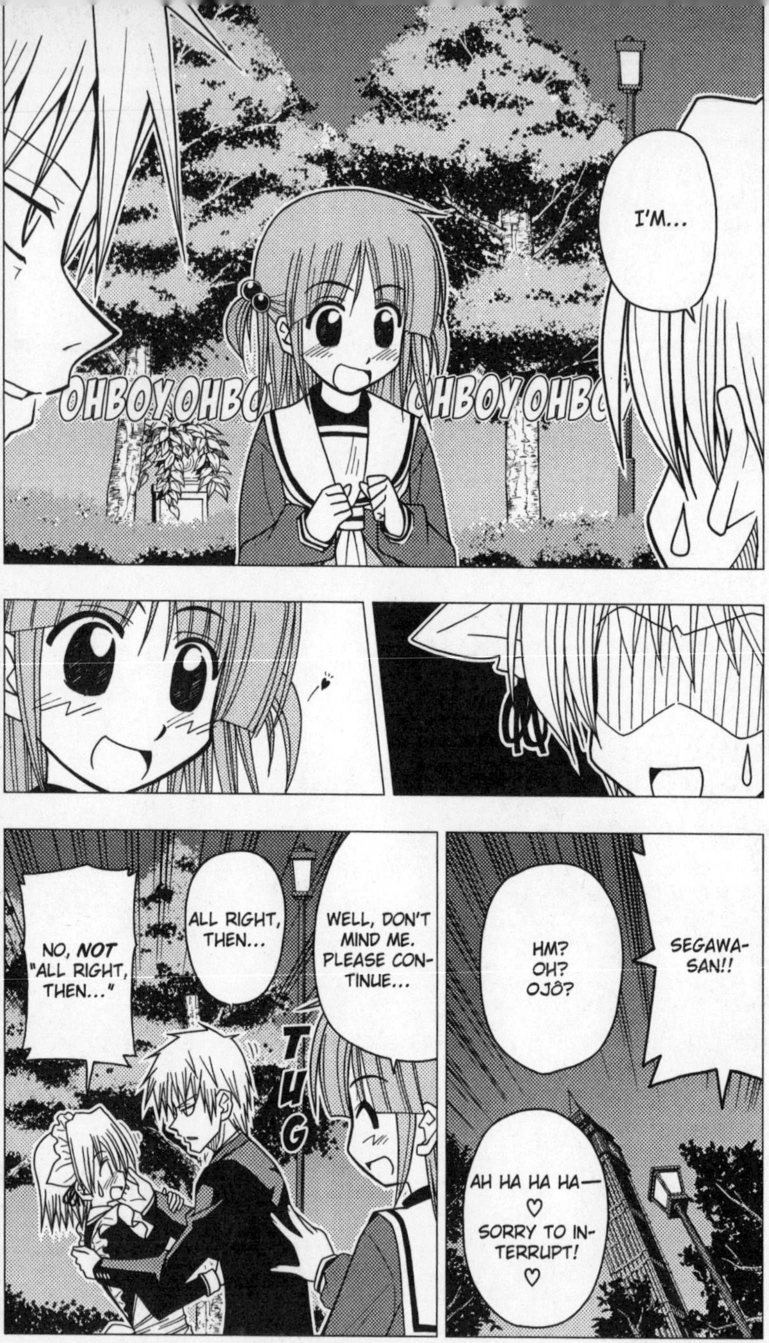
I'M...
OHBOYOHBO
OHBOYOHBO
SEGAWA-SAN!!
HM? OH? OJÔ?
AH HA HA HA— ♡ SORRY TO INTERRUPT! ♡
WELL, DON'T MIND ME. PLEASE CONTINUE...
ALL RIGHT, THEN...
NO, NOT "ALL RIGHT, THEN..."
TUG

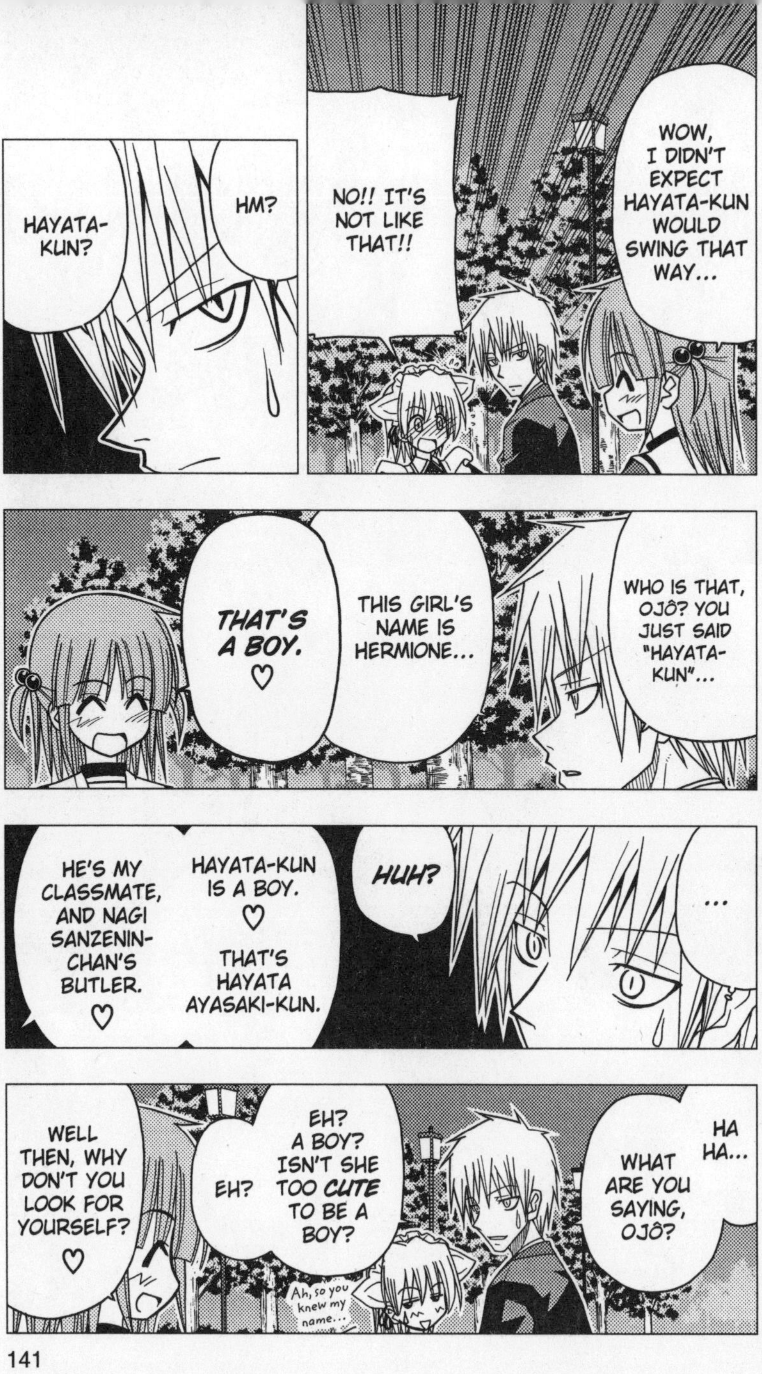

WOW, I DIDN'T EXPECT HAYATA-KUN WOULD SWING THAT WAY...
NO!! IT'S NOT LIKE THAT!!
HM?
HAYATA-KUN?
WHO IS THAT, OJÔ? YOU JUST SAID "HAYATA-KUN"...
THIS GIRL'S NAME IS HERMIONE...
THAT'S A BOY. ♡
...
HUH?
HAYATA-KUN IS A BOY. ♡
THAT'S HAYATA AYASAKI-KUN.
HE'S MY CLASSMATE, AND NAGI SANZENIN-CHAN'S BUTLER. ♡
HA HA...
WHAT ARE YOU SAYING, OJÔ?
EH? A BOY? ISN'T SHE TOO CUTE TO BE A BOY?
EH?
Ah, so you knew my name...
WELL THEN, WHY DON'T YOU LOOK FOR YOURSELF? ♡

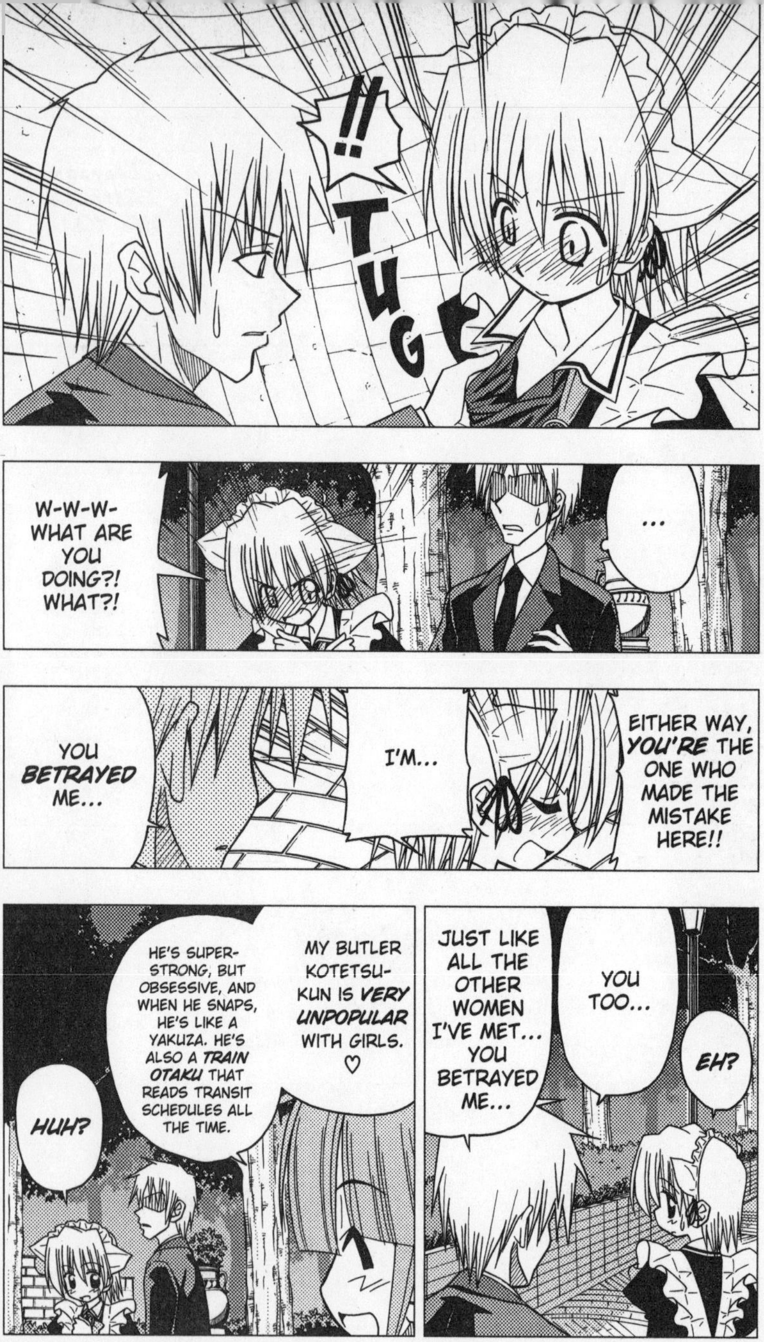

!!
TUG
...
W-W-W-WHAT ARE YOU DOING?! WHAT?!
EITHER WAY, *YOU'RE* THE ONE WHO MADE THE MISTAKE HERE!!
I'M...
YOU **BETRAYED** ME...
YOU TOO...
JUST LIKE ALL THE OTHER WOMEN I'VE MET... YOU BETRAYED ME...
EH?
MY BUTLER KOTETSU-KUN IS ***VERY UNPOPULAR*** WITH GIRLS. ♡
HE'S SUPER-STRONG, BUT OBSESSIVE, AND WHEN HE SNAPS, HE'S LIKE A YAKUZA. HE'S ALSO A ***TRAIN OTAKU*** THAT READS TRANSIT SCHEDULES ALL THE TIME.
HUH?

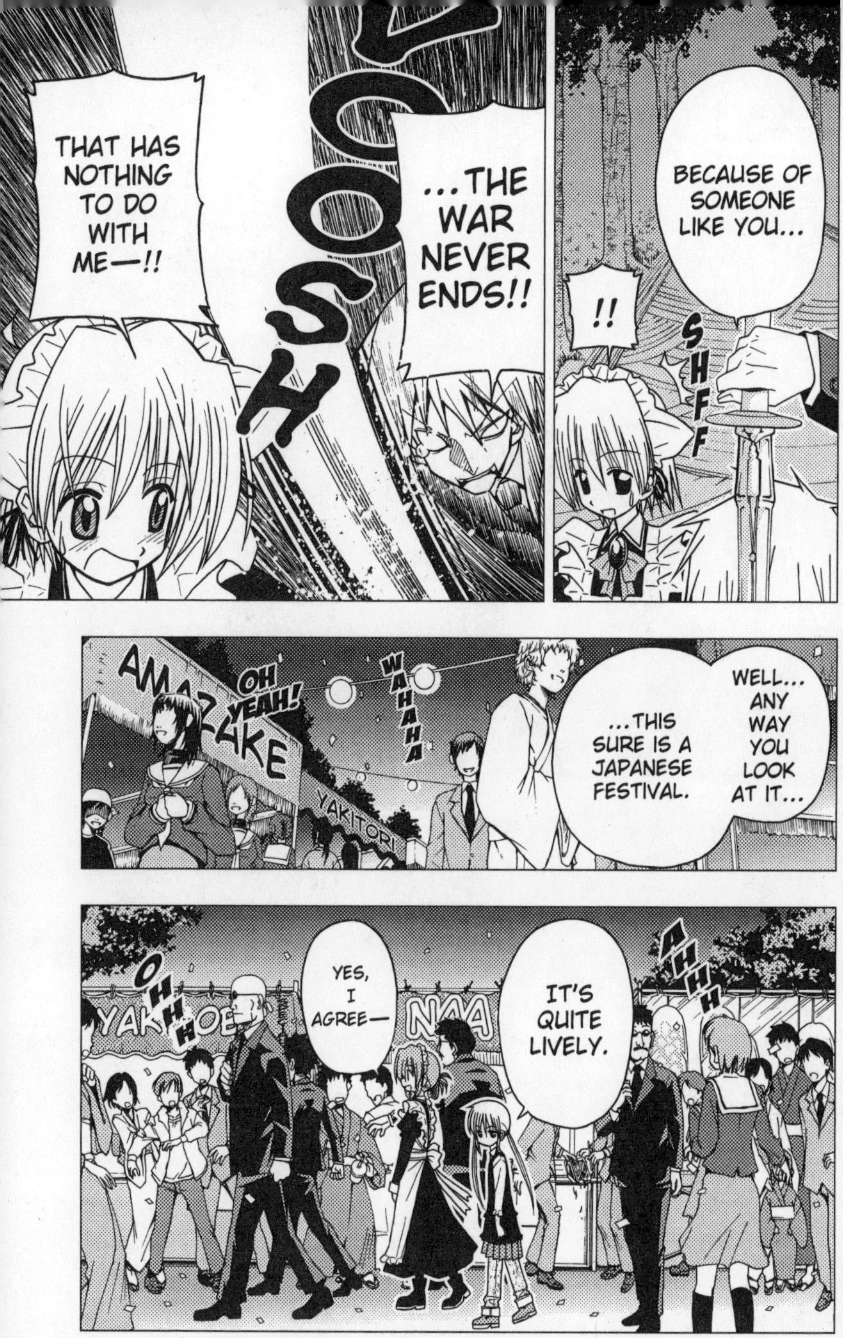

BECAUSE OF SOMEONE LIKE YOU...
!!
SHFF
...THE WAR NEVER ENDS!!
THAT HAS NOTHING TO DO WITH ME—!!
WELL... ANY WAY YOU LOOK AT IT...
...THIS SURE IS A JAPANESE FESTIVAL.
WAHAHA
OH YEAH!
YAKITORI
AHHH
IT'S QUITE LIVELY.
YES, I AGREE—
OHHHH

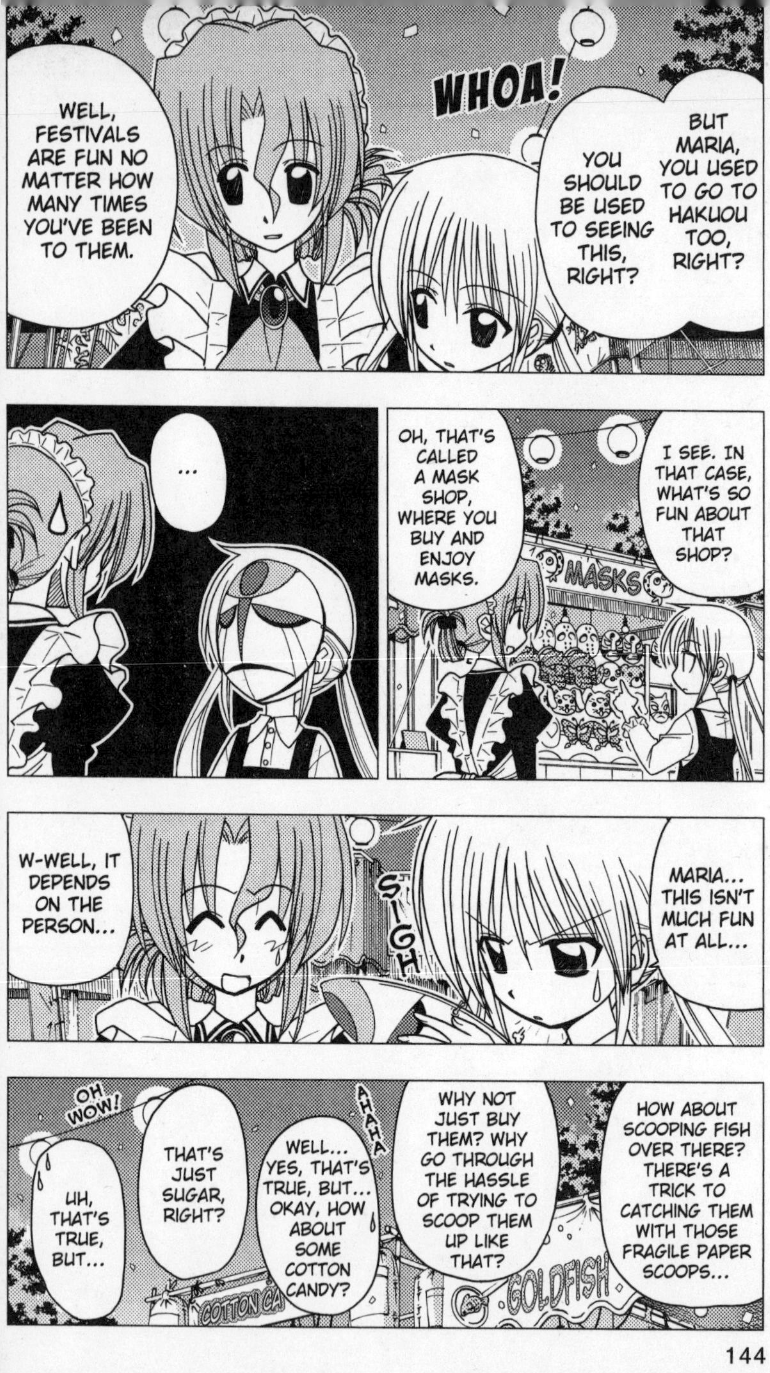

BUT MARIA, YOU USED TO GO TO HAKUOU TOO, RIGHT?
YOU SHOULD BE USED TO SEEING THIS, RIGHT?
WHOA!
WELL, FESTIVALS ARE FUN NO MATTER HOW MANY TIMES YOU'VE BEEN TO THEM.
I SEE. IN THAT CASE, WHAT'S SO FUN ABOUT THAT SHOP?
OH, THAT'S CALLED A MASK SHOP, WHERE YOU BUY AND ENJOY MASKS.
MASKS
...
MARIA... THIS ISN'T MUCH FUN AT ALL...
SIGH
W-WELL, IT DEPENDS ON THE PERSON...
HOW ABOUT SCOOPING FISH OVER THERE? THERE'S A TRICK TO CATCHING THEM WITH THOSE FRAGILE PAPER SCOOPS...
GOLDFISH
WHY NOT JUST BUY THEM? WHY GO THROUGH THE HASSLE OF TRYING TO SCOOP THEM UP LIKE THAT?
AHAHA
WELL... YES, THAT'S TRUE, BUT... OKAY, HOW ABOUT SOME COTTON CANDY?
THAT'S JUST SUGAR, RIGHT?
OH WOW!
UH, THAT'S TRUE, BUT...
COTTON CA

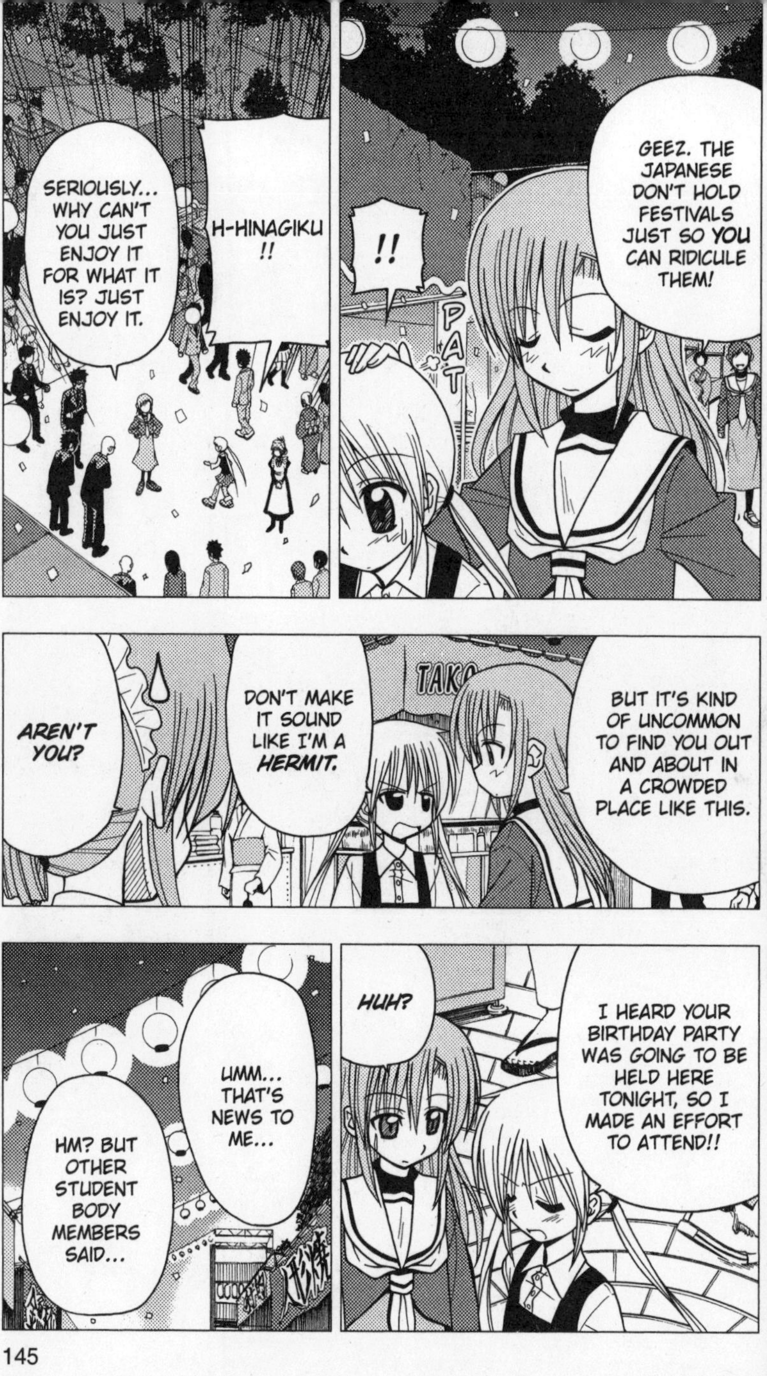
GEEZ. THE JAPANESE DON'T HOLD FESTIVALS JUST SO *YOU* CAN RIDICULE THEM!
!!
PAT
H-HINAGIKU !!
SERIOUSLY... WHY CAN'T YOU JUST ENJOY IT FOR WHAT IT IS? JUST ENJOY IT.
BUT IT'S KIND OF UNCOMMON TO FIND YOU OUT AND ABOUT IN A CROWDED PLACE LIKE THIS.
TAKO
DON'T MAKE IT SOUND LIKE I'M A *HERMIT.*
AREN'T YOU?
I HEARD YOUR BIRTHDAY PARTY WAS GOING TO BE HELD HERE TONIGHT, SO I MADE AN EFFORT TO ATTEND!!
HUH?
UMM... THAT'S NEWS TO ME...
HM? BUT OTHER STUDENT BODY MEMBERS SAID...

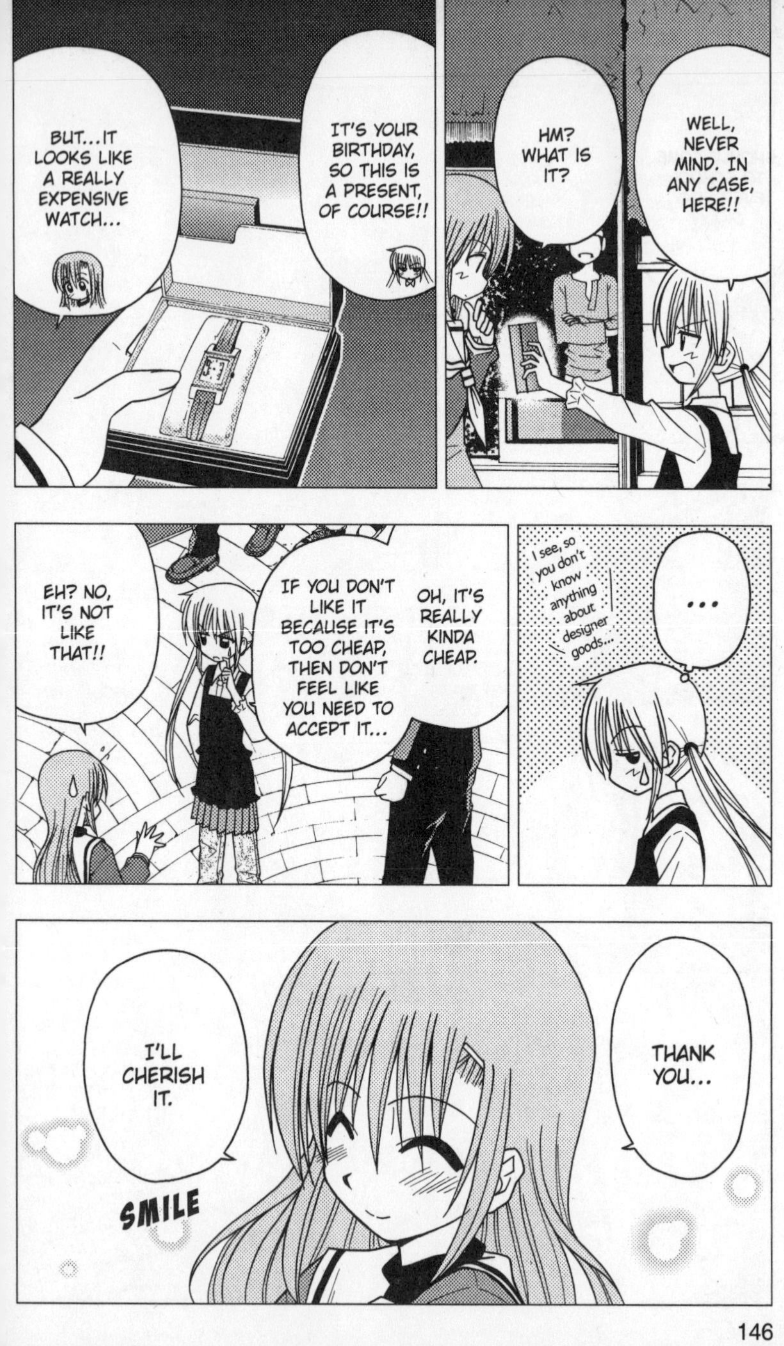
WELL, NEVER MIND. IN ANY CASE, HERE!!
HM? WHAT IS IT?
IT'S YOUR BIRTHDAY, SO THIS IS A PRESENT, OF COURSE!!
BUT...IT LOOKS LIKE A REALLY EXPENSIVE WATCH...
...
I see, so you don't know anything about designer goods...
OH, IT'S REALLY KINDA CHEAP.
IF YOU DON'T LIKE IT BECAUSE IT'S TOO CHEAP, THEN DON'T FEEL LIKE YOU NEED TO ACCEPT IT...
EH? NO, IT'S NOT LIKE THAT!!
THANK YOU...
I'LL CHERISH IT.
SMILE

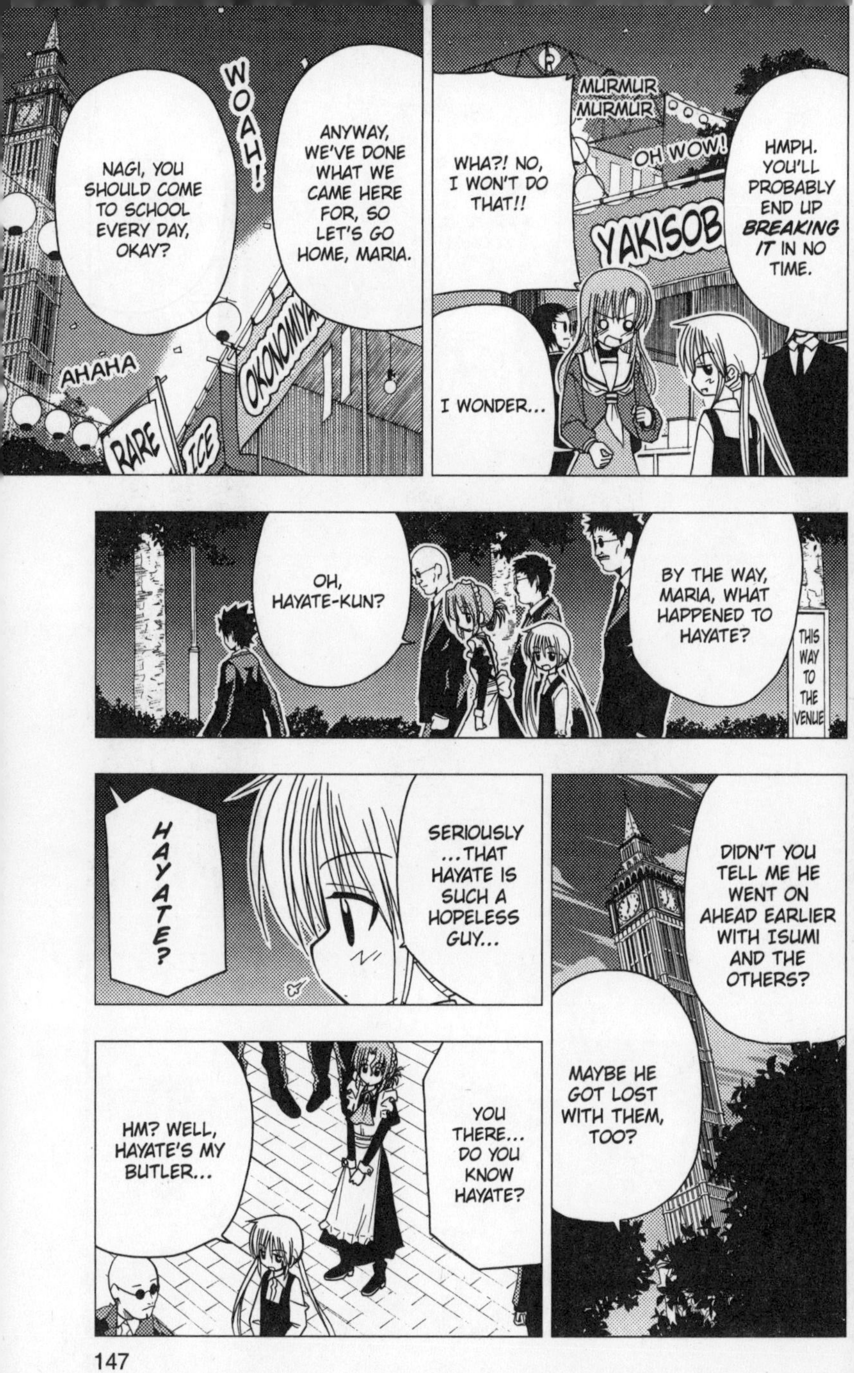
HMPH. YOU'LL PROBABLY END UP *BREAKING IT* IN NO TIME.
OH WOW!
MURMUR MURMUR
YAKISOB
WHA?! NO, I WON'T DO THAT!!
I WONDER...
ANYWAY, WE'VE DONE WHAT WE CAME HERE FOR, SO LET'S GO HOME, MARIA.
WOAH!
NAGI, YOU SHOULD COME TO SCHOOL EVERY DAY, OKAY?
OKONOMIYA
AHAHA
RARE
ICE
THIS WAY TO THE VENUE
BY THE WAY, MARIA, WHAT HAPPENED TO HAYATE?
OH, HAYATE-KUN?
DIDN'T YOU TELL ME HE WENT ON AHEAD EARLIER WITH ISUMI AND THE OTHERS?
MAYBE HE GOT LOST WITH THEM, TOO?
SERIOUSLY ...THAT HAYATE IS SUCH A HOPELESS GUY...
HAYATE?
YOU THERE... DO YOU KNOW HAYATE?
HM? WELL, HAYATE'S MY BUTLER...

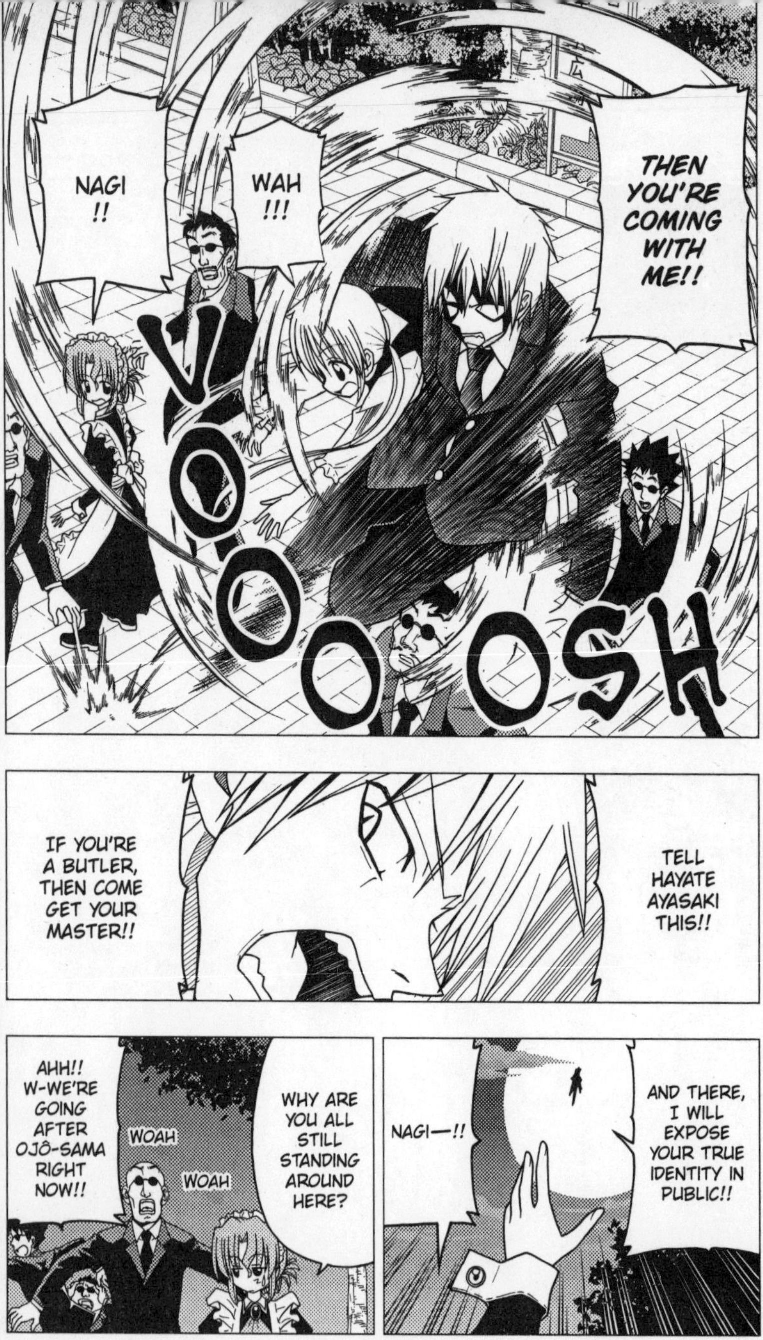
THEN YOU'RE COMING WITH ME!!
WAH !!!
NAGI !!
VOOOOSH
TELL HAYATE AYASAKI THIS!!
IF YOU'RE A BUTLER, THEN COME GET YOUR MASTER!!
AND THERE, I WILL EXPOSE YOUR TRUE IDENTITY IN PUBLIC!!
NAGI—!!
WHY ARE YOU ALL STILL STANDING AROUND HERE?
WOAH
WOAH
AHH!! W-WE'RE GOING AFTER OJÔ-SAMA RIGHT NOW!!

Episode 10:
"A Cruel, Foolish Man's Thesis"

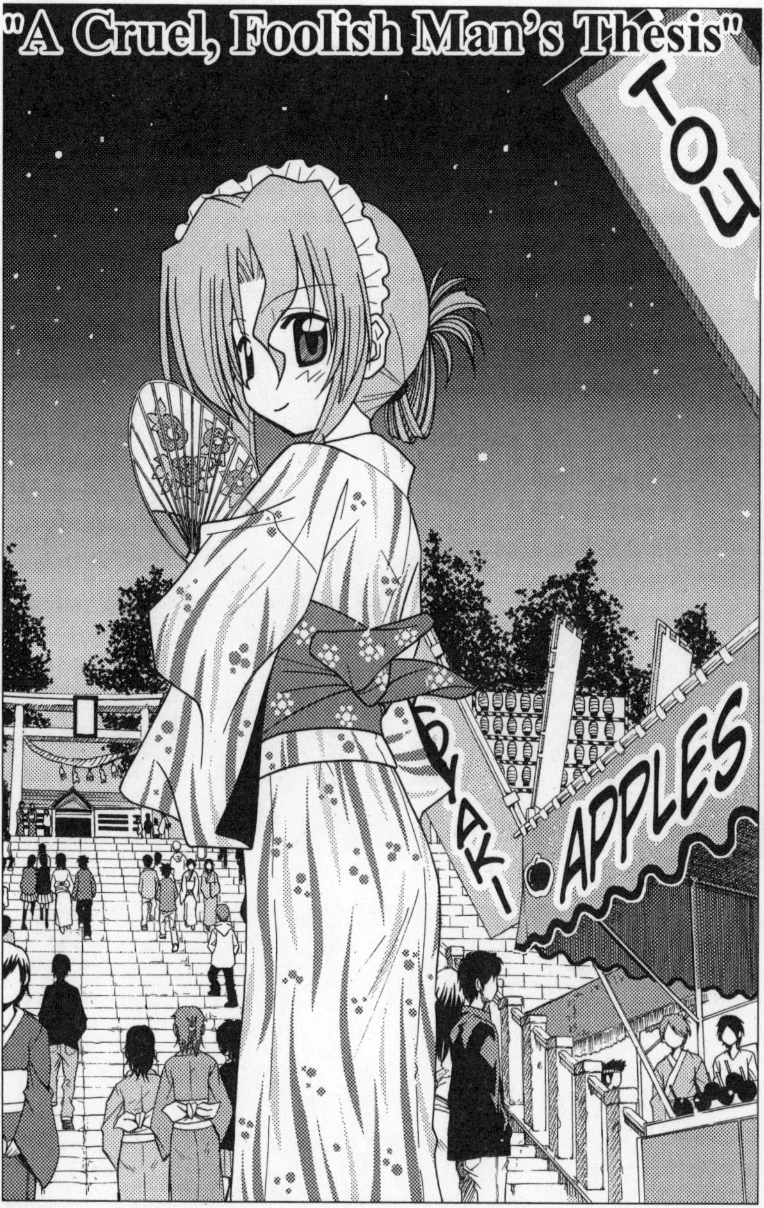
TOU
APPLES

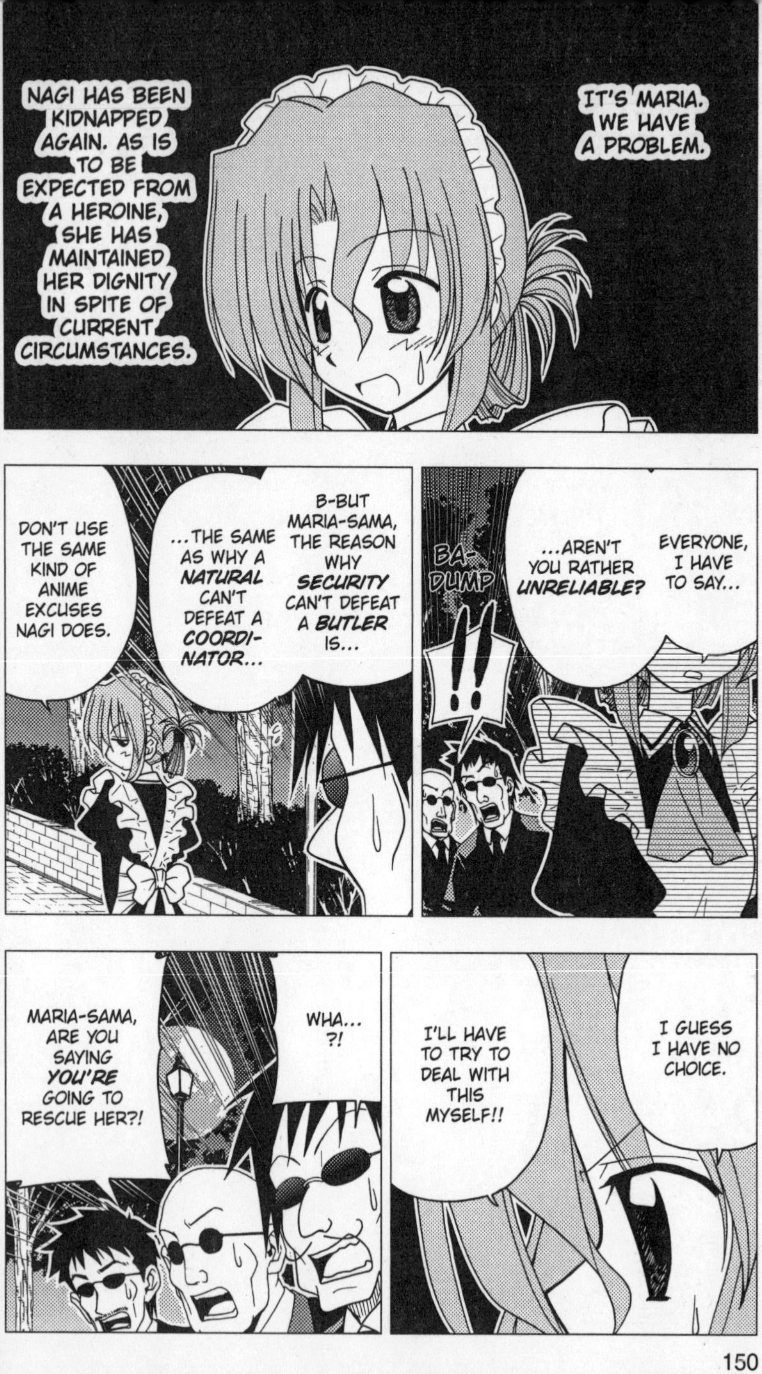
IT'S MARIA. WE HAVE A PROBLEM.
NAGI HAS BEEN KIDNAPPED AGAIN. AS IS TO BE EXPECTED FROM A HEROINE, SHE HAS MAINTAINED HER DIGNITY IN SPITE OF CURRENT CIRCUMSTANCES.
EVERYONE, I HAVE TO SAY...
...AREN'T YOU RATHER *UNRELIABLE?*
BA-DUMP
!!
B-BUT MARIA-SAMA, THE REASON WHY *SECURITY* CAN'T DEFEAT A *BUTLER* IS...
...THE SAME AS WHY A *NATURAL* CAN'T DEFEAT A *COORDINATOR*...
DON'T USE THE SAME KIND OF ANIME EXCUSES NAGI DOES.
I GUESS I HAVE NO CHOICE.
I'LL HAVE TO TRY TO DEAL WITH THIS MYSELF!!
WHA... ?!
MARIA-SAMA, ARE YOU SAYING *YOU'RE* GOING TO RESCUE HER?!

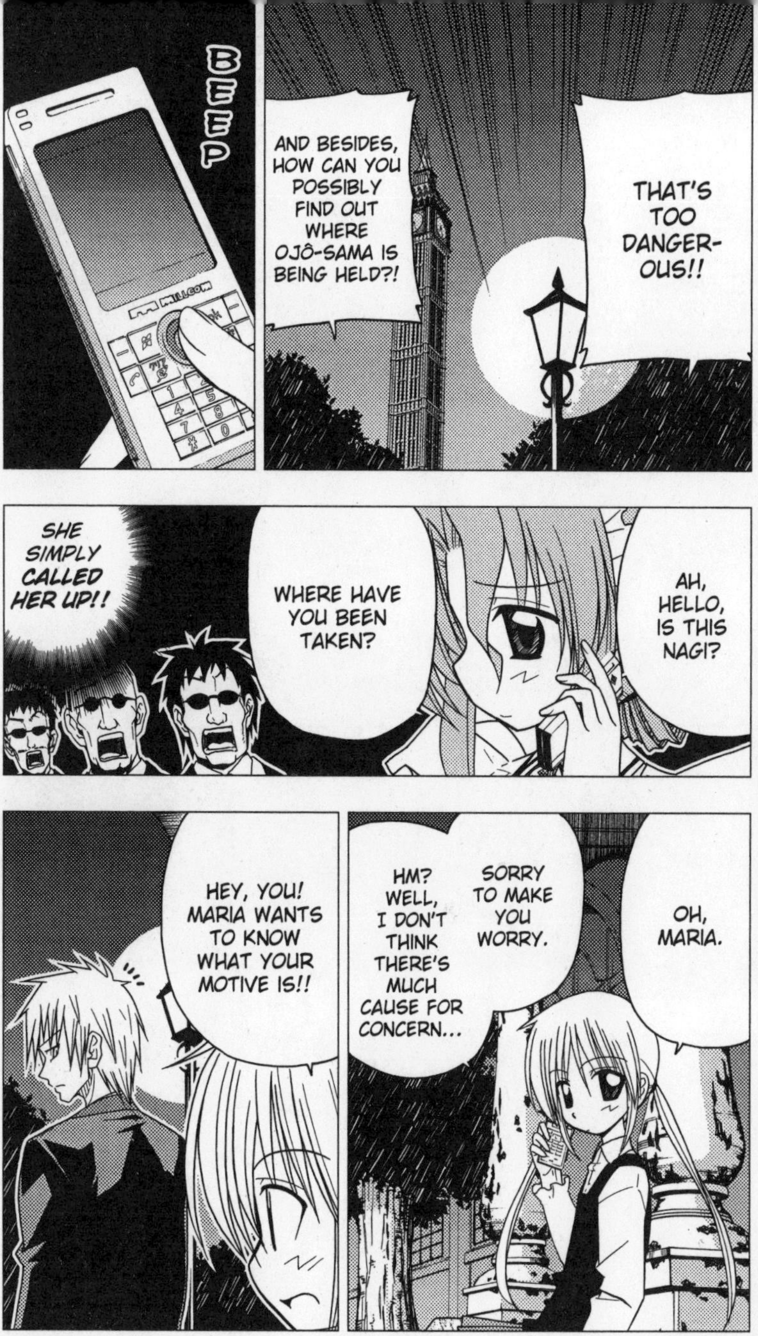
THAT'S TOO DANGER-OUS!!
AND BESIDES, HOW CAN YOU POSSIBLY FIND OUT WHERE OJÔ-SAMA IS BEING HELD?!
BEEP
AH, HELLO, IS THIS NAGI?
WHERE HAVE YOU BEEN TAKEN?
SHE SIMPLY CALLED HER UP!!
OH, MARIA.
SORRY TO MAKE YOU WORRY.
HM? WELL, I DON'T THINK THERE'S MUCH CAUSE FOR CONCERN...
HEY, YOU! MARIA WANTS TO KNOW WHAT YOUR MOTIVE IS!!

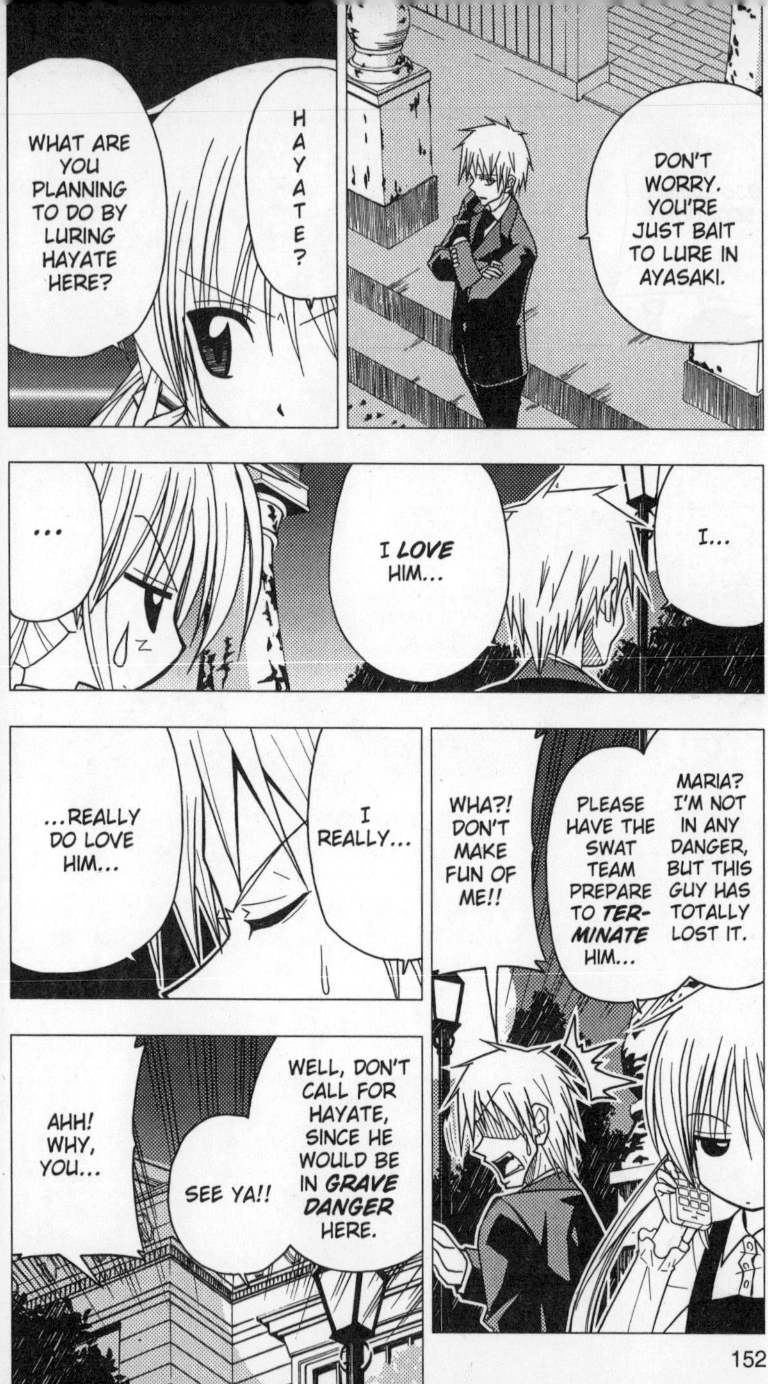

DON'T WORRY. YOU'RE JUST BAIT TO LURE IN AYASAKI.
HAYATE?
WHAT ARE YOU PLANNING TO DO BY LURING HAYATE HERE?
I...
I *LOVE* HIM...
...
MARIA? I'M NOT IN ANY DANGER, BUT THIS GUY HAS TOTALLY LOST IT.
PLEASE HAVE THE SWAT TEAM PREPARE TO *TERMINATE* HIM...
WHA?! DON'T MAKE FUN OF ME!!
I REALLY...
...REALLY DO LOVE HIM...
WELL, DON'T CALL FOR HAYATE, SINCE HE WOULD BE IN *GRAVE DANGER* HERE.
SEE YA!!
AHH! WHY, YOU...

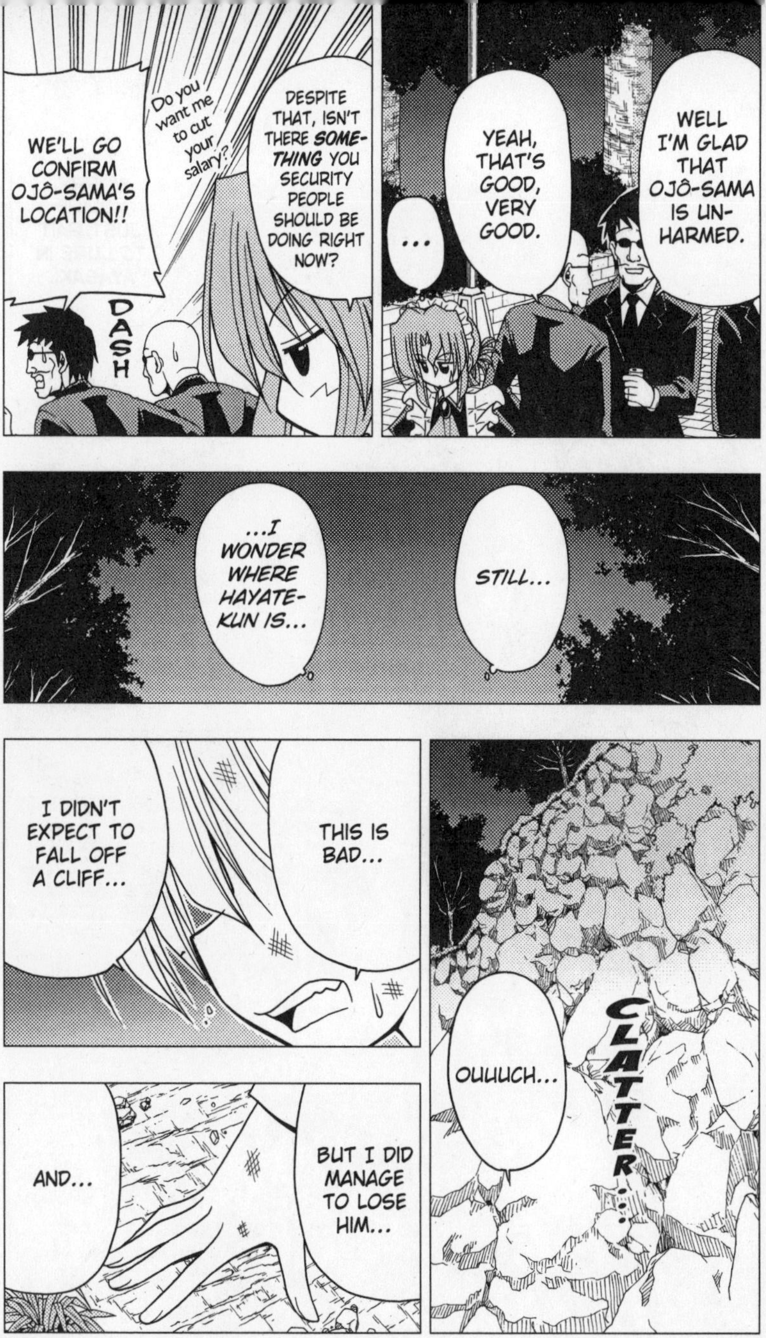
WELL I'M GLAD THAT OJÔ-SAMA IS UN-HARMED.
YEAH, THAT'S GOOD, VERY GOOD.
...
DESPITE THAT, ISN'T THERE SOMETHING YOU SECURITY PEOPLE SHOULD BE DOING RIGHT NOW?
Do you want me to cut your salary?
WE'LL GO CONFIRM OJÔ-SAMA'S LOCATION!!
DASH
STILL...
...I WONDER WHERE HAYATE-KUN IS...
OUUUCH...
CLATTER...
THIS IS BAD...
I DIDN'T EXPECT TO FALL OFF A CLIFF...
BUT I DID MANAGE TO LOSE HIM...
AND...

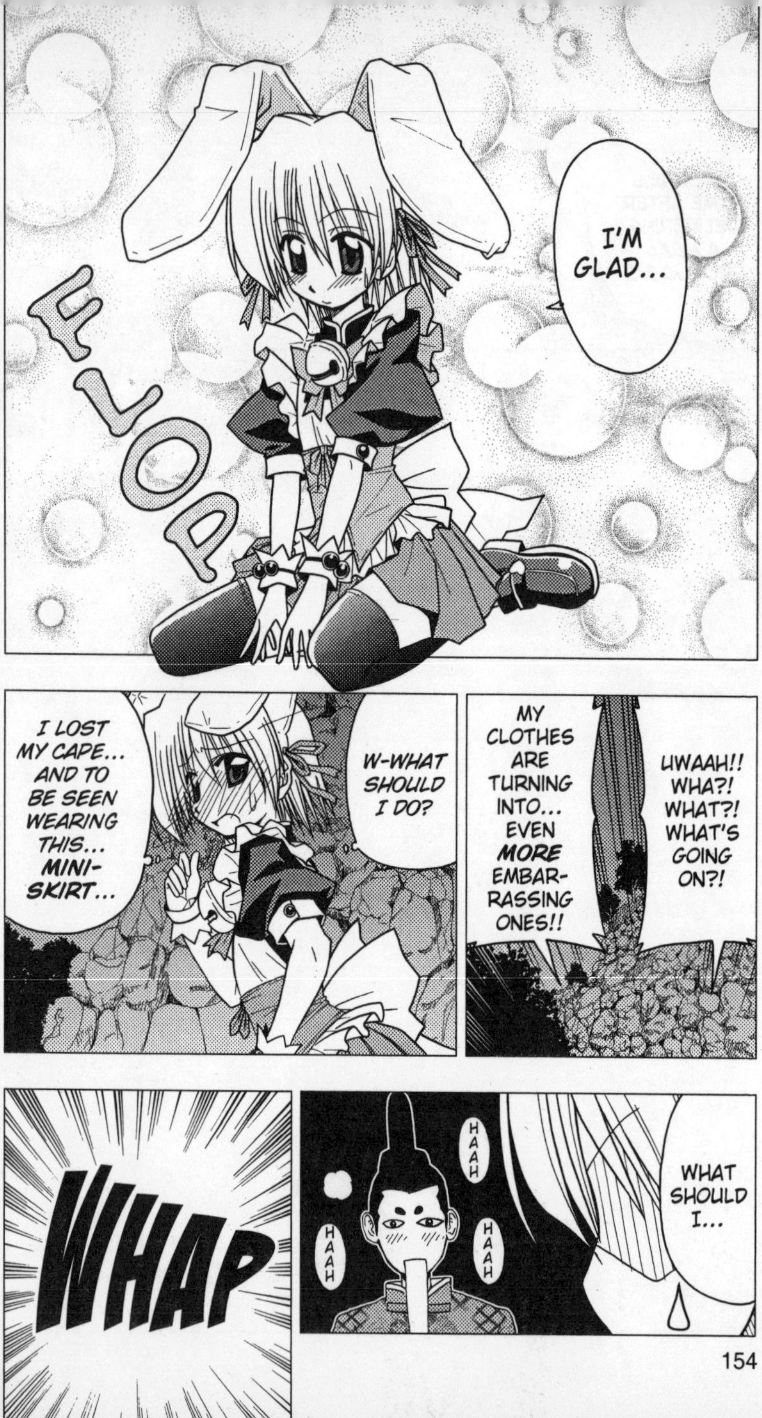
I'M GLAD...
FLOP
UWAAH!! WHA?! WHAT?! WHAT'S GOING ON?!
MY CLOTHES ARE TURNING INTO... EVEN MORE EMBARRASSING ONES!!
W-WHAT SHOULD I DO?
I LOST MY CAPE... AND TO BE SEEN WEARING THIS... MINI-SKIRT...
WHAT SHOULD I...
HAAH
HAAH
HAAH
WHAP

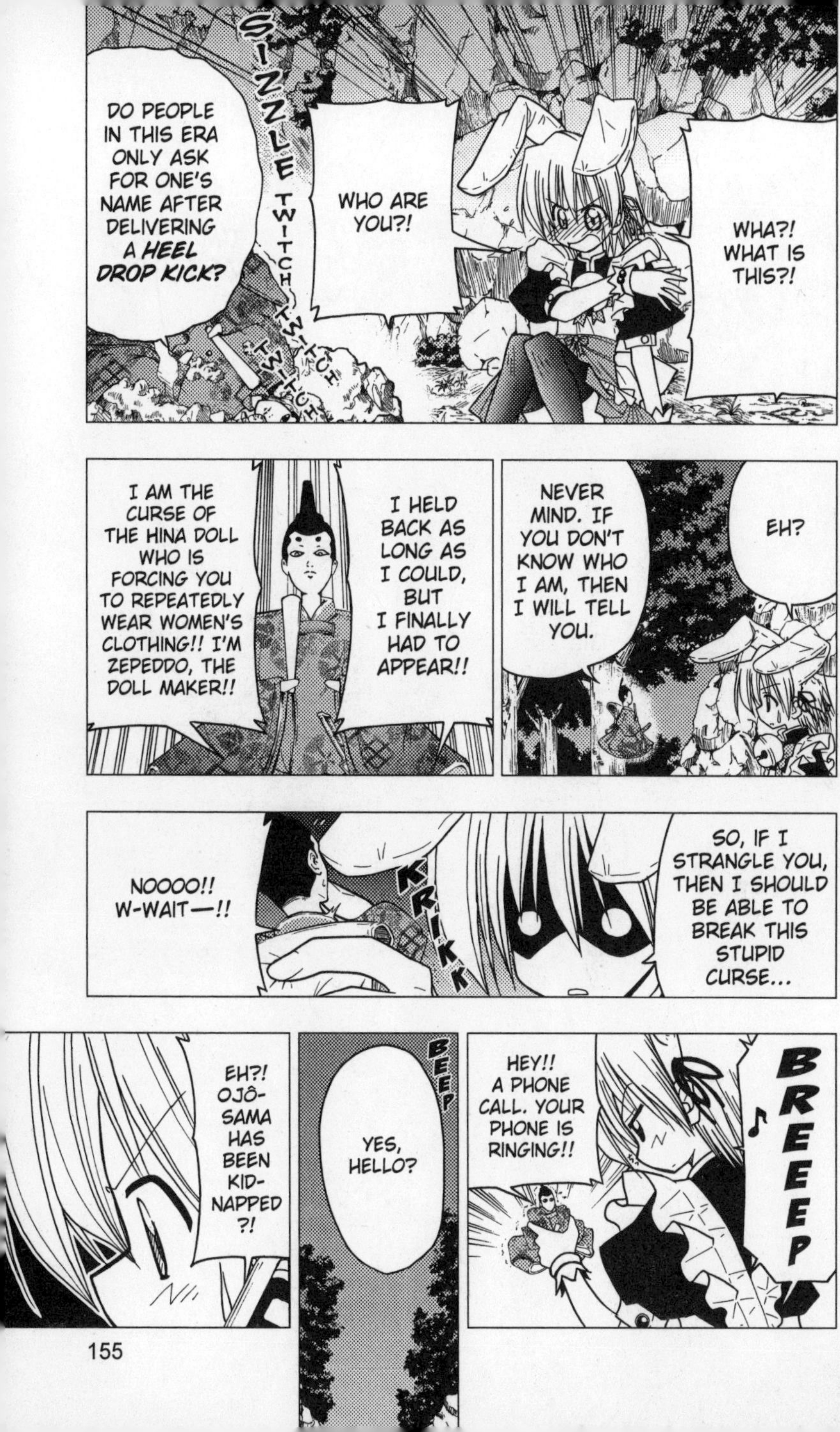
WHA?! WHAT IS THIS?!
WHO ARE YOU?!
SIZZLE
TWITCH TWITCH TWITCH
DO PEOPLE IN THIS ERA ONLY ASK FOR ONE'S NAME AFTER DELIVERING A HEEL DROP KICK?
EH?
NEVER MIND. IF YOU DON'T KNOW WHO I AM, THEN I WILL TELL YOU.
I HELD BACK AS LONG AS I COULD, BUT I FINALLY HAD TO APPEAR!!
I AM THE CURSE OF THE HINA DOLL WHO IS FORCING YOU TO REPEATEDLY WEAR WOMEN'S CLOTHING!! I'M ZEPEDDO, THE DOLL MAKER!!
SO, IF I STRANGLE YOU, THEN I SHOULD BE ABLE TO BREAK THIS STUPID CURSE...
KRIKK
NOOOO!! W-WAIT—!!
BREEEP
HEY!! A PHONE CALL. YOUR PHONE IS RINGING!!
BEEP
YES, HELLO?
EH?! OJÔ-SAMA HAS BEEN KID-NAPPED?!

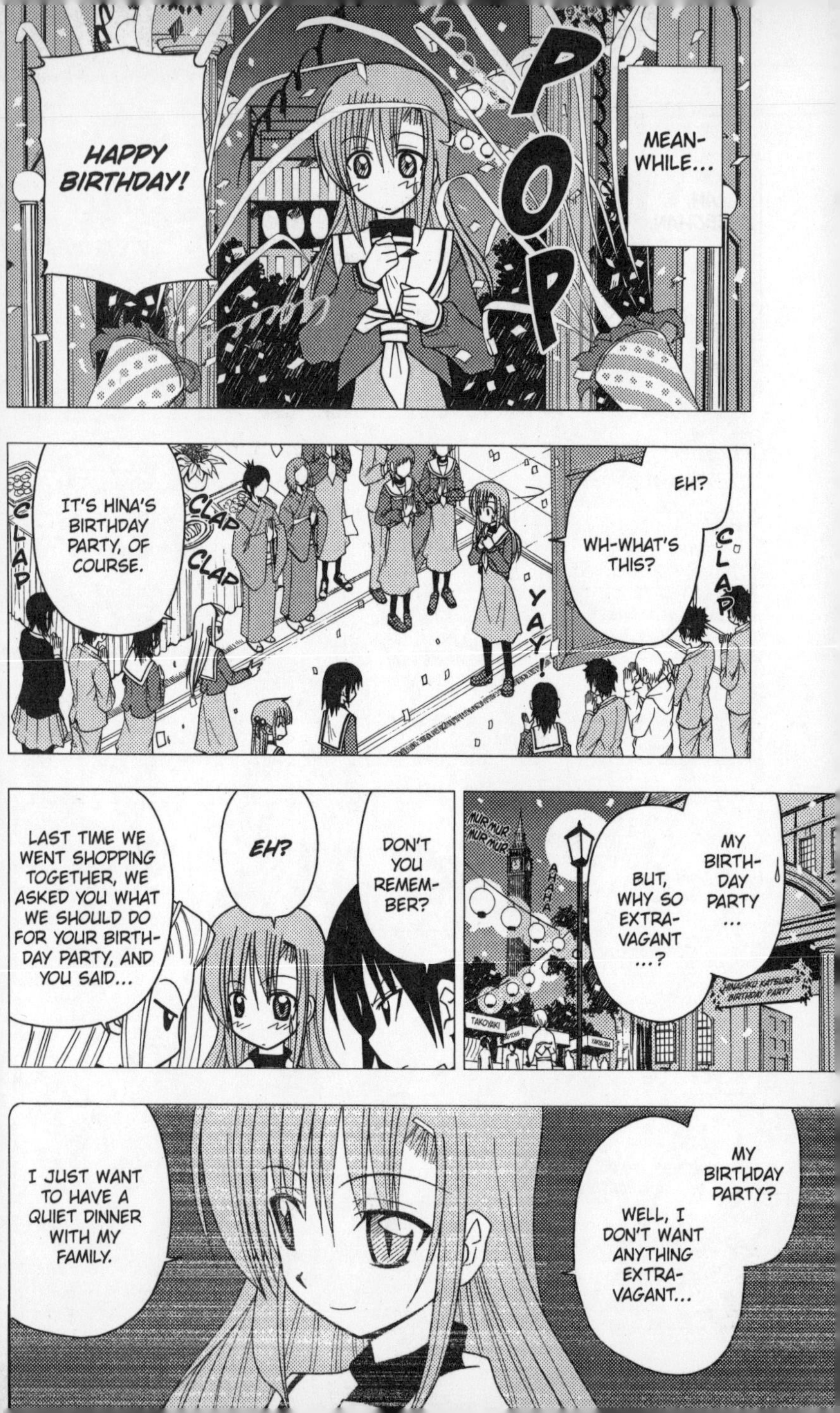
MEAN-WHILE...
POP
HAPPY BIRTHDAY!
EH?
WH-WHAT'S THIS?
CLAP
YAY!
CLAP
CLAP
CLAP
IT'S HINA'S BIRTHDAY PARTY, OF COURSE.
MY BIRTH-DAY PARTY...
BUT, WHY SO EXTRA-VAGANT...?
MUR MUR MUR MUR
AHAHA
HINAGIKU KATSURA'S BIRTHDAY PARTY
TAKOYAKI
DON'T YOU REMEM-BER?
EH?
LAST TIME WE WENT SHOPPING TOGETHER, WE ASKED YOU WHAT WE SHOULD DO FOR YOUR BIRTH-DAY PARTY, AND YOU SAID...
MY BIRTHDAY PARTY?
WELL, I DON'T WANT ANYTHING EXTRA-VAGANT...
I JUST WANT TO HAVE A QUIET DINNER WITH MY FAMILY.

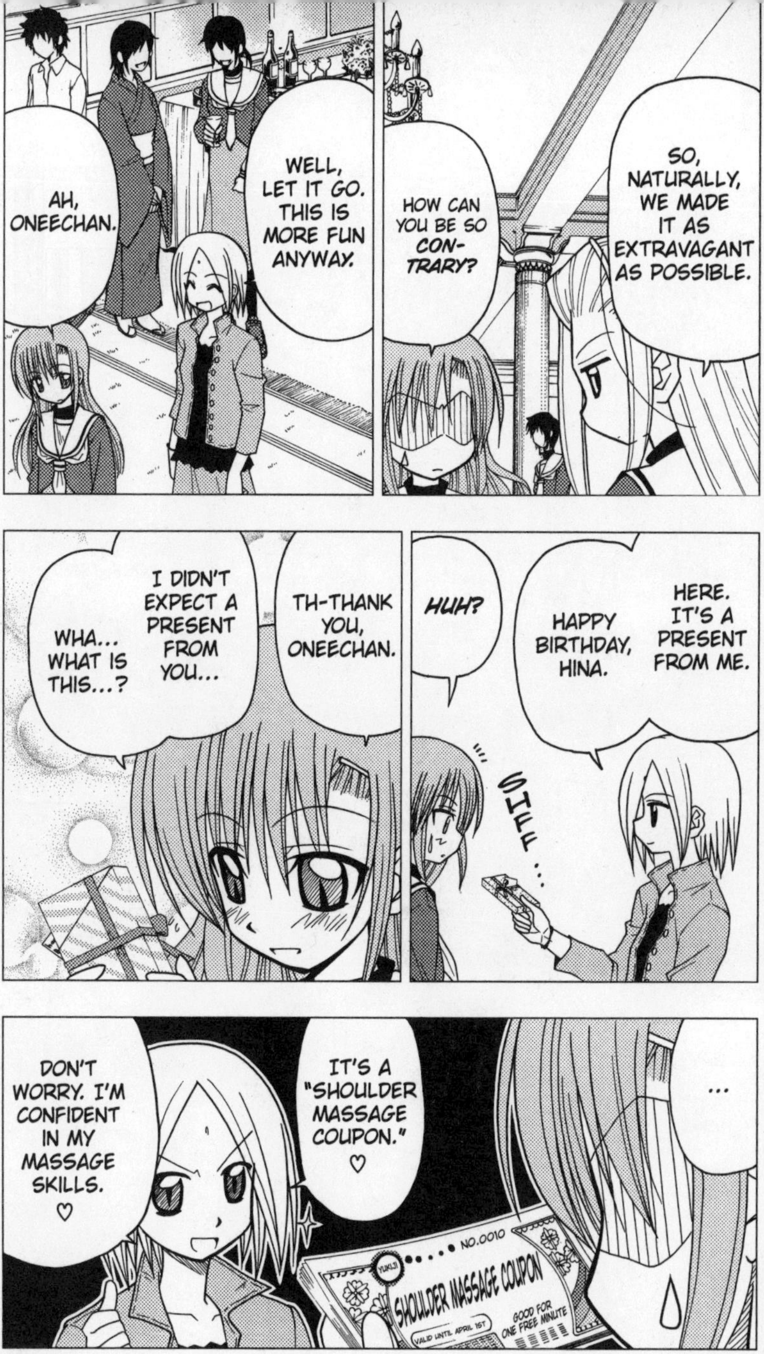
SO, NATURALLY, WE MADE IT AS EXTRAVAGANT AS POSSIBLE.
HOW CAN YOU BE SO CON-TRARY?
WELL, LET IT GO. THIS IS MORE FUN ANYWAY.
AH, ONEECHAN.
HERE. IT'S A PRESENT FROM ME.
HAPPY BIRTHDAY, HINA.
HUH?
SHFF...
TH-THANK YOU, ONEECHAN.
I DIDN'T EXPECT A PRESENT FROM YOU...
WHA... WHAT IS THIS...?
...
IT'S A "SHOULDER MASSAGE COUPON." ♡
DON'T WORRY. I'M CONFIDENT IN MY MASSAGE SKILLS. ♡
NO.0010
YUKIJI
SHOULDER MASSAGE COUPON
VALID UNTIL APRIL 15T
GOOD FOR ONE FREE MINUTE

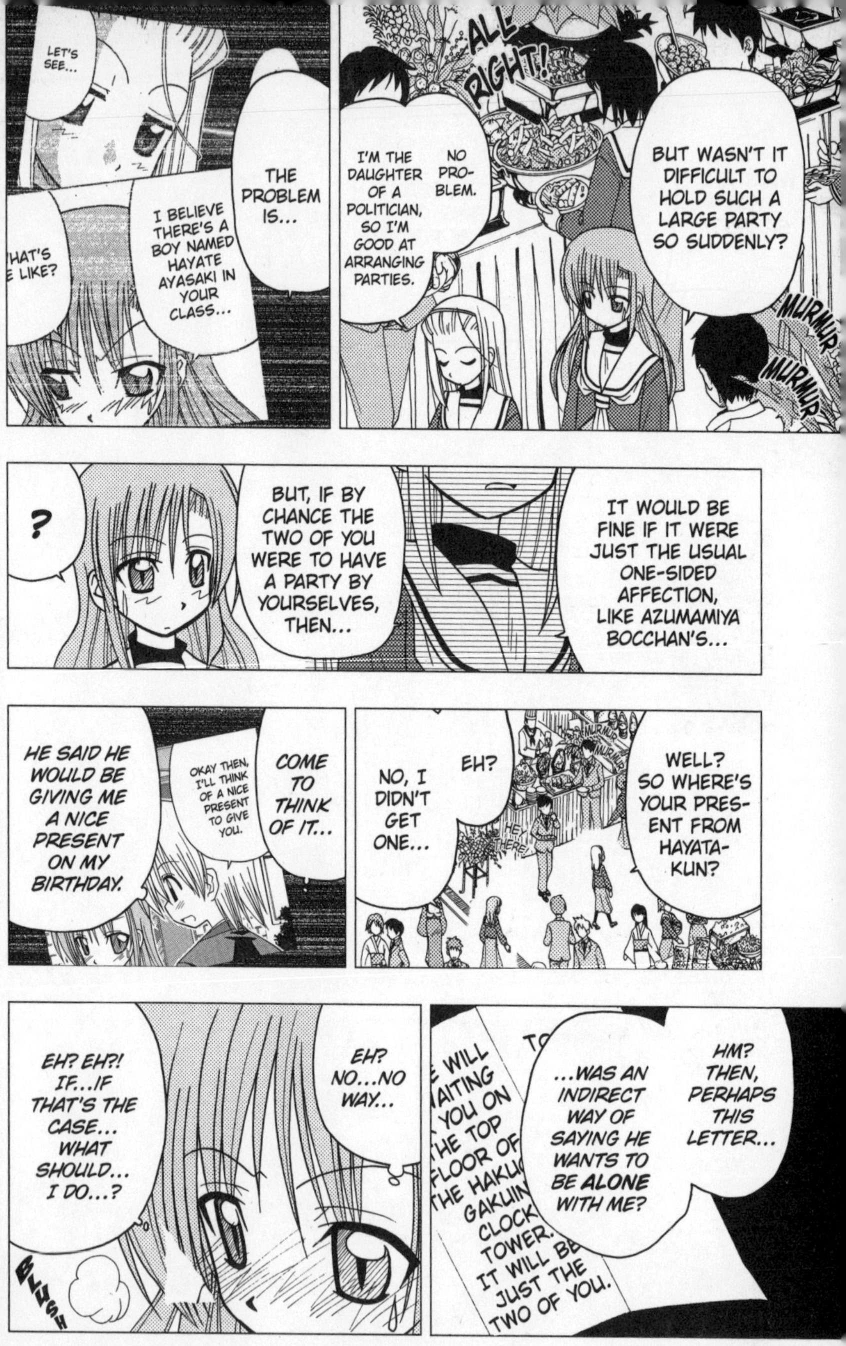
ALL RIGHT!
BUT WASN'T IT DIFFICULT TO HOLD SUCH A LARGE PARTY SO SUDDENLY?
NO PROBLEM.
I'M THE DAUGHTER OF A POLITICIAN, SO I'M GOOD AT ARRANGING PARTIES.
MURMUR
MURMUR
THE PROBLEM IS...
LET'S SEE...
I BELIEVE THERE'S A BOY NAMED HAYATE AYASAKI IN YOUR CLASS...
HAT'S E LIKE?
IT WOULD BE FINE IF IT WERE JUST THE USUAL ONE-SIDED AFFECTION, LIKE AZUMAMIYA BOCCHAN'S...
BUT, IF BY CHANCE THE TWO OF YOU WERE TO HAVE A PARTY BY YOURSELVES, THEN...
?
WELL? SO WHERE'S YOUR PRESENT FROM HAYATA-KUN?
MURMUR
MURMUR
EH?
HEY THERE!
NO, I DIDN'T GET ONE...
COME TO THINK OF IT...
OKAY THEN, I'LL THINK OF A NICE PRESENT TO GIVE YOU.
HE SAID HE WOULD BE GIVING ME A NICE PRESENT ON MY BIRTHDAY.
HM? THEN, PERHAPS THIS LETTER...
...WAS AN INDIRECT WAY OF SAYING HE WANTS TO BE ALONE WITH ME?
TO
E WILL AITING YOU ON THE TOP FLOOR OF THE HAKU GAKUIN CLOCK TOWER. IT WILL BE JUST THE TWO OF YOU.
EH? NO...NO WAY...
EH? EH?! IF...IF THAT'S THE CASE... WHAT SHOULD... I DO...?
BLUSH

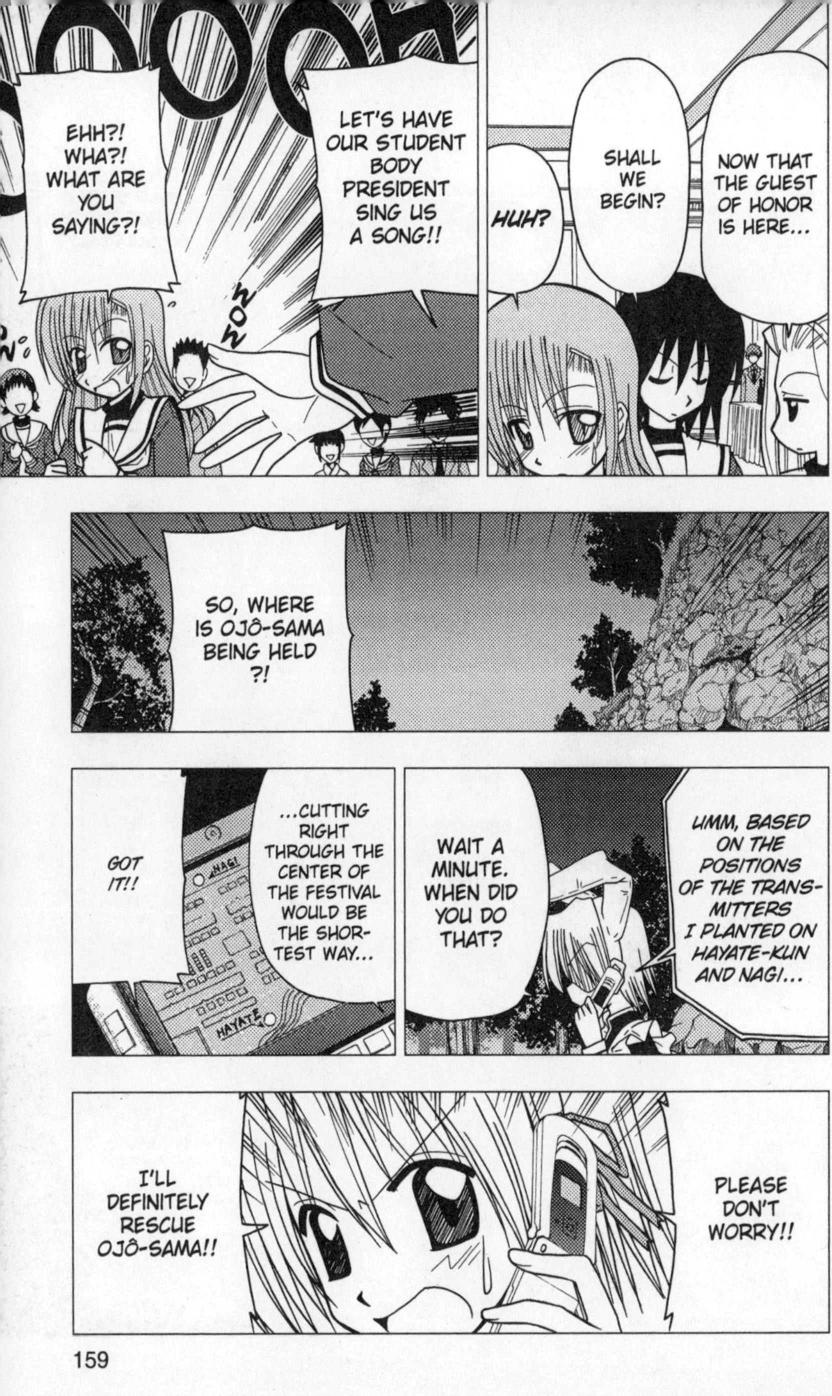
NOW THAT THE GUEST OF HONOR IS HERE...
SHALL WE BEGIN?
HUH?
LET'S HAVE OUR STUDENT BODY PRESIDENT SING US A SONG!!
WOW
EHH?! WHA?! WHAT ARE YOU SAYING?!
SO, WHERE IS OJÔ-SAMA BEING HELD ?!
UMM, BASED ON THE POSITIONS OF THE TRANSMITTERS I PLANTED ON HAYATE-KUN AND NAGI...
WAIT A MINUTE. WHEN DID YOU DO THAT?
...CUTTING RIGHT THROUGH THE CENTER OF THE FESTIVAL WOULD BE THE SHORTEST WAY...
NAGI
HAYATE
GOT IT!!
PLEASE DON'T WORRY!!
I'LL DEFINITELY RESCUE OJÔ-SAMA!!

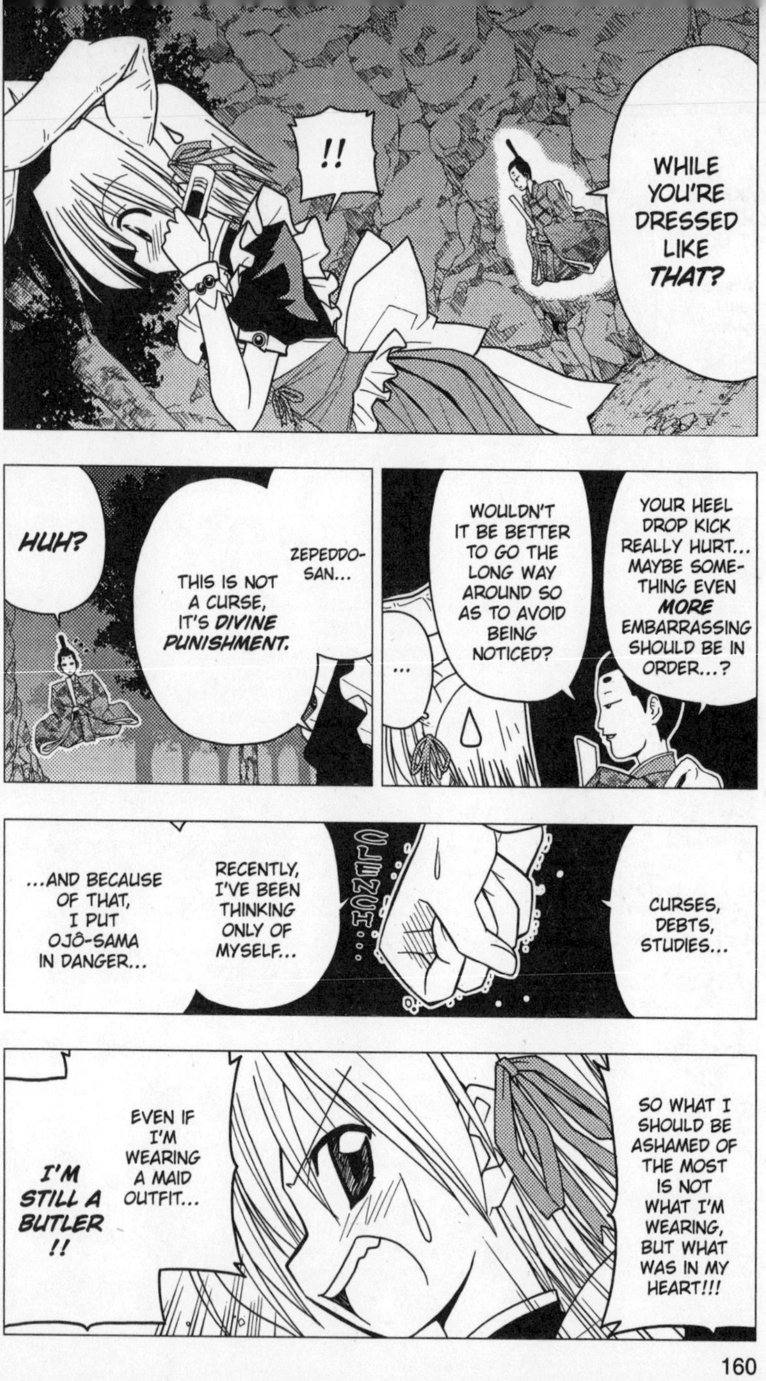
WHILE YOU'RE DRESSED LIKE *THAT?*
!!
YOUR HEEL DROP KICK REALLY HURT... MAYBE SOME-THING EVEN *MORE* EMBARRASSING SHOULD BE IN ORDER...?
WOULDN'T IT BE BETTER TO GO THE LONG WAY AROUND SO AS TO AVOID BEING NOTICED?
...
ZEPEDDO-SAN...
THIS IS NOT A CURSE, IT'S *DIVINE PUNISHMENT.*
HUH?
CURSES, DEBTS, STUDIES...
CLENCH...
RECENTLY, I'VE BEEN THINKING ONLY OF MYSELF...
...AND BECAUSE OF THAT, I PUT OJÔ-SAMA IN DANGER...
SO WHAT I SHOULD BE ASHAMED OF THE MOST IS NOT WHAT I'M WEARING, BUT WHAT WAS IN MY HEART!!!
EVEN IF I'M WEARING A MAID OUTFIT...
I'M STILL A BUTLER !!

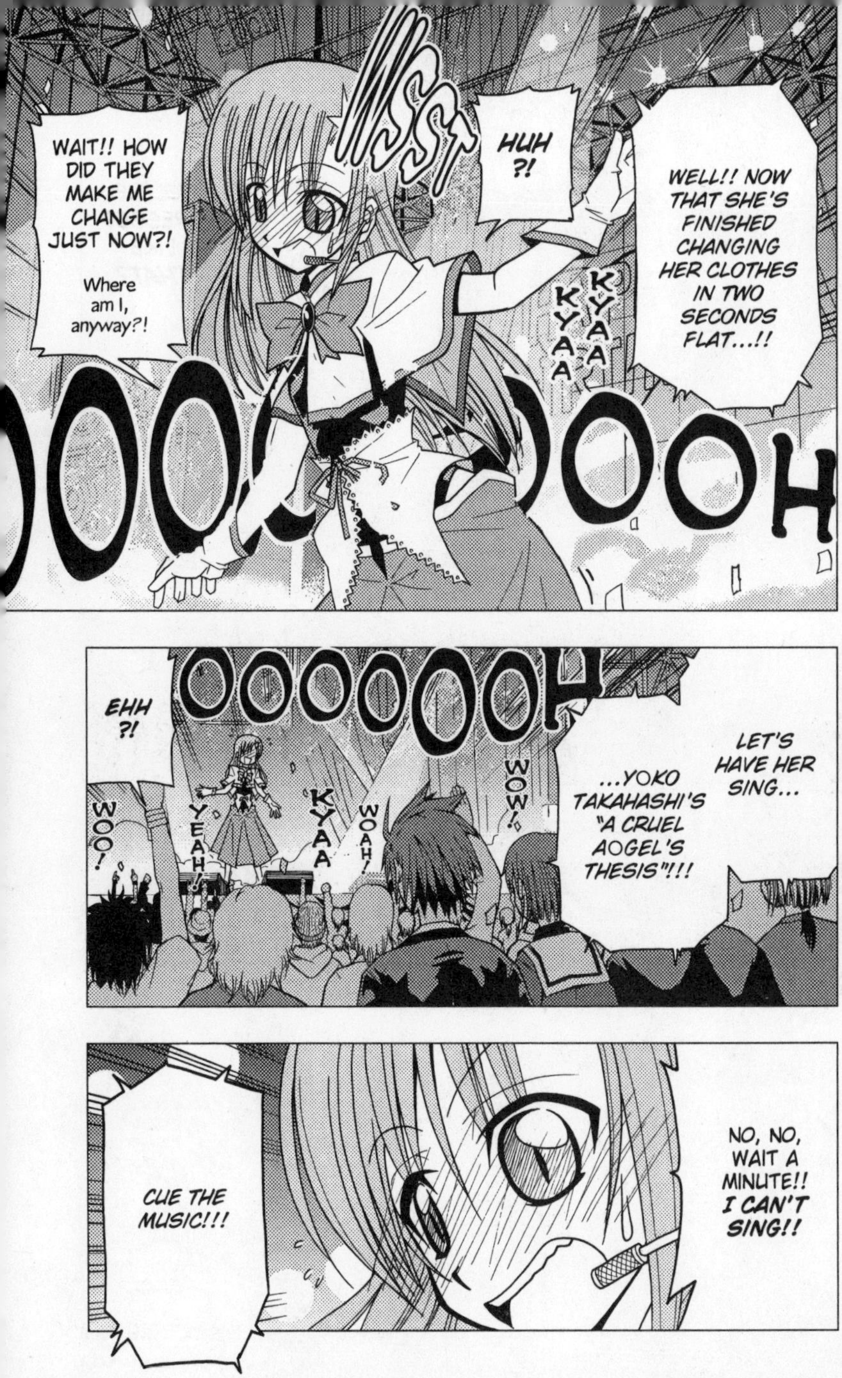
WELL!! NOW THAT SHE'S FINISHED CHANGING HER CLOTHES IN TWO SECONDS FLAT...!!
KYAA KYAA
HUH ?!
WSST
WAIT!! HOW DID THEY MAKE ME CHANGE JUST NOW?!
Where am I, anyway?!
OOOOOOOH
LET'S HAVE HER SING...
...YOKO TAKAHASHI'S "A CRUEL AOGEL'S THESIS"!!!
WOW!
WOAH!
KYAA
YEAH!
WOO!
EHH ?!
OOOOOOOH
NO, NO, WAIT A MINUTE!! I CAN'T SING!!
CUE THE MUSIC!!!

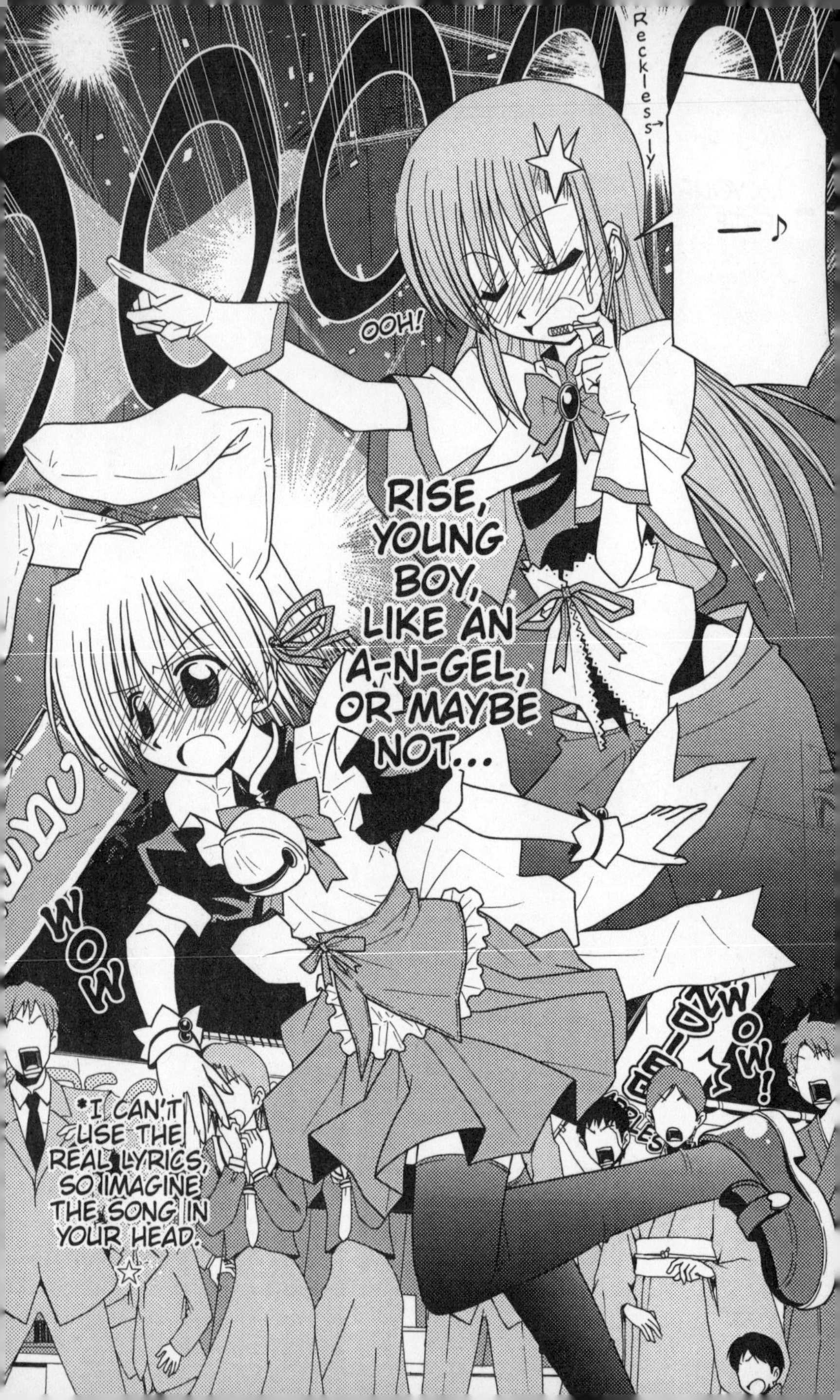
Recklessly
—♪
OOH!
RISE, YOUNG BOY, LIKE AN A-N-GEL, OR MAYBE NOT...
WOW!
WOW
*I CAN'T USE THE REAL LYRICS, SO IMAGINE THE SONG IN YOUR HEAD. ☆

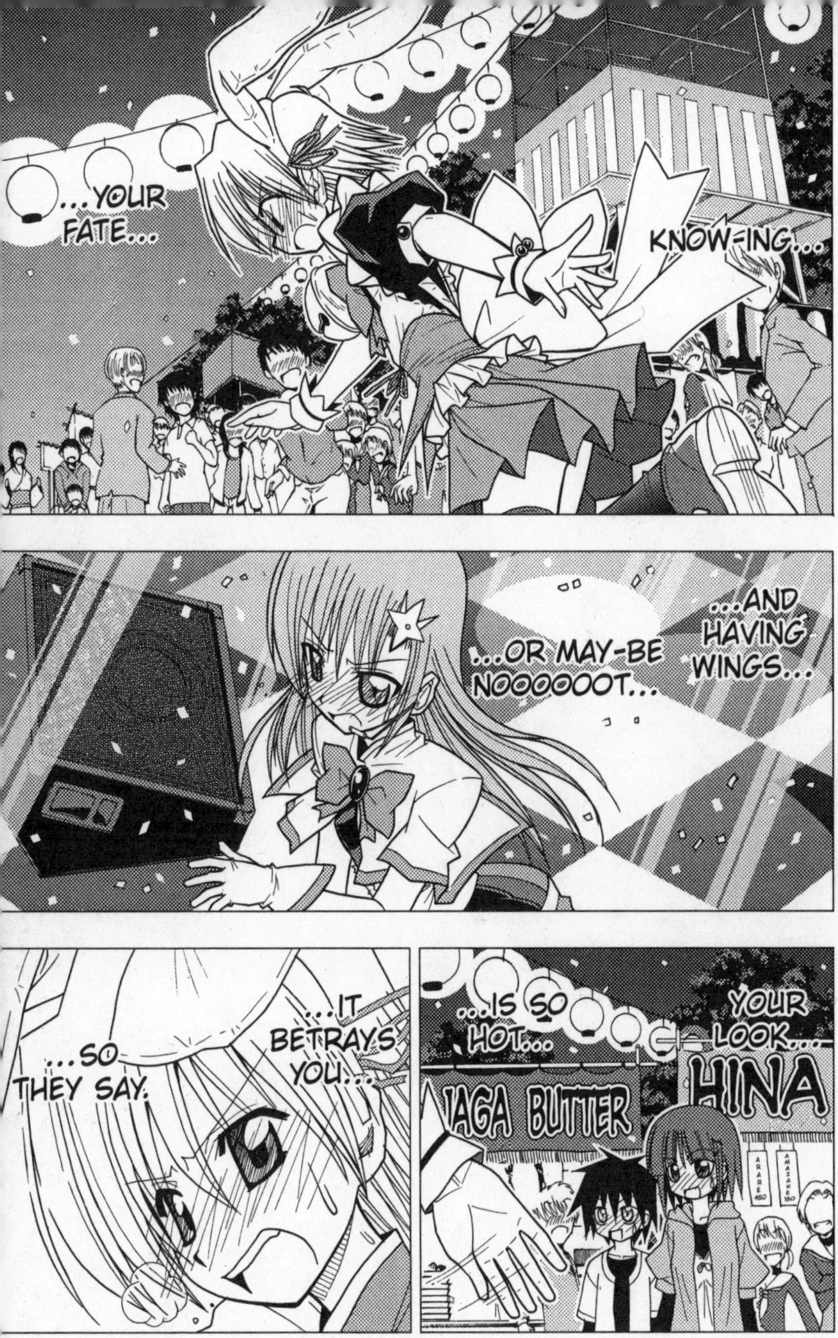
KNOW-ING...
...YOUR FATE...
...AND HAVING WINGS...
...OR MAY-BE NOOOOOOT...
YOUR LOOK...
...IS SO HOT...
HINA
JAGA BUTTER
ARARE 450
AMAZAKE 180
...IT BETRAYS YOU...
...SO THEY SAY.

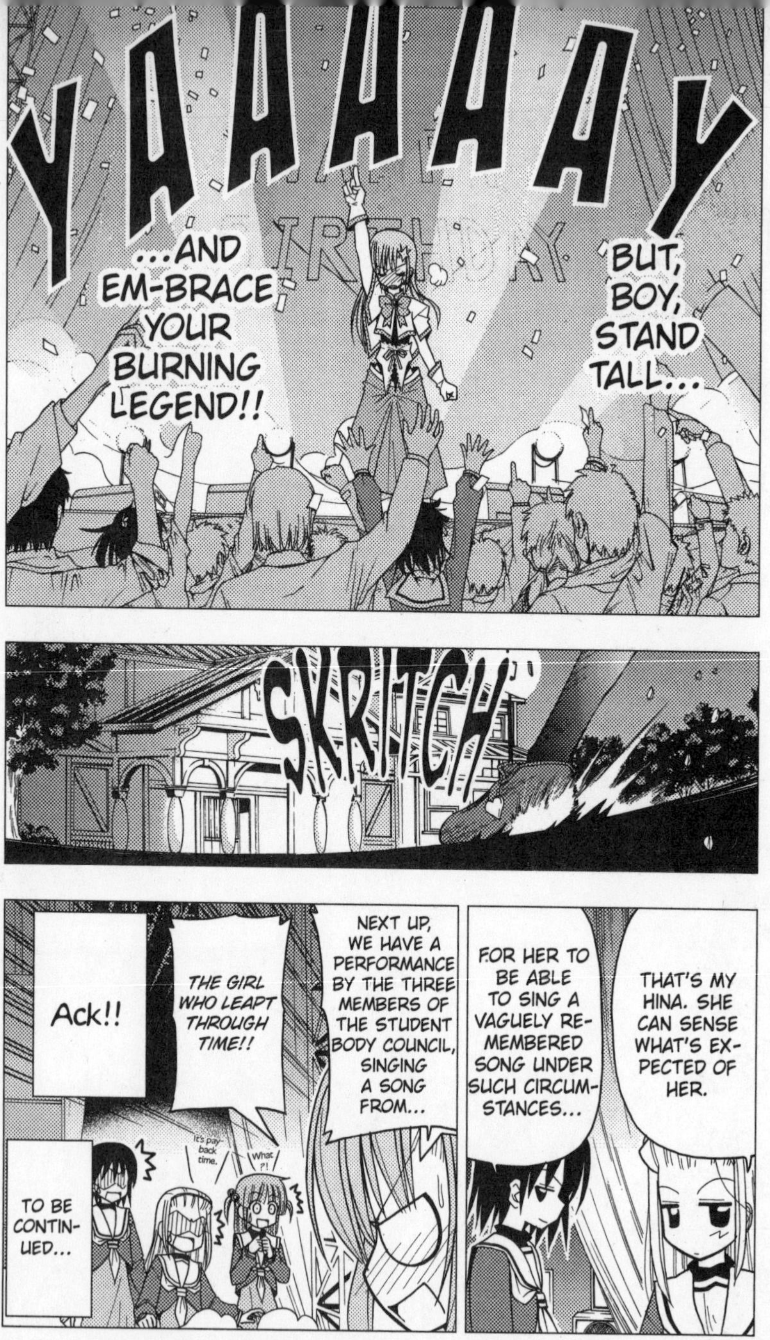
YAAAAAY
BUT, BOY, STAND TALL...
...AND EM-BRACE YOUR BURNING LEGEND!!
SKRITCH
THAT'S MY HINA. SHE CAN SENSE WHAT'S EX-PECTED OF HER.
FOR HER TO BE ABLE TO SING A VAGUELY RE-MEMBERED SONG UNDER SUCH CIRCUM-STANCES...
NEXT UP, WE HAVE A PERFORMANCE BY THE THREE MEMBERS OF THE STUDENT BODY COUNCIL, SINGING A SONG FROM...
THE GIRL WHO LEAPT THROUGH TIME!!
Ack!!
What ?!
It's pay-back time.
TO BE CONTIN-UED...

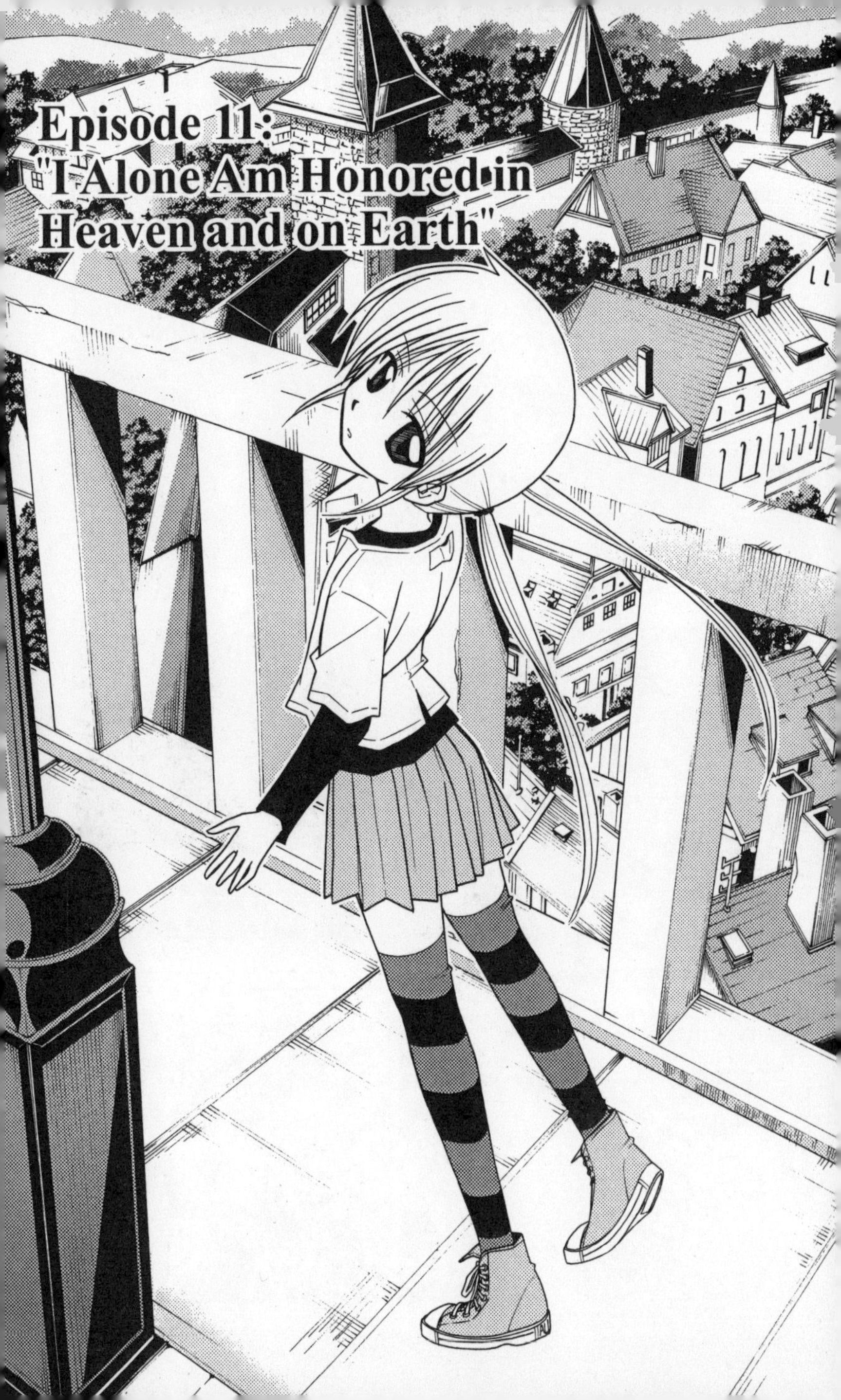
Episode 11:
"I Alone Am Honored in Heaven and on Earth"

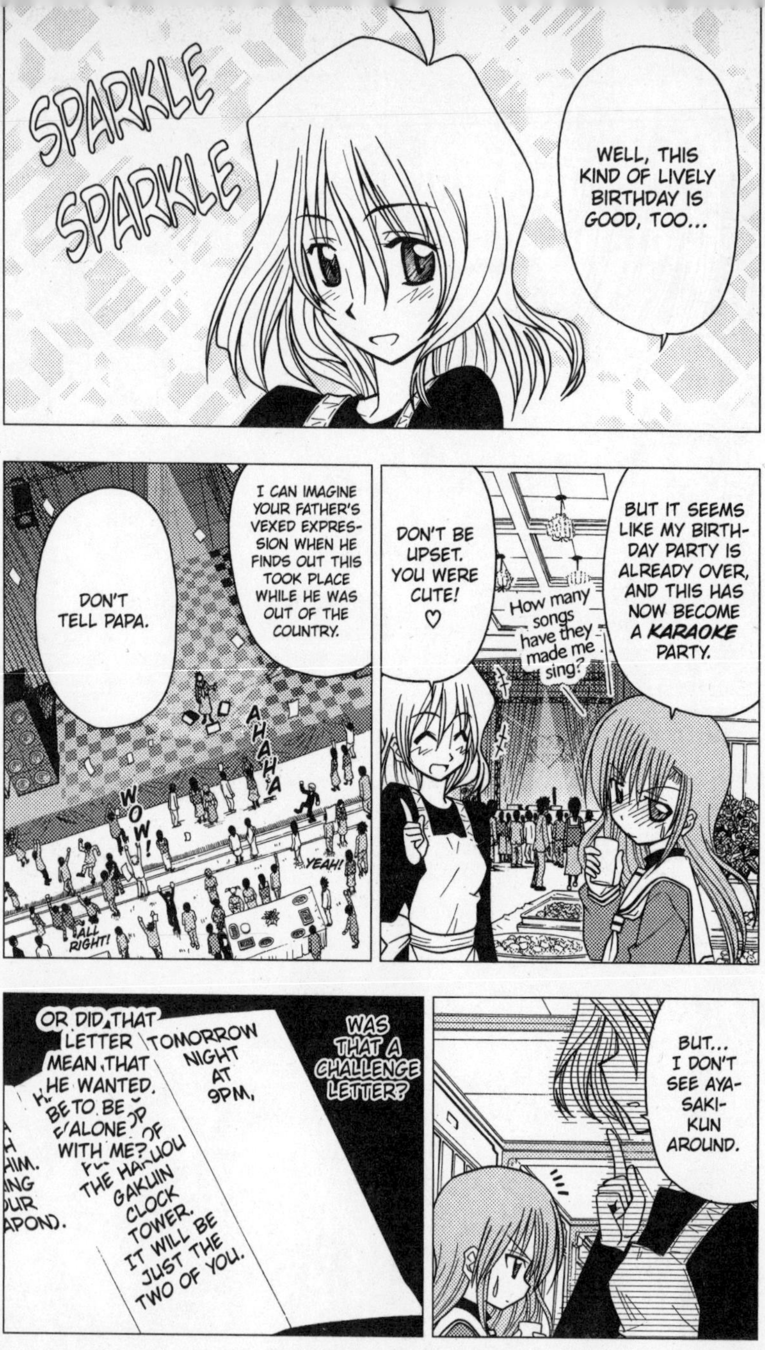
SPARKLE SPARKLE
WELL, THIS KIND OF LIVELY BIRTHDAY IS GOOD, TOO...
BUT IT SEEMS LIKE MY BIRTHDAY PARTY IS ALREADY OVER, AND THIS HAS NOW BECOME A **KARAOKE** PARTY.
How many songs have they made me sing?
DON'T BE UPSET. YOU WERE CUTE! ♡
I CAN IMAGINE YOUR FATHER'S VEXED EXPRESSION WHEN HE FINDS OUT THIS TOOK PLACE WHILE HE WAS OUT OF THE COUNTRY.
DON'T TELL PAPA.
AHAHA
WOW!
YEAH!
ALL RIGHT!
BUT... I DON'T SEE AYASAKI-KUN AROUND.
WAS THAT A CHALLENGE LETTER?
OR DID THAT LETTER MEAN THAT HE WANTED TO BE ALONE WITH ME?
TOMORROW NIGHT AT 9PM,
THE HAKUOU GAKUIN CLOCK TOWER. IT WILL BE JUST THE TWO OF YOU.

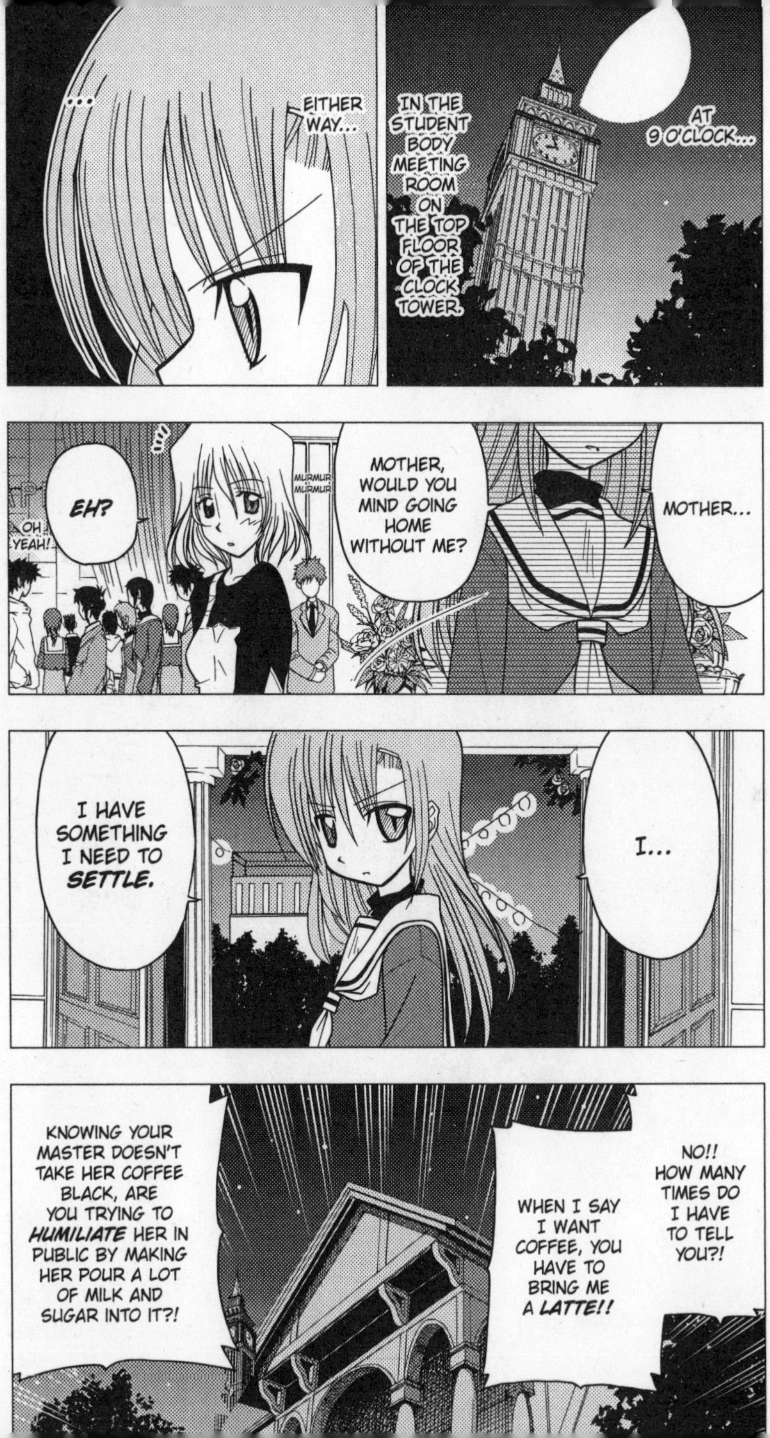
AT 9 O'CLOCK...
IN THE STUDENT BODY MEETING ROOM ON THE TOP FLOOR OF THE CLOCK TOWER.
EITHER WAY...
...
MOTHER...
MOTHER, WOULD YOU MIND GOING HOME WITHOUT ME?
MURMUR MURMUR
EH?
OH YEAH!
I...
I HAVE SOMETHING I NEED TO *SETTLE.*
NO!! HOW MANY TIMES DO I HAVE TO TELL YOU?!
WHEN I SAY I WANT COFFEE, YOU HAVE TO BRING ME A *LATTE!!*
KNOWING YOUR MASTER DOESN'T TAKE HER COFFEE BLACK, ARE YOU TRYING TO *HUMILIATE* HER IN PUBLIC BY MAKING HER POUR A LOT OF MILK AND SUGAR INTO IT?!

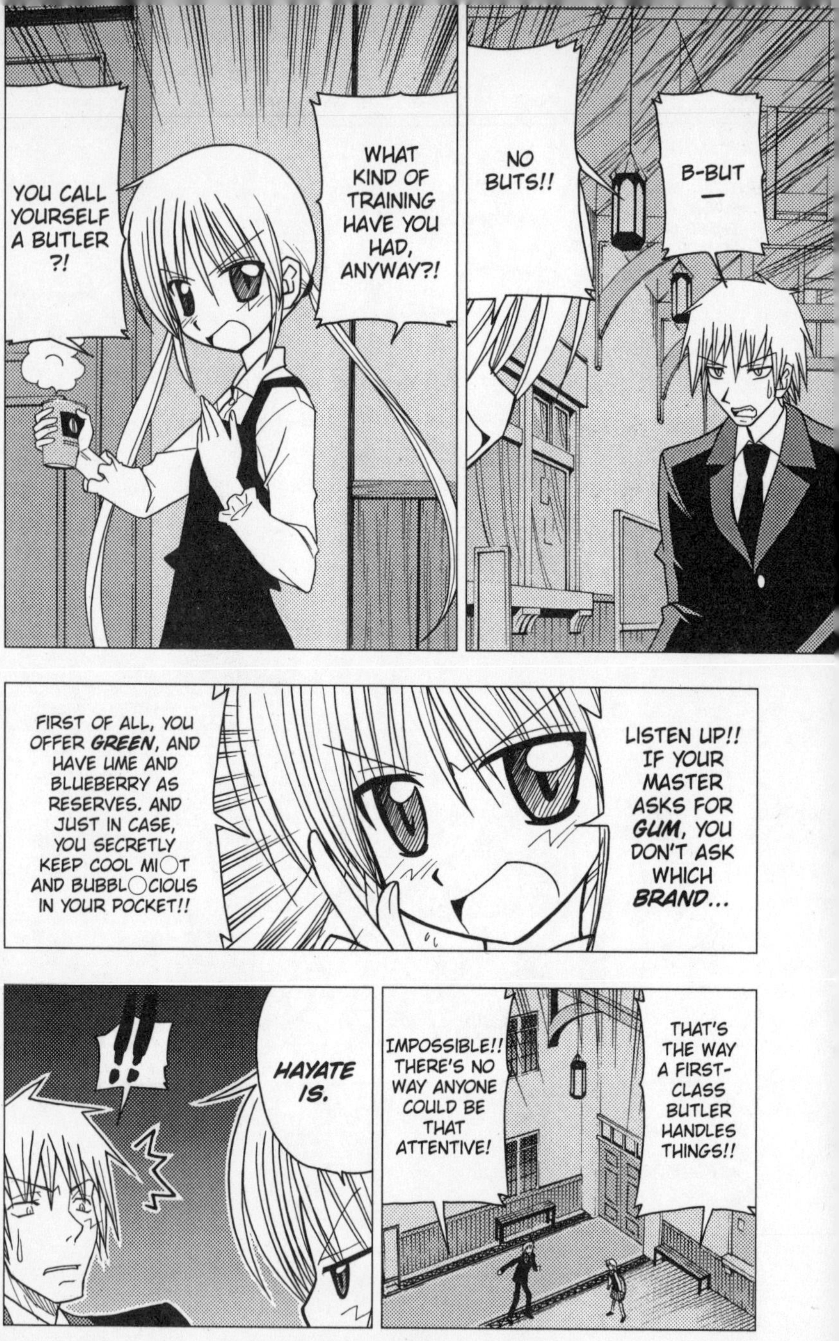
B-BUT —
NO BUTS!!
WHAT KIND OF TRAINING HAVE YOU HAD, ANYWAY?!
YOU CALL YOURSELF A BUTLER ?!
LISTEN UP!! IF YOUR MASTER ASKS FOR GUM, YOU DON'T ASK WHICH BRAND...
FIRST OF ALL, YOU OFFER GREEN, AND HAVE UME AND BLUEBERRY AS RESERVES. AND JUST IN CASE, YOU SECRETLY KEEP COOL MI◯T AND BUBBL◯CIOUS IN YOUR POCKET!!
THAT'S THE WAY A FIRST-CLASS BUTLER HANDLES THINGS!!
IMPOSSIBLE!! THERE'S NO WAY ANYONE COULD BE THAT ATTENTIVE!
HAYATE IS.
!!

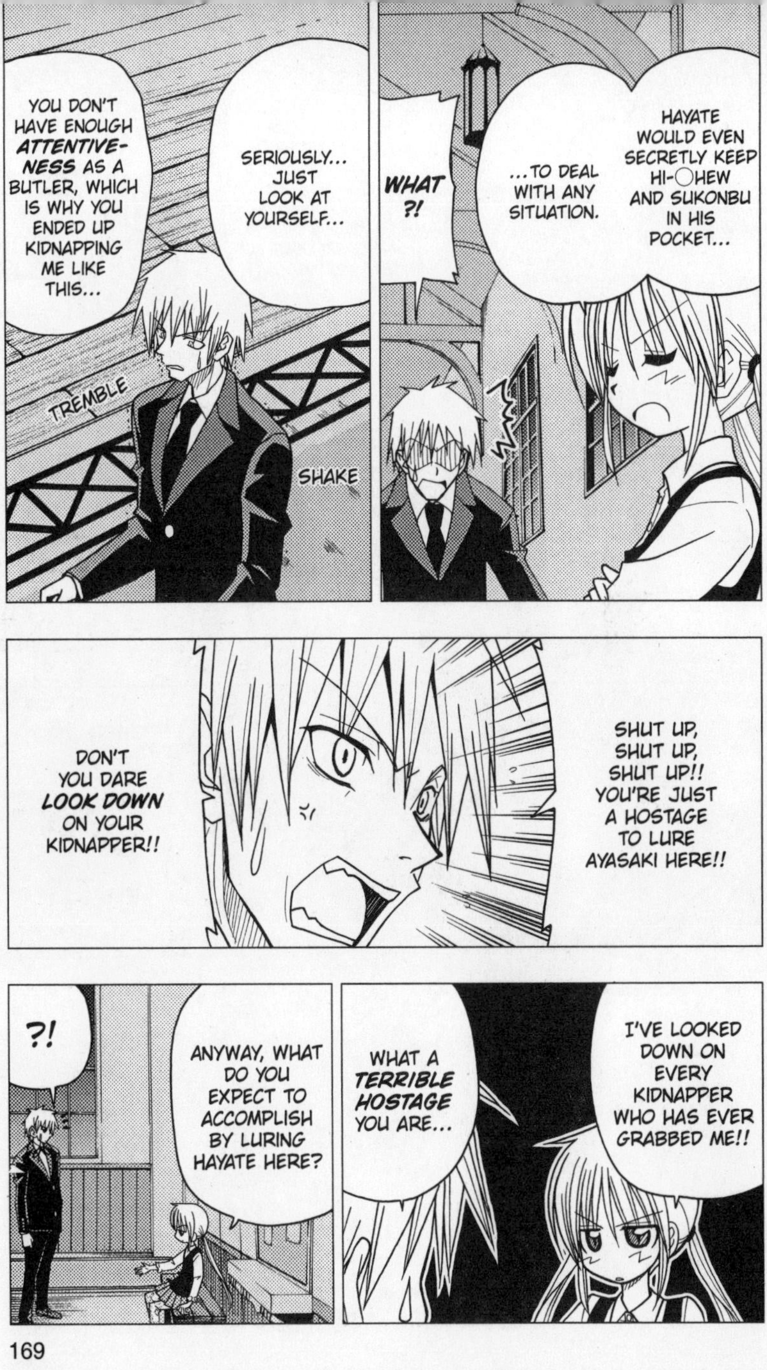
HAYATE WOULD EVEN SECRETLY KEEP HI-◯HEW AND SUKONBU IN HIS POCKET...
...TO DEAL WITH ANY SITUATION.
WHAT ?!
SERIOUSLY... JUST LOOK AT YOURSELF...
YOU DON'T HAVE ENOUGH ATTENTIVE-NESS AS A BUTLER, WHICH IS WHY YOU ENDED UP KIDNAPPING ME LIKE THIS...
TREMBLE
SHAKE
SHUT UP, SHUT UP, SHUT UP!! YOU'RE JUST A HOSTAGE TO LURE AYASAKI HERE!!
DON'T YOU DARE LOOK DOWN ON YOUR KIDNAPPER!!
I'VE LOOKED DOWN ON EVERY KIDNAPPER WHO HAS EVER GRABBED ME!!
WHAT A TERRIBLE HOSTAGE YOU ARE...
ANYWAY, WHAT DO YOU EXPECT TO ACCOMPLISH BY LURING HAYATE HERE?
?!

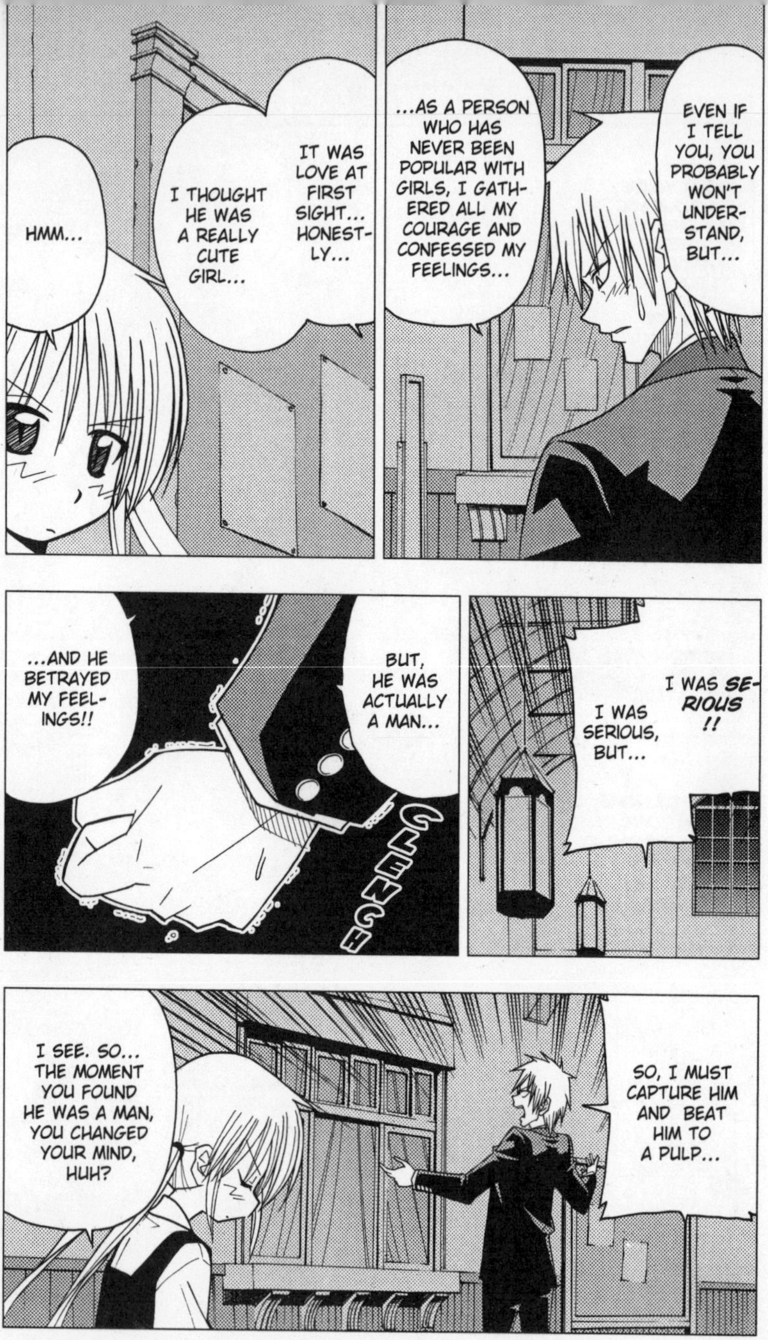
EVEN IF I TELL YOU, YOU PROBABLY WON'T UNDERSTAND, BUT...
...AS A PERSON WHO HAS NEVER BEEN POPULAR WITH GIRLS, I GATHERED ALL MY COURAGE AND CONFESSED MY FEELINGS...
IT WAS LOVE AT FIRST SIGHT... HONESTLY...
I THOUGHT HE WAS A REALLY CUTE GIRL...
HMM...
I WAS SERIOUS!!
I WAS SERIOUS, BUT...
BUT, HE WAS ACTUALLY A MAN...
...AND HE BETRAYED MY FEELINGS!!
CLENCH
SO, I MUST CAPTURE HIM AND BEAT HIM TO A PULP...
I SEE. SO... THE MOMENT YOU FOUND HE WAS A MAN, YOU CHANGED YOUR MIND, HUH?

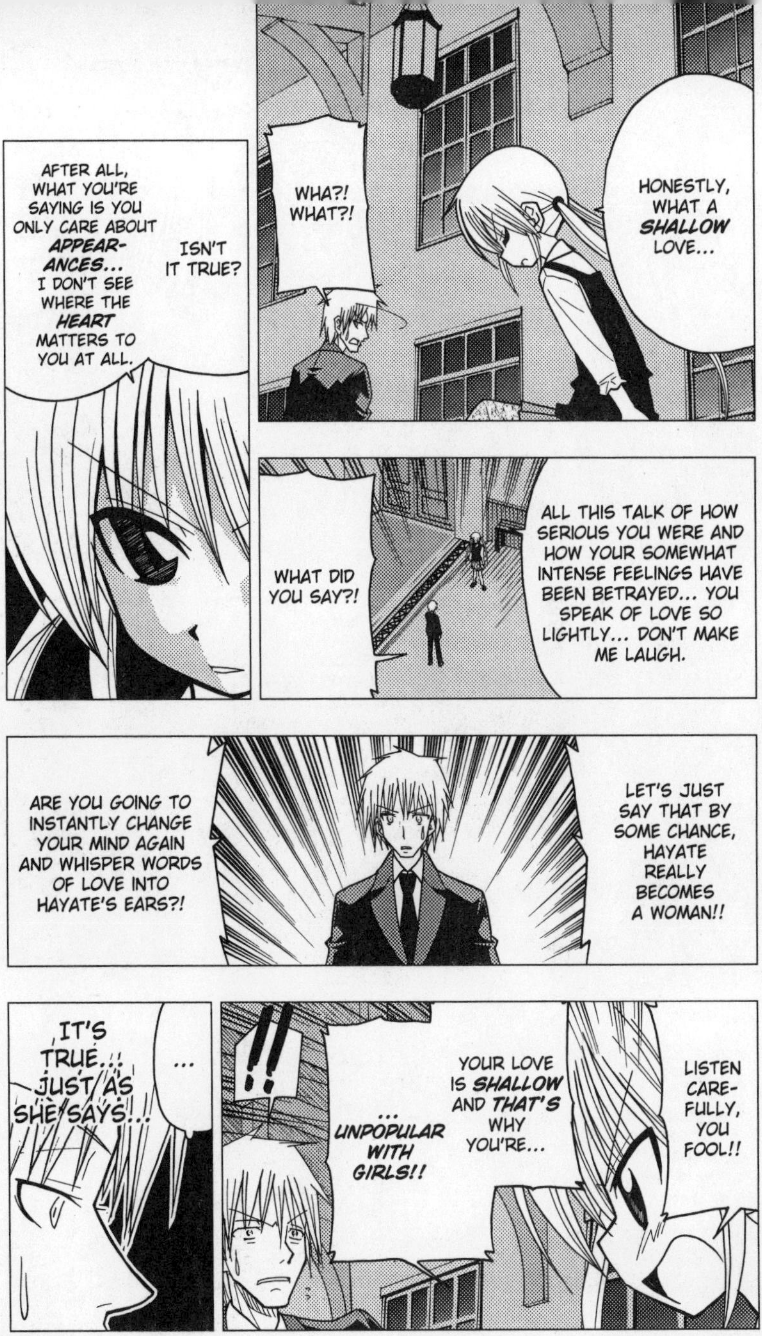
HONESTLY, WHAT A SHALLOW LOVE...
WHA?! WHAT?!
ALL THIS TALK OF HOW SERIOUS YOU WERE AND HOW YOUR SOMEWHAT INTENSE FEELINGS HAVE BEEN BETRAYED... YOU SPEAK OF LOVE SO LIGHTLY... DON'T MAKE ME LAUGH.
WHAT DID YOU SAY?!
AFTER ALL, WHAT YOU'RE SAYING IS YOU ONLY CARE ABOUT APPEARANCES... I DON'T SEE WHERE THE HEART MATTERS TO YOU AT ALL.
ISN'T IT TRUE?
LET'S JUST SAY THAT BY SOME CHANCE, HAYATE REALLY BECOMES A WOMAN!!
ARE YOU GOING TO INSTANTLY CHANGE YOUR MIND AGAIN AND WHISPER WORDS OF LOVE INTO HAYATE'S EARS?!
LISTEN CAREFULLY, YOU FOOL!!
YOUR LOVE IS SHALLOW AND THAT'S WHY YOU'RE...
...UNPOPULAR WITH GIRLS!!
!!
...
IT'S TRUE... JUST AS SHE SAYS...

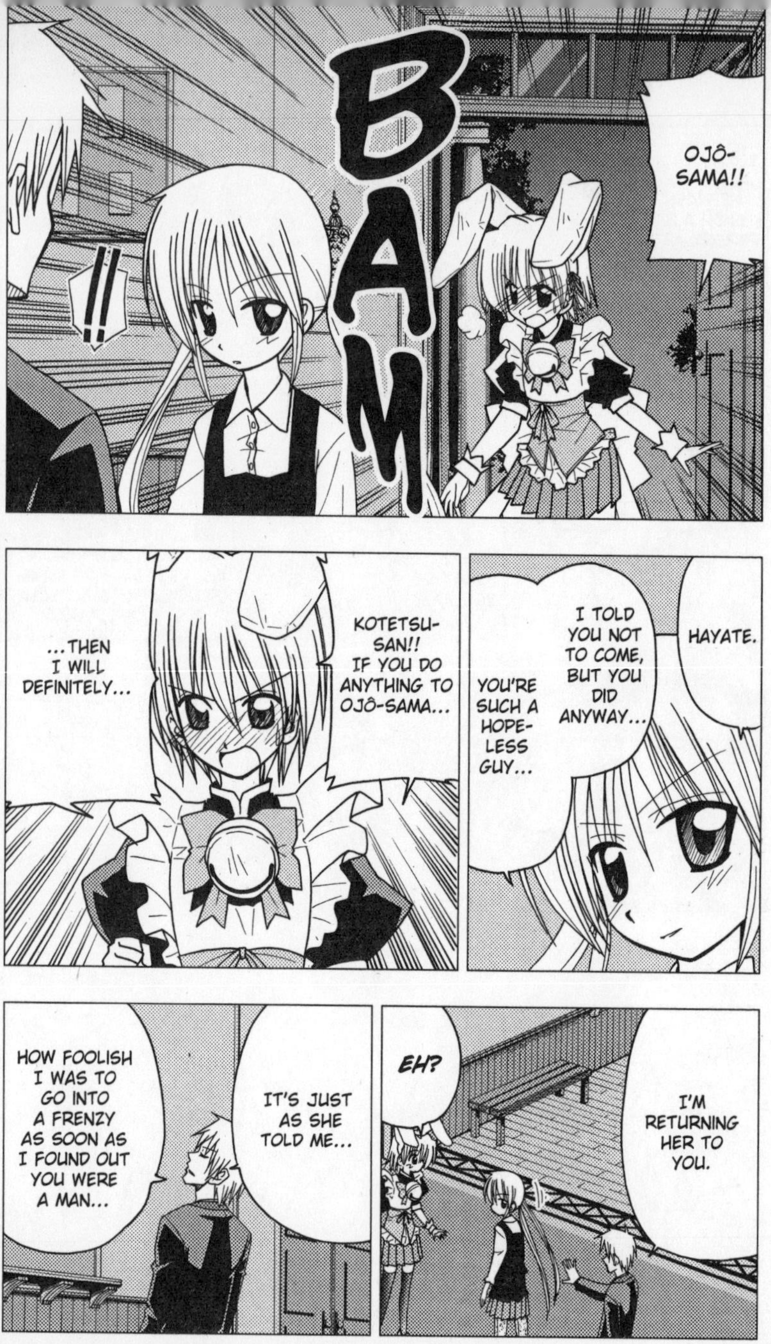
OJÔ-SAMA!!
BAM
!!
HAYATE.
I TOLD YOU NOT TO COME, BUT YOU DID ANYWAY...
YOU'RE SUCH A HOPE-LESS GUY...
KOTETSU-SAN!! IF YOU DO ANYTHING TO OJÔ-SAMA...
...THEN I WILL DEFINITELY...
I'M RETURNING HER TO YOU.
EH?
IT'S JUST AS SHE TOLD ME...
HOW FOOLISH I WAS TO GO INTO A FRENZY AS SOON AS I FOUND OUT YOU WERE A MAN...

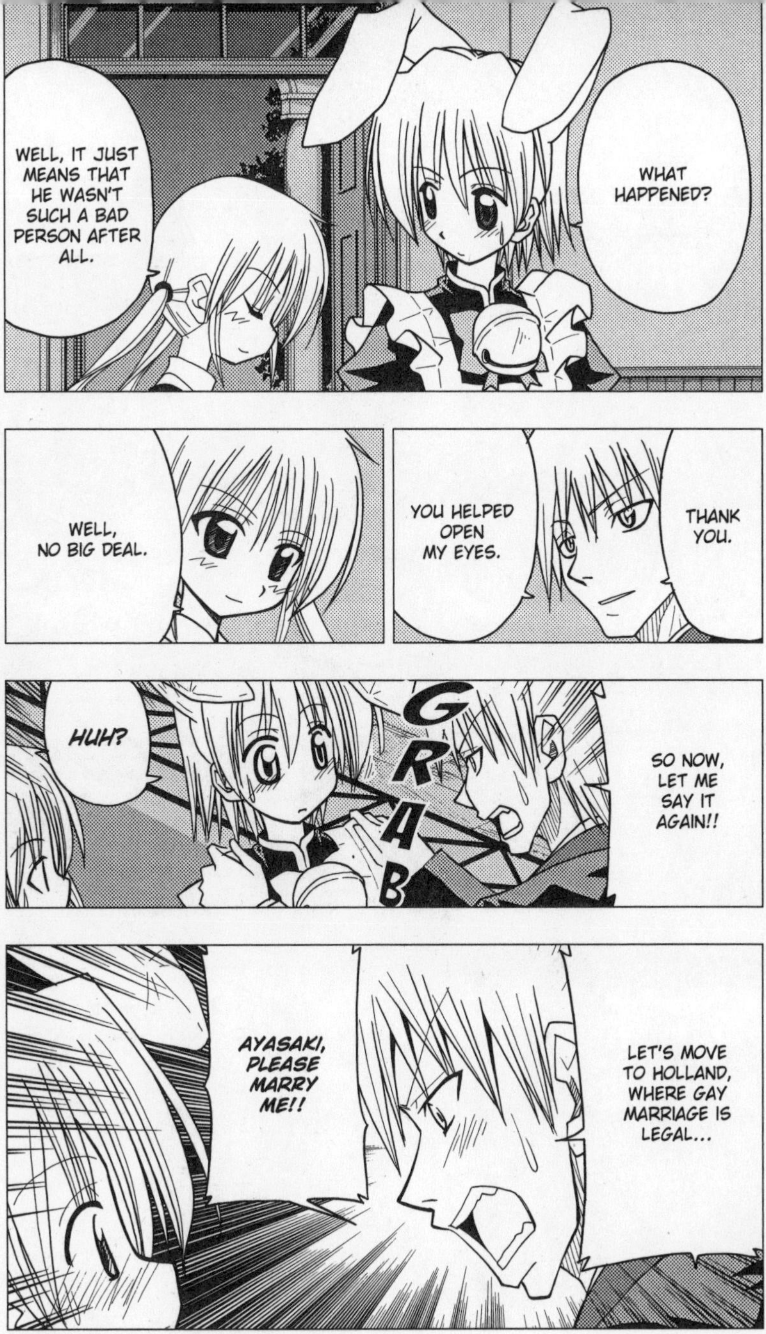
WHAT HAPPENED?
WELL, IT JUST MEANS THAT HE WASN'T SUCH A BAD PERSON AFTER ALL.
THANK YOU.
YOU HELPED OPEN MY EYES.
WELL, NO BIG DEAL.
SO NOW, LET ME SAY IT AGAIN!!
GRAB
HUH?
LET'S MOVE TO HOLLAND, WHERE GAY MARRIAGE IS LEGAL...
AYASAKI, PLEASE MARRY ME!!

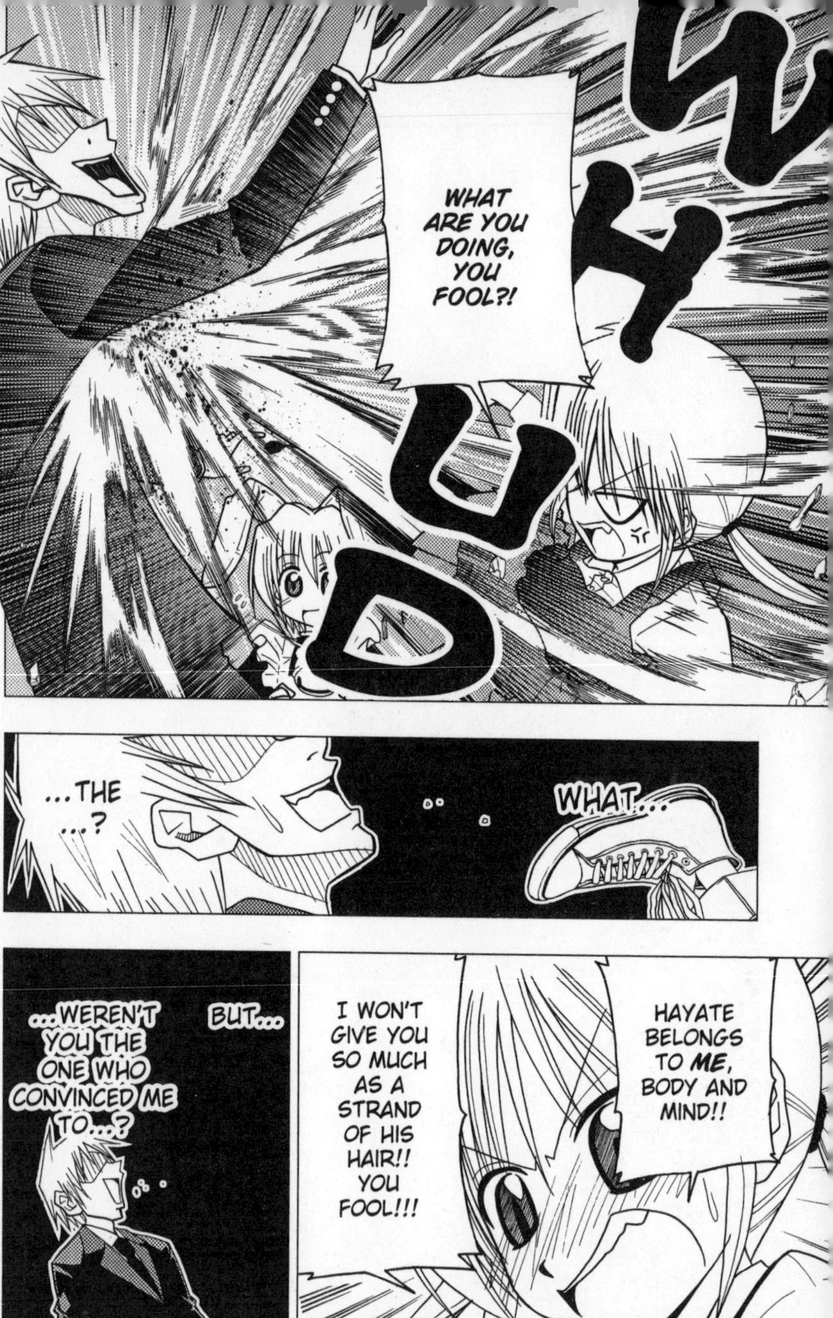
WHAT ARE YOU DOING, YOU FOOL?!
WHAT...
...THE ...?
HAYATE BELONGS TO *ME*, BODY AND MIND!!
I WON'T GIVE YOU SO MUCH AS A STRAND OF HIS HAIR!! YOU FOOL!!!
BUT...
...WEREN'T YOU THE ONE WHO CONVINCED ME TO...?

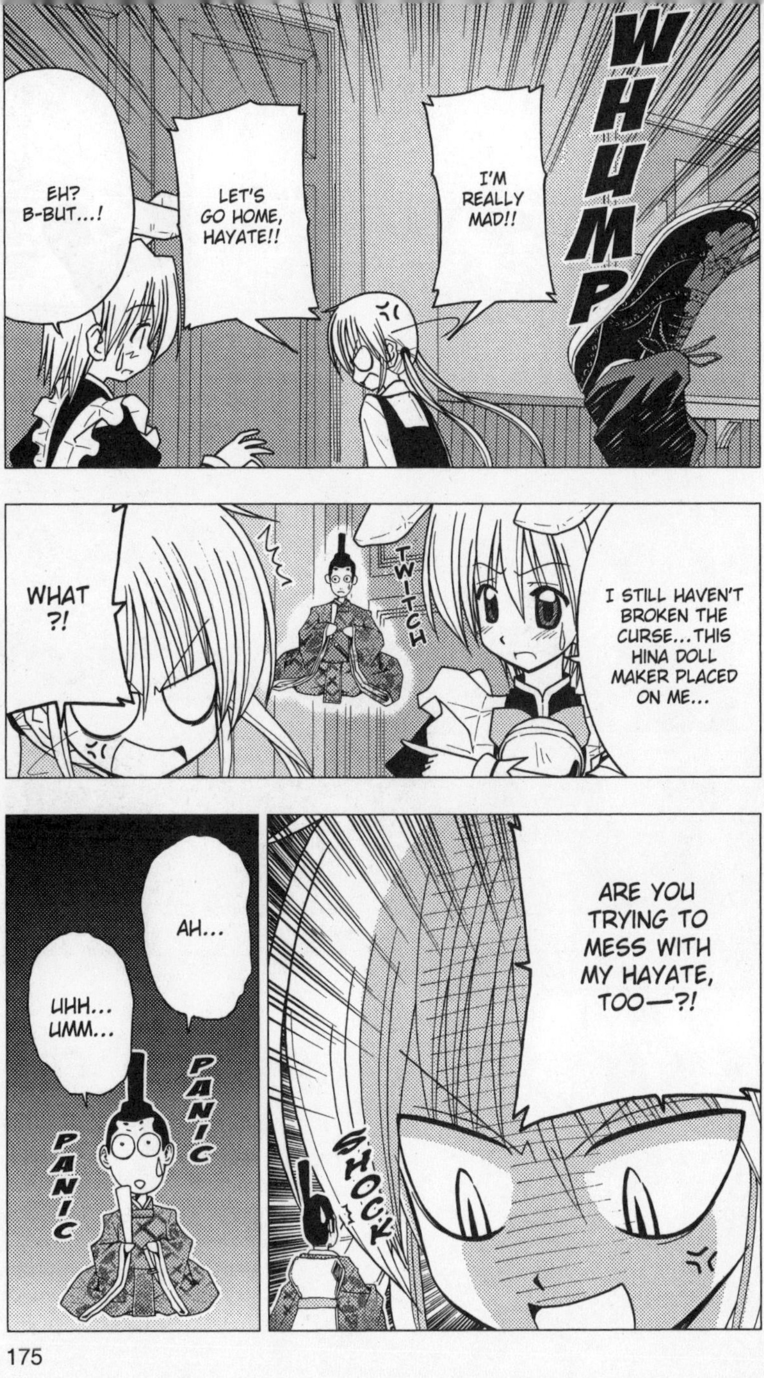
WHUMP
I'M REALLY MAD!!
LET'S GO HOME, HAYATE!!
EH? B-BUT...!
I STILL HAVEN'T BROKEN THE CURSE...THIS HINA DOLL MAKER PLACED ON ME...
TWITCH
WHAT ?!
ARE YOU TRYING TO MESS WITH MY HAYATE, TOO—?!
SHOCK
AH...
UHH... UMM...
PANIC
PANIC

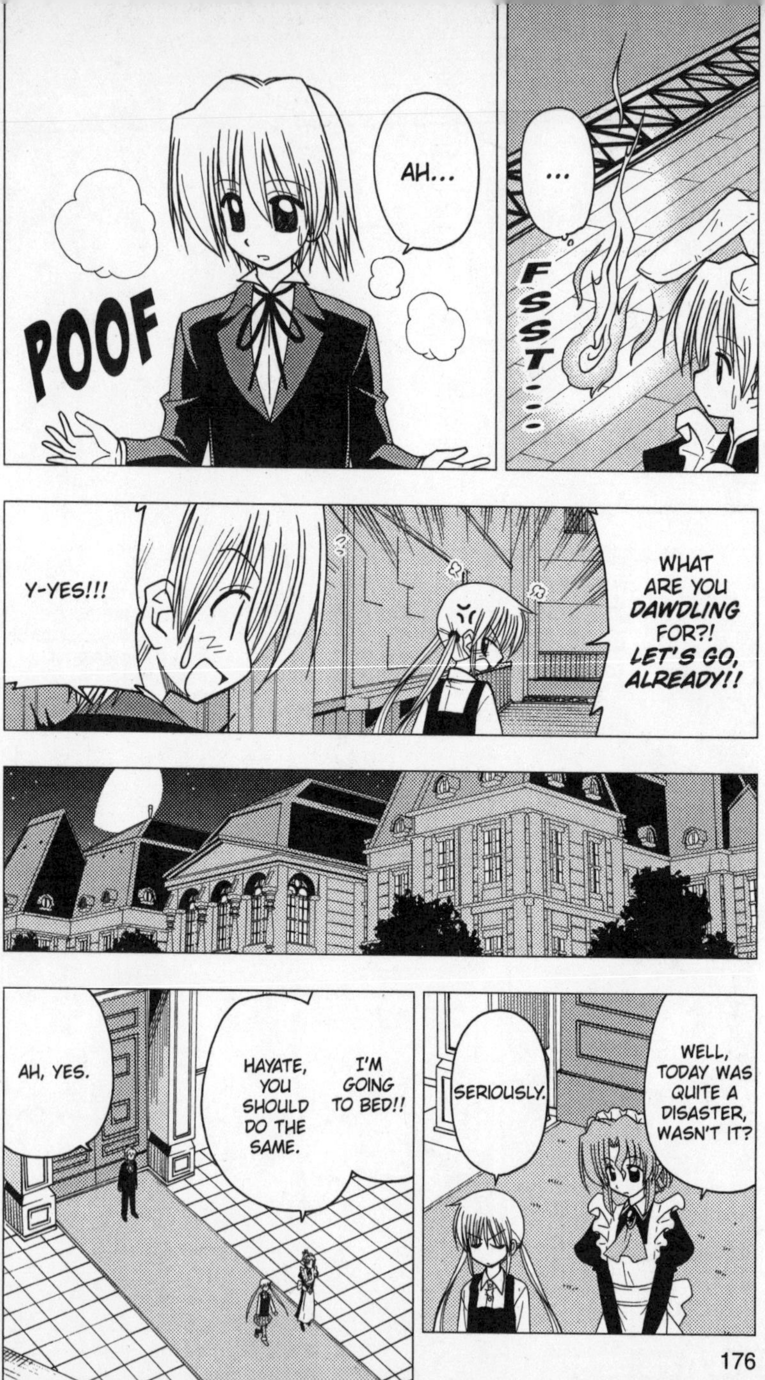
...
FSST...
AH...
POOF
WHAT ARE YOU DAWDLING FOR?! LET'S GO, ALREADY!!
Y-YES!!!
WELL, TODAY WAS QUITE A DISASTER, WASN'T IT?
SERIOUSLY.
I'M GOING TO BED!!
HAYATE, YOU SHOULD DO THE SAME.
AH, YES.

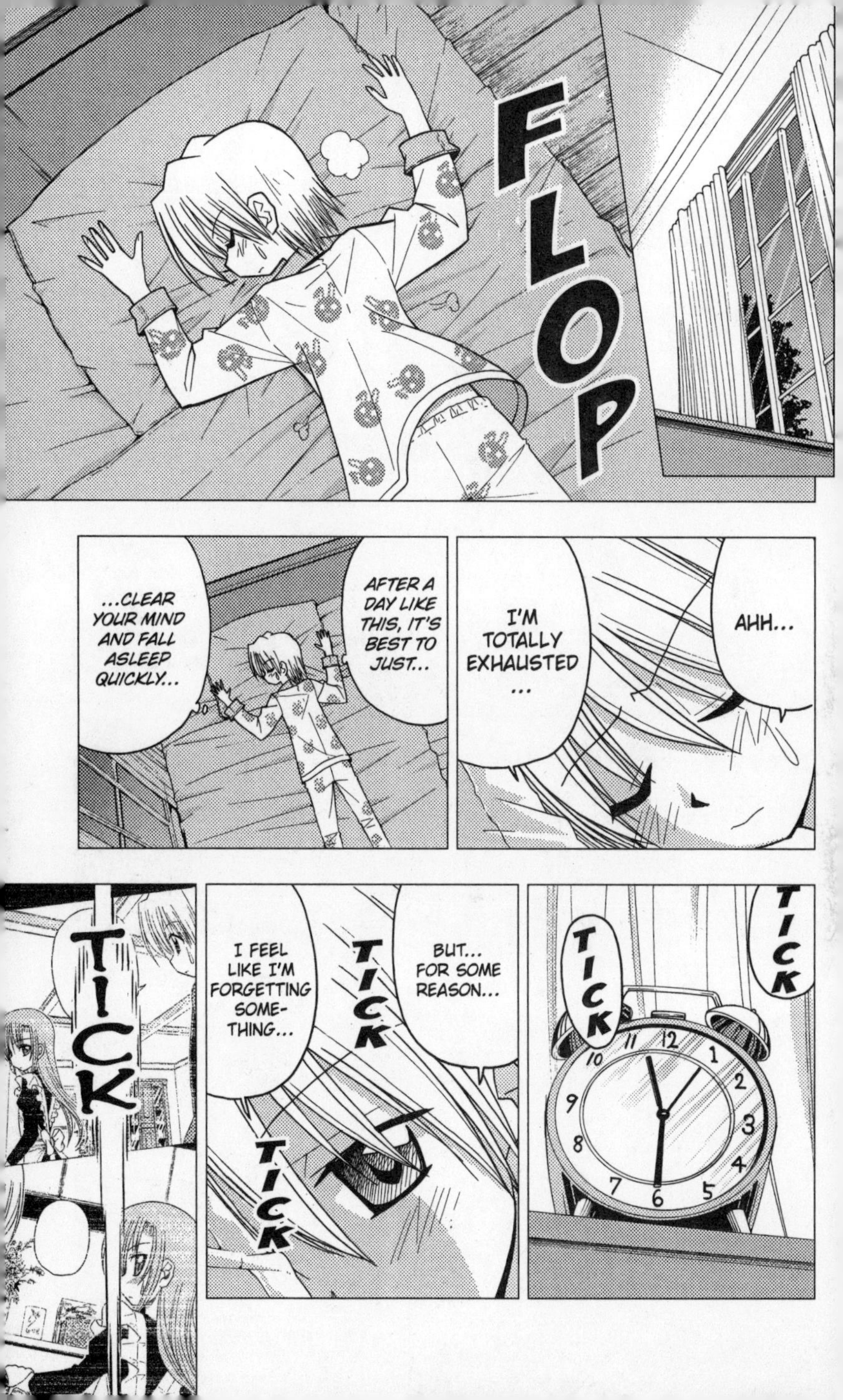
FLOP
AHH...
I'M TOTALLY EXHAUSTED ...
AFTER A DAY LIKE THIS, IT'S BEST TO JUST...
...CLEAR YOUR MIND AND FALL ASLEEP QUICKLY...
TICK
TICK
BUT... FOR SOME REASON...
TICK
I FEEL LIKE I'M FORGETTING SOME-THING...
TICK
TICK

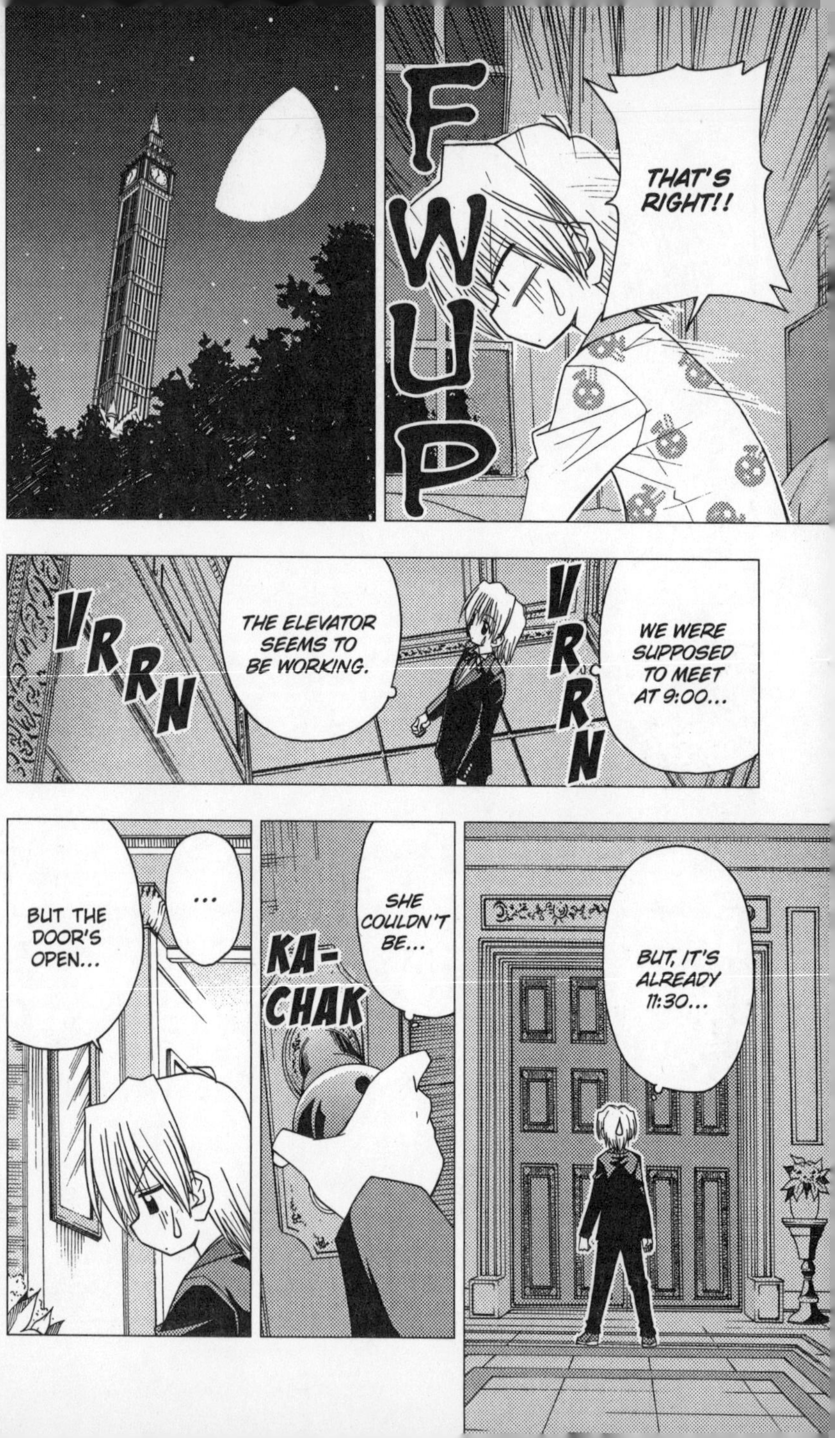
FWUP
THAT'S RIGHT!!
WE WERE SUPPOSED TO MEET AT 9:00...
VRRN
THE ELEVATOR SEEMS TO BE WORKING.
VRRN
BUT, IT'S ALREADY 11:30...
SHE COULDN'T BE...
KA-CHAK
...
BUT THE DOOR'S OPEN...

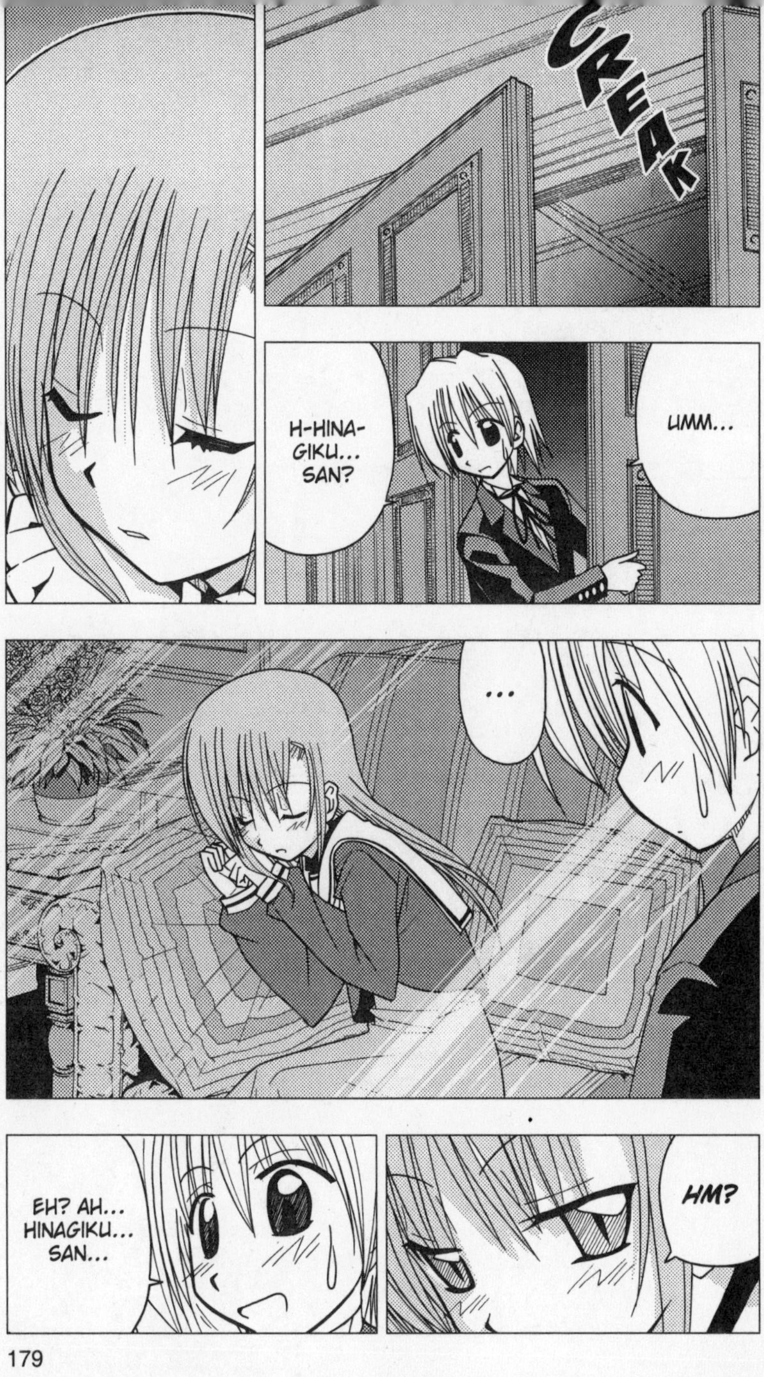
CREAK
UMM...
H-HINA-GIKU... SAN?
...
HM?
EH? AH... HINAGIKU... SAN...

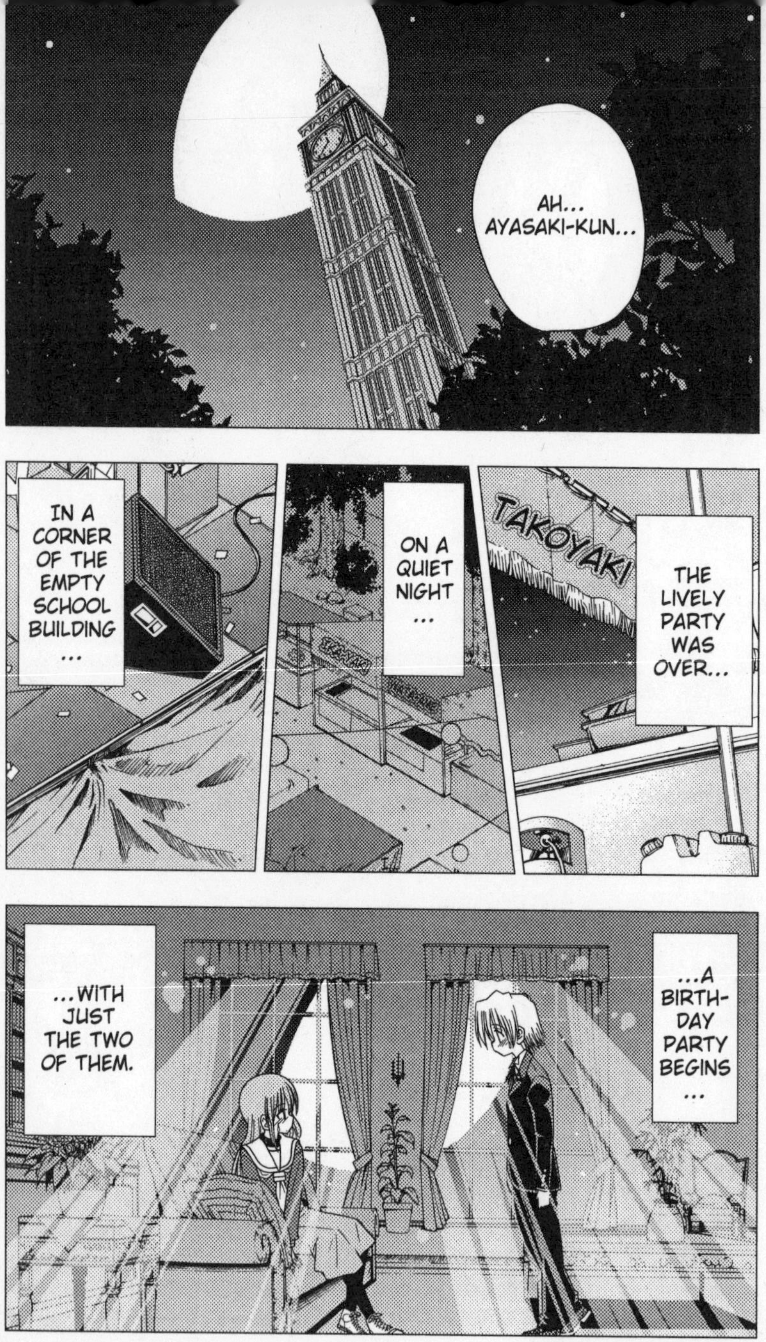
AH... AYASAKI-KUN...
TAKOYAKI
THE LIVELY PARTY WAS OVER...
ON A QUIET NIGHT...
IN A CORNER OF THE EMPTY SCHOOL BUILDING...
...A BIRTH-DAY PARTY BEGINS...
...WITH JUST THE TWO OF THEM.

TO BE CONTINUED

HAYATE THE COMBAT BUTLER

BONUS PAGE

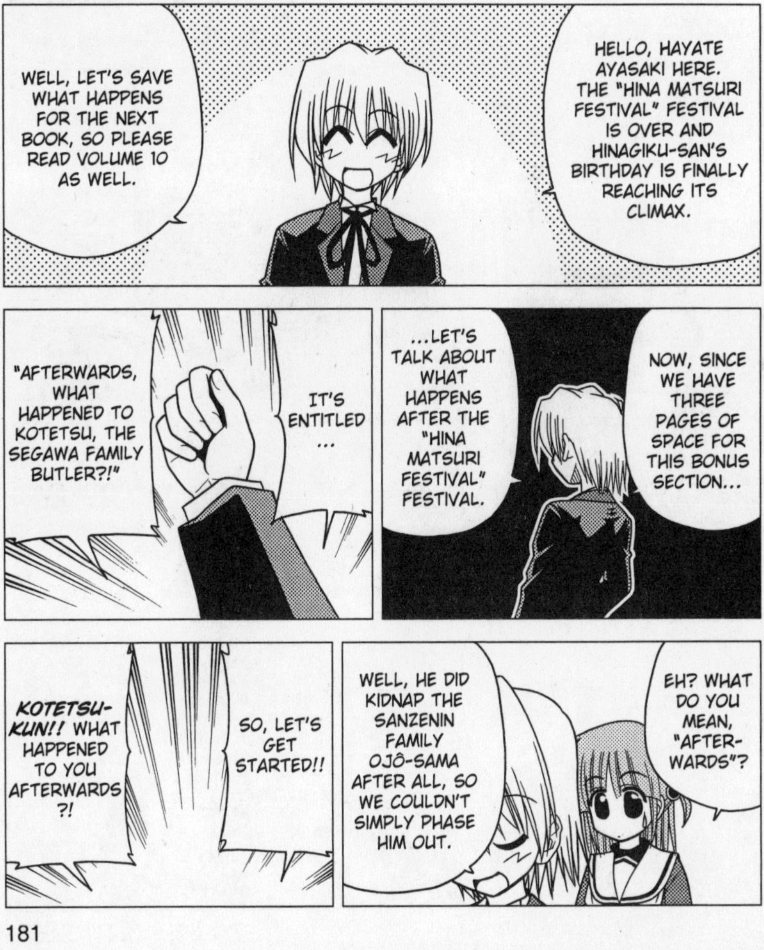
HELLO, HAYATE AYASAKI HERE. THE "HINA MATSURI FESTIVAL" FESTIVAL IS OVER AND HINAGIKU-SAN'S BIRTHDAY IS FINALLY REACHING ITS CLIMAX.
WELL, LET'S SAVE WHAT HAPPENS FOR THE NEXT BOOK, SO PLEASE READ VOLUME 10 AS WELL.
NOW, SINCE WE HAVE THREE PAGES OF SPACE FOR THIS BONUS SECTION...
...LET'S TALK ABOUT WHAT HAPPENS AFTER THE "HINA MATSURI FESTIVAL" FESTIVAL.
IT'S ENTITLED ...
"AFTERWARDS, WHAT HAPPENED TO KOTETSU, THE SEGAWA FAMILY BUTLER?!"
EH? WHAT DO YOU MEAN, "AFTER-WARDS"?
WELL, HE DID KIDNAP THE SANZENIN FAMILY OJÔ-SAMA AFTER ALL, SO WE COULDN'T SIMPLY PHASE HIM OUT.
SO, LET'S GET STARTED!!
KOTETSU-KUN!! WHAT HAPPENED TO YOU AFTERWARDS ?!

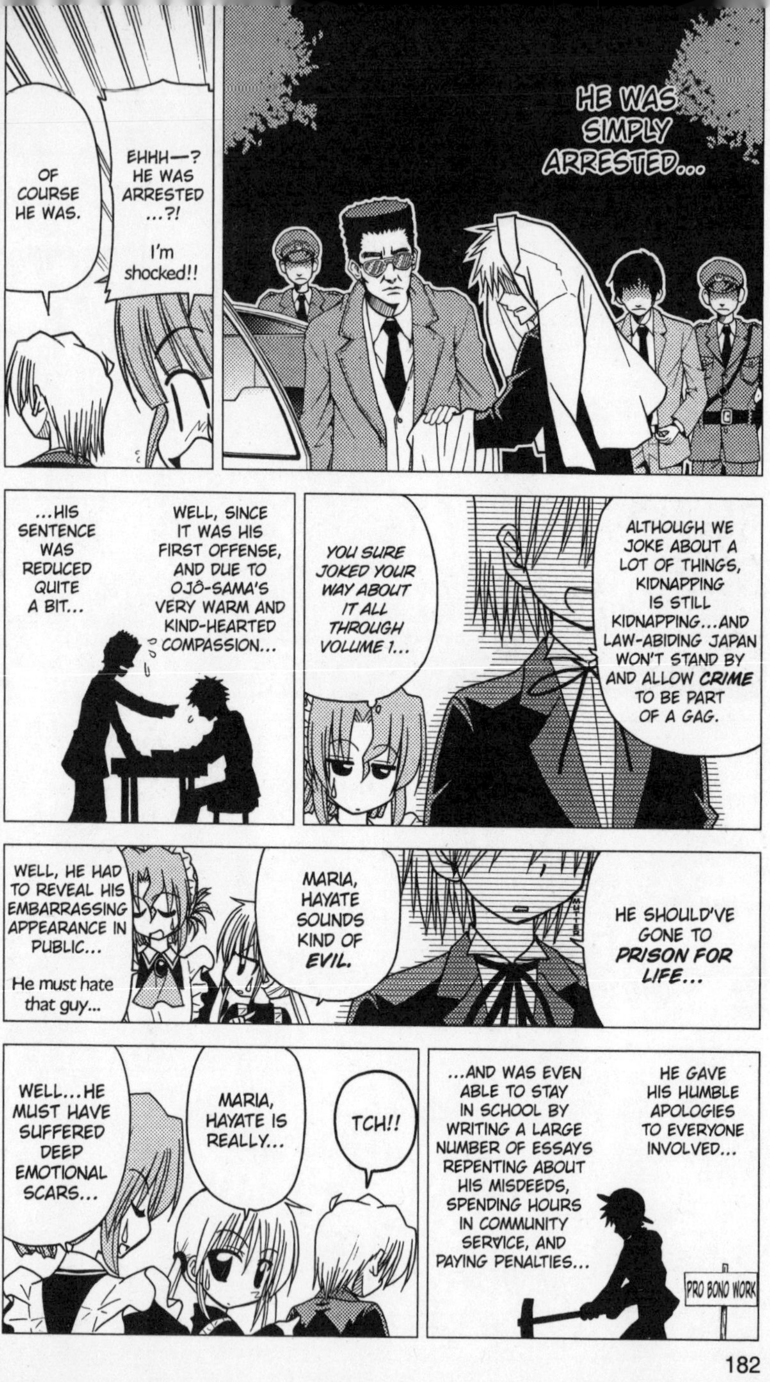
HE WAS SIMPLY ARRESTED...
EHHH—? HE WAS ARRESTED ...?!
I'm shocked!!
OF COURSE HE WAS.
ALTHOUGH WE JOKE ABOUT A LOT OF THINGS, KIDNAPPING IS STILL KIDNAPPING...AND LAW-ABIDING JAPAN WON'T STAND BY AND ALLOW **CRIME** TO BE PART OF A GAG.
YOU SURE JOKED YOUR WAY ABOUT IT ALL THROUGH VOLUME 1...
WELL, SINCE IT WAS HIS FIRST OFFENSE, AND DUE TO OJÔ-SAMA'S VERY WARM AND KIND-HEARTED COMPASSION...
...HIS SENTENCE WAS REDUCED QUITE A BIT...
HE SHOULD'VE GONE TO **PRISON FOR LIFE...**
MUTTER
MARIA, HAYATE SOUNDS KIND OF **EVIL.**
WELL, HE HAD TO REVEAL HIS EMBARRASSING APPEARANCE IN PUBLIC...
He must hate that guy...
HE GAVE HIS HUMBLE APOLOGIES TO EVERYONE INVOLVED...
...AND WAS EVEN ABLE TO STAY IN SCHOOL BY WRITING A LARGE NUMBER OF ESSAYS REPENTING ABOUT HIS MISDEEDS, SPENDING HOURS IN COMMUNITY SERVICE, AND PAYING PENALTIES...
PRO BONO WORK
TCH!!
MARIA, HAYATE IS REALLY...
WELL...HE MUST HAVE SUFFERED DEEP EMOTIONAL SCARS...

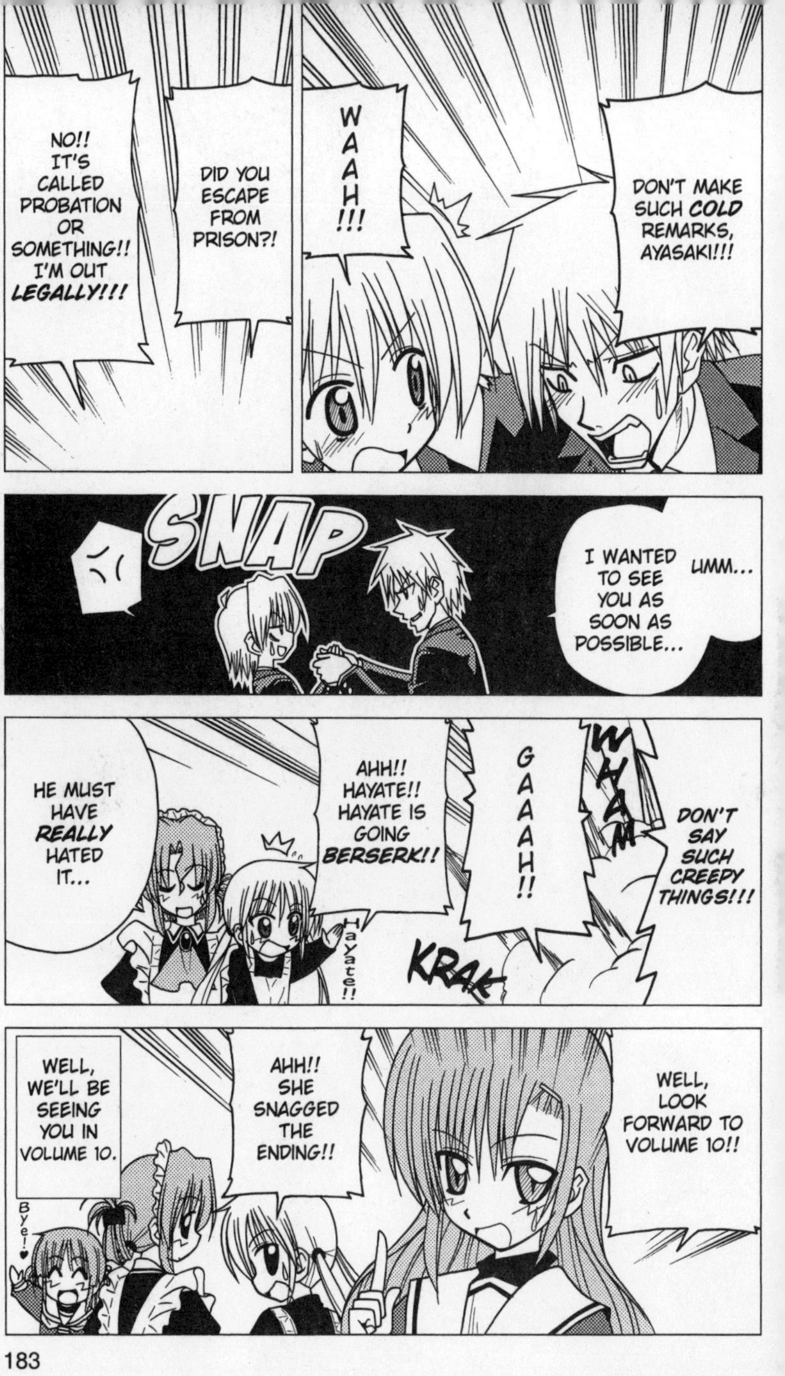
DON'T MAKE SUCH COLD REMARKS, AYASAKI!!!
WAAH!!!
DID YOU ESCAPE FROM PRISON?!
NO!! IT'S CALLED PROBATION OR SOMETHING!! I'M OUT LEGALLY!!!
UMM...
I WANTED TO SEE YOU AS SOON AS POSSIBLE...
SNAP
DON'T SAY SUCH CREEPY THINGS!!!
WHAM
GAAAAH!!
KRAK
AHH!! HAYATE!! HAYATE IS GOING BERSERK!!
HaYate!!
HE MUST HAVE REALLY HATED IT...
WELL, LOOK FORWARD TO VOLUME 10!!
AHH!! SHE SNAGGED THE ENDING!!
WELL, WE'LL BE SEEING YOU IN VOLUME 10.
Bye!♥

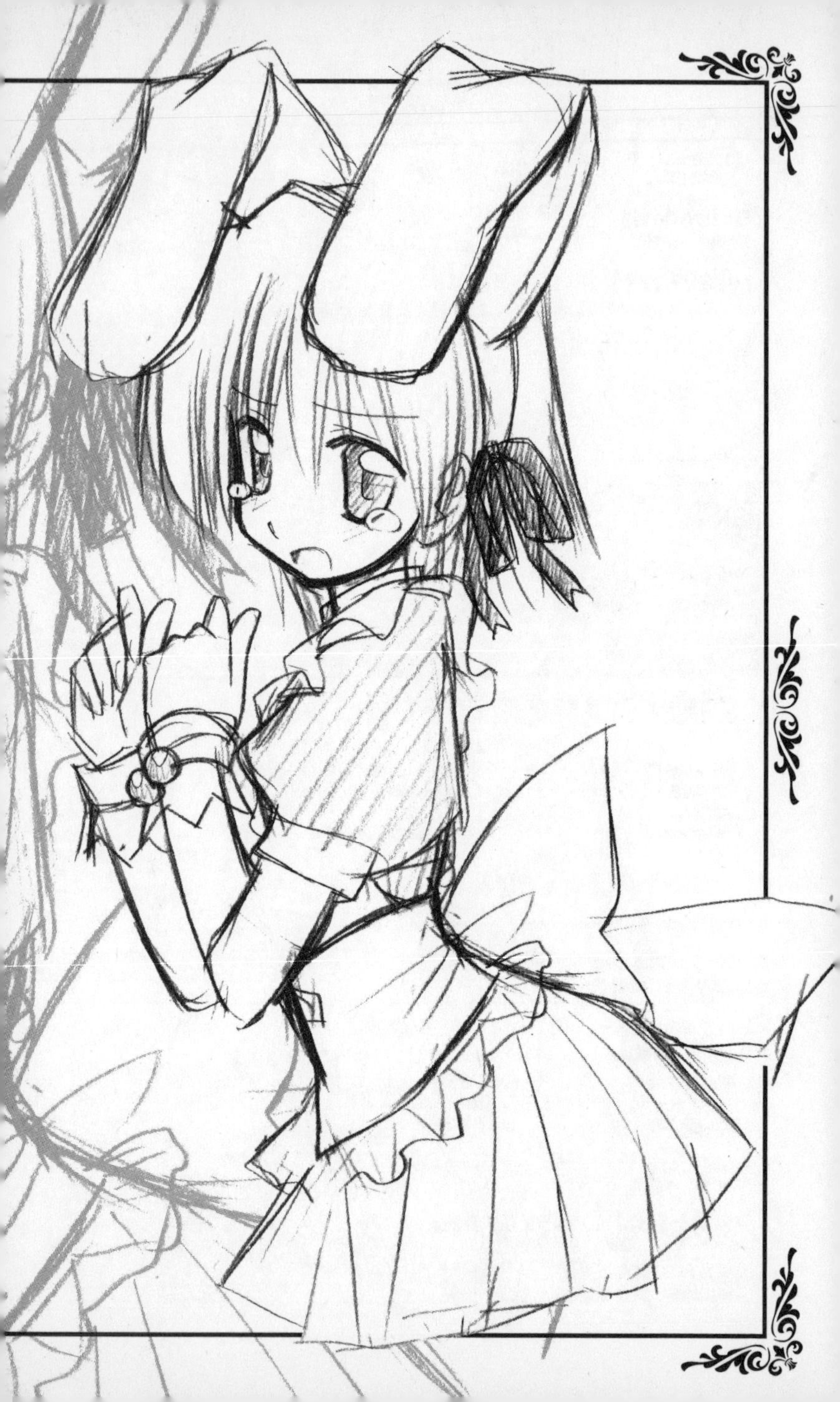

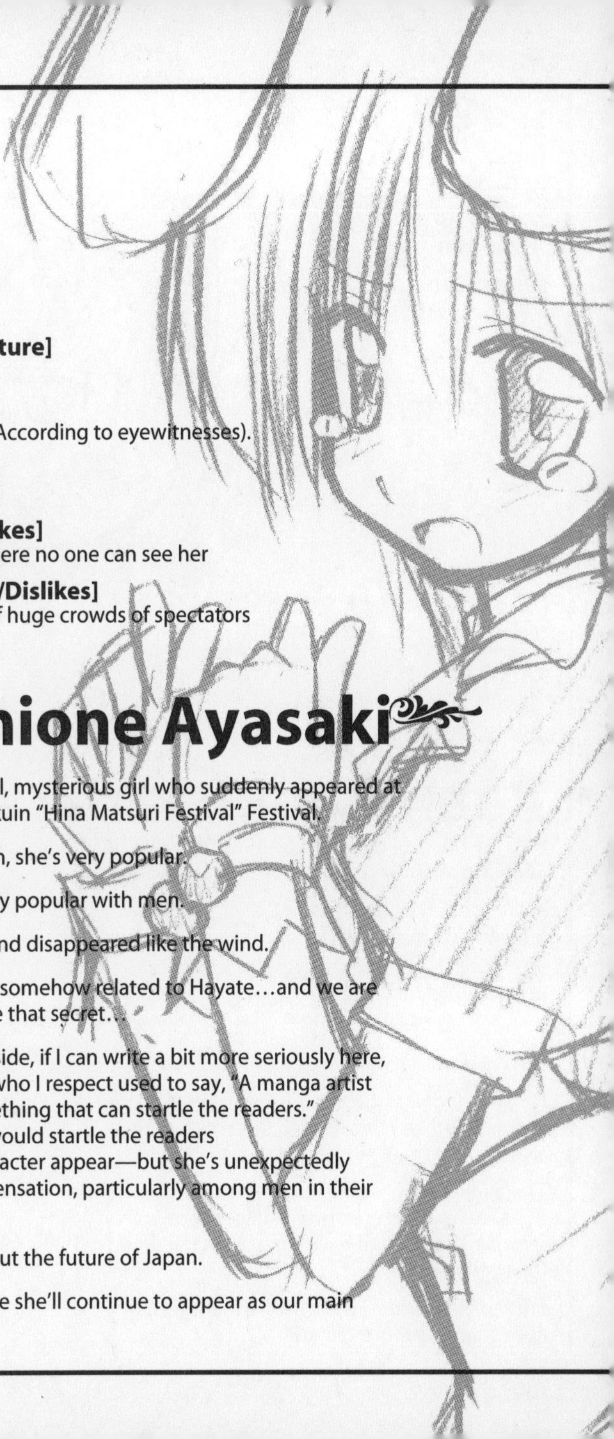

PROFILE

[Age]
?

[Birthday]
?

[Blood Type]
?

[Family Structure]
?

[Height]
About 155 cm (According to eyewitnesses).

[Weight]
Looks very light

[Strengths/Likes]
Quiet places where no one can see her

[Weaknesses/Dislikes]
Being in front of huge crowds of spectators

Hermione Ayasaki

She's a beautiful, mysterious girl who suddenly appeared at the Hakuou Gakuin "Hina Matsuri Festival" Festival.

For some reason, she's very popular.

She's particularly popular with men.

She appeared and disappeared like the wind.

She is probably somehow related to Hayate…and we are going to expose that secret…

Well, all jokes aside, if I can write a bit more seriously here, a manga artist who I respect used to say, "A manga artist should do something that can startle the readers."
So, I figured it would startle the readers
if I had this character appear—but she's unexpectedly become a big sensation, particularly among men in their twenties.

I'm worried about the future of Japan.

Anyway, I'm sure she'll continue to appear as our main heroine.

PROFILE

[Age]
82 (at death)

[Birthday]
January 3rd

[Blood Type]
B (in life)

[Height]
175 cm (in life)

[Weight]
60 kg (in life)

Rean Radiostar ❧

He's the priest of the Alexian Marco Church, also known as "Lord British of Akiba, Rean Radiostar."

His face has changed quite a bit since his first appearance, but…well, let's just say it's because he's a ghost.

His appearance as a ghost reflects his looks when he was 22-23 years old.

He had quite an attractive face.

His knowledge of games and anime reflects the author's own psyche, making this character easy to use and painless to work into any episode.

The original plan was to have him rest in peace during the festival, but for various reasons, I decided to have him stay in this world for a while longer.

For the time being, I think he will make frequent appearances here and there.

HI!!! SO HOW DID YOU LIKE VOLUME 9?

BEFORE I KNEW IT, TWO YEARS HAVE PASSED DOING THIS SERIES, AND IT EXCEEDED ONE HUNDRED EPISODES IN THE WEEKLY MAGAZINE. THIS IS DUE TO THE SUPPORT OF ALL OF YOU. THANK YOU VERY MUCH. I REALLY APPRECIATE IT.

BY THE WAY, WE HELD A CHARACTER POPULARITY POLL IN THE MAIN *SHÔNEN SUNDAY* MAGAZINE. FOR THOSE WHO DON'T READ THE MAGAZINE, I'M PLANNING TO REVEAL TO YOU HOW THINGS WENT, SO PLEASE LOOK FORWARD TO THAT. YOU MIGHT SEE AN UNEXPECTED CHARACTER COME OUT ON TOP!

AT ANY RATE, FOR ME, THE YEAR 2006 WAS A YEAR THAT MADE ME THINK, "A LOT OF THINGS HAPPEN IN LIFE. I HAVE TO TRY MY BEST TO LIVE THIS MOMENT TO ITS FULLEST." I RECALL ONE CHARACTER SAYING, "WELL, HAVE NO REGRETS," SO I WOULD LIKE TO CONTINUE CREATING EACH AND EVERY EPISODE WITH THAT IN MIND.

IN ANY CASE, IT SEEMS THAT I WILL BE EVEN BUSIER IN 2007, SO I WOULD APPRECIATE YOUR CONTINUED SUPPORT.

SEE YOU LATER! ☆

Throwing Away One's Pride

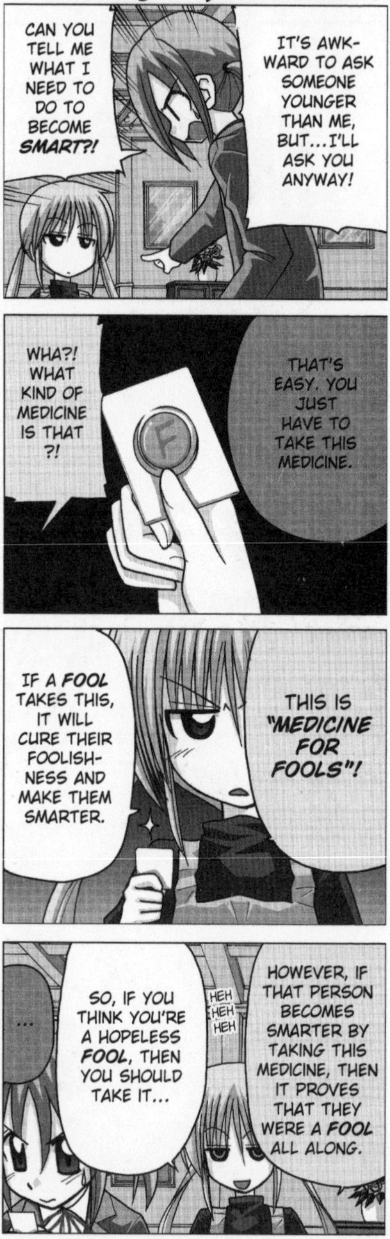
IT'S AWKWARD TO ASK SOMEONE YOUNGER THAN ME, BUT...I'LL ASK YOU ANYWAY!
CAN YOU TELL ME WHAT I NEED TO DO TO BECOME SMART?!
THAT'S EASY. YOU JUST HAVE TO TAKE THIS MEDICINE.
WHA?! WHAT KIND OF MEDICINE IS THAT?!
THIS IS "MEDICINE FOR FOOLS"!
IF A FOOL TAKES THIS, IT WILL CURE THEIR FOOLISHNESS AND MAKE THEM SMARTER.
HOWEVER, IF THAT PERSON BECOMES SMARTER BY TAKING THIS MEDICINE, THEN IT PROVES THAT THEY WERE A FOOL ALL ALONG.
HEH HEH HEH
SO, IF YOU THINK YOU'RE A HOPELESS FOOL, THEN YOU SHOULD TAKE IT...
...

Taking Pride

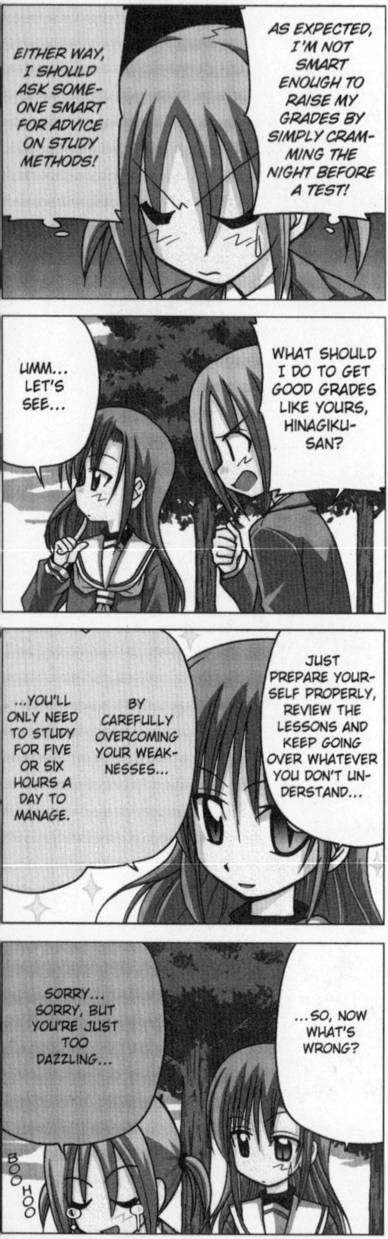
AS EXPECTED, I'M NOT SMART ENOUGH TO RAISE MY GRADES BY SIMPLY CRAMMING THE NIGHT BEFORE A TEST!
EITHER WAY, I SHOULD ASK SOMEONE SMART FOR ADVICE ON STUDY METHODS!
WHAT SHOULD I DO TO GET GOOD GRADES LIKE YOURS, HINAGIKU-SAN?
UMM... LET'S SEE...
JUST PREPARE YOURSELF PROPERLY, REVIEW THE LESSONS AND KEEP GOING OVER WHATEVER YOU DON'T UNDERSTAND...
BY CAREFULLY OVERCOMING YOUR WEAKNESSES...
...YOU'LL ONLY NEED TO STUDY FOR FIVE OR SIX HOURS A DAY TO MANAGE.
...SO, NOW WHAT'S WRONG?
SORRY... SORRY, BUT YOU'RE JUST TOO DAZZLING...
BOO HOO

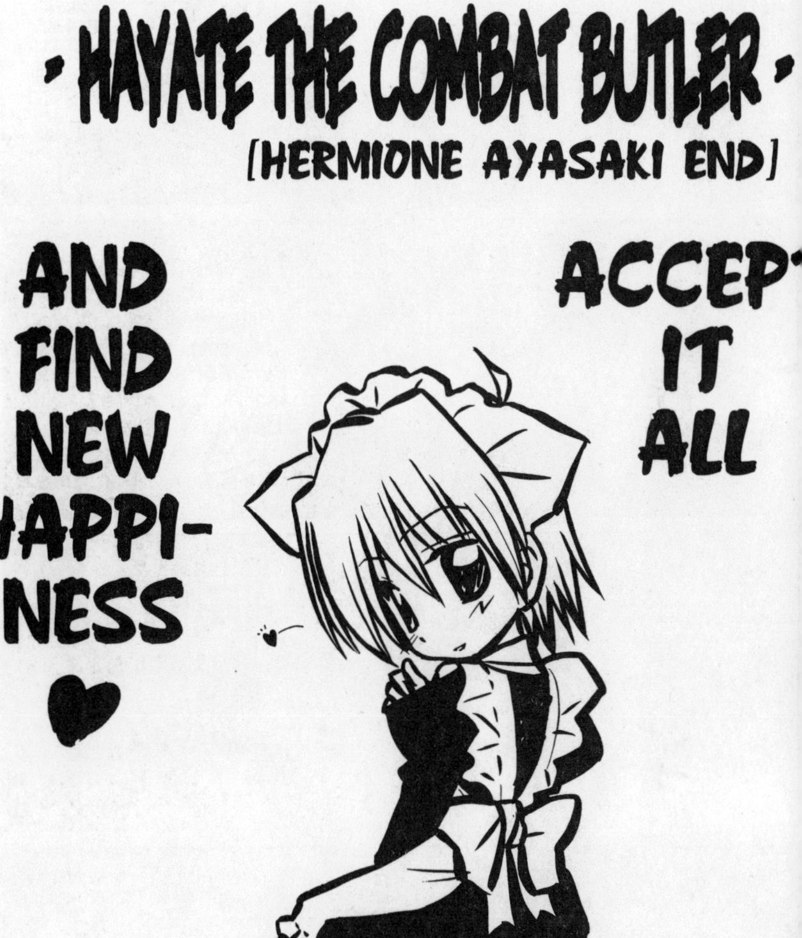
- HAYATE THE COMBAT BUTLER -
[HERMIONE AYASAKI END]
ACCEPT IT ALL
AND FIND NEW HAPPI-NESS ♥

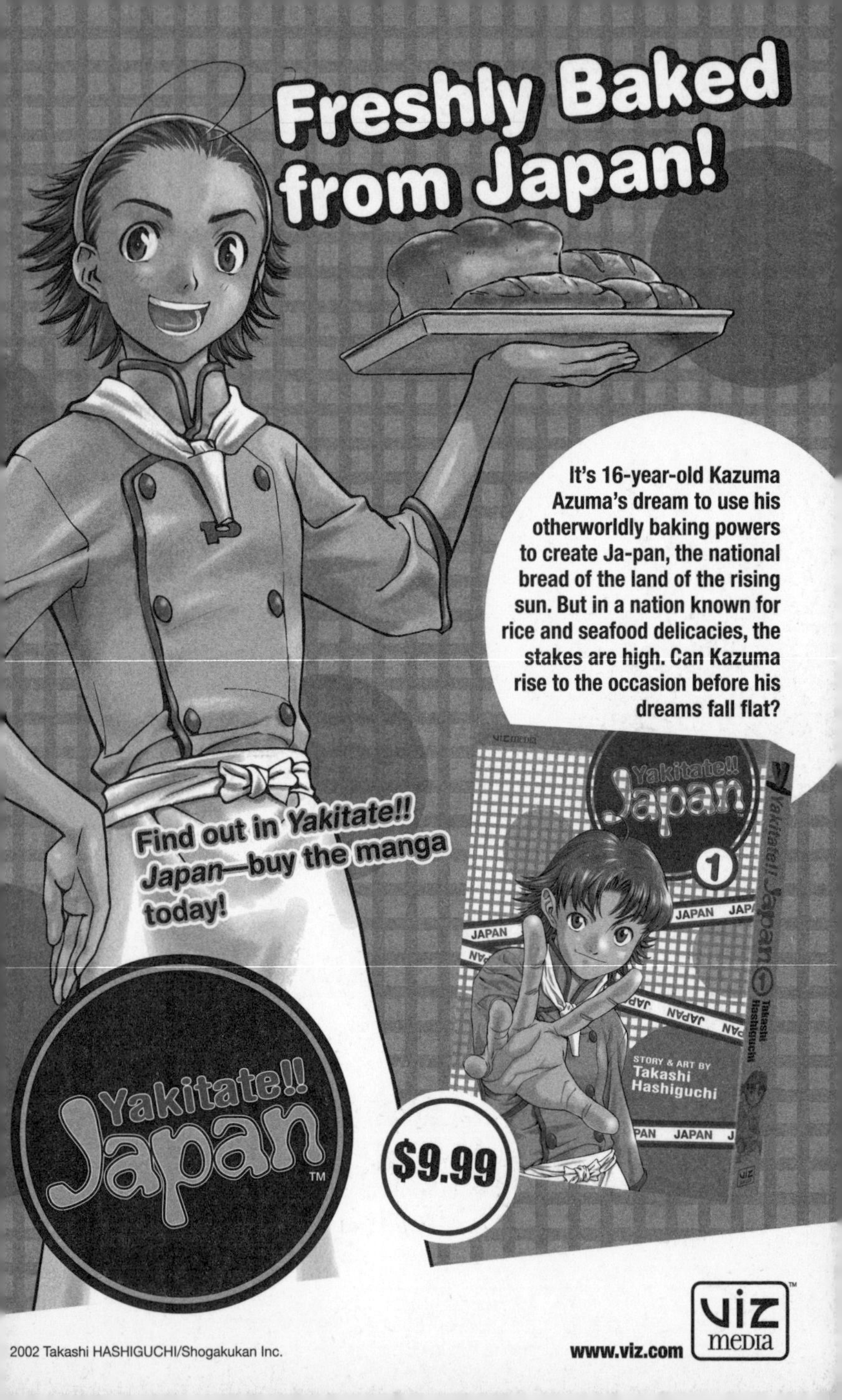

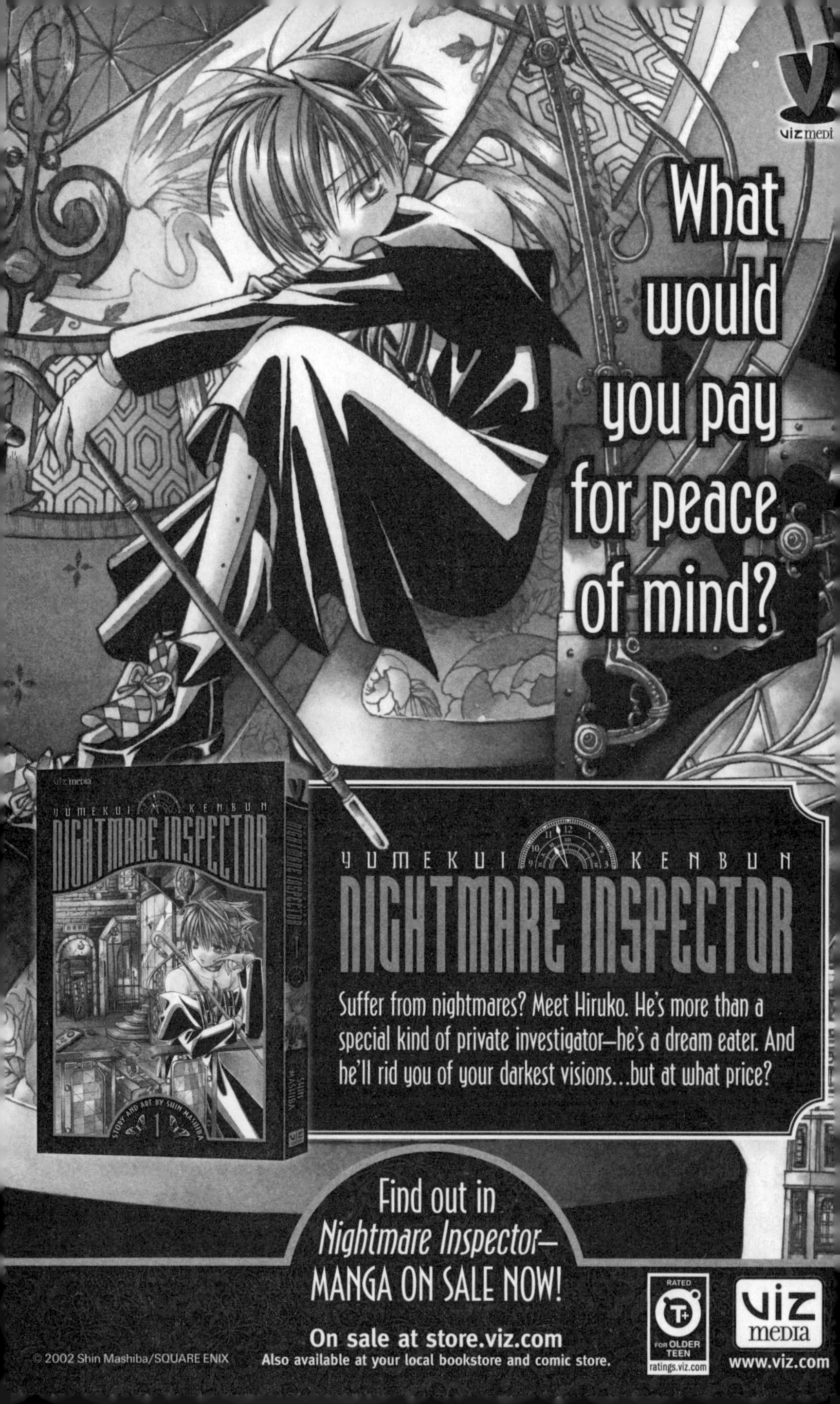

viz media
What would you pay for peace of mind?
viz media
YUMEKUI KENBUN
NIGHTMARE INSPECTOR
STORY AND ART BY SHIN MASHIBA
1
YUMEKUI KENBUN
NIGHTMARE INSPECTOR
Suffer from nightmares? Meet Hiruko. He's more than a special kind of private investigator—he's a dream eater. And he'll rid you of your darkest visions...but at what price?
Find out in *Nightmare Inspector*—
MANGA ON SALE NOW!
On sale at store.viz.com
Also available at your local bookstore and comic store.
© 2002 Shin Mashiba/SQUARE ENIX
RATED T+ FOR OLDER TEEN
ratings.viz.com
viz media
www.viz.com

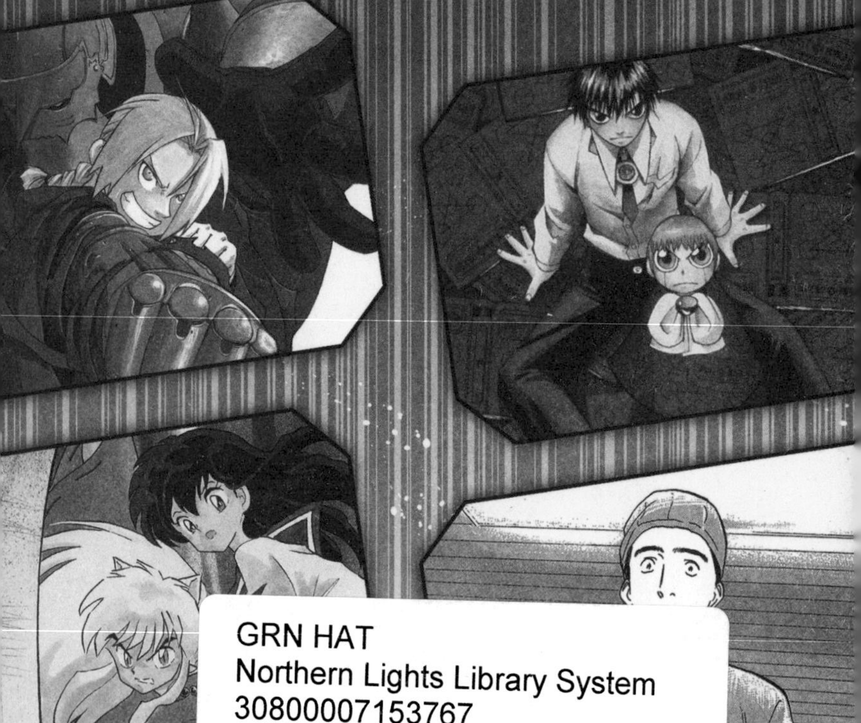